# Lecture Notes in Computer Science 7558

Commenced Publication in 1973
Founding and Former Series Editors:
Gerhard Goos, Juris Hartmanis, and Jan van Leeuwen

Elvira Popescu   Qing Li   Ralf Klamma
Howard Leung   Marcus Specht (Eds.)

# Advances
# in Web-Based Learning –
# ICWL 2012

11th International Conference
Sinaia, Romania, September 2-4, 2012
Proceedings

 Springer

Volume Editors

Elvira Popescu
University of Craiova, Romania
E-mail: popescu_elvira@software.ucv.ro

Qing Li
City University of Hong Kong, China
E-mail: itqli@cityu.edu.hk

Ralf Klamma
RWTH Aachen University, Germany
E-mail: klamma@dbis.rwth-aachen.de

Howard Leung
City University of Hong Kong, China
E-mail: howard@cityu.edu.hk

Marcus Specht
Open Universiteit, Heerlen, The Netherlands
E-mail: marcus.specht@ou.nl

ISSN 0302-9743                    e-ISSN 1611-3349
ISBN 978-3-642-33641-6            e-ISBN 978-3-642-33642-3
DOI 10.1007/978-3-642-33642-3
Springer Heidelberg Dordrecht London New York

Library of Congress Control Number: 2012947343

CR Subject Classification (1998): H.4, H.3, I.2.6, H.5, K.3, D.2, I.2, J.1

LNCS Sublibrary: SL 3 – Information Systems and Application, incl. Internet/Web
and HCI

*Typesetting:* Camera-ready by author, data conversion by Scientific Publishing Services, Chennai, India

Printed on acid-free paper

Springer is part of Springer Science+Business Media (www.springer.com)

# Preface

ICWL is an annual international conference on Web-based learning, which started in Hong Kong in 2002. Since then, it has been held in Australia (2003), China (2004), Hong Kong (2005), Malaysia (2006), UK (2007), China (2008), Germany (2009), China (2010), and Hong Kong (2011). ICWL 2012, the 11th conference in the series, was organized by the University of Craiova, Romania, and was held in the Sinaia mountain resort.

The location chosen for this year was at high altitude, true to the spirit of a high-level conference. Sinaia, also known as the "Carpathian Pearl", is situated in breathtaking mountain scenery, on the Prahova Valley. Blending astonishing natural beauty with picturesque architecture, Sinaia is a formal royal residence, home of the Peles Castle; this is one of the most well-preserved royal palaces in Europe, which served as the summer residence of the first king of Romania, Carol I.

In this rich cultural atmosphere, the conference provided a discussion forum and social networking opportunity for academic researchers, developers, educationalists, and practitioners alike. Latest findings were presented in the areas of: computer-supported collaborative learning; personal learning environments; Web 2.0 and social learning environments; personalized and adaptive learning; game-based learning; deployment, organization, and management of learning objects; semantic Web and ontologies for e-learning; intelligent learner modeling and learning analytics; design, modeling, and implementation of e-learning platforms and tools.

This year we received 105 submissions from 33 countries; while the majority of authors came from Europe, all other continents were represented, resulting in a remarkable international diversity. After a rigorous double-blind review process (in which each paper was reviewed by at least three members of the Program Committee), 28 papers were selected as full papers, yielding an acceptance rate of 26.6%. In addition, 10 more papers were selected as short papers. Moreover, three workshops were held in conjunction with ICWL 2012. The conference also featured two distinguished keynote presentations as well as a panel.

We would like to thank the entire Organizing Committee for their efforts and time spent to ensure the success of the conference. Last but not least, we would like to thank all the authors of the submitted papers, whether accepted or not, for their contribution to maintaining a high-quality conference. We count on your continual support for playing a significant role in the Web-based learning community in the future.

September 2012

Elvira Popescu
Qing Li
Ralf Klamma
Howard Leung
Marcus Specht

# Organization

## Organizing Committee

### Conference Co-chairs

Elvira Popescu                 University of Craiova, Romania
Qing Li                        City University of Hong Kong, Hong Kong,
                               China

### Program Committee Co-chairs

Ralf Klamma                    RWTH Aachen University, Germany
Marcus Specht                  Open University of the Netherlands,
                               The Netherlands
Howard Leung                   City University of Hong Kong, Hong Kong,
                               China

### Workshop Co-chairs

Dickson Chiu                   Dickson Computer Systems, Hong Kong, China
Demetrios Sampson              University of Piraeus & CERTH, Greece
Costin Badica                  University of Craiova, Romania

### Panel Co-chairs

Yiwei Cao                      RWTH Aachen University, Germany
Stefan Trausan-Matu            Polytechnic University of Bucharest, Romania

### Local Organization Committee Co-chairs

Eugen Bobasu                   University of Craiova, Romania
Marius Brezovan                University of Craiova, Romania

### Publicity Co-chairs

Frederick Li                   University of Durham, UK
Sabine Graf                    Athabasca University, Canada
Philippos Pouyioutas           University of Nicosia, Cyprus

### Steering Committee Representatives

Rynson Lau                     City University of Hong Kong, Hong Kong,
                               China
Timothy Shih                   National Central University, Taiwan, ROC

### Registration Chair

Marius Marian                  University of Craiova, Romania

## International Program Committee

| | |
|---|---|
| Marie-Helene Abel | University of Technology of Compiegne, France |
| Maria Bielikova | Slovak University of Technology in Bratislava, Slovakia |
| Liz Burd | University of Durham, UK |
| Dumitru Dan Burdescu | University of Craiova, Romania |
| Yiwei Cao | RWTH Aachen University, Germany |
| Vladimir Ioan Cretu | Polytechnic University of Timisoara, Romania |
| Valentin Cristea | Polytechnic University of Bucharest, Romania |
| Pieter De Vries | Delft University of Technology, The Netherlands |
| Carlos Delgado Kloos | Carlos III University of Madrid, Spain |
| Stavros Demetriadis | Aristotle University of Thessaloniki, Greece |
| Michael Derntl | RWTH Aachen University, Germany |
| Giuliana Dettori | Institute for Educational Technology (ITD-CNR), Italy |
| Darina Dicheva | Winston-Salem State University, USA |
| Erik Duval | Katholieke Universiteit Leuven, Belgium |
| Sandy El Helou | EPFL, Switzerland |
| Baltasar Fernandez-Manjon | Universidad Complutense de Madrid, Spain |
| Adina Magda Florea | Polytechnic University of Bucharest, Romania |
| Dragan Gasevic | Athabasca University, Canada |
| Denis Gillet | EPFL, Switzerland |
| Carlo Giovannella | University of Rome Tor Vergata, Italy |
| Sabine Graf | Athabasca University, Canada |
| Christian Guetl | Technical University of Graz, Austria |
| Eelco Herder | L3S Research Center in Hannover, Germany |
| Pedro Isaias | Universidade Aberta (Portuguese Open University), Portugal |
| Malinka Ivanova | TU Sofia, Bulgaria |
| Mirjana Ivanovic | University of Novi Sad, Serbia |
| Jelena Jovanovic | University of Belgrade, Serbia |
| Vana Kamtsiou | Brunel University, UK |
| Ioannis Kazanidis | Technological Educational Institute of Kavala, Greece |
| Tomaz Klobucar | Institut Josef-Stefan, Slovenia |
| Piet Kommers | University of Twente, The Netherlands |
| Rob Koper | Open University of the Netherlands, The Netherlands |
| Milos Kravcik | RWTH Aachen University, Germany |
| Barbara Kump | Graz University of Technology, Austria |
| Lam For Kwok | City University of Hong Kong, Hong Kong, China |

| Mart Laanpere | Tallinn University, Estonia |
| Jean-Marc Labat | Université Pierre et Marie Curie, France |
| Effie Lai-Chong Law | University of Leicester, UK & ETH Zurich, Switzerland |
| Frederick Li | University of Durham, UK |
| Wei Liu | Shanghai University, China |
| Jacques Lonchamp | LORIA - Equipe ECOO, France |
| Stephan Lukosch | Delft University of Technology, The Netherlands |
| Xiangfeng Luo | Shanghai University, China |
| Katherine Maillet | Télécom SudParis, France |
| Ivana Marenzi | L3S Research Center in Hannover, Germany |
| Alke Martens | PH Schwäbisch Gmünd University of Education, Germany |
| Harald Mayer | Joanneum Research, Austria |
| Pablo Moreno-Ger | Universidad Complutense de Madrid, Spain |
| Xavier Ochoa | Escuela Superior Politécnica del Litoral, Ecuador |
| Toshio Okamoto | University of Electro-Communications, Japan |
| Alexandros Paramythis | Johannes Kepler University Linz, Austria |
| Stefan Gheorghe Pentiuc | Stefan cel Mare University of Suceava, Romania |
| Philippos Pouyioutas | University of Nicosia, Cyprus |
| Francesca Pozzi | Institute for Educational Technology (ITD-CNR), Italy |
| Neil Rubens | University of Electro-Communications, Tokyo, Japan |
| Ruimin Shen | Shanghai Jiaotong University, China |
| Marc Spaniol | Max Planck Institute for Computer Science, Germany |
| Natalia Stash | Eindhoven University of Technology, The Netherlands |
| Karen Stepanyan | University of Warwick, UK |
| Nicolae Tapus | Polytechnic University of Bucharest, Romania |
| Marco Temperini | Sapienza University of Rome, Italy |
| Stefan Trausan-Matu | Polytechnic University of Bucharest, Romania |
| Lorna Uden | Staffordshire University, UK |
| Carsten Ullrich | Shanghai Jiaotong University, China |
| Radu Vasiu | Polytechnic University of Timisoara, Romania |
| Julita Vassileva | University of Saskatchewan, Canada |
| Carlos Vaz de Carvalho | Instituto Politécnico do Porto, Portugal |
| Katrien Verbert | Katholieke Universiteit Leuven, Belgium |
| Lucian Nicolae Vintan | Lucian Blaga University of Sibiu, Romania |
| Riina Vuorikari | European Schoolnet, Belgium |
| Jianxin Wang | Central South University, China |

Fridolin Wild                    The Open University, UK
Martin Wolpers                   Fraunhofer FIT, Germany
Zheng Xu                         Shanghai University, China
Qinghua Zheng                    Xi'an Jiaotong University, China

## Additional Reviewers

Monique Baron                    University Pierre et Marie Curie, France
Tingwen Chang                    Athabasca University, Canada
Moushir El-Bishouty              Athabasca University, Canada
Anna Hannemann                   RWTH Aachen University, Germany
Marco Kalz                       Open University of the Netherlands,
                                 The Netherlands
Michal Kompan                    Slovak University of Technology in Bratislava,
                                 Slovakia
Derick Leony                     Carlos III University of Madrid, Spain
David Maroto                     Carlos III University of Madrid, Spain
Petru Nicolaescu                 RWTH Aachen University, Germany
Zinayida Petrushyna              RWTH Aachen University, Germany
Dominik Renzel                   RWTH Aachen University, Germany
Giang Binh Tran                  L3S Research Center in Hannover, Germany

# Table of Contents

## Learning Objects' Management and Ontologies

## Game-Based Learning

# Personalized and Adaptive Learning

# Feedback, Assessment and Learning Analytics

## Design, Model and Implementation of E-Learning Platforms and Tools

## Pedagogical Issues, Practice and Experience Sharing

# An Approach to Exploit Social Bookmarking to Improve Formal Language Learning

Giuliana Dettori[1] and Simone Torsani[2]

[1] Istituto per le Tecnologie Didattiche del CNR, Genoa, Italy
dettori@itd.cnr.it
[2] University of Genoa, Genoa, Italy
s.torsani@gmail.com

**Abstract.** This paper describes an original approach developed to enrich a formal language learning environment by means of suggestions of related web pages automatically retrieved at run time from social bookmarking sites. The users of the environment are also invited to share within the platform an indication of personal like or dislike, which constitutes a help for the fellow users in the selection of valuable web resources of their interest. This paper describes the aims, structure and operation of the mentioned bookmark-retrieving tool, and summarizes students' use and appreciation of it in a short pilot experimentation. Finally, the critical elements for its successful operation are highlighted.

**Keywords:** Online learning, Language learning, Social bookmarking, Informal learning, Information Extraction, Micro evaluation.

## 1 Introduction

The Internet constitutes an important resource for language learners, allowing them to get in touch with a huge amount of "real" documents which provide a rich variety of examples of language use in contexts of user's interest [1-4]. Moreover, the development of social web (the so-called web 2.0) has added a wealth of possibilities to interact, in a variety of ways, with both people and socially constructed contents around the world [5]. Such contacts (that can be exploited by the learners in individually planned or unplanned, personal way), favour meaning construction, knowledge contextualization and skill practice.

The chaotic richness of Internet resources, however, makes this opportunity difficult to exploit for the learners, because finding interesting materials which may be relevant for learning often entails time-consuming quests among the numerous links retrieved by search engines. Moreover, free Internet explorations may turn out rather detached from a student's current object of formal study, hence giving rise to fragmentary learning experiences which do not help to establish a useful synergy between formal learning path and individual web surfing. This, on the other hand, is very desirable for effective language learning, in which formal and informal situations

E. Popescu et al. (Eds.): ICWL 2012, LNCS 7558, pp. 1–10, 2012.

complement each other, contributing to language competence development in different ways.

In order to overcome these problems, we have worked out an approach to help the users of a formal language learning platform currently in use at university level to automatically detect web pages related to the content of each formal activity, be it focused on grammatical, communicative or cultural topics. To this end, we retrieve suitable suggestions from available social bookmarking sites, and organize a micro-evaluation service within the platform, i.e., the platform's users can express their like or dislike for each suggested link. The choice to search among bookmarks, and the development of a procedure to perform it automatically and effectively, constitutes the element of novelty of our proposal.

We decided to rely on social bookmarking services for this search, rather than on collections of educational materials, because language learners need to get in touch with original documents of diverse nature more than to find extra exercises on grammatical/lexical topics. Social bookmarking sites appear therefore more suitable to the considered task than repositories of educational materials because they offer good quality suggestions on all the variety of aspects that may be of interest for language learners.

Searching in social bookmarking sites, moreover, appears preferable than searching on the web. In bookmark collections, the links retrieved are not discovered by automatic procedures, but chosen, recorded, tagged and evaluated by users for their own benefit [6]. This represents a powerful support to web navigation, thanks to a mix of direct advice, given by the bookmark uploaders, and indirect guidance, that derives from the preferences expressed by the other users through the (usually provided) like/unlike option [7]. Bookmarks can therefore contribute to realize the view of learning proposed by connectivism [8], according to which "*[k]now-how and know-what is being supplemented with know-where (the understanding of where to find knowledge needed)*". Moreover, the voting possibility brings to the fore what has been defined "the wisdom of the crowd", that is, emergence of quality from participants' appreciation [9], and constitutes a practical form of scaffolding for effective web browsing.

Using micro-evaluation of web resources may also contribute to the success of an online learning environment in other ways. As Nielson [10] points out, self study language courses are potentially subject to a quick decrease in motivation and interest; in order to overcome this problem, she suggests to foster human interactions, proper tutoring and a sense of community. Encouraging the participants in an online course to share opinions in synthetic form on the posted websites is a simple but effective way to reveal social presence and suggest the existence of a community of users, even though very loosely structured, and by this means encourage participation and help to overcome the feeling of isolation of individual online study. Moreover, expressing an opinion requires the learners to pay attention to what they consider valuable to support their learning and therefore is an encouragement to develop critical abilities and gain some awareness of their own learning process.

We chose to repeat resource retrieval at each runtime in order to avoid to have a static group of resources for each activity, which would be the case if links were retrieved only once and moved up or down in the displayed list based on user evaluation.

In the next section, the bookmark-based component is described, together with the formal platform on which it was first implemented; some initial findings related to its use are also presented. Some reflections on advantages, limitations and needs for improvement of our proposal conclude the paper.

# 2    Adding Bookmarks in a Formal Learning Environment

## 2.1    Our Starting Point: Traditional Online Language Learning

The CliRe platform, first launched in 2008, is used at the Faculty of Foreign Languages of the University of Genoa (Italy) to complement or substitute the face-to-face classes offered for five different languages (English, French, German, Spanish, Italian for foreigners), with a total of around one thousand registered users [11]. It was developed based on a traditional, non interactive approach and mirrors the organization of typical self-study courses, in which a study subject is divided into units to be tackled sequentially, each focused on a chosen topic.

In this platform, teachers build learning environments for their courses by creating learning units, each of which includes activities aiming to improve knowledge of some topic of grammar (e.g., the past perfect), or vocabulary (e.g., weather forecasting), linguistic functions (e.g., asking for directions), civilization (e.g., the Highlands in the UK), or a combination of them. Learning units are sequenced to form modules. Figure 1 shows the page of a typical unit where the learning activities can be accessed by the users in sequence, by clicking on the icons placed along the dark, curved path.

Learning contents, kind and amount of activities proposed, use of multimedia (recordings and pictures) to help convey or construct meanings, and combination of topics are decided by the teacher, who can partially choose, by these means, a pedagogical approach local to each unit, hence making them more or less alive, fostering some linguistic skill in particular, stimulating reflection, etc.

Students need to complete all the activities of a unit before progressing to the next one, and all the units of a module before moving to the next module. A number of tools (a dictionary, a set of grammar flash cards, etc.) can be attached to each module, so as to provide learners with some support.

After the initial implementation, the system has been progressively improved by adding functional components (e.g., a compound dictionary system) to facilitate and stimulate learning. Such developments also have the research aim to experiment how language learning can be made more effective and pleasant within the context of an autonomous, traditional, non-interactive learning approach [12].

A step along the line of improving language courses run on this platform is the bookmark-based component which represents the contribution of this paper. This social feature is intended not only to provide automatic retrieval of web resources useful for learning but also to foster involvement and feeling of participation, to the advantage of learning.

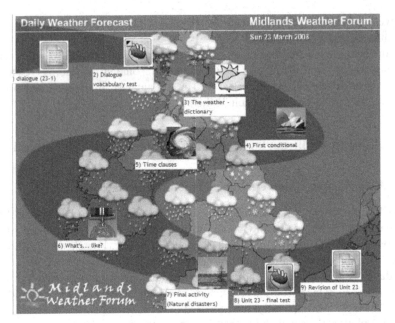

**Fig. 1.** A unit of a formal language learning course on the described platform

## 2.2    The Bookmark-Retrieval Tool

The idea of adding web suggestions to learning activities is appealing but a manual selection and regular updates would result onerous and time-consuming for both teacher and platform manager. Our choice to retrieve resources from social bookmarking portals based on teacher-assigned keywords describing the activities' learning content presents a double benefit: 1) no extra work is required from teachers, apart defining keywords for their activities and 2) automatic extraction is performed on previously selected and shared content, thus (potentially) avoiding, or at least decreasing, problems of spam or incorrect classification connected to plain web browsing with standard search engine.

When a learner starts working on the activity, the system automatically enquires some websites of social bookmarking by using the activity's keywords; only links with more positive than negative appreciation marks are retained. If only a small number of links are obtained in this way, a few more are added by searching on the web. All links detected are then filtered by means of a superficial scan of the content, in order to eliminate spam, dead links, advertisements and duplicates; in the end, between 10 and 15 links are shown. We deemed necessary to set limits on the number of links displayed, in that too many links may result in a distraction and pose the selection problem that we want to avoid, while a small number may result in a too limited choice, missing to meet the desire for deepening of several users. The links retained are displayed by means of the page title, and recorded, together with an id associated with the related activity, so as to speed up and uniform the operation in the next running of the same activity.

The most decisive filter to the collection of links, however, comes from the users' opinions. To this end, a micro-evaluation system was realized, each link being followed by two clickable icons (see Fig. 2) to express positive and negative judgment of the corresponding resource. Each user can vote a resource only once. The evaluations expressed are stored so as to be used at the next retrieval by any platform user.

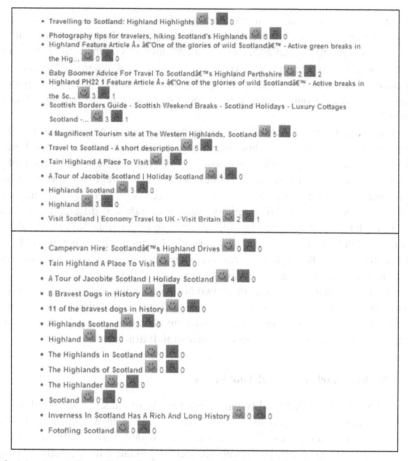

**Fig. 2.** A bookmark list at the end of two learning activities obtained with the tags "Highlands, Scotland, Travel" (upper) and "Highlands, Scotland, History" (lower)

We felt the need to introduce a voting possibility inside the platform, even though bookmarks portals usually have their own, since local votes represent the opinion of fellow course mates, and hence are likely made from a course perspective. The possibility to express a personal evaluation of the bookmarked sites and to see the preferences of the classmates aims not only to provide a useful filter supporting the users in their selection, as pointed out above. It also has relevant educational purposes: to raise curiosity for extra resources, suggesting that learning should not be limited to classroom work; to suggest the users that they are anyway part of a learning community with which they can exchange useful suggestions; to stimulate the users to look at the visited sites with a critical eye in order to meaningfully express their own vote.

## 2.3    Technical Realization

From a technical point of view, this function was developed through a combination of scripting languages and techniques. We exploited Jquery, a Javascript class which is widely used in dynamic social applications to add interactive functions. Through this class, the page containing the activity  calls a script  that queries different social bookmarking websites, then filters and sorts the returned data through previous evaluations and finally outputs them on the activity's page in our language learning platform[13].

Resources are retrieved through an algorithm (made on purpose for this task) which searches different social bookmarking sites at runtime (i.e. every time an activity is loaded), sorts and prints the results. For each web site to be queried our procedure first defines an array of variables, including the regular expression to be used to mine data and a query string, based on the activity's keywords. Then, results are extracted. Since each bookmarking site is organized differently, different technicalities have been designed in order to retrieve as good as possible results, for instance by asking the inquired sites to sort results by popularity, when possible. The algorithm then sorts the collected resources by means of a two-step procedure resulting in a numeric value assigned to each resource of the list.

At the moment, the search is made in two bookmark sites, Digg (http://digg.com/) and xMarks (http://www.xmarks.com/), which offer a good choice of references interesting for language learners, but a higher number of bookmark sites could be used, provided the page structure allows Information Extraction.

## 2.4    The Bookmark-Retrieval Tool in Use

Before testing the described facility with a pilot group of students, we checked what kind of bookmarks were actually retrieved in relation with a variety of learning contents and keyword choices. The outcomes were widely satisfactory in that in all cases we obtained several links to web sites closely related to the activity's topic which can be considered valuable as for richness, accuracy and interest of their content. In most cases, a few improper links were also initially retrieved. These, however, do not constitute a big problem, in that the negative votes assigned by the users make them soon disappear from the list, where they are substituted by newly retrieved (and possibly better) ones.

We found that the typology of the activities' content does influence the amount of good links retrieved. For instance, we always obtained many good links in relation to grammar topics, because many resources containing grammar exercises are currently available on the web and hence it is not rare to meet them. Even better was the adherence of the retrieved links to the assigned keywords when the activity's topic concerned some very well known cultural fact on which there are numerous web sites. On the other hand, pertinent and relevant links were more rare, but never absent, in relation to particular lexical topics, e.g. vocabulary on jobs and professions.

The choice of keywords has an even greater influence on the relevance of the retrieved bookmarks as shown in Fig. 2 and discussed in the next session.

Before opening this component to all online students, we tested it with few students in a beginner and an intermediate course (3 students per level). The choice of two different levels of initial competence had the aim to check if the proposed web extension could result appealing and effective under different conditions.

Beginners were first approaching German, which was completely unknown to them, so that no bias from previous language knowledge could be expected. Moreover, the scarce linguistic competence of beginners makes them still unable to read real documents or listen recordings in the language they are studying; this mostly limits the types of web sites they would be in condition to take advantage of to grammatical and lexical exercises. Intermediate students, on the other hand, worked on English; their competence level allowed more complex activities in the formal course, and also a wider choice of tags for the learning activities, including not only grammatical and lexical but also cultural aspects, likely leading to a richer and more challenging proposal of bookmarks.

None of the students involved had used the platform before, but all of them had familiarity with some social space and hence with the like/dislike voting format. We asked them to work on several units which were suitable for their language level and then to express their opinion on the learning experience, without calling their attention in particular on the bookmark component, because we wanted to see if they would freely make use of, and appreciate, the links and the voting possibility, even without being explicitly requested to do so. All of them were asked to use the platform in a same, short period. At the end of the experience, we collected their opinions by means of semi-structured interviews.

All students in the two groups made use of the bookmark component, visiting more than half of the links displayed (but never all the available ones), and expressed their like or dislike for all sites they visited.

The beginners were offered mostly bookmarks to sites with grammatical exercises, for the reasons explained above. We had defined tags in both English and Italian; as could be easily expected, English keywords yielded more numerous results, not only for the English course but also for the German one, since in general it is easier to find free educational resources addressed to an international audience than to a strictly national one. The mostly grammatical nature of the sites retrieved slightly decreased the students' enthusiasm for this possibility of web navigation, but did not prevent them from making a wide exploration of the links provided. All students started their choice with links having already some "likes", but always continued it including some non-voted one. They explained they had been stimulated to look for external resources because they had found the lessons quite challenging.

The intermediate students found a wider choice of links, since in their case the keywords also included linguistic expressions and cultural topics. The three activities they tackled - Sydney (asking and giving directions), the Tunguska event (reported speech) and Horoscope (could, should, hypothesis and suggestions) - offered nice possibilities to reach out to both grammatical/lexical pages and to cultural ones. The users found web suggestions interesting and enjoyable in general and tended to select web sites that looked most strictly connected with the lesson's linguistic content rather than finding extra information on cultural topics. For the three of them, the number of links visited decreased from the first to the second lesson, but increased again with the third one, due to the fact that they had found this lesson more challenging from the point of view of its linguistic content and hence appreciated the availability of suggestions to make some more practice.

The possibility to complement the official classes with external web pages of various nature was in general perceived as a "pleasant" activity, contributing to building a positive learning climate; this might contribute to foster the learners' interest in the activity, and to indirectly increase their intrinsic motivation [14].

## 2.5    Discussion and Future Improvements

Despite its limited extent, this experience of use resulted encouraging, in that the students were spontaneously inclined to use both the external links and the voting device, and found these possibilities interesting. The preference for visiting sites that had received positive votes from previous users suggests that they tended to consider peers' evaluations potentially useful; analogously, the fact that they tended to resort more to external links when they found the lesson difficult suggests that they viewed favourably complementing the online course with external resources. Further investigations needs to be carried out to check if users' interest remains high over long periods, and how does it vary based on course and users' characteristics. The positive outcomes of this experience, however, show that students' appreciation and actual use are *possible*, and hence our approach is worth being carried on.

It is clear from the above description that the choice of keywords associated to each lesson is a critical point for the success of this bookmark-retrieval tool: keywords need to be defined so as to faithfully mirror the lesson's content and be rich enough to produce a set of bookmarks complementing it from different points of view. They also need, however, to take into consideration the level of language competence that the users are likely to have, in order to avoid that initial difficulties in the use of external resources may discourage the users to resort to the linked web pages even after they have acquired enough competence to do so profitably.

Moreover, very rich sets of keywords usually lead to poor outcomes, in that it is likely difficult to find sites that concern all of them. This may constitute a problem when a compound activity includes more than a topic. For the moment we have overcome this difficulty by asking teachers to revise their activity plan so as to break very rich activities into smaller, homogeneous ones. Another possible way to overcome this problem could be to enhance the implementation by making more than one search round within a same activity, with different sets of keywords.

Also the language in which the keywords are specified has an influence on the outcomes, in that it is it not uncommon to find pages on a given topic in different languages (e.g., grammar exercises may concern English, but also any other language). Hence, it is preferable to use keywords in the target language or at least to specify the target language among them.

The influence of the keywords associated to a learning activity on the bookmarks retrieved is evident in the example presented in Figure 2: even though the tags used in the two cases share two of them and differ just as for the third one, the sets of bookmarks proposed in the two cases is rather different. This highlights another aspect on which some further investigation is necessary, so as to gather useful suggestions to guide and inform teachers' tagging of their lessons.

Being retrieved from social web sites, the set of retrieved bookmarks is not fixed but changes over the time, as everything on the web is in continuous evolution. This however does not appear as a drawback but rather apt to further stimulate users' curiosity, possibly offering some novelty elements at successive processing of a same learning activity.

A critical point for the successful use of this tool is the presence of peers' ratings, because it works as a filter for the bookmarks retrieved. Moreover, they help to create the feeling of belonging to a community of learners and help raising user's interest. This aspect is shared with social spaces in general, and social bookmarking portals in particular: as Hammond and colleagues [6] point out, *"the more they are used, the more value accrues to the system itself and therefore to all who participate in it"*. We can therefore expect students' appreciation and tool usefulness to increase the more the bookmark component will be used.

## 3     Concluding Remarks

A positive point of this bookmark-based tool is the fact that it does not impose much extra burden to either teachers (who just have to define keywords for each activity) or students (who are not obliged for credit to visit any of the suggested bookmarks, if they do not wish so).

Its potentially positive impact on learning derives from the wealth of multi-modal materials, both authentic and created for educational purposes, that the web offers to the learners of almost any language (and certainly for the five languages taught in our formal online learning environment). The suitability of the retrieved links is granted by the content-related keywords defined by the teachers and by the ratings given by fellow users.

Finally, its novelty depends on the fact that, despite its simplicity, the concrete possibility of effective implementation with the current technology, and the actual value of the links retrieved by this mean, the proposed approach to coordinate formal language learning with informal web surfing is at the moment not reported by other authors in the literature.

## References

1. Thomas, M.: Handbook of Research on Web 2.0 and Second Language Learning. IGI Global, Hershey (2010)
2. Dudney, G.: The Internet and the Language Classroom. Cambridge University Press, Cambridge (2007)

3. Murray, D., Macpherson, P.: Using the Web to support Language Learning. Macquire University, North Ryde (2006)
4. Escobar Urmeneta, C., Sánchez Sola, A.: The Internet Classroom Assisstant in pre-service teacher education or learning by doing. In: Piqué-Angodans, A., et al. (eds.) Internet in Language for Specific Purposes and Foreign Language Teaching, pp. 243–258. Universitat Jaume I (2003)
5. Berger, P., Trexler, S.: Choosing Web 2.0 Tools for Learning and Teaching in a Digital World. Libraries unlimited, Santa Barbara, CA (2010)
6. Hammond, T., Hannay, T., Lund, B., Scott, J.: Social Bookmarking tools (I): A general overview. D-Lib Magazine 11(4) (2005),
   `http://www.dlib.org/dlib/april05/hammond/04hammond.html`
   (retrieved January 10, 2012)
7. Millen, D., Yang, M., Whittaker, S., Feinberg, J.: Social Bookmarking and Exploratory Search. In: Bannon, I., Wagner, I., Gutwin, C., Schmidt, K. (eds.) Proc. of the 10th European Conference on Computer Supported Cooperative Work. Springer (2007)
8. Siemens, G.: Connectivism: A Learning Theory for the Digital Age. International Journal of Instructional Technology and Distance Learning, 2(1) (2005),
   `http://itdl.org/Journal/Jan_05/article01.htm` (retrieved January 10, 2012)
9. Surowiecki, J.: The wisdom of crowds. Anchor Books, New York (2005)
10. Nielson, K.: Self-study with language learning software in the workplace: what happens? Language Learning & Technology 15(3) (2011)
11. Torsani, S.: La piattaforma CLiRe: autoistruzione e Web 2.0 (The CLiRe platform: self-instruction and Web 2.0). In: Proceedings of the VII AICLU Conference –Bolzano (2011) (in print; in Italian)
12. Poli, S., Torsani, S.: Toile, bon usage et dictionnaires à la carte. Un exemple d'emploi didactique (Web, good practices, and "à la carte" dictionaries. A case study in the field of Education), Atti delle Seste giornate italiane dei dizionari. In: (Proceedings of the 6th dictionaries Confernece), Università degli Studi di Salerno, April 22-23 92010) (in print; in French)
13. Poli, S., Torsani, S.: Mi piace. Un esempio di evoluzione verso il social networking nell'apprendimento linguistico in rete ("I like it". An example of evolving toward social networking in online language learning). In: Proceedings of the Conference Database, Corpora and Linguistic Teaching, Salerno (2012) (in print, in Italian)
14. Crookes, G., Schmidt, R.: Language Learning Motivation: re-opening the research agenda. Language Learning 41, 469–512 (1991)

# Perceived Support in E-Collaborative Learning: An Exploratory Study Which Make Use of Synchronous and Asynchronous Online-Teaching Approaches

Stefanie Andrea Hillen and Tero Päivärinta

University of Agder, Gimlemoen 25, 4604 Kristiansand, Norway
stefanie.a.hillen@uia.no
Luleå University of Technology, 97187 Luleå, Sweden
tero.paivarinta@ltu.se

**Abstract.** This study compares four different learning environments for e-collaborative learning in two European countries related to the dimension of student's mutual support. The theoretical baseline is Vygotsky's zone of proximal development (ZOPD) and the socio-genetic approach of Piaget. The analyzed data are based on questionnaires collected over the time period of an entire semester including four different courses at the master's level. These courses applied different e-collaborative approaches including a variety of tools for supporting communication. It is assumed that these courses including communication tools e.g. virtual face-to-face meetings enhance the chances for better communication, and finally, for mutual support of students themselves. The objective is to investigate how the different environments have affected the students' perception related to different e-collaborative learning platforms in the dimensions of social support, information exchange, and task support.

**Keywords:** e-collaborative learning, mutual support, blended learning.

## 1 Introduction to Online Teaching Applications, Objectives of the Study and Theoretical Framework on E-Collaboration

### 1.1 Orientation about Online Teaching Applications

The differentiation between synchronous and asynchronous online-teaching applications is taken as a decisive and distinct attribute in online teaching. Empirical research uses this distinction and makes it thereby difficult to analyze and compare teaching effectiveness with their underlying instructional models. On the one hand the term asynchronous online teaching is predominantly used for the application of Learning Management Systems (LMS) in teaching. This kind of learning uses preferentially online discussion-boards as one way of constructing knowledge (Salmon, 2004).

On the other hand synchronous online-teaching by video-conferencing is more seen as capturing lessons in a digital format. This classification does not mirror

E. Popescu et al. (Eds.): ICWL 2012, LNCS 7558, pp. 11–20, 2012.
© Springer-Verlag Berlin Heidelberg 2012

appropriately the potential and variety of application modes in online teaching. Even if these criteria seem obvious this distinction has to be seen rather analytically. Instead of looking for the separating factor between these approaches, this research project wants to open up alternative perspectives in online teaching through an integrated e-collaborative learning approach. A continuum of these approaches is necessary to explore, including a variety of physical tools and pedagogical means which target on different objectives in online teaching should replace this dichotomy.

## 1.2    Objectives of the Study and Theoretical Framework on E-Collaboration

Major goals of collaborative learning are to support social interaction and encourage learner's cognitive processes (Ertl, Kopp, & Mandl, 2005). The cognitive dimension of collaborative learning processes is "… as comprising two relatively independent cognitive systems which exchange messages. It can also be viewed as a single cognitive system with its own properties." (Dillenbourg et al., 1996, p. 3). The research group of Ertl differentiates between three specific mechanisms in collaborative learning, that is, to raise cognitive conflicts, the need for elaborated explanations and negotiations and the co-construction of knowledge.

Regarding social interactions Cecez-Kezcmaniv and Webb (2000) mention that "… by enabling social interactions via an electronic medium, unrestrained by space, time and pace, web technologies actually expand and transform the social interaction space of collaborative learning. Students can work together, achieve shared understanding, and cooperatively solve problems in the new web-mediated environment." The study of Martinez et al. (2002) analyzes the collaboration among students applying different educational designs and tools in online-teaching. One of the results is that the students "… developed new collaborative attitudes beyond the ones they reflected in the initial questionnaire" (Martinez et al., 2002, p. 632). At any rate, e-collaboration does not automatically secure effective learning or improve learning processes and outcomes. Rather, it offers just extended chances for collaborative learning. "These benefits, however, are only achieved by active and well-functioning learning teams." (Soller, et al., 1998). In addition, the impact of collaborative learning cannot easily be transferred to e-collaborative learning.

One phenomenon in e-collaboration is virtual distance which affects the efficacy of collaboration in groups (Lojeski & Reilly, 2008; Lojeski et al., n.d., p. 1). Virtual distance is "… a perceived, psychological distance that accumulates when individuals and team members rely heavily on electronic communication." (Lojeski, et al., n.d., p. 8). "When Virtual Distance is high, team members do not share knowledge with one another. Therefore, they do not collaborate or reflect upon lessons learned from any given work initiative or project." (Lojeski et al., n.d., p. 24). Lojeski mentions various factors which contribute to reduce (f2f communication) or contribute to enhance (cultural differences) the perceived virtual distance. It is important to reduce virtual distance so that virtual socialization can take place as one prerequisite for learning in virtual rooms (Salmon, 2004). Face-to-face (f2f) communication, para-verbal and non-verbal communication are crucial elements in communication processes. A specification in the concept of virtual distance is the one named 'communicative distance' (Lojeski & Reilly,

2008, p. 33ff) which can be explained as the perception or feeling of being separated because of the lack of opportunities for common meaning making. Hence, the choice of an appropriate communication tool is crucial to reduce 'communicative distance'.

If students communicate only by means of text-based discussion boards a reduction of stimulation of senses is occurring which is called channel reduction[1]. This relates to the filter-theory according Döring (2000, p. 355). The opportunity to enhance visual and nonverbal parameters in online-communication by video which include gesture, mimic and *contextual* information, will reduce the 'filter-effect' in electronic based communication.

The blended learning courses mentioned above applied different e-collaborative approaches, including a variety of tools for supporting e-communication. It is assumed that these courses including various communication tools e.g. virtual face-to-face meetings enhance the chances for better communication, and finally, for mutual support of students themselves.

Empirical research has shown that computer-based communication enhances the interaction between learners and increases critical thinking in online discussions (Derry, Levin, & Osana, 2000; Gokale, 1995). According to Vygotsky (1978) one explanation can be seen in the model of ZOPD. In collaborative online teaching this includes the students' colleagues, and teachers as well as the technology supporting communication and interaction as well as access to information. From Piaget's point of view (socio-genesis) the individual cognitive development is seen as a process of equilibration as reaction to external disturbance (cognitive conflicts) induced by social interactions. Lehtinen (2003) remarks that both approaches are essential theoretical foundations for collaborative learning.

To analyze the participation in collaborative learning processes seen as a social interaction process it is analytically divided in three aspects, an action which contributes to learning; information exchange, task support, and social support. The types are adapted of Haythornthwaite's approach (2000, 2002, 2003):

*Collaborative work with information exchange:* To guarantee learning, information has to be shared and circulated to increase the ability of (re-) constructing knowledge by members of the learning community. One prerequisite for learning is the members' perceived 'safe' community. This 'enables' the participant to ask 'dumb' questions.

*Task support:* Task support is any activity to try to accomplish the objectives given by the online community and the teacher and /or the teaching objectives. Online distributed learners need means to accomplish these exchanges as well as means to deliver the end-products like papers, or presentations. (Haythornthwaite, 2002). But task support is more than just the technical infrastructure it is the use of the competence of the people involved considering the idea of ZOPD.

*Social and emotional support:* "Although information exchange is the key to learning environments, communities are not built on instrumental exchanges only." (Haythornthwaite, 2002, p. 172). Social support of peers in e-collaborative learning is needed because of the missing learning and interaction opportunities learners are used to having compared to traditional learning situations. When examining a learning

---

[1] A reduction of information take place through constrained communication channels (para-verbal, non-verbal and visual). This loss of information have an impact on the perception of the collaboration partner (Döring, 2000, p. 355).

community there is a need to analyze the social and emotional support given between the participants. This is because "… information exchange, social support and task support relations are the three major categories of interaction, that are important for building and sustaining learning communities." (Haythornthwaite, 2002, p. 175).

This study asks how the different environments have affected students' perception related to e-collaborative learning in the dimension of social support, information exchange and task support. These dimensions are chosen as dependent variables because they are seen as a prerequisite for e-collaborative learning (Gorghiu, Lindfors, Gorghui & Hämäläinen, 2011; Haythornthwaite, 2000, 2002, 2003; Kopp, Matteucci, & Tomasetto, 2012).

If focusing on the mutual support based on (virtual) socialization that students had experienced during the course, it must be said that these processes lead to stronger or weaker ties between the collaborative learners. Therefore it is not useful to polarize because the strength or weakness of ties leads to different functionalities in collaborating communities. Weak ties are primarily functional; they enable access to new information (exchange of content related information) which stretches over the current knowledge status quo of the single student (Granovetter, 1973, p. 137). Strong ties are rather of an emotional and social nature because they can be traced back to tight relationships (Wellmann & Wortley, 1990, p. 566).

"It is important for individuals to have such a balance of ties in their networks: Weak ties provide exposure to a range of ideas and viewpoint, and strong ties provide the social and emotional support needed to support work in the online environment" (Haythornthwaite, 2000, p. 221).

## 2     Techniques of Inquiry, Settings, Research Methods, and Research Question

For the purpose of data collection two different questionnaires (Q1,2) were applied (see Table 1). The first one (Q1) was used before the course started to gain access to the students' 'general attitude'[2] to online learning. The second one (Q2) aims at the representation of the perception of the students during the courses with respect to satisfaction, social support, information exchange and task support. These questionnaires were applied voluntarily after each lecture over a time period of an entire semester.

The settings of the different Platforms (A-D) followed the idea of blended learning, realized by e-collaborative learning combined with on-campus lectures. Beside on-campus lectures the course settings differed mostly by their synchronous (Platform C, D) and asynchronous teaching (Platform A, B) offers and learning opportunities. The tools to be used in the University courses in IS and EDU (Platform C, D) included an Intelligent round table camera[3], Wikispaces, Fronter etc. The VET students' courses (Platform A, B) used primarily asynchronous learning platforms (discussion boards)

---

[2] The students' general attitude of the different platforms A,C,D have been significantly different towards online learning (pre-test). Conference Paper Earli 2012 SIG 6/7: Attitude, Satisfaction and Support in Blended Learning Approaches (accepted paper).

[3] Microsoft LiveMeeting see http://www.microsoft.com/online/de-de/prod-Livemeeting.aspx

in combination with three on-campus sessions. The VET2 students used additionally prescheduled (sound based) Skype meetings without a camera[4]. The applied e-collaboration tools were didactically adjusted to the curricula, the pre-knowledge and the experience of the involved students e.g. the EDU students received additionally two introduction courses how to participate using LiveMeeting (see Table 2).

Even if it appears that a distinction in these approaches were done by their synchronicity and the tools applied it has to be stressed that the focus were on the opportunities given by these different setting for the mutual support of students, interactions and learning in the dimensions of task support, social support, and information exchange which is presumably seen as a prerequisite for e-collaborative learning (see section 1.2). A qualitative study analyzes these dimensions supported by asynchronous learning opportunities as well[5]. An additional analysis is planned for the learning journals of the students.

Thus, the main research hypothesis is: The four e-collaborative learning approaches differ in respect to the perceived task support, social support, and information exchange by the students.

**Table 1.** Stages of inquiry (selected for this paper)[6]

| Stage 1 | Data collection tool | Stage 2 | Data collection tool |
|---|---|---|---|
| Analysis over all approaches (A-D) on all dep. variables | | Analysis between single approaches on one dep. variable | |
| Information support (dep.v.) | Q2 | | |
| Social support (dep.v.) | Q2 | Social support (dep.v.) | Q2 |
| Task support (dep.v.) | Q2 | | |
| General satisfaction (dep.v.) | Q2 | | |
| General attitude (dep.v.) | Q1 | | |

## 3    Data Sources, Materials and Findings

The data collection is based on n=53 students. This includes the questionnaires about the 3 dimensions of support and students' general satisfaction. The master students are from 2 different universities in Europe and are enrolled in 4 different master's program courses and belong to 3 different departments (Education, VET, Information Systems). In addition, verbal data is collected by discussion boards, and learning journals over the period of an entire semester as well as examination results.

---

[4]  This is a restriction by the provider for group meeting sessions.

[5]  Conference paper ECER 2012, Cadiz, Spain: The role of discussion boards in e-collaborative learning (accepted paper).

[6]  The development of the tools for data collection and the data collection itself was conducted by the authors.

**Table 2.** Database[7]

| Blended learning approach | Students (n) | University | Question-naires2 (N) | Tools[8] | Artifacts[9] |
|---|---|---|---|---|---|
| Platform A (VET1) | 23 | Germany | 29 | OC; R; | D; G |
| Platform B (VET2) | 7 | Germany | 15 | OC, R; S | D; G |
| Platform C (EDU) | 13 | Norway | 21 | OC; LM | V; G |
| Platform D (IS) | 10 | Norway | 59 | OC; LM;W | V; G; D; J; |
| Total | 53 | | 124 | | |

A non-parametric test[10] was used to analyze the e-collaborative learning approaches named platform A-D. One test was conducted for each dependent variable: social support, information exchange, and task support. While all three hypotheses had to be rejected, the hypothesis with the dependent variable 'social support' (see Table 3) was just barely not to be confirmed with a p-value of 0.057.

**Table 3.** Kruskal-Wallis test over all approaches to the dimension of 'social support'[11]

| Blended learning approach | N (delivered questionnaires) | Average rang | Social support |
|---|---|---|---|
| Platform A (VET1) | 29 | 50,24 | |
| Platform B (VET2) | 15 | 68,87 | |
| Platform C (EDU) | 21 | 76,36 | |
| Platform D (IS) | 59 | 61,97 | |
| Total of N | 124 | | |
| Chi- Square | | | 7,50 |
| df | | | 3 |
| Asympt. significance | | | ,057 |

The effect size was = 0.061, that is, 6% of the differences of the average rang can be explained by the different blended learning approaches[12]. Even if this group difference is not significant it has to be interpreted as evidence to be further investigated in a single study. The first analysis (see Table 3) was conducted by a Kruskal-Wallis test over all platforms but not individually between these groups. An additional analysis by a single non parametric-test was carried out - each with two platforms using an

---

[7] see footnote 6.

[8] Tools: R = Reader (LMS), asynchronous text based tool;
OC = On Campus lectures; S = Skype, synchronous video-tool, LM = LiveMeeting, synchronous video tool; W = Wiki, asynchronous text based tool.

[9] Artifacts: D = students' Discussion boards, G = students' Grades, V = Video-taped lecture, J = students' learning Journals.

[10] A non-parametric test had to be chosen because of the data's distribution.

[11] The presented enquiry is based on the master thesis of Lecher (2012).

[12] From Cohen's (1988, p. 27) point of view this has to be treated as a low effect size. An average or high effect size is between 0.5 and 0.8.

apriori-hypothesis[13] which can be verified or falsified. This test confirmed a statistical significant (p=0,018) difference between platform A and C (C applied LiveMeeting) regarding the dependent variable 'social support' (see Table 4.). It is to be stressed that the single tool application was not in focus; rather the entire course (approach) included all communication chances and tools which were proposed and used for the analysis. With regard to enhancing the readability, just one tool was mentioned.

**Table 4.** Individual Kruskal-Wallis test to the dimension of 'social support'[14]

| Experiment | N (delivered questionnaires) | Average rang | Social support |
|---|---|---|---|
| Platform A (VET1) | 29 | 21,43 | |
| Platform C (EDU) | 21 | 31,12 | |
| Total of N | 50 | | |
| Chi- Square | | | 5,643 |
| df | | | 1 |
| Asympt. significance | | | ,018 |

An additional analysis was conducted applying a Kruskal Wallis test to examine the 'general satisfaction' both Platforms C and D ranked significantly higher (p =0.00) than the others.[15] These platforms C and D were using the tool 'LifeMeeting' which is an intelligent face to face (f2f) communication tool.

## 4    Conclusions and Scientific and Scholarly Significance of the Study

Referring to Haythornthwaite (2000) it can be concluded that the average ranking *of all* the three relevant dimensions of support (task, information, and social) for well-functioning virtual learning groups has been perceived stronger in IS and EDU (Platform C,D) than in the learning approaches of VET1 and VET2 (Platform A, B)[16]. According to Granovetter (1973) it can be concluded that in both learning approaches VET1 and 2 less stronger or less weaker ties have been developed over one entire semester compared to IS and EDU.

One exception to these results was indicated by the learning approach of VET2 (Platform B) regarding 'social support'. In VET2 the perceived 'social support' was ranked in second place with 68,87 (see Table 3) that is, they have built stronger ties compared to IS students (Platform D). From Granovetter's (1973) point of view,

---

[13] An apriori hypothesis is an assumption, formulated before the analysis is conducted to be able to predict a presumed result (Bortz & Döring, 2006, p. 379). Platform A – Platform C: p=0,018 < 0,05.

[14] see footnote 11.

[15] Accepted Conference Paper Earli 2012 SIG 6/7: Attitude, Satisfaction and Support in Blended Learning Approaches.

[16] These results over all dependent variables are not shown in this paper.

strong ties generate social support whereas week ties are rather content related. So it can be concluded that stronger ties have been developed in VET2 or were already there before (because the master's students had eventually met one another before - during their bachelor studies). In addition, they have used synchronous, sound based Skype-meetings for communication.

If we take the theoretical construct of virtual distance into account it may be assumed that the perceived virtual distance of the VET1and 2 students was higher. Support is based on the estimation of the other(s). Using primarily text-based communication[17] the psycho-social background of the collaborative partner is hardly visible because of channel reduction[18], potentially leading to a negative impact on the perceived virtual distance; hence, this can have hampered support. The mostly asynchronous and text-based interaction of the VET1 and VET2 students might explain the lower values of perceived support (task, information and social) compared to those of EDU and IS.

Continuing this argumentation the average and higher ranking of IS and PED approaches (Platform C; D) can be explained by the implemented communication tools in combination with the methodical conception of the courses. The ratio of presences' of EDU students was around 80 % and 73 % of the IS students. Beside the actual f2f interactions, LiveMeeting was applied which is quite close to natural f2f conversations. Because of the less reduced interaction chances (less channel reduction) the virtual distance was presumable perceived less high. At any rate, the general satisfaction was significantly highest (p= 0,00) with the platforms C (EDU) and D (IS) (see section 3), having most actual and most virtual f2f interactions. Summarizing these findings and conclusions one can say that the significance of the study relies on the evidence that e-collaborative learning needs more than a well-designed instructional model with a variety of technological tools. The challenge is not just to investigate synchronous or asynchronous online tools as competitive or complementary but to stress social aspects as well. Understanding the phenomenon 'support' -for instance being able to validate the meaning of stronger and weaker ties in e-collaboration- can help instructional designers and facilitators to better design and support collaborative activities to enhance learning processes.

# References

1. Bortz, J., Döring, N.: Forschungsmethoden und Evaluationen für Human- und Sozialwissenschaftler, 4th edn. Springer, Heidelberg (2006)
2. Brody, C.M., Davidson, N.: Introduction: Professional development and Cooperative learning. In: Brody, C.M., Davidson, N. (eds.) Professional Development for Cooperative Learning- Issues and Approaches, State University of NY Press, Albany (1998)

---

[17] VET2 students have worked 67% of their time virtually asynchronously whereas the VET1 students have worked 100% virtually asynchronously beside their three on campus sessions.

[18] A reduction of information take place through constrained communication channels (paraverbal, non-verbal and visual).This loss of information have an impact on the perception of the collaboration partner (Döring, 2000, p. 355).

3. Bruffee, K.A.: Sharing our toys - Cooperative learning versus collaborative learning. Change, 1–2, 12–18 (1995)
4. Cecez-Kecmanovic, D., Webb, C.: Towards a communicative model of collaborative web-mediated learning. Australian Journal of Educational Technology (1), 73–85 (2000), http://www.ascilite.org.au/ajet/ajet16/cecez-kecmanovic.html retrieved June 08, 2011 )
5. Cohen, J.: Statistical Power Analysis for the Behavioral Science, 2nd edn. Lawrence Erlbaum, New Jersey (1988)
6. Derry, S.J., Levin, J.R., Osana, H.P.: Fostering students' statistical and scientific thinking: Lessons learned from an innovative college course. American Educational Research Journal 37(3), 747–775 (2000)
7. Dick, W., Cary, L.: The systematic design of instruction, 3rd edn. Harper Collins, New York (2000)
8. Dillenbourg, P., Baker, M., Blaye, A., O'Malley, C.: The evolution of research on collaborative learning. In: Spada, E., Reiman, P. (eds.) Learning in Humans and Machine: Towards an Interdisciplinary Learning Science, pp. 189–211. Elsevier, Oxford (1996)
9. Döring, N.: Kommunikation im Internet: Neun theoretische Ansätze. In: Batinic, B. (ed.) Internet für Psychologen, 2nd edn., pp. 345–379. Hogrefe, Göttingen (2000)
10. Ertl, B., Kopp, B., Mandl, H.: Supporting Collaborative Learning in Videoconferencing using Collaboration Scripts and Content Schemes (Research report No. 176). Germany: Ludwig-Maximilians-University, Department of Psychology, Institute for Educational Psychology, Munich (2005)
11. Gorghiu, G., Lindfors, E., Gorghiu, L.M., Hämäläinen, T.: Acting as Tutors in the ECSUT On-line Course - How to Promote Interaction in a Computer Supported Collaborative Learning Environment? Procedia Computer Science 3(1), 579–583 (2011)
12. Gokhale, A.A.: Collaborative Learning Enhances Critical Thinking. Journal of Technology Education 7(1), 22–31 (1995)
13. Granovetter, M.S.: The Strength of Weak Ties. American Journal of Sociology 78(6), 1360–1380 (1973)
14. Haythornthwaite, C.: Online Personal Networks: Size, Composition and Media Use among Learners. New Media Society 2(2), 159–226 (2000)
15. Haythornthwaite, C.: Building social networks via computer networks: Creating and sustaining distributed learning communities. In: Renninger, K.A., Shumar, W. (eds.) Building virtual Communities: Learning and Change in Cyberspace, pp. 159–190. Cambridge University Press, Cambridge (2002)
16. Haythornthwaite, C.: Supporting distributed relationships: social networks. In: Joinson, A.N., McKenna, K., Postmes, T., Reips, U.D. (eds.) The Oxford Handbook of Internet Psychology, pp. 121–138. University Press, Oxford (2003)
17. Jonassen, D.H.: What are cognitive Tools? In: Kommers, P.A.M., Jonassen, D.H., Mayes, J.T. (eds.) Cognitive Tools for Learning, pp. 1–6. Springer, Heidelberg (1991)
18. Kopp, B., Matteucci, M.C., Tomasetto, C.: E-tutorial support for collaborative online learning: An explorative study. Computers & Education, 58(1), 12–20, 3270–3273 (2012)
19. Lecher, R.: E-Kollaboratives Lernen im Studium - Eine Pilotstudie. Johannes Gutenberg University Mainz. Unpublished master thesis (2012)
20. Lehtinen, E.: Computer Supported Collaborative Learning: An Approach to Powerful Learning Environments. In: De Coerte, E., Verschaffel, L., Entwistle, N., van Merrienboer, J. (eds.) Powerful Learning Environments: Unravelling Basic Components and Dimensions, pp. 33–55. Elsevier, Oxford (2003)

21. Lojeski, K.: Virtual Distance. A proposed model for the study of virtual work. Stevens Institute of Technology. Dissertation (2006)
22. Lojeski, K.S., Reilly, R.: Uniting the Virtual Workforce: Transforming Leadership and Innovation in the Globally Integrated Enterprise. John Wiley & Sons, New Jersey (2008)
23. Lojeski, K.S., Reilly, R., Dominick, P.: The Role of Virtual Distance in Innovation and Success. System Sciences (35), 25–34 (2006)
24. Lojeski, K.S., London, M., Reilly, R.: The Role of Virtual Distance and Group Learning: A Case Study from Big Pharma and Financial Services (n.d.), http://www.industrystudies.pitt.edu/pittsburgh11/documents/Papers/PDF%20Papers/7-6%20Sobel%20Lojeski.pdf (retrieved January 17, 2012)
25. Panitz, T. (1996), http://www.londonmet.ac.uk/deliberations/collaborative-learning/panitz-paper.cfm (retrieved June 08, 2011)
26. Piaget, J.: Meine Theorie der geistigen Entwicklung. Beltz, Weinheim/Basel (2003)
27. Reigeluth, C.M.: Instructional design: What is it and why is it? In: Reigeluth, C.M. (ed.) Instructional Theories and Models: An Overview of Their Current Status, pp. 1–36. Lawrence Erlbaum, Hillsdale (1983)
28. Rockwood, R.: Cooperative and collaborative learning. National Teaching and Learning Forum 4(6) (1995) (retrieved June 2011), http://home.capecod.net/~tpanitz/tedsarticles/coopdefinition.htm
29. Roschelle, J., Teasley, S.: The construction of shared knowledge in collaborative problem solving. In: O'Malley, C.E. (ed.) Computer Supported Collaborative Learning, pp. 69–97. Springer, Heidelberg (1995)
30. Säljö, R.: Learning as the use of tools: a sociocultural perspective on the human-technology link. In: Littleton, K., Light, P. (eds.) Learning with Computers: Analysing Productive Interaction, pp. 144–161. Routledge, London (1999)
31. Salmon, G.: E-moderating, 2nd edn. The key to teaching and learning online. Routhledge Falmer, London (2004)
32. Soller, A., Goodman, B., Linton, F., Gaimari, R.: Promoting Effective Peer Interaction in an Intelligent Collaborative Learning System. In: Goettl, B.P., Halff, H.M., Redfield, C.L., Shute, V.J. (eds.) ITS 1998. LNCS, vol. 1452, pp. 186–195. Springer, Heidelberg (1998)
33. Vygotsky, L.S.: Mind in society: The development of higher psychological processes. Harvard Business Press, Cambridge (1978)
34. Wellman, B., Wortley, S.: Different Strokes from Different Folks: Community Ties and Social Support. American Journal of Sociology 96(3), 558–588 (1990)

# How to Get Around with Wikis in Teaching

Zuzana Kubincová and Martin Homola

Comenius University, Faculty of Mathematics, Physics and Informatics,
Mlynská dolina, 84248 Bratislava, Slovakia
{kubincova,homola}@fmph.uniba.sk

**Abstract.** Wikis were showed to be an interesting and powerful tool in education, supporting tasks starting from project management, collaborative data management, etc., up to more elaborate tasks such as collaborative production of lecture notes, reports, and essays. On the other hand, most wiki softwares were not created as educational tools in the first place, hence their application in curricula with groups of students faces some obstacles which need to be dealt with. These include motivating the students to engage with the tool, boosting collaboration between students, supervising and tracking student's activity, and evaluation. A number of tools were developed to enable or ease these tasks for the teacher. This paper takes a look on selected tools developed with this aim with two main goals: to produce a concise list of functionalities that are needed, and to compare and evaluate the tools that are available.

**Keywords:** wiki, teaching, collaboration, tools.

## 1 Introduction

The advent of Web 2.0, with its various tools for content creation and sharing, has generated an increased interest in employing these tools in education [4]. Among these tools are wikis, a sort of collaborative websites whose content is not created by some webmaster but instead it can be directly contributed by the users. Wikis have great potential especially for any collaborative activity and they have been successfully applied in teaching and learning in various ways from maintaining project pages, and obtaining feedback on course materials, to collaborative lecture notes construction and co-writing exercises [3,14,9,4].

On the other hand, wikis were not originally conceived as educational tools, to be used by a group of students for specific tasks with educational goals whose work is supervised and evaluated by the teacher. Most wikis offer only basic features that can support the tasks the students and especially the teachers have to carry out in fostering and keeping track of the students' activity and their educational progress which is to be evaluated and assessed. This fact makes more sophisticated uses of wikis difficult for the educators, if not impossible with larger groups of students. This problem was noted by researchers [14] and multiple tools that can support the educational process with wikis were proposed and developed either as plugins or extensions of existing wikis (e.g., Co-Writing Wiki [1,2], EdDokuWiki [9,10], and Tracking Bundle for MediaWiki [7]) or as self-standing wiki-based educational systems (e.g., ClassroomWiki [5,6]).

E. Popescu et al. (Eds.): ICWL 2012, LNCS 7558, pp. 21–30, 2012.

These tools can be useful in organization and evaluation of student's work, but some of their features can also have significant impact on the learning outcome. On the other hand, they were often designed to support specific needs faced by a specific group of teachers tackling a specific application of a wiki in the educational process. In this paper, we build on the experience with these tools, and we look at the problem from a broader perspective. We first concentrate on the process in which a wiki is typically applied in education, and we study the tasks faced by students and teachers as well. Our attention is then shifted towards features and functions that can be useful in supporting these tasks. We produce a list of possible features, that were either described in the literature but also based on our own experience. Finally, we get back to the existing tools and evaluate them in order to find out which of these functionalities they currently offer. This study maybe useful for the potential user of these tools, who is trying to select the best tool for her needs (albeit not all of the tools are freely available). More importantly, the list can help the developers to extend their tools or to build new tools with improved versatility and more universal applicability. Our survey of these tools is based on the published research reports and partly on direct communication with the authors.

## 2    Use of Wikis in the Educational Process

In this section we take a look on the goals and especially tasks placed on students and teachers engaged with a wiki in an educational process. We start from student's point of view passing the phases of work carried out by the students. Then we look on the tasks required from the teacher.

### 2.1    Student's Tasks

Wiki-based assignments are typically collaborative content development tasks, inherent to the nature of wikis. As such, the work has to be split somehow at the beginning, then content is built which includes some interaction between students. Additionally, students may be involved in self assessment and/or peer review to strengthen reflection and social learning.

**Material study:** the assignment may often involve study of materials that are to be processed or in which useful information is found. This is usually placed as the very first step in the process [14,10] however the materials will likely be referred to also later in the process.

**Work planning:** typically the assignment is placed on a group of students who first have to split up the work among themselves and possibly plan the content structure thus exercising important competencies such as group management and collaborative tasks planning [14,10,2].

**Writing/content development:** the principal task in which text is written, other content developed and put in place. Each student may work on her own part as assigned during the planning phase, incorporating feedback from others, however deeper collaboration patterns in which students exchange their parts, or take turns in passes are also possible. It is important to note that while content-wise this phase is principal, and is often perceived as such by the students, it need not necessarily carry the majority of pedagogical goals, especially if emphasis is placed on the latter phases.

**Social interaction:** an important part of the process is interaction during which students communicate, comment on the work of others, ask questions and share ideas. Comparing one's point of view on the subject with others enhances social learning and enables consensus to be formed, thus this phase is very important [3,14,8]. Wiki tools are well equipped for this task, however, engagement in interaction may not be granted for many students who may see it as unnecessary work.

**Peer review and peer assessment:** one of the most effective strategies to reinforce interaction and social learning is to ask students to review and comment on the work done by others [14]. Students benefit from understanding the others view point on the topic and from getting feedback on their own work. To further reinforce and simplify this process, students may be asked to rate the work of their colleagues on some scale [10,2].

**Self assessment:** to foster critical perception of one's own work students may be asked to rate as well the work done by themselves [2,1]. As explained later on, this may also ease the evaluation process for the teacher.

## 2.2  Teacher's Tasks

A number of tasks has to be coped by the teacher as well. The assignment needs to be communicated to the students and typically students have to be broken into smaller teams. During the content development students have to be coordinated in order to maintain desired levels of collaboration and interaction, and to avoid free riding, student apathy, and other common problems associated with online group learning [11]. In addition the collaborative work has to be evaluated which is a non-trivial task.

**Instruction:** the assignment can easily be delivered as a wiki page. In these instructions, the teacher not only describes the scope of the work to be done, but also has to carefully guide the students to act collaboratively and to interact. Wiki tools allow to comment on any page, hence it is good if the students may ask additional questions and get answers from the teacher so the assignment may become interactive. In addition, the teacher may add further instructions during the supervision of students placed directly into the students work-in-progress pages as special wiki templates [7]. Students then react to these contextual, or just-in-time instructions by carrying out the indicated changes and removing the template.

**Group formation and interaction policy:** in large groups, some students may feel that there is too little space for them to contribute [7], hence it is strongly desired to split them into smaller groups [14,5,11]. While theoretically, groups can be self-organized by students, a number of reports stress on well balanced groups carefully selected by the teacher which may improve the collaboration outcome [5,11].

**Supervision:** collaborative writing and content creation takes time, and the whole process has to be supervised by the teacher in order to avoid leaving the work to the last moment which many students tend to do and which would marginalize the collaborative goals. Tracking of students contributions and interactions allows the teacher to understand better the dynamics of student's learning and to provide a proactive and timely scaffolding to the students or groups [6]. Student's motivation has to be built via feedback and other means and collaboration with other students has to be encouraged. Formative intermediate feedback can improve student's performance and learning outcome: hence it is useful to split also the evaluation in multiple (e.g., weekly or biweekly) phases [7].

**Assessment:** assessment of a collaborative assignment is a difficult task [14,10,7], an increased number of edits has to be inspected and multiple aspects have to be evaluated and then combined. These include content quality, collaboration, communication, cross-referencing, and possibly more. As already noted, intermediate evaluation may improve motivation, and it also reduces the momentary workload placed on the teacher.

## 3   Functionality to Support Wiki-Based Learning

As wikis were not originally conceived as educational tools, they do not provide many functions needed for comfortable integration into the educational process. As pointed out by previous research, many useful functionalities are lacking [14]. In this section we list the most interesting functions that would be useful to integrate into a typical wiki implementation in order to support the educational process and its goals, and ease the tasks placed on teachers and students.

**Instruction delivery support:** instructions and assignments may be easily delivered as wiki pages, however, additional support of contextual just-in-time instruction may be beneficial. To certain extent this can be achieved by dedicated editor templates created by the teacher [7], but clearly there is space for further research.

**Group management:** breaking students into smaller groups is highly desired [14,1,10] but most wikis do not support this function. Apart from users, also the wiki pages they are supposed to work on should be part of the group [7] and even a dedicated group homepage gathering the groups recent activity was proven useful [6,1]. Automated group formation tools can be used to balance group members [5]. Access control and group roles can also be useful in some learning scenarios.

**Writing aids:** there is open space for equipping wikis with various writing aids such as spell checkers, thesauri, literature tracking and sharing tools, etc. Currently we only found mentions of incorporating a WYSIWYG editor [6]. This can ease writing, on the other hand, wikitext languages are quite simple and learning them can be considered a useful skill in the digital age. Tools for resolving conflicts and other aids for collaborative writing [12] may also be useful.

**Content archiving:** in certain cases archiving previous runs of the course, cleaning the wiki for new cohort of students while enabling the teacher to browse older runs of the course would be useful.

**Motivation and collaboration boosting:** to motivate student's engagement, the assignment is usually made part of overall assessment including interaction processes such as cross-linking, peer review, etc. Additional tools useful for motivating students and fostering collaboration include monitors showing online presence of their colleagues [1] and automatic reminders of planned activities [6]. Another option that can be useful is to introduce student's profile pages with visualization of their progress and achievements.

**Social interaction:** communication between users is typically supported in wikis via discussion pages (e.g., in MediaWiki), which are edited as any other page (i.e., messages are directly written into the page). While this is an effective form of communication, automated tracking and evaluation of student's interaction calls for structured discussion in form of messages or comments [1,10] which can be more easily processed. Typical implementation would include comments under each page and peer to peer messages between students. More elaborate one would allow to create fora on any topic and comment on them [6].

**Activity tracking:** the tools provided by a typical wiki for user's activity tracking include revision history and revision diffs. Typically it is possible to browse history of each page, and as well overall recent changes in the wiki. Once students groups are added to a wiki, filtering revisions by the group should be added to ease tracking of group activity. As the number of revisions can be high, additional filters, such as arbitrary time window can be very useful [7]. Basic revision difference visualization can be enhanced by highlighting the contribution of each user by unique colors, which facilitates the teacher in the process of examining the revisions [1].

Besides for changes in the pages (active usage), other activities should be tracked, such as frequency of user's access of a page and time spent there (passive usage), hyperlinks between the pages and also with outside sources, social interaction and communication [6,14]. To support data analysis, this information should be visualized in form of charts and diagrams [14,1,7].

**Teacher assessment:** assessment capabilities are not part of wikis but for teachers they can be very useful. Basic option would be to add evaluation (points, grades, comments) to each student once or multiple times per course [10]. Another option is to add evaluation to every revision and to compute the overall result by some formula [7]. This evaluation can also be structured (i.e., multiple aspects evaluated for each revision separately) [7] or possibly data recorded from tracking passive usage and social activities, can be part of the formula [14,1]. As the number of revisions can be high, some form of grouping partial revisions before assigning the points may also be useful.

Other useful features that could facilitate assessment include integration with some anti-plagiarism tools, or analyzers that can detect excessive similarities between different students' output. Also assessment questionnaires may be useful, especially with distance courses.

**Self assessment:** basic self assessment can be readily implemented via revision comments which are common in wikis. Enhancements may include adding numerical self evaluation of each revision's relevance to overall group task and incorporating this into revision filters and grading formulae [1].

**Peer assessment:** peer review and peer assessment in form of commentary can be easily implemented via the social layer. This can be further enhanced by adding user, page, revision and comment rating facilities [1,10]. Again, the recorded data can be incorporated into the final grading formula [1].

## 4    Existing Tools

As most wikis were not originally aimed at educational uses, a number of lacking functionalities that would be useful in the teaching scenarios were identified, as we summarize in previous section. Given the usefulness of wikis, this problem was already addressed by some implementations. In this section we review and compare ClassroomWiki, Co-Writing Wiki, EdDokuWiki, and Tracking Bundle for MediaWiki.

### 4.1    ClassroomWiki

ClassroomWiki [5,6] was developed at the University of Nebraska-Lincoln. It was developed as an research prototype and it is not being used at the parent university any longer. Unlike its preceding prototype I-MINDS [13] in which most of the students' activities was based on synchronous collaboration, this wiki-like collaborative environment was designed as an asynchronous tool mainly used for collaborative writing. In contrast to the following tools, ClassroomWiki was developed from scratch, i.e., it is not based on any existing wiki implementation. Together with wiki it offers other functionalities such as fora and announcements which are composed into an unified collaborative learning environment.

Students and teachers are assigned different roles with distinct rights. Student's view is similar to a regular wiki with versioning and revision tracking, comparison and visualization. A distinctive feature is a WYSIWYG editor for wiki pages which is not a standard for regular wikis which normally prefer wikitext (a simple markup language) editors. In the topic-based forum students can discuss their plans and contributions with other group members as well as communicate with the teacher.

ClassroomWiki adds significant functionalities for the teacher: students activity tracking and visualization which includes active usage (number of words added, changed or deleted), passive usage (number of page and revision history views) and interaction (number of topics created in fora and number of messages posted). An assessment tool is provided by which the student's contribution to the group task can be evaluated. The evaluation is based on combination of data from student's activity tracking with the peer rating results. The teacher is also able to create survey forms which are then filled in by the students.

A distinctive feature offered by ClassroomWiki is the automated group formation tool. Based on collaborative learning theories [11,3], the tool enables to optimize the distribution of students into groups in the way that improves the collaborative learning outcome.

### 4.2    Co-Writing Wiki

Co-Writing Wiki [1,2], developed at the Graz University of Technology, is aimed as tool to support collaborative writing with self assessment, peer reviewing, social awareness and other enhancements. It is based on the open source ScrewTurn Wiki.

Students arrive on a dedicated assignment homepage, where they can see revisions done by other students (of the same group), these revisions can be browsed, difference visualized, and each revision can be commented upon and rated, which is used for the peer assessment process. The assignment homepage also includes contribution charts where they can track their contribution to the collaborative task and compare it with other group members as well as with progress of other groups. To boost social awareness, information about group members currently online is also showed.

The teacher is able to explore the activity of each group on their assignment. Each group member is assigned a unique color by which her part of contribution to the assignment pages is marked up. A unique feature is the history player which allows the teacher to go over a selected wiki-page as a slide show and keep track of particular student's contributions by following her color. Useful statistics is also showed which goes beyond usual wiki statistics: number of revisions made, characters changed, but also links created by each student. Visualization charts are also provided to the teacher including contribution chart, navigation graph, and social network graph. The teacher is also able to send feedback to the students and to evaluate their contribution.

The Co-Writing Wiki dedicates special attention to self assessment and peer assessment. When editing a wiki page, the student is asked to indicate her intention (add text, delete text, change style) and also to rate the significance of the edit towards the group's final goal. After the new revision of the assignment Wiki-page is posted, other group members are allowed to review it (using comments) and rate it. This internal peer review process can be configured to be mandatory. Moreover, there is a special tool by which students assess the final product of other groups. This assessment is structured into so called assessment rubrics. The teacher then can take the peer review and peer assessment into account during the final grading.

## 4.3   EdDokuWiki

EdDokuWiki [9,10], developed at the University of Craiova, is an extension of the popular open-source system DokuWiki with additional features related to collaborative learning and evaluation of student's work which were triggered by the experience with DokuWiki in teaching. This tool is not yet released, but it is already being used in courses at its parent university.

Students are enabled to peer review the others' contributions, rate wiki-pages, add comments, as well as to rate comments they receive. The comments rating is particularly interesting. It is supposed to indicate the utility of the feedback received from peers, and the teacher can take it into account during grading.

For the teacher, this tool enables to track and summarize students' interactions with the wiki, including time and frequency of accesses, pages created and edited by each student, internal and external links added, comments added, comment and page ratings, and number of characters changed. This summary allows the teacher to grasp the level of students engagement with the wiki and the evaluation of the students by her peers. The teacher is then allowed to give grading and also individual textual feedback to the student using a dedicated interface which is also a part of this tool.

## 4.4  Tracking Bundle for MediaWiki

Tracking Bundle [7] is an extension for MediaWiki that offers tools for students activity tracking and assessment. This open-source tool was developed at the Comenius University of Bratislava and it was released via the MediaWiki extension matrix service.

This tool is especially visible for the teacher and it allows to create student groups and to track and evaluate the student's activity within the group. The groups are built on top of MediaWiki users and the same user can independently participate in multiple

**Table 1.** Concise comparison of the existing tools functionalities

|  | CRW | CWW | EDW | TB |
|---|---|---|---|---|
| **Groups** | | | | |
| Creation and Management | Y | Y | (Y) | Y |
| Group Homepage | Y | Y | | |
| Automatic formation | Y | | | |
| Access control | | Y | (Y) | |
| **Motivation** | | | | |
| Online presence monitor | | Y | | |
| Activity reminders | Y | | | |
| **Writing aids** | | | | |
| WYSIWYG editor | Y | | | |
| **Social layer** | | | | |
| Discussion pages | | | | (Y) |
| Comments | | Y | Y | |
| Per revision comments | | Y | | |
| Fora | Y | | | |
| **Tracking** | | | | |
| Active interaction | Y | Y | Y | Y |
| Passive interaction | Y | | | |
| Links | | Y | Y | |
| Graphical visualization | | Y | | Y |
| Revision diff. visualization | | Y | (Y) | (Y) |
| **Self and peer assessment** | | | | |
| Self assessment | | Y | | |
| Peer review | Y | Y | Y | (Y) |
| Page rating | | | Y | |
| Other groups rating | | Y | | |
| Comment rating | | | Y | |
| **Teacher assessment** | | | | |
| Overall | Y | Y | Y | Y |
| Per revision/action | | Y | | Y |
| Structured | Y | Y | | Y |
| Configurable | | | | Y |
| **Distribution** | | | | |
| Open source | | | | Y |
| Based on wiki | own | ScrewTurn Wiki | DokuWiki | MediaWiki |
| Platform | Java | ASP.NET | PHP | PHP |

groups (e.g., respective to two distinct courses). Users but as well wiki pages of interest are assigned to the group.

Using the tracking tool, the teacher is able to view the activity for each group as a chronological listing of revisions of pages related to the group. Additional filters (e.g., time intervals, selected users or pages only, etc.) can be applied to break down the number of revisions showed. The teacher is also able to assess each revision by points. A distinctive feature of this tool is that the assessment is structured into multiple categories which are configurable (the three predefined categories are new content, modified content, and grammar/editing). Final grading of each revision is then computed by a dedicated formula, which is also fully configurable by the user.

In addition the tool provides summarization of the results in tables and useful visualization in form of charts, including chronological activity in time, shares of points earned by different students (i.e., how many points each of the students earned), but as well shares of student's points by different categories (i.e., how many points of each type the student earned). Same filters can be applied on the visualizations as well, so for instance the score earned during any selected time period or only the score respective to selected wiki-pages can be visualized.

### 4.5  Comparison

In Section 3 we have gone through a number of features which may facilitate the applications of wikis in teaching. Many of these are already supported by some of the tools described above. In Table 1 we present a comparative summary of the four tools. The columns are respective to ClassroomWiki (CRW), Co-Writing Wiki (CWW), EdDokuWiki (EDW), and Tracking Bundle (TB). By "Y" we indicate if the tool provides dedicated functionality which supports the feature and "(Y)" indicates that the feature is already supported by the underlaying wiki software on top of which the tool was built.

## 5  Conclusions

Employing wikis in educational practice is a rewarding experience, it contributes to development of important skills and competencies including team work and collaboration and it boosts social learning and thus improves the learning outcome. In this paper we have inspected the process associated with educational applications of wikis, focusing on the tasks placed on students and teachers and especially on the useful supportive features which the wiki-based learning environment should provide.

Out of these features, many have been already implemented in the existing supportive tools such as ClassroomWiki, Co-Writing Wiki, EdDokuWiki, or Tracking Bundle for MediaWiki. This includes group management, activity tracking, teacher assessment but also self assessment, peer review, and other features.

But there is also a number of features that we have identified, to our best knowledge, not yet implemented in any wiki-based learning environment. This includes profile pages for users which would visualize students' overall progress and their achievements, more writing aids, content management and archiving, plagiarism detection tools. In addition, we see significant space for improvement of existing tools for activity tracking and assessment with more advanced functions such as grouping of multiple revisions before evaluation, and better visualization options. Providing for such features would surely be useful for the students and for the teachers who are dealing with wiki assignments in their courses.

# References

1. AL-Smadi, M., Höfler, M., Gütl, C.: Enhancing wikis with visualization tools to support groups production function and to maintain task and social awareness. In: Procs. of ICBL 2011, Antigua, Guatemala (2011)
2. AL-Smadi, M., Höfler, M., Gütl, C.: Integrated and enhanced e-assessment forms for learning: Scenarios from alice project. In: Procs. of Special Track on Computer-based Knowledge & Skill Assessment and Feedback in Learning Settings (CAF 2011), ICL 2011, Piestany, Slovakia (2011)
3. Cress, U., Kimmerle, J.: A systemic and cognitive view on collaborative knowledge building with wikis. The International Journal of Computer-Supported Collaborative Learning 3(2) (2008)
4. Homola, M., Kubincová, Z.: Taking advantage of Web 2.0 in organized education (a survey). In: Procs. of ICL 2009, Villach, Austria (2009)
5. Khandaker, N., Soh, L.K.: Classroomwiki: a collaborative wiki for instructional use with multiagent group formation. IEEE Transactions on Learning Technologies 3(3), 190–202 (2010)
6. Khandaker, N., Soh, L.K., Miller, L.D., Eck, A., Jiang, H.: Lessons learned from comprehensive deployments of multiagent CSCL applications I-MINDS and ClassroomWiki. IEEE Transactions on Learning Technologies 4(1), 47–58 (2011)
7. Kubincová, Z., Homola, M., Janajev, R.: Tool-supported assessment of wiki-based assignments. In: Procs. of CSEDU 2012, Porto, Portugal (2012)
8. Mosel, S.: Self directed learning with personal publishing and microcontent. In: Microlearning 2005. Insbruck University Press (2005)
9. Popescu, E.: Students' acceptance of Web 2.0 technologies in higher education: Findings from a survey in a romanian university. In: Procs. of DEXA 2012 (2010)
10. Popescu, E., Manafu, L.: Repurposing a wiki for collaborative learning – pedagogical and technical view. In: System Theory, Control, and Computing, ICSTCC (2011)
11. Roberts, T.S., McInnerney, J.M.: Seven problems of online group learning (and their solutions). Educational Technology & Society 10, 257–268 (2007)
12. Sefranek, J., Kravcik, M.: A model of collaborative writing. Cognitive Systems 4(3-4), 401–428 (1997)
13. Soh, L.-K., Liu, X., Zhang, X., Al-Jaroodi, J., Jiang, H., Vemuri, P.: I-MINDS: An Agent-Oriented Information System for Applications in Education. In: Giorgini, P., Henderson-Sellers, B., Winikoff, M. (eds.) AOIS 2003. LNCS (LNAI), vol. 3030, pp. 16–31. Springer, Heidelberg (2004)
14. Trentin, G.: Using a wiki to evaluate individual contribution to a collaborative learning project. J. Comp. Assisted Learning 25(1), 43–55 (2009)

# Wiki – A Useful Tool to Fight Classroom Cheating?

Zoran Putnik[1], Mirjana Ivanović[1], Zoran Budimac[1], and Ladislav Samuelis[2]

[1] Department of Mathematics and Informatics, Faculty of Science,
University of Novi Sad, Serbia
{putnik,mira,zjb}@dmi.uns.ac.rs
[2] Department of Computers and Informatics, Faculty of Electrical Engineering and Informatics,
Technical University of Kosice
ladislav.samuelis@tuke.sk

**Abstract.** As a part of the activities of Chair of Computer Science, Department of Mathematics and Informatics various types of eLearning activities have been applied for the last eight years. Using open source LMS system Moodle, we started with a simple repository of learning resources, went over creation of eLessons, quizzes, and glossaries, but recently also started using elements of Web 2.0 in teaching. Usage of forums, blogs, and wikis as simulation of classroom activities proved to be very successful and our students welcomed these trends. What we didn't expect, but what we gladly embraced was the fact that usage of Wikis helped us fighting cheating in teamwork assignment solving. Namely, practice of application of teamwork at several courses was spoiled by students who didn't do their part of the task. Yet, their teammates covered for them and only later, within a survey about their satisfaction with the course, complained about the fact. Usage of Wikis for assignment solving combined with the ability of LMS Moodle to reveal all of the activities and history of changes, enabled us to separate actual doers and non-doers for each of the assignments, to the satisfaction of both teachers and students.

**Keywords:** eLearning, Wiki, cheating.

## 1    Introduction

Since year 2003 when for the first time introduced to LMS Moodle, members of the Chair of Computer Science at the Department of Mathematic and Informatics, University of Novi Sad, tried to use it in everyday teaching activities [6].

At first, Moodle system was used in its' simplest form – being just a repository of learning material. Over the years, we progressed through several phases:

- development of eLessons presenting all of the resources and topics in a different, active, and usually multimedia form;
- introduction of quizzes for self-testing, and glossaries of unknown, or more difficult terms and notions for each topic;
- using Moodle for management of assignments: their submission, evaluation, assessment, and keeping the database of grades per student and per assignment;

E. Popescu et al. (Eds.): ICWL 2012, LNCS 7558, pp. 31–40, 2012.

- using chats and forums to simulate classroom activities – discussions on certain topics and research about given issues, and finally
- Using Wikis for joint work on team assignment solving, again with the ability to evaluate, asses, and grade the assignments.

Our good experiences with LMS Moodle compelled us to study it more and get involved with it in a various activities and ways. Both scientific and educational reasons required involvement in several projects using Moodle as a basic experimental educational space: multilateral project of Serbia, Czech Republic, and Greece, bilateral project between Serbia and Slovenia, and four projects funded by international educational associations. As a result of those projects, several newly developed courses emerged, and also two booklets about Moodle have been written. These activities convinced us that Moodle is the right choice for us, for eLearning. After about eight years of using it at the level of Chair of Computer Science, system has been raised to the faculty level, and for the last year, all of the five departments of Faculty of Science are successfully using Moodle for teaching [8].

The rest of the paper is organized as follows: second section presents current research and dilemmas in the field of prevention of classroom cheating. The third section presents our experiences with LMS Moodle, and gives a more detailed view on the development of the ways in which we are using it. Section four is the central section of this paper, explaining the way in which Moodle helped us fighting cheating, mostly by restricting the ability to avoid dedicated activities on homework team assignments. In the last section we share some conclusions, and present insight into opinions and comments we received by students after applying this technique.

## 2    Related Work

Cheating among students is not a new thing, and it is a problem since forever. New technical developments we encounter every day in information-communication technology, gave an additional bust to it. Various evidence of this can be found in research papers, discussions about this are conducted at workshops and conferences.

In [9], it has been reported that "... as many as 75% to 90% of nursing college students surveyed claim they have participated in some form of academic dishonesty during their academic program of study ...". Besides the usual "dishonesty on an examination" or "plagiarism", notion of "sharing work in a group" is mentioned as an example of dishonesty. Similar attitude has been reported in [2], [14], and [17].

Even more astonishing results are given within frequently cited [13], where McCabe gives statistics that about 45% of faculty students admitted they "turned in work done by another" at least once in the past year, while at the same time astounding 98% of them sees such a behavior as "moderate or serious cheating". Similar results can be found in [18], where author gives evidence that "... two thirds of students cheat on tests, and 90% cheat on homework". Since our paper deals with the same type of cheating behavior, and tries to give one possible model of avoiding it, we were disappointed to find out that were not alone with such a problem.

Being more precise, it seems there is evidence that students with lower grades tend to cheat more often, which – if we're discussing teamwork – adds additional burden on good students and "better parts" of a team. For example, in [16] it's been said that "… research has particularly investigated cheating in the classroom, and confirmed that people with low grade point average (GPA), who have more to gain, cheat more than students with high GPA." As a suggestion, and supported by findings in [11], it was proposed that "… it has been demonstrated that cheating behavior can be reduced by increasing the costs of being caught."

Interesting opinion we can read in [5] putting some question marks on findings considering student cheating: "… results indicate that students do not understand what constitutes cheating and are much more likely to report cheating post-definition."

With all of the criticism of dishonesty in schools, some warnings about the reasons causing such a behavior can be found. For example, in [18] the author criticizes situations when given assignments are, by opinion of students, "meaningless", or when the only reason for solving them is the grade they receive. Since this way motivation for best work fades, while desire to beat the system and cheat increases, author suggests "… as teachers we must try … to work with students to create assignments that engage their lives, interests, and individual intellectual questions."

While trying to follow the above suggestion and create meaningful and creative assignments, in this paper we are also trying to confront research results discussing a role Internet and its' services have in growth of cheating behavior. Namely in [7], editor commenting a connection of Internet with plagiarism and cheating claims that what was once a sporadic problem, becomes a problem "of epidemic proportions."

In this paper we are going to present how Internet services, namely learning management systems and usage of Wikis, can help in preventing cases of "submitting someone else's work", "not doing their part of teamwork assignment", but also "covering other persons cheating".

## 3     Evolution of Usage of LMS Moodle

LMS Moodle was at the Department of Mathematics and Informatics used at first just as a simple repository of teaching resources. One of the courses, "Software Engineering", was selected for an experiment. Students were instructed on how to register, access the course, and download lectures. After some minor introductory problems, usage of Moodle in such a form was established as a "normal" thing for our students.

Knowing that none of the even slightly advanced features of LMS are used this way, we decided to improve number and type of eLearning facilities used. As a part of the course "Elective Seminar – eLearning", we offered a possibility to students to help us in adjusting existing teaching material for "Software Engineering" course in appropriate Moodle forms. This way we managed to prepare: eLessons, glossaries, and quizzes for each of 25 topics within a course. In years to come we had enough students to prepare and arrange several versions of each important topic at every course we had selected, and so created a satisfactory distance learning environment.

We also, rather easily, managed to incorporate Moodle grading system and assignments into our everyday teaching practice. Complaints concerning inability to submit their solutions to a given assignments on time, and at the given place disappeared after introduction of "file upload" system within Moodle. It enabled everyone to submit a solution at any given time within a given time-frame. This functionality was very welcomed by our students. Moodle grading system gave us a chance to assess each student for each of their activities, and to inform them about the outcomes! Privacy protection of Moodle was also welcomed, since everyone is able to see only their personal grades, no one else being able to see and compare the assessments [10].

After several years of successful usage of Moodle, elements of Web 2.0 grabbed our attention and we decided to start using forums and Wikis to simulate classic classroom activities. Forums were intended for discussions, role-playing games, and similar [15]. At first, we tried live chats, yet problems with synchronicity of access and obligations of students, forced us to give up on that. Namely, activity was first introduced at master level of studies, where most of students are already employed. So, we switched to asynchronous method of communication, the thing forums do perfectly. The best examples were courses on "Privacy, Ethics, and Social Responsibility" [20] and "Introduction to eBusiness". Assignments were given to students, with the appropriate time-frame to participate in discussion on given topic(s) and each of their posts was graded. Transparency and "fairness" of grading was provided be open and visible number of points per post. Combination of several such graded forums and individual assignments of "file upload" type produced the final grade.

The final activity type we introduced so far was usage of Wikis for team assignments solving within "Software Engineering" course, a part of long-lasting international project [1], [3], [4]. The main emphasis here is on the fact that assignments solved continuously over the semester through teamwork were defined as one of the milestones of the course. Ability to participate in teamwork is not only useful for maturation and development of students, but is also a quality highly required by local employers in the Balkan region.

During the first several years of delivering course, assignment solutions were submitted on paper, by the team leader. Afterward we switch to file uploading within the Moodle system. Finally, after being "warned" by students about the problems they have within the teams, and continual pleads to try to solve those problems, we started experimenting with usage of Wikis.

Problem can be best explained by students' own words, we received within a survey dealing with the satisfaction of the course: *"Out of 7 assignments, our team solved the first 4, more or less jointly. All of the team members participated up to their abilities. Yet, after that, 2 out of 4 team members decided to be satisfied with the number of points gained and decided to quit. The rest of us continued to work on the next assignment, but that was not only much more difficult, but also convinced the third team member to quit also! So – I was left to solve the final 2 assignments all by myself! It was very difficult, and the difference between grades does not reflect at all the difference in the workload invested!*

*I know that I was able to report this to lecturers, and it would be better for me personally, but you must understand that we are friends, being in the same class through secondary school AND faculty, and that I simply CAN'T do that. Please find some way to solve this problem, since I'm informed by my fellow students that I'm not the only person with this problem. It is a common behavior within almost any team!"*

## 4    Case-Study

Provoked by the above statement, we tried to check its' truthfulness. After the semester was finished, we asked our students to fill out a survey consisting of few simple questions concerning the teamwork. We asked students to rate the following points:

1. How do you rate difficulty of the assignments? (1 – too easy / 5 – too difficult)
2. Did you find the assignments motivating? (1 – not at all / 5 – very much)
3. Do you think that working in a team was valuable for gaining realistic experience? (1 – not at all / 5 – very much)
4. How often did you wish to change a member of a team with some other member, or just "fire" her/him? (1 – very often / 5 – never)
5. Do you think that assignments solving would be easier, better, and more successful if you have done it alone? (1 – not at all / 5 – very much)
6. Did all of the team members participated equally in assignment solving? (1 – not at all / 5 – very much)

Results of the survey definitely confirmed mischievous behavior within team assignments solving. Here are the results for that same year, and for the following year, i.e. for the time before we decided to switch to Wikis with the assignments.

**Table 1.** Results of a survey concerning teamwork assignments

| | 2009 | 2010 | We want |
|---|---|---|---|
| How do you rate difficulty of the assignments? | 3.41 | 3.25 | 3 |
| Did you find the assignments motivating? | 3.52 | 3.21 | 5 |
| Do you think that working in a team was valuable for gaining realistic experience? | 4.15 | 4.29 | 5 |
| How often did you wish to change a member of a team with some other member, or just "fire" her/him? | 2.3 | 1.64 | - |
| Do you think that assignments solving would be easier, better, and more successful if you have done it alone? | 2.22 | 1.79 | 1 |
| Did all of the team members participated equally in assignment solving? | 2.17 | 2.14 | 5 |

Or, if we try to state the above survey results in a sentence, it would be something like the following: Assignments are of just appropriate difficulty, not too motivating, but valuable as an experience. Since some of the members of a team were not doing their duty, I wished very often to fire them from the team, but we didn't do it, since it would be very difficult to solve those assignments alone!

What's more important, opinions of students concerning „equal participation" of all team members, convinced us to try to find a solution for the problem of students trying to avoid their duties. After our own and some other experiences found in related literature about cheating prevention and also checking on the abilities of LMS Moodle, we decided to change a few things in our methodology.

First, it was the simple and "brutal" thing for which we received (many) protests by (some of the) students: teams were no longer self-formed by students, but randomly determined by Moodle. Interesting but expected fact is that the most of the protests came from students recognized and identified during the lectures by their tendency to avoid work and obligations.

We expected some conflicts because of possible incompatibilities within a team, related to random composition of groups. For that purpose, we allowed for team members to agree and let go off an individual with whom they are not satisfied. While this was just a recovery plan to cover all possibilities of a workflow, in practice some of the teams used this opportunity. Yet, *never* for reasons of social or character incompatibility, but always for reasons of non-participation in assignment solving. So far, students that were fired either managed to find their place in some other team, or quit attending classes for this course, but we feel that some organized procedure should be defined in such a case.

Another worry came because of the possible question about how much of the *team* are we left with, or we just turned into a group of individuals? Still, our feeling is that random composition of a team is what our students will be faced with in a real life, so that they should be trained for it, and introduced with that fact as soon as possible.

The second thing we changed was that the assignments were no longer submitted in their final form, as a file uploaded into Moodle system, but rather were developed online, via Wiki resource of LMS Moodle.

Technically speaking, the newly established working procedure was as follows:

- members of teams are randomly selected by Moodle i.e. students are assigned to teams of a size we determined in advance;
- assignments are declared one by one, and were to be solved within a given timeframe (which is never less than two weeks);
- only the members of a certain team have the access to their solution, and they have access to NO other solution, so there is no copying of others' solution;
- after the deadline, lecturers check the solution and grade it;

Yet, this is not the end – the assessment of each individual student is a rather complicated story. After grading a solution as a whole, and assigning certain number of points to it, comes the assessment of each of the participants of a team. LMS Moodle for Wiki resource has an ability to show the complete history of development of a solution. Each access of each participant of a team is recorded and can be checked. For each access, Moodle shows when it happened, from which IP address, by which Moodle account/team participant, and the most important thing – what has been done by that person. All of the changes, additions, or deletions are recorded, so the development of the whole solution can be followed step-by-step. This facility gave us a chance to determine the appropriate personal grade for each of the team members, according to their individual contribution to the final solution. Our experiences with this kind of grading and assessment have been considered and published in several papers, for example [12], [15].

Let us also take a look into two graphs showing students behavior as the deadline for submitting the assignment solution approaches. The following graph shows the number of accesses by students as time went by through the semester. Peeks that can be seen on the graph correspond to the moments when 5 assignments were to be completed. The first one is the highest since it represents the deadline for submitting the first assignment, and the highest workload for the second assignment. As can be seen from the graph, the rest of the peeks were getting much lower, since this type of work became a "normal" thing for our students as semester went on. Drop-out rate of students was *not* too large, so it didn't have to much influence on the graph. In fact, after being awarded zero points for the first assignment, the majority of non-doers started participating in assignment solving.

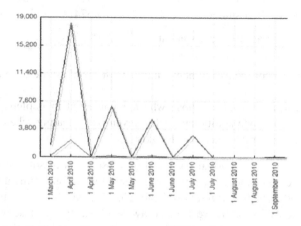

**Fig. 1.** Individual number of accesses to Wiki activity during semester

This kind of assessment caused a large workload for the lecturers, but to us it seemed worthwhile. Individual assessment was of course subject of some students' discussions and complaints, but no more than any other kind of grades we awarded during the semester. And, to our satisfaction, after approximately two finished assignments, cheating stopped! Non-doers were either dismissed from teams, or started working and giving their contribution to assignment solution.

This fact also solved our dilemma about how students should act within a team. There was always a possibility that there are some "passive" team members, who were valuable for the team functioning, yet not active with the wiki activity. While the activity itself asked for *active* involvement within a team and *strong and enthusiastic* work, there was a possibility that not all of the students are suited for this kind of achievements. Still, as the assignments went on, the participation of team members gets more and more equal, and just with the slightly less rigid assessment of contributions, we reached the stage where both lecturers and students were satisfied.

The second interesting thing we would like to present here is the actual difference in number of accesses visible in the previous graph. How much our students got used to Wiki and its usage in assignment solving, can be recognized by the next table, showing the difference in number of accesses for solving the first and the second assignment. While this fact perhaps is not directly connected to cheating behavior and our "fight" to lower it, it shows how fast the newly introduced activity became a regular type of obligation for our students.

**Table 2.** Analysis of student behaviour while solving the first two assignments

| Parameter | Assignment 1 | Assignment 2 |
|---|---|---|
| Total number of accesses | 19229 | 7691 |
| Total number of changes | 1398 | 1217 |
| Number of accesses per student | 0 – 574 | 0 – 821 |
| Average number of accesses per student | 154 | 118 |

Later, for the rest of the assignments, numbers dropped a little bit more, but not so drastic.

Just as a curiosity, for all of those who are interested in implementation of our model, let us mention one additional "rather inventive" cheating scheme our students tried to implement after introduction of Wikis.

— While checking the individual participation of students in solving one of the assignments, we have noticed that within the only few seconds time difference, from the same IP address, *two different* students added certain comments to the solution.
— When we checked further, we became aware of the fact that actually the whole team of four members, worked on the same assignment during the afternoon, accessing LMS Moodle from the same IP address. It was of course possible that the whole team met and worked at the same place, and while that was not our actual idea of teamwork, it would be allowed.
— Yet, when we faced the team members with our findings, they admitted that actually only one person did the whole thing. This was possible because the other team members gave her their usernames and passwords. Still, after being confronted with the rest of the class, they apologized and promised not to do it again.
— That was the only case of such kind of behavior, so either all of the rest of students were obeying the rules, or they invented some even more clever method of cheating, which we haven't discovered.

## 5    Conclusion

Our experience with the usage of LMS Moodle, confirms with the conclusions and experiences of other authors. It *does* help lecturer a lot, enables her/him to *innovate* and *improve* its' teaching material over the years, while keeping it always available to students, and enables her/him to be at all times available to students for questions and comments. Still, at the same time it creates a huge workload for lecturers – if the usage of LMS is to be performed correctly.

Ability to have all of the resources available to students at all times, be in constant contact with them through forums, instant messages, and e-mail communication within LMS Moodle, and to have administration of grades and achievements of students always perfectly precise, is something usually taken for granted with any LMS used.

What we tried to show in this paper, is the ability to use LMS Moodle for something it's not originally intended for, to prevent part of cheating intentions of students. While this required additional effort, it was rather worthwhile. In the beginning, we had to grade 10-15 submitted assignments, each of 15-20 pages, which is a large workload by itself. After our intervention, we had an additional work of establishing which member of the team did which part of the work, and this assumed by our estimation going additionally through the paper 2 or 3 times back and forth. Still, as a result we achieved just what we had in mind. Those who didn't actually want to participate in assignments solving, but wanted to be covered by their team-mates, quit and helped us assess the others fairer and more precise. Some of the others, after being caught for not working on the first few assignments, changed their minds and started participating on further ones. Finally, those who worked from the beginning received the exact grades they deserve. What we would also like to be able to assess is the difference between number of students who were able to pass the exam due to cheating in previous years, and those who became active because of "wiki approach". So far, we do not see a possibility to compare these two groups, yet over time perhaps some additional ideas might come to us.

The same survey that started the whole research was distributed to all of the students after finishing the course. While the other grades for course activities were more or less similar (so we will not present them here), comments and assessments concerning the teamwork and assignments were much better. What's more important, students were more satisfied with the fairness of their grades. The question about "equal participation in assignment solving" received much higher grade, above 4 (on the scale from 1 to 5). In other words, our idea was gladly accepted. Looking from teacher's position, we feel that *not* much of the experiences came because of the novelty of the approach, and that the similar results will be repeated over the years. This opinion is partly confirmed by not-yet-finished school year, when we tried the same approach again, but we still do not have complete data about the experience.

# References

1. Bothe, K., Schützler, K., Budimac, Z., Putnik, Z., Ivanović, M., Stoyanov, S., Stoyanova-Doyceva, A., Zdravkova, K., Jakimovski, B., Bojic, D., Jurca, I., Kalpic, D., Cico, B.: Experience with shared teaching materials for software engineering across countries. In: Proc. of Informatics Education Europe IV, IEE-IV 2009, Freiburg, Germany, pp. 57–62 (2009)
2. Bowen, R.W.: Academic Dishonesty Cancels Academic Freedom. Change 38(1) (2006)

3. Budimac, Z., Putnik, Z., Ivanović, M., Bothe, K., Schuetzler, K.: Conducting a Joint Course on Software Engineering Based on Teamwork of Students. International Journal on Informatics in Education, 17–30 (2007) ISSN 1648-5831, doi:10.1.1.149.2118
4. Budimac, Z., Putnik, Z., Ivanović, M., Bothe, K., Schuetzler, K.: On the Assessment and Self-assessment in a Students Teamwork Based Course on Software Engineering. CAE, Computer Applications in Engineering Education 19(1), 1–9 (2011), doi:10.1002/cae.20249
5. Burrus, R.T., McGoldrick, K., Schuhmann, P.: Self-Reports of Students Cheating: Does a Definitionof Cheating Matter? Journal of Economic Education 38(1), 3–16 (2007)
6. Chair of Computer Science, Department of mathematics and Informatics, Faculty of Science, LMS Moodle home-page, http://perun.pmf.uns.ac.rs/moodle/
7. Duggan, F.: Plagiarism: Prevention, Practice and Policy. Assessment & Evaluation in Higher Education 31(2), 151–154 (2006)
8. Faculty of Science, Novi Sad, LMS Moodle home-page, http://moodle.pmf.uns.ac.rs/
9. Faucher, D., Caves, S.: Academic Dishonesty: Innovative Cheating Techniques and the Detection and Prevention of Them. Teaching and Learning in Nursing 4, 37–41 (2009)
10. Ivanović, M., Welzer, T., Putnik, Z., Hoelbl, M., Komlenov, Ž., Pribela, I., Schweighofer, T.: Experiences and privacy issues - usage of Moodle in Serbia and Slovenia. In: Interactive Computer Aided Learning, ICL 2009, Villach, Austria, pp. 416–423 (2009)
11. Kerkvliet, J., Sigmund., C.L.: Can We Control Cheating in the Classroom? Research in Economic Education 30(4), 331–334 (1999)
12. Komlenov, Ž., Budimac, Z., Putnik, Z., Ivanovic, M.: Wiki as a Tool of Choice for Students' Team Assignments. Int. J. of Information Systems & Social Change (IJISSC) 4(3) (to appear)
13. McCabe, D.: Cheating Among College and University Students: A North American Perspective. International Journal for Educational Integrity 1(1) (2005)
14. Paulos, L.: Breaking the Rules. Scholastic Choices 22, 10–13 (2007)
15. Putnik, Z., Budimac, Z., Komlenov, Ž., Ivanovic, M., Bothe, K.: Wiki Usage in Team Assignments for Computer Science Students. In: Proc. of CompSysTech 2011, International Conference on Computer Systems and Technologies, Vienna, Austria, June 16-17, pp. 596–601 (2011), doi:10.1145/2023607.2023706
16. Schwieren, C., Weichselbaumer, D.: Does Competition Enhance Performance or Cheating? A Laboratory Experiment, Journal of Exonomic Psychology 31, 241–253 (2010)
17. Sorensen, D.: Cheating in the News. Caveon Test Security Newsletter 3, 207 (2007)
18. Stephens, J.: Justice or Just Us? What to Do About Cheating. Carnegie Foundation for the Advancement of Teaching (2004)
19. Williams, B.: Trust, Betrayal, and Authorship: Plagiarism and How to Perceive Students. Journal of Adolescent & Adult Literacy 51(4), 350–354 (2007/2008)
20. Zdravkova, K., Ivanović, M., Putnik, Z.: Experience of Integrating Web 2.0 Technologies. Educational Technology Research & Development 60(2), 361–381, doi:10.1007/s11423-011-9228-z

# Project-Based Learning with eMUSE

## An Experience Report

Elvira Popescu

University of Craiova, Computers and Information Technology Department,
A. I. Cuza 13, 200585 Craiova, Romania
popescu_elvira@software.ucv.ro

**Abstract.** Project-based learning (PBL) is an instructional model
rooted in constructivist principles, according to which learning is driven
by cognitive conflict and knowledge is constructed by the individual,
through collaborative efforts and social interactions. Therefore relying on
a social learning environment for implementing a PBL scenario appears
beneficial. The approach is illustrated by means of eMUSE, a learning
platform which aggregates several Web 2.0 tools and provides support
for both students and teachers (common access point to all the social
software components, basic administrative services, learner monitoring
and graphical visualizations, evaluation and grading support). The implementation of a PBL scenario with eMUSE is described and an experimental study is presented, involving 45 undergraduate students enrolled
in a "Web Applications' Design" course. The scenario enactment is successful and the results of the study are encouraging in terms of subjective
learner satisfaction, motivation, learning gain and involvement.

**Keywords:** project-based learning, Web 2.0, social learning
environment.

## 1 Introduction

Project-based learning (PBL) is a student-centered instructional approach, in
which learning is organized around projects. These projects involve complex,
challenging and authentic tasks, on which students work relatively autonomously
(with the teacher playing the role of facilitator) and over extended periods of
time. The students collaborate in various design, problem-solving, decision making and investigative activities, the final goal being a realistic product or presentation [7].

Thomas [14] identified five characteristics which define PBL and make it different from other models that involve projects:

1. *Projects are central, not peripheral to the curriculum* (the project does not
   serve to provide examples, practical applications or extensions of concepts
   previously taught by other means; instead, students learn the main concepts
   of the curriculum via the project)

E. Popescu et al. (Eds.): ICWL 2012, LNCS 7558, pp. 41–50, 2012.
© Springer-Verlag Berlin Heidelberg 2012

2. *Projects are focused on questions or problems that drive students to encounter (and struggle with) the central concepts and principles of a discipline* (the "driving question" should "be crafted in order to make a connection between activities and the underlying conceptual knowledge that one might hope to foster" [2])

3. *Projects involve students in a constructive investigation* (the project activities should involve construction of knowledge, new understandings and new skills by the students, not simply an application of already-learned information or skills)

4. *Projects are student-driven to some significant degree* (projects are not scripted by the teacher, do not take predetermined paths and do not have predetermined outcomes; students have more autonomy and responsibility towards their own learning)

5. *Projects are realistic, not school-like* (projects are authentic, real-life challenges in terms of topic, tasks, student roles, context of work, artifacts, final product, evaluation criteria).

Paper [14] presents a comprehensive review of studies on PBL, categorized according to their research goal: i) evaluating the effectiveness of PBL; ii) describing the implementation process and the associated challenges; iii) assessing the role of individual student differences in PBL; iv) improving the efficiency of PBL by various interventions. Based on all these studies, PBL appears as a popular, beneficial and effective instructional method, enhancing the quality of students' learning (who are more capable of applying the knowledge in novel contexts), as well as their planning, communicating, problem solving, and decision making skills. Some drawbacks are also acknowledged: students may have difficulties in self-directed situations (e.g., initiating inquiry, directing investigations, managing time), especially in complex projects, so providing support to students in "learning how to learn" is essential [14].

PBL has its roots in constructivism, constructionism, cooperative and collaborative learning, active learning, expeditionary learning, as well as situated cognition [7], [14]. PBL is also closely related to problem-based learning and the line between them is frequently blurred; however, they are not identical: PBL focuses on the end-product and on the skills acquired during the production process, while problem-based learning has as goal finding the solution to the ill-defined problem and usually includes a tutorial ingredient (students are guided by a facilitator who plays the role of a coach). However, they are both led by the following constructivist principles: i) understanding is an individual construction and comes from our interactions with the environment; ii) learning is driven by cognitive conflict or puzzlement; iii) knowledge evolves through social negotiation [13].

Since PBL has a strong social component, the emergent social media tools can be used to support communication and collaboration in the PBL framework [4]. Indeed, during the last couple of years there have appeared a few studies investigating the use of Web 2.0 tools for PBL: [1], [6], [8], [10], [16]. The approach presented in this paper is new in that an integrated social learning environment (called eMUSE) is used as support tool for collaborative activities and co-construction of knowledge, rather than single Web 2.0 tools in the studies mentioned above.

More details regarding the eMUSE platform can be found in the next section. Subsequently, in section 3, we describe the instructional scenario that we conceived for a "Web Applications' Design" class, following the PBL principles detailed above; the roles fulfilled by eMUSE and the selected Web 2.0 tools for communication, collaboration, learner tracking and assessment support are also discussed. The designed PBL scenario is put into practice in section 4: an experimental study involving 45 undergraduate students is presented and discussed. The students' opinion about their learning experience (as elicited by means of questionnaires applied at the end of the study) is reported in section 5. The results are very encouraging in terms of subjective learner satisfaction, motivation, learning gain, quality of teamwork and involvement; some scenario improvements are also proposed based on the students' feedback. Finally, section 6 concludes the paper, outlining future research directions.

## 2   An Overview of eMUSE Platform

eMUSE is a social learning environment which integrates several Web 2.0 tools (wiki, blog, microblogging tool, social bookmarking tool, media sharing tools). Its name (empowering MashUps for Social E-learning) comes from the underlying technology: the Web 2.0 tools are integrated into the platform by means of mashups [3]. eMUSE was built in order to support both the students and the instructor to manage their activity on several disparate social media tools. The platform retrieves students' actions with each Web 2.0 tool (such as *post_blog_entry, post_blog_comment, upload_youtube_video, post_delicious_bookmark, add_delicious_friend_to_network, add_slideshare_document, create_picasa_album, post_tweet, revise_wiki_page, upload_wiki_file* etc.) and stores them in a local database for further processing.A detailed rationale underlying eMUSE can be found in [12]. Fig. 1 provides an overview of the platform, featuring a student page and an instructor page.

The main functionalities offered to the instructor include:
- configure the course, by setting up the associated social learning scenario and selecting the Web 2.0 tools to be used
- student management (course enrolment, centralized access to students' accounts on each Web 2.0 tool, grading information)
- collect data on students' activity, search and browse students' actions, visualize course statistics, detailed charts of student involvement and comparative evaluation
- configure grading scheme: define grading categories (i.e., individual contributions, peer feedback, communication skills etc.) and assign different weights to each action type inside each category, based on the particularities of the course; the overall score will be a weighted sum of all defined categories.

Similarly, the main functionalities provided to the student include:

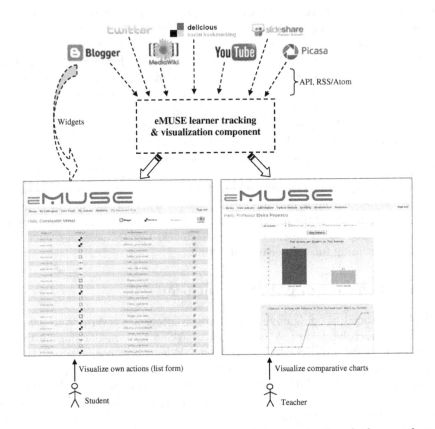

**Fig. 1.** eMUSE overview - integration of Web 2.0 tools in the platform and student/instructor screenshots

- an integrated learning space, with a common access point to all the Web 2.0 tools selected by the teacher, including detailed usage and instructional guidelines
- updates of the latest peer activity
- a summary of each student's involvement, including pie/bar/line charts, evolution over time, comparisons with peers, as well as aggregated data
- a preliminary score computed based on the recorded student activity, following instructor-defined criteria.

It is worth noting that eMUSE is different from the so-called "mash-up personal learning environments" (platforms that support learners in building their own PLE, such as MUPPLE [15] and PLEF [5]), since the Web 2.0 components are chosen by the teacher and the platform offers the built-in monitoring functionality. Furthermore, eMUSE is not aimed at replacing a learning management system (LMS); it is designed as a dedicated support tool for social interaction and collaborative learning, which could be integrated with any course / project and could be run in parallel with an LMS. Even if some LMS nowadays integrate social media tools (e.g., blog and wiki in Moodle or Sakai), the range of available components is limited and they are built-in tools, often providing less functionalities than a fully-fledged external Web 2.0 application (which students are already familiar with). Hence eMUSE occupies a well defined niche in the landscape of Web 2.0-enhanced learning spaces [12].

Before the start of the course, the instructor can configure the learning environment by selecting the Web 2.0 tools to be used by the students, according to the learning scenario that will be adopted. In the next section we will detail one of the several instructional scenarios that can be supported by eMUSE, namely a PBL setting.

## 3   Designing the PBL Scenario

The context of the PBL scenario is a course on "Web Applications' Design" (WAD), delivered to 4th year undergraduate students in Computer Science. The project task is the development of an authentic Web application, such as a virtual bookstore, an online auction website, a professional social network, an online travel agency etc. The students must perform all the stages of real-life application development, starting with system analysis and requirements specification and continuing with design, implementation and testing. Therefore learners have a lot of freedom in developing the projects, by selecting the desired functionalities and shaping the final product. Students are expected to use their programming skills as well as their project management and software engineering knowledge that they have acquired from previous courses; at the same time, students have the opportunity to learn the main concepts of the WAD curriculum, as well as construct new knowledge and skills by means of the challenges they encounter throughout the unfolding of the project. Students have to collaborate in teams of 4-5 peers, each of them taking various real-life roles in different stages (system analyst, database specialist, interface designer, application architect, programmer, tester, project manager). Due to the complexity of the tasks, the project spans over the whole semester. Both the final product and the continuous collaborative work carried out week-by-week counts towards students' grades.

The PBL scenario is implemented in blended mode: there are weekly face-to-face meetings between each team and the instructor (for checking the project progress, providing feedback and answering questions) and for the rest of the time students have to use eMUSE as support for their communication and collaboration activities. Four Web 2.0 tools are selected from the platform:

1. *Blogger* - for documenting the progress of the project (i.e., a kind of "learning diary" - reporting each accomplished activity, describing problems encountered and asking for help, reflecting on their learning experience); publishing ideas, thoughts, interesting findings (project-related); communicating with the peers, providing solutions for peers' problems, critical and constructive feedback, interacting with other teams

2. *MediaWiki* - for collaborative writing tasks among the members of a team; gathering and organizing their knowledge and resources regarding the project theme; clearly documenting each stage of the project as well as the final product

3. *Delicious* - for storing links to resources of interest for the project (i.e., a kind of "personal knowledge management tool"); sharing discovered bookmarks with peers; tagging and rating the collected resources; checking the resources shared by peers (and especially by own team members)

4. *Twitter* - for staying connected with peers and posting short news, announcements, questions, status updates regarding the project [12].

One of the advantages of using eMUSE over the disparate Web 2.0 tools for PBL relies on the monitoring and visualization functionalities provided by the platform - thus the teacher could follow the progress of each team, instead of just seeing the final product. Hence the instructor can take into account the communication and collaboration activities of each student (e.g., blog posts and comments, wiki entries and files etc.), as they are reported in eMUSE; moreover, an indicative score is automatically computed by the platform based on teacher-defined criteria. Therefore the contribution of each student to the final result can be better assessed and valued. At the same time, due to the provision of comparative evaluations and continuously updated overviews of latest activity, student competitiveness and motivation are also enhanced. Finally, by offering a convenient access to the tools, eMUSE provides a reduction in the time and effort needed for the tool management task, both for the students and the instructor, who can thus focus on the actual PBL tasks.

## 4 Putting the PBL Scenario into Practice

The enactment of the PBL scenario took place in the first semester of the 2010-2011 academic year. 45 students from the University of Craiova were enrolled in the WAD course and consequently participated in our study. In the first week, students were grouped into 11 teams and assigned the project tasks; they were given clear guidelines regarding the unfolding of the project, the grading criteria, as well as the utilization of the Web 2.0 tools. Both the students and the instructor used eMUSE (and the integrated social media tools) on a regular basis throughout the semester. At the end of the project, eMUSE recorded about 1700 valid student actions.

The distribution of actions over time is illustrated in Fig. 2a, as it appears to the instructor in eMUSE, at the end of the semester. As we can see, the lowest amount of actions were recorded in week 1 (when the first meeting with the students took place and they were introduced to the tools and the project assignments); weeks 12&13 (during winter holidays); and week 16 (when the final project presentation and assessment was scheduled, right at the beginning of the week). Conversely, the highest activity periods include week 2 (when most students started using their accounts and setting up their social networks, and

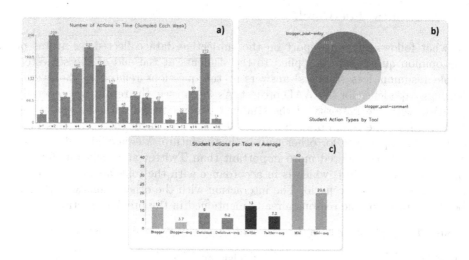

**Fig. 2.** Examples of student actions charts at the end of the semester (as provided to the instructor in eMUSE): a) Total number of actions per week; b) Distribution of action types for Blogger (posts vs. comments); c) Comparison between the contributions of a 10-grade student and the class average

when the novelty enthusiasm was also at its peak); week 15 (the last week before the final product presentation, when some students tried to do some last minute contributions and all students finalized their project documentation on the wiki); and week 5 (in which students had to finalize their software requirements specification, written as a collaborative document on the wiki).

According to Fig. 2b, the number of blog comments is half the number of blog posts, which means that the student interaction on the blog was not very high. Indeed, when analyzing the actual content of the blog posts, we could see that only a small part contain questions or requests for feedback from the peers; instead students mostly used the blog to report on what they have done in the current week. Furthermore, the interaction between the teams is quite limited, most of the blog comments being written by the initial poster's teammates. This can be explained by the fact that teams had different tasks, hence different interests and problems; moreover, as resulted from students' after-course interviews, they did not have enough time to follow the work of other teams since their own project was quite time-consuming.

Fig. 2c illustrates the number of actions performed by a student who obtained the maximum grade (10 out of 10) for this project activity; as we can see, he had significantly more contributions than the course average (which turned out to be the case for most top students). This can be explained by the fact that the level of involvement with a course/project is a good indicator of the performance level. We plan to perform also a more in-depth analysis in order to investigate the statistical correlations between the number of actions on the Web 2.0 tools and students' final grades.

## 5   Students' Feedback

In what follows, we will report on the subjective data collected by means of the opinion questionnaire applied to the students at the end of the semester. Table 1 summarizes students' answers at the questions related to the overall learning experience for the WAD project. As we can see, the results are generally positive, with the majority of the students being satisfied with the use of the PBL method, the teamwork, the Web 2.0 tools, and eager to repeat this kind of learning experience for other courses in the future. MediaWiki and Blogger were generally considered more important than Twitter and Delicious for the purpose of this project, which is in accordance with the roles assigned for each of them in the PBL scenario. The interaction with the other teams was judged below average, for the reasons already mentioned in the previous section.

**Table 1.** Sample items from the post-study questionnaire and associated responses

| Question | Student answers |
|---|---|
| Which of the 4 Web 2.0 tools did you consider most important for your project? | *Blogger:* 20% *MediaWiki:* 62.22% *Delicious:* 4.44% *Twitter:* 13.33% |
| Which of the 4 Web 2.0 tools did you consider least important for your project? | *Blogger:* 8.89% *MediaWiki:* 6.67% *Delicious:* 44.44% *Twitter:* 40% |
| Assess your overall satisfaction with the use of the 4 Web 2.0 tools for the WAD project | *Very satisfied:* 15.56% *Satisfied:* 55.56% *Neutral:* 24.44% *Dissatisfied:* 4.44% *Very dissatisfied:* 0% |
| Evaluate your experience of working in teams for the WAD project | *Very good:* 26.67% *Good:* 55.56% *Neutral:* 17.78% *Bad:* 0% *Very bad:* 0% |
| What was the level of interaction with the other teams? | *Very high:* 4.44% *High:* 15.56% *Average:* 42.22% *Low:* 26.67% *Very low:* 11.11% |
| Would you like this PBL method to be used for other courses too? | *Definitely yes:* 40% *Probably yes:* 35.56% *Neutral:* 13.33% *Probably not:* 6.67% *Definitely not:* 4.44% |

Table 2 includes students' comparison of the PBL approach applied at WAD with a traditional project. According to these self-reported measures, PBL represents an improvement in terms of learning gain, motivation, enjoyment, involvement, teamwork quality and overall satisfaction. However, the study time and learning effort reported by the students seem to be the same or even higher than in case of traditional projects; this is probably triggered by the complexity of the assignments and the lack of experience with the PBL method and the social learning environment, but is also in line with the increased motivation and involvement of the students.

When asked to comment on the drawbacks of their learning experience, the main issues mentioned by the students were:

– In a couple of teams there was a lack of cooperation and a low level of involvement from peers. This can be frustrating in any scenario in which students have to rely on the work of their peers who refuse to collaborate. A solution would be to try to engage students even more and increase their accountability by adding multiple checkpoints throughout the project; this would also discourage the practice of activity peak at the end of the semester.
– The amount of time and effort necessary for accomplishing the project was deemed too high by some of the participants. This can be explained by the fact that these PBL settings were a premiere for the students, so they needed

**Table 2.** Students' self-reported comparison of the PBL approach applied at WAD with a traditional project

|  | A lot lower | Somewhat lower | The same | Somewhat higher | A lot higher |
|---|---|---|---|---|---|
| Learning gain | 2.22% | 4.44% | 26.67% | 46.67% | 20% |
| Study time | 2.22% | 8.89% | 46.67% | 28.89% | 13.33% |
| Motivation | 6.67% | 2.22% | 24.44% | 51.11% | 15.56% |
| Overall satisfaction | 4.44% | 2.22% | 17.78% | 55.56% | 20% |
| Learning effort | 2.22% | 15.56% | 46.67% | 24.44% | 11.11% |
| Enjoyment | 2.22% | 8.89% | 33.33% | 46.67% | 8.89% |
| Involvement | 0% | 4.44% | 33.33% | 46.67% | 15.56% |
| Quality of teamwork | 4.44% | 2.22% | 28.89% | 35.56% | 28.89% |
| Interaction with other teams | 8.89% | 15.56% | 53.33% | 17.78% | 4.44% |

some time to get accustomed with the tasks as well as the new collaborative environment.

- The summaries and statistics available in eMUSE are quantitative only and some students feared that this could lead to an inflation of low-quality contributions ("post hunting" as one student put it). However, this actually happened only in a limited number of cases in our study, since students were clearly informed that in the end it will be the quality of their contributions that will matter most towards their final grade. As future work, we plan to extend the platform with an annotation mechanism (e.g., add ratings, tags or comments by peers and instructor for each student action), to include also the quality component.

## 6  Conclusion

The paper described the successful implementation of a PBL scenario in the framework of a social learning environment. As opposed to the related studies mentioned in the Introduction, which rely on single Web 2.0 tools, our approach is based on an integrated platform (eMUSE) including four such tools, with additional monitoring and visualization functionalities.

The proposed scenario followed the five PBL criteria mentioned in section 1: centrality, driving question, constructive investigations, autonomy, and realism. The flexibility of the tasks and of the social environment helped students be in control of their own learning and acquire knowledge construction skills.

Based on the success of the experiment and the positive feedback received from the students, we are currently applying the same method for this year's WAD course (refined according to the improvements mentioned in the previous section). As future work, following the ideas in [9] and [11], we plan to further explore the process of high level knowledge co-construction; by using content analysis and social network analysis, we want to extend the investigation of the patterns and quality of online interactions during PBL.

**Acknowledgments.** This work was supported by the strategic grant POSDRU/89/1.5/S/61968, Project ID 61968 (2009), co-financed by the European Social Fund within the Sectorial Operational Program Human Resources Development 2007 - 2013.

The author would like to thank Dan Cioiu and Alin Ilie, former students at the University of Craiova, for their contribution to the early stage implementation of the eMUSE prototype.

# References

1. Ardaiz-Villanueva, O., Nicuesa-Chacón, X., Brene-Artazcoz, O., Sanz de Acedo Lizarraga, M.L., Sanz de Acedo Baquedano, M.T.: Evaluation of computer tools for idea generation and team formation in project-based learning. Computers & Education 56(3), 700–711 (2011)
2. Barron, B.J.S., et al.: Doing with understanding: Lessons from research on problem- and project-based learning. The Journal of the Learning Sciences 7, 271–311 (1998)
3. Beemer, B., Gregg, D.: Mashups: A literature review and classification framework. Future Internet 1(1), 59–87 (2009)
4. Boss, S., Krauss, J.: Reinventing project-based learning: Your field guide to real-world projects in the Digital Age. International Society for Technology in Education (2008)
5. Chatti, M.A., Agustiawan, M.R., Jarke, M., Specht, M.: Toward a Personal Learning Environment Framework. International Journal of Virtual and Personal Learning Environments 1(4), 66–85 (2010)
6. Cheong, C., Tandon, R., Cheong, F.: A project-based learning internship for IT undergraduates with social support from a social networking site. In: Proc. ISECON 2010, 27(1389) (2010)
7. EduTechWiki: Project-based learning, http://edutechwiki.unige.ch/en/Project-based_learning (last accessed on January 16, 2012)
8. Grippa, F., Secundo, G.: Web 2.0 project-based learning in Higher Education - some preliminary evidence. Int. J. Web Based Communities 5(4), 543–561 (2009)
9. Heo, H., Lim, K.Y., Kim, Y.: Exploratory study on the patterns of online interaction and knowledge co-construction in project-based learning. Computers & Education 55, 1383–1392 (2010)
10. Kim, P., Hong, J.S., Bonk, C., Lim, G.: Effects of group reflection variations in project-based learning integrated in a Web 2.0 learning space. Interactive Learning Environments 19(4), 333–349 (2011)
11. Koh, J.H.L., Herring, S.C., Hew, K.F.: Project-based learning and student knowledge construction during asynchronous online discussion. Internet and Higher Education 13, 284–291 (2010)
12. Popescu, E.: Providing collaborative learning support with social media in an integrated environment. World Wide Web (2012), doi: 10.1007/s11280-012-0172-6
13. Savery, J.R., Duffy, T.M.: Problem-based learning: An instructional model and its constructivist framework. Educational Technology 35, 31–38 (1995)
14. Thomas, J.W.: A review of research on project-based learning (2000), http://www.bie.org/research/study/review_of_project_based_learning_2000
15. Wild, F.: Mash-Up Personal Learning Environments. iCamp project deliverable (2009), http://www.icamp.eu/wp-content/uploads/2009/01/d34_icamp_final.pdf
16. Wilson, T., Ferreira, G.M.S.: Using open educational resources and Web 2.0 tools to support ethical reasoning in information and computer sciences project-based learning. The Higher Education Academy (2010)

# Annotation Tool for Enhancing E-Learning Courses

Bernardo Pereira Nunes[1,2,3], Ricardo Kawase[2], Stefan Dietze[2],
Gilda Helena Bernardino de Campos[3,4], and Wolfgang Nejdl[2]

[1] Department of Informatics - PUC-Rio - Rio de Janeiro, RJ, Brazil
bnunes@inf.puc-rio.br
[2] L3S Research Center, Leibniz University Hannover, Germany
{nunes,kawase,dietze,nejdl}@l3s.de
[3] Central Coordination for Distance Learning - PUC-Rio - Rio de Janeiro, RJ - Brazil
{bernardo,gilda}@ccead.puc-rio.br
[4] Education Department - PUC-Rio - Rio de Janeiro, RJ, Brazil
gilda@ccead.puc-rio.br

**Abstract.** One of the most popular forms of learning is through reading and for years we have used hard copy documents as the main material to learn. With the advent of the Internet and the fast development of new technologies, new tools have been developed to assist the learning process. However, reading is still the main learning method that is an individual activity. In this paper we propose a highlighting tool that enables the reading and learning process to become a collaborative and shared activity. In other words, the highlighting tool supports the so-called active-reading, a well-known and efficient means of learning. The highlighting tool brings to the digital environment the same metaphor of the traditional highlight marker and puts it in a social context. It enables users to emphasize certain portions of digital learning objects. Furthermore, it provides students, tutors, course coordinators and educational institutions new possibilities in the teaching and learning process. In this work we expose the first quantitative and qualitative results regarding the use of the highlight tool by over 750 students through 8 weeks of courses.

**Keywords:** e-Learning, Active-Reading, Online-Annotations, Evaluation, User Feedback.

## 1 Introduction

In the last decade we have witnessed an accelerated development of technologies that led us to create new forms of communication, learning situations and social skills. This advance in technology also stimulated a rapid growth of information and made a huge amount of information available anytime and anywhere. A flood of information is delivered every minute, making us to read more frequently than previous generations. However, the cognitive strategies that involve the learning process have not changed so fast. Still today, the so-called *active reading* [1] is the most prominent mean for learning and for stimulating critical thinking. Active reading involves mainly the actions of reading and annotating.

Annotating hard copy documents is a natural activity that involves direct interaction with the document and that is known to support understanding and memorization [2].

E. Popescu et al. (Eds.): ICWL 2012, LNCS 7558, pp. 51–60, 2012.
© Springer-Verlag Berlin Heidelberg 2012

The term annotation comprises several techniques such as underline, circle or highlight important or confusing keywords and phrases; or writing notes to summarize or raise questions found in the text.

Nowadays, most of the queries with the purpose of learning are conducted on reference Web sites like Wikipedia as well as the debates around it, through the means of discussion forums, social networks or even e-mails that shifted the learning process from a paper-based activity and solitary task to a Web-based activity [5] and collaborative task.

However, due to limitations of the annotations tools on the Web, learners end up with a large collection of scattered digital resources. In most cases, annotations are out of context, written down on a piece of paper, on a separated digital document or e-mail, which impairs the information retrieval and the learning process.

The problem identified here is twofold. First, learners have a problem in contextualizing the annotations of a given online document. Second, the natural annotation activities are not supported in the Web. To overcome these problems we proposed an online annotation tool for online courses. We built our annotation tool upon the expertise learnt from the many pros and cons found in predecessor tools (see Section 2). Our annotation tool provides learners means to highlight any portion of the learning material available online. We decided for a minimalistic approach where users can intuitively make use of the tool, just by doing the same they would do when reading a hard copy document.

In addition to the highlighting, we provide two possible semantics for an annotation: *confusing* or *important*. In this way learners can not only better guide learning process, but also provide valuable feedback to the contents' authors. We assume that the contents' authors are constantly working with the students as a more capable pair. Thus, from the semantic-annotation done by students, the tutors can track students' development during the course.

In this paper we describe the technologies involved in the deployment of the tool applied on the online courses. Additionally, we present quantitative results of usage from a community of over 750 learners subscribed to the courses where the tool was available, together with qualitative results collected from a questionnaire.

The remainder of this paper is organized as follows. In the next Section, we review related work on past experiences and studies regarding online annotations. Section 3 describes the methodology involved in the online courses available in our system and Section 4 explains in details the usage of the highlight tool. In Section 5, we briefly describe the metrics used to collect students' feedback followed by a quantitative and qualitative results in Section 6. Finally, we present our conclusions and future directions in Section 7.

## 2   Related Work

In our work we define an annotation as any additional content that is directly attached to a resource and that adds some implicit or explicit information in many different forms [7]. This definition is in line with the definitions set forth by MacMullen [10] and Marshall [11].

Annotations are a common practice usually accompanying a reading task. They serve for different purposes. The most frequent annotations are used for signaling, supporting memorization and interpretation or for triggering reflection. Annotations also occur in many different forms: highlights, circles, symbols, writings, to name but a few. Each form of annotation is embedded with a certain use. Highlighting for example is mostly used to emphasize the importance of a certain part of the document. The same metaphor holds for encircling or underlining text. On the other hand, a strikethrough indicates that something is wrong, misplaced or not relevant. Also, to create relations between elements, lines and arrow-signals are used. In this work we focus on the highlight annotation metaphor which goals are to emphasize a certain portion of learning objects and classify it as important or confusing.

Vannevar Bush in the Memex [4] has long ago envisioned the benefits of electronic and automatic annotations. By relating all documents that users have read and attaching their annotations to these documents, individuals could organize and refind information resources in an associative manner, together with any earlier annotations. Although some Hypertext systems provide rich forms of annotations with categories, directions and multi-links, supporting associative trails, today's Web does not provide such functionalities. Information consumers have limited possibilities for writing and sharing comments on regular Web pages. As a result, a lot of time and effort is wasted when users try to comprehend the different formats of how people comment online resources. In the end, the work around solution is sending comments via e-mail [12].

In order to provide an unified standard for online annotations, as an extension of the open hypermedia Arakne Environment [3], the Fluid Annotations projects [13] deploys an online annotation system that supports in-context annotations. Their work focused on understanding the best metaphors to present digital annotations in terms of visual cues, regarding interactions, accommodation and animated transactions. Their work provides valuable feedback to the community for implementing usability and manipulation of annotations. Their main approach consists in accommodate annotations in between lines. Differently, we believe that disrupting the original information layout turns out to be more disruptive than beneficial.

Diigo is a more complete and commercial annotation tool. Diigo provides a toolbar with which users can highlight text or attach 'inline sticky notes' to Web pages. Despite the wealth of features, Diigo cannot boost a big user population. According to online user comments, this is due to both usability issues and the fact that all annotations are public by default. For a collaborative setup, reliability on the collaborators is a major issue for the beneficial outcomes of using the tool. Thus, a rather limited and trustful network of users is the best audience for a collaborative annotation tool.

In a past work, we have analyzed readers' annotation behavior during the learning process. In this way, we could fully comprehend the desired annotation features needed on the web. We conducted a field-study examining the paper-based annotations of 22 PhD students and pos-Docs in their own work environment [6]. For each participant, we looked at the last 3 research papers or articles that they have printed and read. In total we have collected 66 articles, covering a total of 591 pages of text. We found 1778 annotations and an average of 3.08 annotations per page. Out of these 1778 annotations, over 81% of them were simply highlights.

In addition to that, we have previously developed an in-context annotation tool for the broad audience, namely SpreadCrumbs [8]. Similar to Diigo the tool provides a toolbar that allows users to annotate with a floating sticky note on any Web page. Additionally, users were provided with searching and sharing functionalities within their social networks with great privacy control. In an oriented user study we have evaluated the usability of the tool, and most important, the benefits on online annotations in the tasks of refinding information [9]. The outcomes suggested that users of the annotation tool could refind information over two times faster. Furthermore, the usage of the browsers' 'find' functionality (CTRL+F) drops from an average of 53.5% to only 17.2%.

Despite the benefits of the cited tools, none has reached a great audience. We believe that the excess of functionalities given by these tools is the main responsible for this failure. This failure increases the time of the learning process of the tools, and since the benefits are not perceived in a short-term use, users are most likely to abandon it. Also the inexistence of a smaller and trustful network with common interests imposes a barrier for the catch up of collaboration and mutual benefits of exchanging annotations. Considering these past experiences, we implemented an online highlight tool that (a) provides students a way to make their own annotations; (b) that allows the teachers to assess students' interaction in the content; and (c) that allows the contents' authors to improve and match the content of the course as students highlight the text.

## 3   Online Courses

The distance course 'Technology applied in Education' is designed for postgraduate students who wish to achieve literacy not only in information technology, but also to deepen the knowledge of it in the classroom. The course is aimed to those who are teachers in the educational public network in Brazil and aims to generate knowledge, promote teacher development and educational reform.

The first two editions of this course were held in 2006-2007 and 2009-2010 and resulted in the specialization of over 6000 teachers, distributed throughout Brazil. Although the main structure of the course is kept the same, each version of the course incorporates new tools and means of communication available, in order to suit current needs and prepare teachers to use and create new learning situations in their future lectures.

The 'Technology applied in Education' course is available all over Brazil and in the current version has over 750 subscribed students. Along with, the course has over 50 tutors that are responsible for monitoring, evaluating and teaching through our Learning Management System (LMS). Each tutor has a group of maximum 30 students. The course is delivered through online lectures, discussion forums, Web seminars and practical projects that support learning by doing.

Accordingly, we have deployed, in each edition of this specific course, several tools that can help students and teachers in the learning process. In this manner, here, we introduce the 'highlight tool', a simple yet powerful annotation tool, that has demonstrated a huge potential to improve and facilitate the learning process and course management.

For instance, the highlight tool has been demonstrated to be very useful to support the creation of courses focused on individual needs. Since the annotations are available to tutors, they can provide to each student additional materials or even create discussion

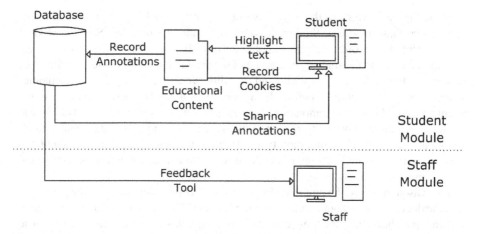

**Fig. 1.** The workflow shows the annotation process realized by a student. The annotations are stored in the LMS database and locally via cookies. All the annotations are available for analysis in the Staff Module.

forums to solve unexpected misunderstandings. This kind of tool allows us to create a non-mass course, adapting the structure of each content to fit students' needs and reach the goals of each lecture.

## 4    The Highlight Annotation Tool

The highlight tool is a reformulation of the traditional highlight pen used to emphasize excerpt of texts in hard copy documents. Usually, this pen is used to highlight relevant passages of text or passages that must be reviewed and easily found later. However, regardless of how good the highlight is, it will still have its own limitations.

With the advent of the Internet and the development of new technologies, simple tools like highlight pen could be redesigned to aggregate new possibilities of use and overcome its original use. Obviously, the first main difference from the traditional highlight pen is the fact that highlighted texts can be shared over the Internet. Consequently, all annotations done by the readers of a book could be sent to the publisher, which could analyze it and, if it is the case, update the next edition of a book.

For example, we commonly find typing errors in books, so this tool could help to correct them. In the e-learning context, this tool is even more powerful because students can share annotations between them and the teachers. The tool is boosted with an administration view, where teachers can analyze all the annotations done by their students. In this manner, teachers can have an overview of the content from the point of view of the students.

Moreover, teachers can discuss topics that most students thought confusing or even give more information about topics that they annotated as interesting. With the traditional highlight pen it would be impossible due to the time one would take to verify each annotation done by each student in a hard copy document. Hence, the highlight pen improves the whole learning development by assisting both learners and teachers within their tasks.

In the Figure 1, we show the workflow of the highlight tool. The highlight tool consists in two main modules, Student Module and Staff Module. The Student Module is responsible for recording all the annotations done by a student. The process is triggered at the moment the student selects one of the available highlight pens (*confusing* or *important*). For matters of simplicity and usability, we adopted only the two semantic-annotations types mentioned before. However, the tool can be customized to use different colors and semantic-annotations types. Furthermore, before start the use of these tools, we introduced a brief description of its usage in order to ensure their understanding about each semantic-annotation type. Once the annotation is done, the annotated area is recorded in the LMS database. A copy of the annotation is also stored in the users' computer via cookies.

The reason to record the annotations in the users' computer is because they can also read the document when not connected to the Internet. Although this is an online course and one must have Internet connection to participate, this decision was made because in many regions in Brazil the Internet connection is dial-up or over satellite, thus, many students prefer to download the document, read, make their annotations and later connect again and participate online. In this manner, we record students' interactions twice, one in our database and another in their computers (via browsers' cookies).

The Staff Module is responsible for presenting the staff members (tutor, contents' author, course coordinator) highlighted texts in the online content (see Figure 2). In addition to that, an interface presenting statistics by course and type of annotation (confusing or important) help staff members to create and improve learning situations that better fits the students' needs. The tool can be installed in any document available in the Learning Management System (LMS), where we record all the annotations done by each student.

## 5    Evaluation

In order to evaluate the Highlight tool, we collected quantitative usage statistics and qualitative feedback from the learners. To assess qualitative feedback we set up an online questionnaire with 17 questions. We distributed the questionnaire to all students subscribed in the online courses that had access to the highlight tool. The questionnaire was not mandatory and was completely anonymous. We divide the questionnaire in five different tiers of questions, namely: usage, satisfaction, application, collaboration and future use.

- **Usage.** The questions regarding usage collect feedback regarding the students' access frequency to the online courses, the usage of the highlight tool and revisitation to the annotations.
- **Satisfaction.** Satisfaction covers the students' personal feeling regarding the tool concerning utility of the tool, if it supported their studies and easiness of use.
- **Application.** The questions of the application tier collect feedback considering possible applications and activities to be done on top of the annotations. For example, 'Is it beneficial to provide extra material for the annotations that are marked as important/confusing?'.

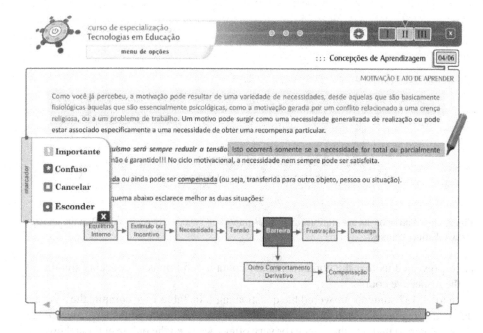

**Fig. 2.** Student Module. Example of annotations realized by a student. On top, an annotation marked as important(yellow) followed by an annotation marked as confusing(red).

- **Collaboration.** In terms of collaboration, although the tool did not provide any means for the students to exchange annotations, the questionnaire inquire them about their will to share and collaborate with other students. As one example, among the collaboration-related questions, we asked if they would like to have access to other students' annotations.
- **Future Use.** Finally the questions regarding future use address general opinions and inquire the students about their desires and plans to use the highlight tool in future courses.

For each question, the participants had to choose their agreement on a 5-point Likert scale.

## 6   Results

We collected the data from the first two courses where the tool was available. Each course consists of the main document - the one that can be annotated - together with other activities described in Section 3, and has a time-span of approximately eight weeks. We gathered the students' interaction during these 8 weeks. The first course consisted of a document containing 43 pages, while the second had 65 pages. In total we collected 279 annotations where 88% were marked as important. In Figure 3 we discriminate the annotations (important) by course and by page in each learning object. We did not find any correlation between the number of annotations marked as confusing and important. A thorough analysis of the portion of the most important-annotated

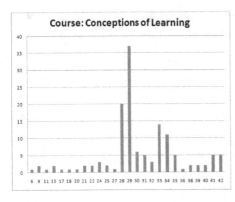
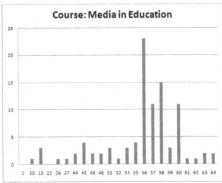

**Fig. 3.** Distribution of the annotations marked as important (y-axis) by page (x-axis) in the content of two distinct courses

pages, revealed us that the contents mainly contain definitions of concepts significant to the respective course.

In total, 132 students answered the questionnaire. In Table 1 we compile the answers distinguishing them by tear and agreement. Over 75% of the students that answered the questionnaire stated that they often (or very often) accessed the online content, however only 25% stated to use the highlight tool with the same frequency.

From the Satisfaction tier, over 77% agreed or strongly agreed that the highlight tool contributed to their learning process. Also, over 75% of the participants considered the tool straightforward to use.

Regarding the annotations and further activities that should be provided to the students, over 50% of the questionnaire participants agreed (or strongly agreed) that it is important to have further materials, discussion forums and other extra activities on the annotated topics. Peculiarly, the students considered on the same degree of agreement (without significant difference), that these activities would be helpful for both types of annotations, confusing or important.

Although the first goal of highlight tool is to provide students an individual method to support active-reading and refinding information, collaboration and communication also plays a major role in the learning process. Over 63% of the participants strongly agreed or agreed that collaborative features, as for example, sharing annotations and accessing other students' annotations, would definitely be beneficial during the learning process. By sharing annotations, or merely visualizing colleagues' highlights, students

**Table 1.** Results of the user experience questionnaire

|                      | Favor   | Neutral | Against |
|----------------------|---------|---------|---------|
| Usage                | 54.23%  | 23.81%  | 21.96%  |
| Utility/Satisfaction | 66.14%  | 20.11%  | 13.76%  |
| Application          | 51.72%  | 25.79%  | 22.49%  |
| Collaboration        | 63.49%  | 23.81%  | 12.70%  |
| Future Use           | 53.57%  | 25.40%  | 21.03%  |

can have a better overview on the importance of some portions of the learning objects, and also on the portions that raised more questions among her learning group. Shared annotations improve the individual learning and boost the online group discussion as well.

Finally, over 53% of the participants would recommend the tool for colleagues and are also willing to use the tool in the next courses.

## 7   Conclusion

In this paper we present the highlight tool that aims to assist students in their learning process. As we demonstrated in this paper, once the annotations are recorded and available online, students, teachers/tutors, contents' authors and course coordinators can use this information to improve the content taught and the student's learning experience. The tool was deployed in an e-learning course with over 750 students that actively used it. Through the use of the tool the tutors could create new discussion topics to handle some students questions or to extend topics that was marked as interesting.

The annotations also contributed to improve the content available to the students. The contents' author reviewed the passages of the text that were very often marked as confusing or important. The texts that were marked as confusing are being reformulated. The texts that were marked as important are being expanded and in the next version of the course a complimentary material will be available for the students.

Finally, in the point of view of the course coordination or even of the institution, the tool is important to give feedback about the student needs, content quality and the continuity of the course. Through the use of this tool, the teachers can go beyond the group needs but also address individual needs of each student.

Through the feedback collected in our user evaluation, we conclude that the tool had a positive impact in the learning process and, moreover, students are willing to continue using the tool. As future works, we intend to expand the tool to recommend complimentary materials and enable collaborative features to enhance communication, facilitate social reading and to bring students closer, in order to improve the whole learning experience.

**Acknowledgement.** This research has been co-funded by the European Commission within the eContentplus targeted project OpenScout, grant ECP 2008 EDU 428016 (cf. http://www.openscout.net) and by CAPES (Process $n^o$ 9404-11-2).

## References

1. Adler, M.J., Doren, C.V.: How to Read a Book. revised edn. Simon and Schuster, New York (1972)
2. Bernstein, M., Van Kleek, M., Karger, D., Schraefel, M.C.: Information scraps: How and why information eludes our personal information management tools. ACM Trans. Inf. Syst., 26(4), 24:1–24:46 (2008)
3. Bouvin, N.O.: Unifying strategies for web augmentation. In: Proceedings of the Tenth ACM Conference on Hypertext and Hypermedia: Returning to our Diverse Roots: Returning to our Diverse Roots, HYPERTEXT 1999, pp. 91–100. ACM, New York (1999)

4. Bush, V.: As we may think. The Transatlantic Monthly (July 1945)
5. Chatti, M.A., Jarke, M.: The future of e-learning: a shift to knowledge networking and social software. Int. J. Knowledge and Learning 3(4/5), 404–420 (2007)
6. Kawase, R., Herder, E., Nejdl, W.: A Comparison of Paper-Based and Online Annotations in the Workplace. In: Cress, U., Dimitrova, V., Specht, M. (eds.) EC-TEL 2009. LNCS, vol. 5794, pp. 240–253. Springer, Heidelberg (2009)
7. Kawase, R., Herder, E., Papadakis, G., Nejdl, W.: In-Context Annotations for Refinding and Sharing. In: Filipe, J., Cordeiro, J. (eds.) WEBIST 2010. LNBIP, vol. 75, pp. 85–100. Springer, Heidelberg (2011)
8. Kawase, R., Nejdl, W.: A straightforward approach for online annotations: Spreadcrumbs - enhancing and simplifying online collaboration. In: Filipe, J., Cordeiro, J. (eds.) WEBIST, pp. 407–410. INSTICC Press (2009)
9. Kawase, R., Papadakis, G., Herder, E., Nejdl, W.: The impact of bookmarks and annotations on refinding information. In: Proceedings of the 21st ACM Conference on Hypertext and Hypermedia, HT 2010, pp. 29–34. ACM, New York (2010)
10. Macmullen, W.J.: Annotation as process, thing, and knowledge: Multi-domain studies of structured data annotation. Technical report, in ASIST Annual Meeting (Charlotte, NC, 2005), ASIST (2005) (in review)
11. Marshall, C.C.: Annotation: from paper books to the digital library. In: DL 1997: Proceedings of the Second ACM International Conference on Digital Libraries, pp. 131–140. ACM Press, New York (1997)
12. Pirolli, P.: Information Foraging Theory: Adaptive Interaction with information. Oxford University Press, New York (2007)
13. Zellweger, P.T., Mangen, A., Newman, P.: Reading and writing fluid hypertext narratives. In: Proceedings of the Thirteenth ACM Conference on Hypertext and Hypermedia, HYPERTEXT 2002, pp. 45–54. ACM, New York (2002)

# Teaching Culture as Social Constructivism[*]

Cat Kutay[1], Deirdre Howard-Wagner[2], Lynette Riley[3], and Janet Mooney[3]

[1] Computer Science and Engineering, The University of New South Wales
ckutay@cse.unsw.edu.au
[2] Dept. of Sociology and Social Policy, University of Sydney
deirdre.howard-wagner@sydney.edu.au
[3] The Koori Centre, University of Sydney
{lynette.riley,janet.mooney}@sydney.edu.au

**Abstract.** Teaching complex learning domains such as cultural awareness relies on individual perspectives. In this paper we present the process and technology to develop an online system to share multiple experiences of Aboriginal Culture in NSW, Australia within a social-constructivist framework.

The focus of the material is the Kinship system used for thousands of years in this region. This topic exemplifies the knowledge used to maintain societies and provides the setting for social conflict with the non-Aboriginal people who came here in recent history.

We are using stories from the community to augment the learning material. Using innovative web services, teachers can select the stories that are relevant to their course, and link these within a range of scenarios being developed. The scenarios enable students to select the way they relate to the characters, listen to their stories, and become aware of their own role in the community.

**Keywords:** Indigenous Knowledge, Community Narrative, Cultural Awareness.

## 1    Introduction

The paper describes the design and implementation of an online cultural training workshop based around the complex Kinship system used in NSW, Australia. It is to be used at Sydney University as part of the professional training of lawyers, teachers and social workers and at Edith Cowan University for health workers. The project arose from the fact that Australian Aboriginal and Torres Strait Islander people are still alienated and dispossessed within a highly affluent western society and their culture and values are rarely considered in decision-making.

Since commerce and education now involve the sharing of information electronically across the globe, it is important that Indigenous people are not excluded. Hence this research proposes software architectures and web services that can provide an

---

[*] The Australian Government Office for Learning and Teaching has provided support for this project/activity. The views in this project do not necessarily reflect the views of the Office.

E. Popescu et al. (Eds.): ICWL 2012, LNCS 7558, pp. 61–68, 2012.

environment in which Indigenous people will share knowledge for the maintenance of their culture and the education of others, while maintaining control of what is presented and how this is done.

The project is based on a face-to-face presentation developed by Riley [14] with the aim of making it available to many more people as a video and then enhances it with community narratives. In particular we wish to reflect where possible the Aboriginal knowledge sharing process, traditionally through interwoven stories, song and dance at a community ceremony or corroboree [13]. These dances provide for re-enactment and an environment for experiential learning of the subject matter. While web services provide a form of mediation that is representational and more static than previous methods of knowledge sharing [15] this medium does provide ability to combine material from many informants [6]. Furthermore we wish to emulate a performance, and develop the individual narratives into a coherent story, in this case using simulation or game environments.

## 2    Learning Design

We have developed an online workshop that teaches NSW Aboriginal culture relating to certain aspects of life, such as knowledge sharing protocols and communications strategies between distant groups. The understanding of these aspects of the Aboriginal culture is crucial for Australian professionals who will work with Aboriginal people as colleagues and clients. This knowledge is diachronic in that it presents the evolution of the culture and the environment over time. This differs to mainstream teaching that is concerned with generalising in a synchronic form, analysing processes and material at a certain point in time but differing contexts.

The original presentation has proved highly successful and has previously been evaluated, but the focus of this work is now to evaluate the process of converting the material to online format, and how to provide a learning format that is more interactive and incorporates the knowledge of the community, not just an individual. In particular, we wish to support the updating of information to mimic the changing choice of stories presented at Aboriginal ceremonies, to present material that relates to the changing conditions.

A video of this original presentation has been developed and is now online. Further information has been added to update the workshop, by linking new information to time slots in the presentation. Also the interactive role-plays have been presented as short flash videos with simple user interaction, and inserted into the workshop.

At the end of the original presentation students are placed in a European context that conflicts with the new knowledge they now have. We wish to expand this aspect of the learning for the online workshop by adding more stories of such experiences, and immersing students in relevant role-plays. The online workshop has been reviewed with feedback for improvement, and the next stage of the project is to run more workshops and assist users to upload their narratives and link them to the appropriate section of the workshop video.

The site will be a combination of Aboriginal people's experience, including those of students and staff at the Koori Centre, University of Sydney and Aboriginal elders, forming a community narrative. Additionally non-Aboriginal academics from professional teaching areas are involved in the project to ensure the resources are appropriate for use in their degree structure.

As we collect these resources we are co-developing the simulation worlds and learning scenarios to fit the stories that are available so far.

# 3    Learning Style

The focus of the learning system development is twofold. Firstly we wish the Aboriginal students and community members involved in this project to view themselves as knowledge givers, or teachers [17]. Secondly we want the learning to match the learning style used by Aboriginal people. Using story telling for learning has benefits for retention within highly diverse and complex-structured knowledge systems. We are not describing knowledge about a single cause and effect, but a highly interwoven knowledge system and its resilience during a long period of ignorance by European invaders. This knowledge is highly significant for Aboriginal people in Australia, and we want the students to engage and learn.

Furthermore, we are developing the workshop to be integrated into University courses to provide an introduction to Aboriginal Kinship across the disciplines. Hence some standard learning methods are being integrated, such as reflective questions. The main topics are relationships and interaction, as understanding relationships is the first priority in teaching Kinship and narratives are used to emulate the process used by Aboriginal teachers within the context of sharing Aboriginal knowledge.

The use of narrative content is a way to teach ([7] and [1]) and respect traditional storytelling methods ([3] and [10]). As this research is based on a social constructivist approach to teaching and learning, which presumes students learn through active formation of their own knowledge rather than by memorising or absorbing ideas from presentations by a single teacher [16], learning is through experimentation and opportunities for students to create their own 'worlds', in this case as scenarios.

The knowledge in this learning environment is provided in a manner that supports Indigenous knowledge sharing processes ([8] and [11]) as part of the process of elevating Indigenous knowledge as a legitimate knowledge system. These are:

- **Community-based:** Upload and link of stories from multiple authors (with accrediting of ownership) to provide a community narrative
- **Coherent:** Provide a consistent framework into which individuals can insert their stories to form part of the knowledge sharing on that theme
- **Context:** Allow individuals to see and here where their stories will be presented, and retain this consistent context over time
- **Ownership:** Tag material and providing permanent links to author's information[9]
- **Methodology:** Focus on experiential learning rather than theoretical
- **Format:** Use multimedia so that visual and audio elements are available for learning, as well as text format

- **Diachronic:** Provide for continually updating of content through additional comments, modules and clipping videos to enable diachronic analysis
- **Immersive:** Opportunity for students to immerse in the environment they are learning about
- **Interactive:** Opportunity for students to try things for themselves and get feedback that is advisory rather than specific or didactic
- **Teaching methods:** Provide for teachers and learners to use different approaches to knowledge to help retention and understanding, such as abstraction, analogy and humour

We will now describe how we are implementing this learning process online.

## 4     Workshop Design

The software being developed is highly modular so that we can support different applications, for instance non-video focus material can be used in future for implementation within other topic areas, while retaining audio/video support for comments. The web services include the ability to 'chop' and annotate the video so the Kinship workshop can be presented in segments, and interactive games interleaved where required.

We explain here briefly the next stage of the development, as this will be crucial for satisfying the learning criteria listed above. The learning environment will be a virtual world scenario, which will provide links to a set of stories types. The instructor will select the specific stories relevant to their domain. Students will go through relevant interactive scenarios after viewing the workshop.

The methodology used in the software development is Action Research, a process of continual iteration through different forms of evaluation, and consultations with the various stakeholders. In this project the interface and simulations are developed in stages with regular feedback from Aboriginal community members [5], who are also developing their information technology skills in line with the evolving system.

The evaluation involved the following steps and the results will be summarised in the section below. We have evaluated and improved the presentation to suit the understanding of students who will be adding narratives and staff who will be using the online version in their teaching. The presentation was then recorded and evaluated by a group of teaching staff, which resulted in the video material being edited and futher material linked to the site. Then it was requested that we provide a more interactive version of the role-play games, and this was developed and interleaved into the online modules, using video clipping. The resultant web services are:

1. The introductory content evaluated by:
   (a) Face-to-face presentation evaluated and improved
   (b) Videos from presentation reviewed and edited
   (c) Additional material added to or inserted into video
2. Tools to update the video with comments that are tagged using XrML standards for annotation [9] and themes developed from:

(d) Workshops held with Aboriginal people to gather types of material that will be added

(e) Selection of comments added and tested in the system

3. Interface usability improved by:

(f) Collected reviews by IT and cultural experts

(g) User testing run and all issues noted

4. Support incorporation of the narratives into games:

(h) Isolate themes that link stories through discussion with community members

(i) Workshops with Aboriginal students to gather thematic areas of stories that will be added

A further request by users was for an interface to review the narratives already collected, sorted by their themes, etc. This Narrative Interface has been developed and undergone user testing. It allows users to listen to a selection of stories sorted by tags in a non-interactive environment. We still need to develop culturally suitable graphical icons to improve the search mechanism.

## 4.1    Simulation Design

The simulation system has been designed with separate components (and related tools) for content development, scenario modeling and teaching support and feedback, using the experience from game based e-learning system and modular online learning and assessment tools such as Adaptive E-Learning [2]. We have separated the design into:

1.  Narratives: the content of the learning derived from the database repository
2.  Scenarios: the context of the virtual worlds or eLearning interface including learning paths
3.  Teaching goals: the consciousness we aim for in the students or the goals of the learning supported by learning paths and feedback authoring tool

For this we need to provide interfaces for novice users to:

1.1  Chose relevant contributed stories, author scenarios and develop teaching support and assessment
2.1  Select and run single user scenarios on website
3.1  Develop a range of automated 'bots' for prototype insertion of stories into a 3D multi-player environment

The final stage is to develop a multi-player Virtual World as an extension of the single-player scenarios using some of the agents and narratives from that system.

## 5    Teaching Framework

While retaining the diversity of views that are being collected on the themes we need to ensure the experiences do not become stereotypical. Hence much discussion has been held with community members, including elders, looking at the content or themes to be covered in the material.

The teaching aims for a consciousness that will be developed through the creation of the scenarios (including those in the introductory material) and through reflective questions linked to the uploaded narratives. We are considering some minimal scoring systems (e.g. does the user listens to the correct people) due to their motivational nature, and so provide a simple evaluation of the users' achieved level of learning.

In particular there are two aspects of consciousness that we want to deal with: providing students with an experience from an Aboriginal person's kinship knowledge; and the experience of how people relate within and between cultures. The first is simply gathering the relevant stories. The second aspect is more difficult and is being developed through the design of state charts.

### 5.1    Evaluation

The evaluation of the project so far follows on from the evaluation of the original presentation, and looks at two aspects of teaching:

1. Can the online web system provide the teaching approach used in the original face-to-face presentation?
2. Can we extend that presentation through additions web resources?

The first goal has been achieved through providing the video online after editing, and had been verified by users as coving the content well and in a viewable format. We have also been able to provide a simulation of the interactive sections online to the satisfaction of the instructor who designed the exercises.

We explain now how we have extended the workshop in line with each of the aspect of Indigenous knowledge sharing listed above (where relevant), and how these are incorporated into the existing online system:

- **Community:** Commenting and narrative interface provides tools to link stories to the workshops and store for use in games, after moderation
- **Coherency:** Workshop provides themes and subthemes that are used to tag narratives, as well as other tags such as cultural context, subject area, specific location in space or time and cultural relation to listener
- **Context:** The workshop provides an interface for displaying stories in sequence, and a separate narrative search interface for viewing stories by tags. However, the third stage of simulation gaming will provide the main context for learning from these stories
- **Ownership:** The repository retains information about the author or contributor (possibly an audio file) and the context in which they wish this story to be heard, and presents it with this information and in this context
- **Methodology:** The information is presented entirely as stories and discussion, then presented firstly in a simple sorting interface and then as roles in the simulation scenarios. Authors can include some reflective questions with their stories that are displayed after the story is finished, but these are not assessed

- **Format:** The format is similar to YouTube in that users can view the material in multimedia format, but the site links these into learning environments and simulations
- **Diachronic:** Users can upload comments (eg external links) and stories

The next stage of the project, to incorporate simulation and role-play games into the system will provide:

- **Immersive:** The simulation will present learning material and narratives in a gaming environment
- **Interactive:** The generic simulation interactions have been designed and will be implemented by computer agents within the simulations

The teaching framework has been design [12] to consider the different ways of presenting information, including:

- **Abstraction:** In the workshop Aboriginal views and processes are presented and then an explanation is given of how this is enacted within the culture to preserve the specific society and the environment in which the peoples live; and then present how this varies from non-Aboriginal culture
- **Analogy:** An aspect specific to Aboriginal culture is selected, then students are asked how this aspect could be enacted in mainstream culture and how this would affect relations, responsibilities or survival within the new cultural context
- **Humour:** The stories offered by Aboriginal users that relate to the themes of the workshop are frequently told with humour, so this style will be common on the site, as it makes some difficult issues easier to deal with

# 6    Conclusion

The story formats and protocol used by traditional cultures for knowledge sharing (see [8]) can be emulated in software to some extent. Further research is needed to unify these features within systems that are easy for novice users to tailor to the theme they wish to develop online, and to support the multimedia formats that users may prefer. While much work still needs to go into this project, we envisage great benefits.

The software will be published as open-source under the Creative Commons Attribution-Noncommercial-ShareAlike 3.0 Australia Licence (CCL) and the teaching guidelines will be published on the final workshop site. It is expected the project will continue as part of the University of Sydney development programs.

By working with similar existing oral collection projects at other universities, such as Edith Cowan University, we will be able to verify the flexibility of our system as we progress. This requires the initial design to include options to add and change features.

As well as providing a means to save stories for future generations that convey the knowledge of existing Indigenous communities, the environment will also support the experience of urban culture. The stories that are shared in the contemporary Aboriginal culture include family histories or genealogies, moral stories, and life experience, for example the Bringing Them Home Oral History Project [4]. Such stories are important in the education of the next generation of Australian children and their parents.

# References

1. Andrews, D., Hull, T., De Meester, K.: Storytelling as an instructional method: research perspectives. Sense Publishers, Rotterdam and Taipai (2010)
2. Ben-Naim, D., Bain, M., Marcus, N.: Visualization and Analysis of Student Interactions in an Adaptive Exploratory Learning Environment. CEUR Workshop Proceedings, Berhard Beckert (2008)
3. Bradley, J.: Singing saltwater country. Allen & Unwin, Sydney (2010)
4. Bringing Them Home, http://www.nla.gov.au/digicoll/bringing-them-home-online.html (accessed June 2012)
5. Cronin, D., Jebakumar, L.: Indigenous Methodology: Indigenous research and the academy. Social Policy Research Centre Newsletter 109 (November 2011)
6. Donovan, M.: Can Technological Tools be Used to Suit Aboriginal Learning Pedagogies? In: Dyson, L.E., Hendriks, M., Grant, S. (eds.) Information Technology and Indigenous People, pp. 93–104. Idea Group Inc., Miami FL (2007)
7. Egan, K.: Teaching as story telling: an alternative approach to teaching and curriculum. University of Chicago Press, Chicago (1998)
8. Holcombe, S.: Indigenous Ecological Knowledge and Natural Resources in the Northern Territory, A report commissioned by the Natural Resources Management Board, NT (2009), http://law.anu.edu.au/ncis/SH%20IEK%20Guidelines.pdf (accessed May, 2012)
9. Hunter, J.: Rights Markup Extensions for the Protection of Indigenous Knowledge. In: The 11th International World Wide Web Conference - Global Community Track, Honolulu (2002)
10. Kutay, C., Ho, P.: Story Telling for Cultural Knowledge Sharing. In: Proceedings of the Third International Workshop on Story-Telling and Educational Games (STEG 2010), Shanghai, China, December 28–34 (2010)
11. Kutay, C.: HCI study for Culturally useful Knowledge Sharing. In: 1st International Symposium on Knowledge Management & E-Learning (KMEL), Hone Kong (2011)
12. Kutay, C., Mooney, J., Riley, L., Howard-Wagner, D.: Experiencing Indigenous Knowledge On-line as a Community Narrative. In: Mackinlay, L., Nakata, M. (eds.) Australian Journal of Indigenous Education, vol. 40S (2012) (accepted April 10, 2012)
13. Langton, M.: Grandmothers' Law, Company Business and Succession in Changing Aboriginal Land Tenure Systems. In: Yunipingu, G. (ed.) Our Land is Our Life, pp. 84–117. University of Queensland Press, St Lucia (1997)
14. Riley, L., Genner, M.: Bemel-Gardoo: Embedding cultural content in the science and technology syllabus. In: Two Way Teaching and Learning: Toward Culturally Reflective and Relevant Education, pp. 119–155. ACER Press (2011)
15. Verran, H., Christie, M.: Using/Designing digital technologies of representation in Aboriginal Australian knowledge practice. Human Technology 3(2), 214–227 (2007)
16. Vygotsky, L.S.: Mind and society: The development of higher mental processes. Harvard University Press, Cambridge (1978)
17. Yunkaporta, T.: Aboriginal pedagogies at the cultural interface. PhD thesis, James Cook University (2009), http://eprints.jcu.edu.au/10974/ (accessed February 2011)

# From LMS to PLE: A Step Forward through OpenSocial Apps in Moodle

Evgeny Bogdanov[1], Carsten Ullrich[2], Erik Isaksson[3],
Matthias Palmer[3], and Denis Gillet[1]

[1] Ecole Polytechnique Fédérale de Lausanne, 1015 Lausanne, Switzerland
{evgeny.bogdanov,denis.gillet}@epfl.ch
[2] Shanghai Jiao Tong University, 200030 Shanghai, China
ullrich_c@sjtu.edu.cn
[3] Uppsala University, Box 256, 751 05 Uppsala, Sweden
{erikis,matthias}@kth.se

**Abstract.** Bringing flexibility and extensibility into Learning Management Systems) is crucial because it gives teachers and students a free choice of technologies and educational materials they want to use for their courses. The paper presents a solution via enabling widgets (OpenSocial apps) within Moodle. Our first Moodle plug-in allows teachers to freely choose a set of tools they want to use in their courses though students can not change widgets proposed by teachers. This environment was evaluated with students within several courses. Even though the environment was perceived as useful by students, they still lacked their own personalization. We describe how the future plug-in tackles this problem.

**Keywords:** widgets, learning management systems, personal learning environments, flexible education.

## 1 Introduction

In the confrontation of the two worlds with Learning Management Systems (LMSs) on one pole and Personal Learning Environments (PLEs) on the other one a compromise is needed. Both have their pros and cons. LMSs are controlled and managed by universities, they are widespread and can be found in almost every university, students and teachers are used to them. The main critics to LMSs come from lifelong learning perspective. First, LMSs are not flexible to be personalized by learners themselves, impose a specific learning process and an environment on students, and, second, they are disconnected from the Internet cloud of information [9,5]. These limitations gave birth to PLEs, where learners are in the full control of their learning process and can construct their learning environments themselves by aggregating tools and content required for their specific tasks [7]. However, a PLE also has several disadvantages. First, it requires a rather steep learning curve and strong self-motivation, because students need to understand how a learning process works before they start to take a full advantage of the provided flexibility or even use it [6]. The second reality is that LMSs

E. Popescu et al. (Eds.): ICWL 2012, LNCS 7558, pp. 69–78, 2012.

are popular in universities, students are used to them and they are reluctant to learn (migrate to) new environments. This paper argues that instead of offering PLEs as an alternative environment to LMSs [8,4] they should be seen as a complementary technology that would augment the current capabilities of LMSs by providing more flexibility and personalization to their users, which would shrink the gap between the two competing worlds.

The paper discusses how the main PLE components can be brought into LMS via widgets that are portable Web applications implemented with HTML, CSS and JavaScript. Several different standards exist for widgets. We adopted OpenSocial apps specification for our work[1], however other standards can be used in a similar manner (both OpenSocial apps and widgets are used interchangeably in the paper). Our main goal was to bring the benefits of PLE to students and teachers but, at the same time, decrease as much as possible the amount of new things/environments they will have to learn or interact with - a requirement requested by several teachers. With widgets, students and teachers become flexible in personalizing their environments and can bring much more functionality into LMSs than is available there by default. For this task, we developed plug-ins for a popular LMS - Moodle.

The rest of the paper is organized as follows. In Section 2 we introduce in more details the Moodle platform, describe the limitations it has and show how our solution tackles these limitations. In Sections 3, 4 we describe how the plug-in was used in the university courses and how students perceived it. Section 5 highlights the possible improvements of the existing plug-in and introduces a new plug-in that encompasses these improvements. Section 6 provides an overview of related work and Section 7 concludes the paper.

## 2　Moodle Plug-in Description

Moodle is a popular LMS to manage courses that is the de-facto standard among many Educational Institutions. It is a plug-in based PHP application that can be extended by installing additional modules. These modules have to be installed on a Moodle server by a system administrator. The Moodle view, as shown to students and teachers, consists of a main center area and a rather narrow right column with blocks (Fig. 3). The center area contains main course resources, such as a wiki page, a forum, a lesson, a quiz, etc. The right block contains some helper plug-ins that a teacher can add to every center page, e.g., a calendar, upcoming events, latest news, a recent activity, etc. These are to extend and enrich the functionality of the main center page.

The Moodle flexibility and adaptability is achieved via visual themes and server side plug-ins, thus an intervention of system administrators is required every time a change should be done. Teachers and students are not involved in the process of the customization. Teachers, for example, can not add or remove plug-ins on their own. Differently from Moodle plug-ins, widgets are client-side

---

[1] http://docs.opensocial.org/display/OSD/Specs

applications that can be added to a system by skipping server side installation, which makes them easy to add.

We have two parts of the OpenSocial plug-in for Moodle. The first one adds a new module to Moodle, which is similar to the standard pages module[2]. Once it is installed to Moodle, a teacher can add a "Widget space" to the course, specify a set of widgets for it, and choose whether 1, 2 or 3 column view should be used for widgets display (Fig. 1). The resulting outcome (as displayed to students) is the page with widgets shown in the iGoogle similar fashion, where students can work with several widgets simultaneously (Fig. 2). The second part of the plug-in adds a new block to Moodle[3]. The teacher can add widgets to the right column for already existing in Moodle wiki pages, lessons, forums, etc. (Fig. 3).

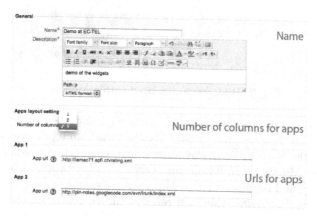

**Fig. 1.** A teacher creates a space with widgets for a course

One of the main benefits of this plug-in is the big pool of available widgets that can be used by teachers. Thus, once the OpenSocial plug-in is installed in Moodle, a teacher can achieve the needed functionality without bothering system administrators with server-side plug-ins installation. The plug-in enhances the flexibility in choosing the resources and tools according to the course specifics: teachers can easily add and remove widgets needed for a course, develop their own ones, etc. Widgets can be found in the existing widget repositories (iGoogle Directory, ROLE Widget Store, etc.). Teachers can re-use existing educational resources and learning objects from external websites. Depending on the desired integration level, teachers can either use an iFrame widget that simply integrates a website URL or develop their own widgets that provide a deeper integration.

From the implementation perspective, the plug-in consists of two main parts. The first part is an engine that renders OpenSocial apps on a page. This engine is a JAVA-based Apache Shindig[4] which represents a reference open-source implementation of the OpenSocial specification. The second part is a PHP module

---

[2] https://github.com/vohtaski/shindig-moodle-mod
[3] https://github.com/vohtaski/shindig-moodle-block
[4] http://shindig.apache.org

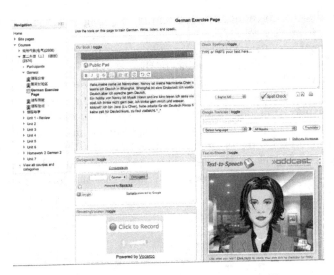

**Fig. 2.** Widgets as displayed within Moodle

that is responsible for a configuration of a page with widgets, adding and removing them to/from the page and gluing Moodle with Shindig engine. OpenSocial API provides the standardized way to retrieve and exchange information between different Moodle installations and other social networks, which improves data portability and interoperability. More precisely, widgets can query Moodle for data via Shindig engine: they can retrieve the currently logged in user, the current course, its participants as well as save and get arbitrary data. The privacy and security are managed via Shindig engine and it is in the full control of university administrators. However, a widget installed within a course runs on behalf of the teacher who added it and can retrieve/update information that teachers can normally do in their courses. Thus, teachers are responsible for checking the trustfulness of a widget, before adding it into their environments. The ability to retrieve a course information and its participants is achieved via OpenSocial Space extension[5] that allows widgets to adapt to the specific context of the course (contextual widgets). For example, a wiki widget can save data for a course and restrict access to only people engaged in this course. The same wiki widget will behave differently being added to another course: it will have a different wiki history and a different list of participants.

## 3    Usage at the Online College of Shanghai Jiao Tong University

The Moodle plug-in has been used at the distance university of Shanghai Jiao Tong University (SJTU School of Continuing Education, SOCE). SOCE students are adult learners who study for an associate or bachelor degree [6]. The college

---

[5] http://docs.opensocial.org/display/OSD/Space+Proposal

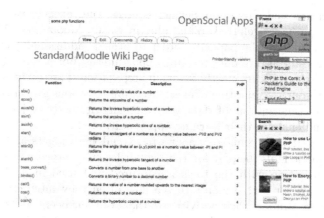

**Fig. 3.** Widgets as blocks on the right

implements blended learning, i.e., students can come to classrooms in person to attend live lectures or watch the lectures live through the Web. All lectures are recorded and available for subsequent non-live view. Teaching and learning follows a traditional pattern and is very teacher-centric, with most students watching the lectures rather passively. Within the ROLE project[6], we investigated how to use existing technologies and tools to provide a larger amount of opportunities for interaction and creation. For instance, tools like Voice Recorders and Text-to-Speech allow foreign language students to practice their pronunciation by recording themselves and comparing their speech to the "original" one. Other tools, such as collaborative text editors enable students to work on joint texts in an easier manner than by using forums. A large percentage of the widgets used in SOCE are existing Web pages that train very specific domain knowledge, such as the usage of German articles and French verbs, or visualize data structures such as linked lists.

The Moodle plug-in has been used at SOCE since August 2011 to add ROLE technology via widgets to a number of courses in the domain of foreign languages as well as computer science. The precise courses are "Business English", "English Newspaper Reading", "Data Structures", "German" and "French". Fig. 2 contains screenshots of a Moodle page. In the lectures "Business English" and "English Newspaper Reading" the teacher used the ROLE approach in several ways. Firstly, and in a similar manner to the other lectures, by converting existing resources into widgets suitable for use in training students for various aspects of business English, such as writing CVs, business emails, etc. Secondly, in order to make the course more realistic, the teachers used a role play scenario in which students set up fictitious companies and products. Students were then instructed to create a web page for their company and a slide set presenting their products. The resources were uploaded in Moodle and students used a rating widget to assess resources authored by their peers.

---

[6] http://www.role-project.eu

In the German and Computer Science courses, the teachers used the PLE (during the courses we referred to the plug-in within Moodle as PLE and we will use this naming in the paper) in order to provide additional exercises, and during the semester also to offer training opportunities, but ostensibly the PLE was utilised by the students mostly for exam preparation. The teachers converted existing web resources consisting of exercises training various aspects of German grammar and visualizations of data structure algorithms to aid the students understand and enhance their learning opportunities.

The usage of ROLE technology allows to extend the widgets and embedded tools with functionality helpful for the overall learning process. For instance, the users' interaction with the tools is captured and used in a visualization which allows teacher and students to see how often they interacted with the resources and to compare their activities to those of their peers. Without ROLE technology, these activities would have been much more difficult to implement in Moodle. While the integration of external exercises is possible with link lists, this approach does not allow to collect interaction data about how often the students actually used the exercises.

## 4  Evaluation

The current section describes the results of a questionnaire that was conducted with students who were using the described plug-in in the courses at SJTU university. Our main goals were to find out whether students see a value in using PLE components brought via the OpenSocial apps and whether they look for more flexibility, i.e., they can manage widgets on their own.

20 students responded to the questionnaire with approximately half of the students coming from the French course and the other half from the German course. In general, students perceived the PLE to be useful for their learning tasks (Fig. 4). They found it to be helpful to learn in an independent manner, to accomplish work more effectively and they would like to use it in the future.

The second answer we wanted to get was whether students are looking for more personalization and flexibility. The questionnaire showed that students feel comfortable in organizing their own environment for learning by customizing the list of widgets offered by teachers, assembling their own sets of widgets for their learning tasks and to search for existing sets of tools (Fig. 4). In Fig. 5 one can see how students rated the tools that were offered by teachers in the PLE. Even though the majority of widgets were useful for students, a number of them (Listen to your pronunciation, Record yourself, Spell check, Activity visualization) were not highly appreciated by several students. This indirectly confirms the fact that students were looking for more flexibility: they would prefer not to have some widgets at all or probably replace them with other alternatives. It seems as the functionality to remove/hide some widgets on the page or to replace them would be appreciated by some students.

| | strongly disagree 1 | 2 | neutral 3 | 4 | strongly agree 5 | Total |
|---|---|---|---|---|---|---|
| I find a PLE useful for my work. | 0 | 0 | 2 (10%) | 7 (35%) | 11 (55%) | 20 |
| I accomplish my work more effectively with a PLE than with the learning technology I am currently using. | 0 | 0 | 2 (10%) | 8 (40%) | 10 (50%) | 20 |
| I find the exercises provided in the PLE helpful for my learning. | 0 | 0 | 2 (10%) | 8 (40%) | 10 (50%) | 20 |
| It is easy for me to use a PLE. | 0 | 0 | 3 (15%) | 6 (30%) | 11 (55%) | 20 |
| I find the exercises provided in the PLE helpful for preparing my exam. | 0 | 0 | 2 (10%) | 7 (35%) | 11 (55%) | 20 |
| It is clear to me how to assemble a PLE using widgets. | 0 | 0 | 9 (45%) | 7 (35%) | 4 (20%) | 20 |
| I find using a PLE frustrating. | 4 (20%) | 3 (15%) | 6 (30%) | 4 (20%) | 3 (15%) | 20 |
| I find interacting with a PLE requires a lot of my mental effort. | 5 (25%) | 4 (20%) | 5 (20%) | 5 (25%) | 2 (10%) | 20 |
| Using a PLE improves my motivation for learning. | 0 | 0 | 6 (30%) | 8 (40%) | 6 (30%) | 20 |

| | strongly disagree 1 | 2 | neutral 3 | 4 | strongly agree 5 | Total |
|---|---|---|---|---|---|---|
| Using a PLE enables me to learn in an independent manner. | 0 | 0 | 5 (25%) | 7 (35%) | 8 (40%) | 20 |
| I predict that I would frequently use a PLE if I had access to it. | 0 | 0 | 4 (20%) | 7 (35%) | 9 (45%) | 20 |
| It were useful if I could combine tools for my own learning/work task. | 0 | 0 | 4 (20%) | 6 (30%) | 10 (50%) | 20 |
| It were useful if I could find an existing set of tools for my own learning/work task. | 0 | 0 | 5 (25%) | 7 (35%) | 8 (40%) | 20 |
| It were useful if I could replace some tools that were by default in PLE. | 0 | 0 | 6 (30%) | 9 (45%) | 5 (25%) | 20 |
| Finding an existing set of tools for my own learning/work task is more useful than creating it by myself. | 0 | 0 | 5 (25%) | 7 (35%) | 8 (40%) | 20 |
| The PLE helps me in organizing my learning better. | 0 | 0 | 4 (20%) | 8 (40%) | 8 (40%) | 20 |
| The PLE gives me more freedom to follow my preferred learning style. | 0 | 0 | 4 (20%) | 6 (30%) | 10 (50%) | 20 |

**Fig. 4.** Questionnaire results

| | low 1 | 2 | average 3 | 4 | high 5 | Total |
|---|---|---|---|---|---|---|
| Collaborative text editor | 0 | 1 (5%) | 3 (15%) | 10 (50%) | 6 (30%) | 20 |
| Translator | 0 | 0 | 2 (10%) | 10 (50%) | 8 (40%) | 20 |
| Business dictionary | 0 | 0 | 3 (15%) | 8 (40%) | 9 (45%) | 20 |
| Text-to-speech | 0 | 1 (5%) | 2 (10%) | 8 (40%) | 9 (45%) | 20 |
| Listen to your pronunciation | 2 (10%) | 0 | 3 (15%) | 8 (42%) | 6 (31%) | 19 |

| | low 1 | 2 | average 3 | 4 | high 5 | Total |
|---|---|---|---|---|---|---|
| Record Yourself | 3 (15%) | 0 | 3 (15%) | 8 (42%) | 5 (26%) | 19 |
| Spell Check | 2 (10%) | 1 (5%) | 1 (5%) | 9 (45%) | 7 (35%) | 20 |
| Multiple Choice Exercises | 0 | 1 (5%) | 1 (5%) | 12 (60%) | 6 (30%) | 20 |
| Other exercises | 0 | 1 (5%) | 3 (15%) | 10 (50%) | 6 (30%) | 20 |
| Activity visualization | 1 (5%) | 2 (10%) | 3 (15%) | 8 (42%) | 5 (26%) | 19 |

**Fig. 5.** Tools as rated by students on a scale from 1 (not useful) to 5 (very useful)

## 5 Future Steps

The plug-in described earlier in this paper takes several steps forward in turning Moodle into a PLE. We will now describe a future plug-in that brings in an actual PLE into Moodle, from a PLE installation running side-by-side with Moodle, while maintaining integration with Moodle through its Web services (Fig. 6).

The embedded PLE has improved personal aspects. Students can add widgets (from an integrated widget store) alongside those chosen by the teacher, which is difficult to enable in the existing plug-in because Moodle requires additional access rights, which students normally do not have. Students can also change the preferences of any widget, configuring it to their needs, overriding the teacher's preferences. Furthermore, widgets can be rearranged and resized.

A dashboard is added to the bottom of the Moodle page and contains widgets that are chosen by the student without teacher's involvement. The dashboard is available independently of the course, which means that students can add widgets that they can access in every course. Outside of Moodle, the dashboard can be accessed on any Web page by means of a bookmarklet (i.e., a Web browser bookmark or favorite that executes a small piece of JavaScript on the current Web page; in our case, the script loads the dashboard). This provides a ubiquitos (cross-organizational) access to the PLE for students which is an important part of lifelong learning [9].

This new plug-in does not integrate with Moodle database. Instead, the plug-in retrieves a token that it passes on to the PLE, allowing the PLE to access Moodle Web services [3] on the authenticated user's behalf. In this way, the embedded PLE is able to access information such as course metadata and participants, and make that information available to widgets. The PLE augments this with support for widgets to store data within the context of a course, similar to the App Data and Media Items of OpenSocial, and other functionality that would not be available from Moodle alone, such as real-time communication. The interface provided to widgets is generic rather than Moodle-specific, and it is possible to implement similar integration that offers the same widget interface also for other LMSs.

As the PLE installation is actually running side-by-side with Moodle, it is possible to access it without Moodle. While it is desirable to keep everything within the same Website (which the embedding of the PLE achieves), it is in some cases better to access the PLE separately. The UI overhead of Moodle page layout is avoided, leaving more screen real estate for the widgets. Additionally, it is possible that the standalone PLE (in this case without the full access rights to the course) could be used as a means to attract students to the course, by giving a taste of what the course is about.

Finally, there are some technological aspects that should make this kind of integration a cleaner solution, although being more complex than integration directly with Moodle database. The more loosely-coupled integration via Moodle provided interfaces is likely (but not certainly) to offer better isolation to changes in Moodle as new versions become available. More importantly, it may be easier to convince administrators to allow the installation if it only integrates with Moodle through its provided interfaces. As this simultaneously reduces the dependency on Moodle, it could also be the first step in leaving the world of LMSes completely, making a PLE-only solution possible.

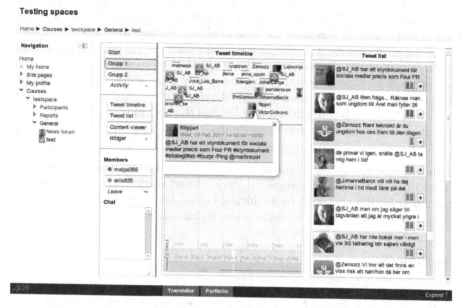

**Fig. 6.** A mock-up of the embedded PLE plug-in for the future step

## 6    Related Work

The earlier work of the authors [6] investigated the usage of a PLE in a similar setting (a French course at SOCE), but with significant differences. First, the PLE was implemented in an external system (Liferay[7]) which was not integrated into the school LMS, thus introducing an additional layer of complexity due to the different user interface and additional log in. Also, the used ROLE technology was still in a very early stage. The paper [1] investigates the applicability of social media platforms within an academic context. More specifically, a social media platform Graasp[8] was used to serve as a stand-alone PLE to augment and enrich the offer of learning tools provided by universities. Through the notion of a space it allowed learners to aggregate and organize both institutional and external resources within different contexts and to conduct learning activities in these contexts. It should be noted that widgets usage is not limited to language learning. Widgets approach is used for teaching chemistry, programming, etc. For example, widgets are used to conduct remote control labs [2].

## 7    Conclusion

The paper presented an approach to extend the existing LMS Moodle with a plug-in enabling OpenSocial apps to run within Moodle. Introducing these apps

---

[7] http://liferay.com
[8] http://graasp.epfl.ch

allows to bring PLE functionalities to LMS, namely, flexibility in managing tools used by people for their learning goals and aggregation of external resources from the Internet. The first version of the plug-in allows teachers to freely choose a set of tools for their courses. The plug-in was used within several courses by students and the questionnaire showed that students find this environment useful, however they still look for more personalization where they can manage apps themselves. The new plug-in that is currently under development is planned to tackle this problem. Thus, our future plans are to finalize the new plug-in, introduce it to students within the courses and evaluate it.

**Acknowledgments.** The research work described in this paper is partially funded through the ROLE Integrated Project; part of the Seventh Framework Programme for Research and Technological Development (FP7) of the European Union in Information and Communication Technologies.

# References

1. Bogdanov, E., Limpens, F., Li, N., El Helou, S., Salzmann, C., Gillet, D.: A Social Media Platform in Higher Education (2012) (accepted to Educon Conference)
2. Bogdanov, E., Salzmann, C., Gillet, D.: Widget-Based Approach for Remote Control Labs. In: 9th IFAC Symposium on Advances in Control Education (2012)
3. Conde, M.A., Aguilar, D.A.G., Pozo de Dios, A., Penalvo, F.J.G.: Moodle 2.0 web services layer and its new application contexts 73, 110–116 (2010)
4. Moedritscher, F., Neumann, G., Garcia-Barrios, V.M., Wild, F.: A web application mashup approach for eLearning. In: OpenACS and LRN Conference (2008)
5. Severance, C., Hardin, J., Whyte, A.: The coming functionality mash-up in Personal Learning Environments. In: Interactive Learning Environments (2008)
6. Ullrich, C., Shen, R., Gillet, D.: Not Yet Ready for Everyone: An Experience Report about a Personal Learning Environment for Language Learning. In: Luo, X., Spaniol, M., Wang, L., Li, Q., Nejdl, W., Zhang, W. (eds.) ICWL 2010. LNCS, vol. 6483, pp. 269–278. Springer, Heidelberg (2010)
7. Van Harmelen, M.: Personal Learning Environments. In: Sixth IEEE International Conference on Advanced Learning Technologies ICALT 2006, vol. 16(1), pp. 815–816 (2006)
8. Van Harmelen, M.: Design trajectories: four experiments in PLE implementation. Interactive Learning Environments 16(1), 35–46 (2008)
9. Wilson, S., Liber, O., Johnson, M., Beauvoir, P., Sharples, P., Milligan, C.: Personal Learning Environments: Challenging the dominant design of educational systems. Journal of eLearning and Knowledge Society 2(1), 173–182 (2007)

# A Mashup Recommender
# for Creating Personal Learning Environments

Alexander Nussbaumer[1], Marcel Berthold[1], Daniel Dahrendorf[2],
Hans-Christian Schmitz[3], Milos Kravcik[4], and Dietrich Albert[1,5]

[1] Knowledge Management Institute, Graz University of Technology
{alexander.nussbaumer,marcel.berthold,dietrich.albert}@tugraz.at
[2] imc information multimedia communication AG
daniel.dahrendorf@im-c.de
[3] Fraunhofer Institute for Applied Information Technology
hans-christian.schmitz@fit.fraunhofer.de
[4] Lehrstuhl Informatik 5, RWTH Aachen University
kravcik@dbis.rwth-aachen.de
[5] Department of Psychology, University of Graz, Austria

**Abstract.** This paper presents an approach and an integrated tool that
supports the creation of personal learning environments suitable for self-
regulated learning. The rationale behind this approach is an ontology
of cognitive and meta-cognitive learning activities that are related to
widgets from a Widget Store. Patterns of such learning activities allow
for providing the user with appropriate recommendations of widgets for
each learning activity. The system architecture follows a Web-based approach and includes the Mashup Recommender widget and its backend
service, the ontology available through a Web service, the Widget Store
with its interface to retrieve widgets, and the integration into the learning environment framework. The pedagogical approach regarding the
usage of this technology is based on self-regulated learning taking into
account different levels between guidance and freedom. A quantitative
and qualitative evaluation with teachers describes advantages and ideas
for improvement.

**Keywords:** personal learning environments, recommender, widget,
mashup, ontology, learning activities, self-regulated learning.

## 1 Introduction

In the recent years a trend became very popular to create small applications for
specific purposes with limited functionalities. Online catalogues containing hundreds of thousands of such applications appeared for mobile and desktop area.
Due to this huge amount finding applications for learning purposes in these catalogues becomes more and more difficult. A second trend became popular in
the technology-enhanced learning area, that systems and technology appeared
that allow to create learning environments by mashing up such small applica-

E. Popescu et al. (Eds.): ICWL 2012, LNCS 7558, pp. 79–88, 2012.

tions. For example iGoogle[1] allows to choose from a large amount of widgets that can be included in the Google state page. Apache provides frameworks that allow to add widgets to a personal space (Shindig[2], Wookie[3]). Other approaches investigate the possibilities of mashup environments specifically for learning purposes, how environments can be created that support learning tasks (for example the eMUSE system [1]). Though there are many activities to create small applications and mashup technologies, there is still a lack of support to create pedagogically sound learning environments consisting of small applications.

The European research project ROLE[4] aims to achieve progress beyond the state of the art in providing personal support of creating user-centric responsive and open learning environments. Learners should be empowered to create and use their own personal learning environments (PLE) consisting of different types of learning resources. According to Henri et al. [2] PLEs refer to a set of learning tools, services, and artifacts gathered from various contexts to be used by the learners. A user requirements study revealed that PLEs are not seen as persistent environments, but they should evolve according to the learner's objectives and achievements [3]. Unlike traditional Learning Management Systems (LMS) where content and tools are predefined for the learner, PLEs are based on soft context boundaries with resources and tools being added at run time [4].

In order to provide some help with self-created PLEs, different recommendation approaches have been proposed in [5]. A tool (Binocs) is described that recommends learning content using federated search in the background. Another tool is proposed that recommends learning activities, in order to provide guidance through the learning process. Finally a tool is described that recommends whole sets of widgets based on settings of other people. In our case an important goal of PLEs is the aspect that they should be suitable for self-regulated learning (SRL). Such an SRL-enabled environment should support learners in certain meta-cognitive activities, such as goal setting, self-evaluation, self-monitoring, or task strategies [6]. To this end, a PLE should contain widgets that are usable to perform these or similar cognitive and meta-cognitive learning activities. Therefore it is required that the compiled environment contains respective widgets. While some learners can create such environments on their own without any help, many learners need assistance and help on different levels.

The aim and purpose of the Mashup Recommender is to recommend widgets for PLEs, so that they are suitable for SRL. To this end, a template approach has been developed, where a set of learning activities is available and for each learning activity specific widgets are recommended. This paper describes the theoretical basis, the technical approach, the support strategies used with this technology, and an initial evaluation with teachers.

---

[1] http://www.google.com/ig

[2] http://shindig.apache.org/

[3] http://incubator.apache.org/wookie/

[4] http://www.role-project.eu

## 2    Theoretical Background

The basic assumption of creating good PLEs is that the assembly of widgets to a widget bundle should follow a pedagogical approach. While widget containers typically allow for compiling PLEs in a completely free way, our approach suggests that the creation of widget bundles should follow a pedagogical approach that is based on underlying educational constructs related to widgets. Assembling widgets to a PLE then follows some guidelines which underlying constructs should be contained and how they should be assembled [7].

A model for SRL in the context of PLEs has been proposed in [8]. This approach is based on a modified version of the cyclic model for SRL as proposed by Zimmerman [9]. It states that SRL consists of four cognitive and meta-cognitive phases (or aspects) that should happen during the self-controlled learning process, which are planning the learning process, search for resources, actual learning, and reflecting about the learning process. In addition to these phases and in order to operationalise them, a taxonomy of learning strategies and learning techniques (in short SRL entities) has been defined and assigned to the learning phases. Following the ideas presented in [10], learning strategies and techniques are defined on the cognitive and meta-cognitive level and are related to the cyclic phases in order to define explicit activities related to SRL. Furthermore, learning techniques have been assigned to widgets stating that these techniques are supported by the respective widgets.

In order to compile pedagogically meaningful PLEs, the assembly of widgets should reflect the underlying learning strategies and techniques. In contrast to existing approaches where just widgets are compiled to a bundle, our approach proposes to start with the consideration which SRL entities should be supported by the PLE. In a second step widgets should be found for the selected SRL entities and added to the widget space. Because of the relations between SRL entities and widgets, widgets can be recommended for a PLE. The pedagogical approach how to create a PLE based on these considerations is described in Section 4.

In contrast to collaborative recommendation approaches that are based on social usage data to generate recommendations, this approach is based on a pre-defined ontology. The advantage of this approach lies in the fact that the leaner's attention can be drawn to meta-cognitive aspects of learning even if other learners do not follow these aspects.

## 3    Technical Approach and Implementation

For the technical realisation of the approach described above a service-oriented design has been chosen that allows for integration with a widget container. The system architecture of the Mashup Recommender (see Figure 1) consists of a front-end and several backend services. The front-end or user interface is realised as a widget to be included in an Open Social widget container. In this widget the learner selects SRL entities and gets other widgets recommended that can be included in the current widget space. SRL entities are organised in templates that bundle SRL entities. A template store holds different templates ensuring that different pedagogical approaches are realised. An authoring tool allows for creating, modifying and deleting such templates in a Web-based environment. The backend service is responsible for the recommendation logic. When the Mashup Recommender widget requests widgets for a learning activity, then the backend service assembles such a list. Therefore it requests widget functionalities from the Ontology Service which translates learning activities to technical functionalities needed to perform the learning activity. Next step is to contact the Widget Store for getting widgets which have assigned the respective functionalities. These widgets are returned back to the Mashup Recommender widgets.

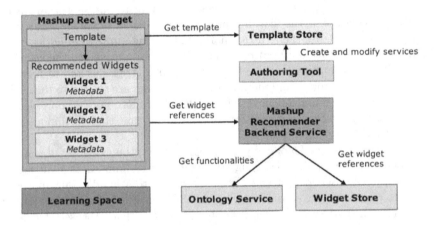

**Fig. 1.** Mashup Recommender Architecture

## 3.1  Widget Store

The ROLE Widget Store [11] is one of the basic components needed for the Mashup Recommender functionality. It provides a catalogue of learning widgets that can be used for the self-compiled PLE. In contrast to existing Web widgets stores (e.g. iGoogle[5]) it has specific features to support the learning processes. The ROLE Widget Store allows learners to search for appropriate learning tools which can be included in existing learning environments. Furthermore, the Widget Store allows for assigning widgets with tool functionalities from the ROLE ontology in order to specify their possible usage. Domain concepts from the DB-Pedia repository can also be assigned to each widget, which allows for describing the domain the widget can be used for. A high-level classification of widgets is the so-called tool categories which classifies all widgets along a seven categories. Accessing the Widget Store can be done in two ways. First it provides a Web-based user interface which allows for searching and adding widgets to the widget

---

space. Second, it also provides a REST interface which allows for search widgets according to one of the above mentioned vocabularies (tool categories, tool functionalities, domain concepts). The second one is the important feature for the Mashup Recommender, because it can search for widgets fitting to the ontology entities.

## 3.2  Ontology and Ontology Service

In order to make the learning strategies and techniques available in a technical sense, an ontology has been created that contains these SRL entities. On top there are learning phase and each learning phase is related to learning strategies. The learning strategies are related to learning techniques, which in turn are related to tool functionalities. The relation to tool functionalities is important, because they are the connection to the widgets in the widget store, where widgets are related to the same tool functionalities.

The ontology is modelled in RDF format, which allows to define each entity and the relations between the entities. In order to expose this ontology to other services, a Web service is used (Joseki) which makes available this RDF file using a SPARQL interface. In this way, other services can access the ontology with SPARQL queries and get the results in XML or JSON format.

## 3.3  Mashup Recommender Backend Service

The Mashup Recommender backend service is the access point for the related widget. If the Mashup Recommender widget searches for widgets for specific SRL entities, it queries the backend service. The service then, queries the ontology service, in order to retrieve the related tool functionalities. Using these tool functionalities it asks the Widget Store for related widgets and gets a list of references and metadata of matching widgets. Using this information the service compiles a list of all retrieved widget references and metadata and sends it back to the Mashup Recommender widget.

## 3.4  Mashup Recommender Widget and Widget Space

The Mashup Recommender widget is the place where the user gets the recommendations and adds recommended widgets to the current widget space. It can be used in the two contexts iGoogle and ROLE SDK. Though implemented as Open Social Widget, it needs specific features of these containers that must provide an API to include new widgets. iGoogle provides an URL that can be used to include a new widget and the ROLE SDK provides a messaging mechanism to notify the container that a new widget should be integrated. The Mashup Recommender widget dynamically detects the container and adds the selected widget accordingly. Figure 2 show a screenshot how a new widget is included.

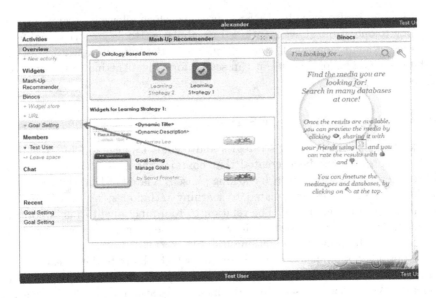

**Fig. 2.** Mashup Recommender Widget and ROLE SDK

## 3.5   Template Store and Authoring

There are three operation modes possible which are specified in each template. First, in a template learning activities can be freely defined and associated with widgets directly. In this case no backend infrastructure is needed and the template author has maximum freedom. Second, SRL entities are taken from the ontology. In this case the ontology service is questioned for the respective functionalities and the widget store returns the associated widget. Third, the categories of the widget store can be used as template entities, and then all widgets from the Widget Store are returned related to each category. In this way, the widget store is represented as a widget in the widget space.

In order to create a new template or to modify an existing template, a tool has been developed for this purpose (see Figure 3). This tool displays the ontology as a graph and lets the user select single SRL entities in order to add them to a template.

A template can be constructed in three different ways. First there is an ontology available which connects learning strategies and learning techniques with functionalities of widgets. The learning strategies and techniques are used as template elements. By clicking on such an element, the associated widget functionalities are used to retrieve according widgets from the Widget Store. Second template type consists for learning activities that are freely defined and hardwired with widgets. The third type consists of the tool categories of the Widget Store. In this last case the same widgets are displayed as in the Widget Store where the same tool categories are used, which actually implements the Widget Store as widget in the current space (Figure 3).

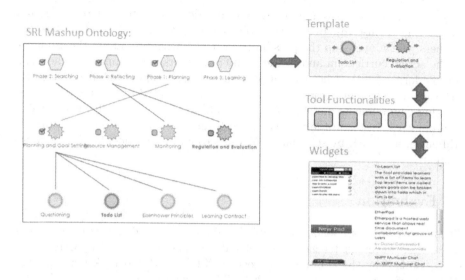

**Fig. 3.** Authoring Tool. This diagram schematically shows the authoring process. On the left side the ontology is displayed whose elements can be added to the template on the right side.

## 4    Guidance Strategies

The Mashup Recommender can be used to provide guidance on different levels and for different stakeholders. A high level of guidance is the preparation of complete predefined PLEs based on a specific template by a teacher or tutor. Then the tutor can share this PLE with her students who can use it and also modify it. A lower level of guidance can be provided if the teacher just shares the template with the students, so that they have to create their own PLE. For example, a teacher could select the SRL entities *goal setting, resource searching, note taking, debating,* and *reflecting* for a template. Then teachers or learners using this template could easily search for widgets for each of these SRL entities and include them in a PLE. In this way the PLE consists of widgets for each SRL entity.

Learning strategies are on a higher abstraction level, which results in a greater number of widgets that can be recommended. Learning techniques are on a lower abstraction level, which leads to a smaller number of related widgets that can be recommended. While in the first case the learner gets more widgets recommended and thus less guidance, in the second case the level of guidance is higher because of the smaller number of recommended widgets. In the case of hard-wired assignment of widgets to freely defined learning activities the level of guidance can also freely be set. In case of using the Widget Store tool categories, the level of guidance is rather small, because all available widgets are assigned to seven template elements.

The creation of the templates is typically done by a teacher or tutor, not by learners themselves. In this way, the teacher provides the guidance for the learners, which opens up the possibility for the teachers to adjust the guidance to the actual curriculum and to the group of learners. This approach leads to a specific form of SRL, where a teacher still provides scaffolding. The reason for the approach arose in the testbeds where teachers wanted to provide predefined learning environments and learners had problems to create their own learning environments. Instead of letting the control fully by the teacher, this approach still encourages SRL by stimulating learners to find their widgets in a guidance context.

## 5 Evaluation

The Mash-Up Recommender was introduced and evaluated as part of two workshops where in sum 29 teachers participated. The first workshop (21 participants) was organised by the European project NEXT-TELL[6] and took place in Bad Waltersdorf, Austria, in December 2011. The second workshop (8 participants) was organised as part of the AHA Konferenz[7] in Vienna, Austria, in April 2012. Both workshops consisted of three parts, (1) an introduction of the Mashup Recommender's theoretical concept, (2) a hands-on-session to make the participants familiar with this software, and (3) subsequent discussion on the approach of the Mashup Recommender and formal evaluation with a questionnaire.

Quantitative feedback using a questionnaire was provided by 13 participants. The answering format ranged from strongly disagree (1) to strongly agree (6) with higher values indicating stronger agreement. Figure 4 shows a positive overall impression of the Mash-Up Recommender. The overall score was computed by the mean of the four individual items. Teachers reported the least agreement concerning creating their own template. However, the other items were evaluated more positively, which is the first indication of relevance and usefulness of this recommender approach.

Qualitative feedback was provided by all 29 participants, which gave more detailed insight. This kind of feedback was provided by the participants as free comments, discussion contributions, and spontaneous feedback while working with the Mashup Recommender. In general the participants understood the idea of the Mashup Recommender and reacted very positively to it. They saw its main advantage in the psycho-pedagogical underpinning regarding the SRL concept. In this way orientation for teachers and learners is provided to guide them through a large number of widgets, because a large number of available widgets might distract them from learning without any kind of guidance. Most of the teachers also highlighted that the Mashup Recommender covers meta-cognitive aspects of learning, which seems to be more important than ever, especially having life-long learning in mind.

---

[6] http://www.next-tell.eu
[7] http://www.ahakonferenz.at/

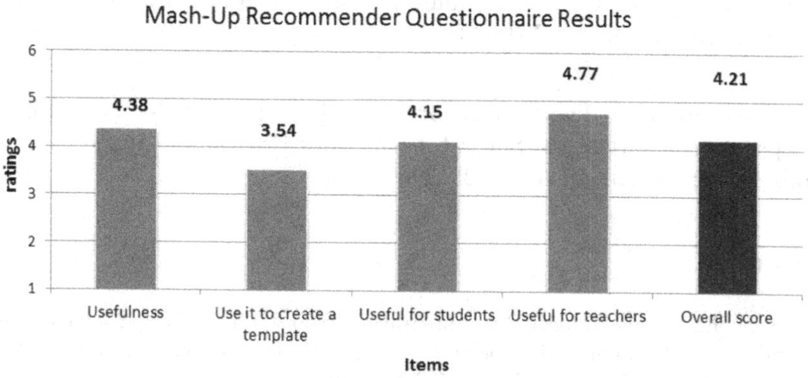

## Mash-Up Recommender Questionnaire Results

**Fig. 4.** Evaluation Result

Still some teachers raised concerns about the additional effort they have to invest in order to understand the Mashup Recommender functionality completely. They mentioned that this could be a barrier to get going with this new technology. That is why the teachers were in favour of getting tutorial material such as an online course or a specific workshop where concrete lessons could be planned using the Mash-Up Recommender.

## 6    Conclusion and Outlook

This paper presented an approach and an integrated tool that supports the creation of PLEs suitable for SRL. The approach is based on an ontology of SRL entities that are also connected with widgets from the ROLE Widget Store. Templates consisting of such ontology entities can be created, which allows for search widgets. In this way a widget space can be created that can be used for various cognitive and meta-cognitive learning activities. An evaluation of this approach with teachers showed that they consider it useful and would use it in their courses.

Since all components have open interfaces, they can also be used by other widgets or services. For example, the Mashup Recommender backend service can be queried to get widget recommendations for ontology entities, the Ontology service can be asked to get tool functionalities for certain entities, or the Mashup Recommender widget can be asked to retrieve widget recommendations for external (virtual) templates.

Possible further work could focus on the use of usage data by feeding back the information which widget in the PLE has actually been used. Specific hints can be given, if a widget already included in the widget space is not used. In this case it can be recommended to use this widget in a specific way (for the use with a certain learning strategy or technique). Additionally, the recommendation strategy can be improved by not only use ontology information, but also collaborative usage data by taking into account the information which widget has been selected for which SRL entity.

**Acknowledgements.** The work reported has been partially supported by the ROLE project, as part of the Seventh Framework Programme of the European Commission, grant agreement no. 231396.

# References

1. Popescu, E., Cioiu, D.: eMUSE - Integrating Web 2.0 Tools in a Social Learning Environment. In: Leung, H., Popescu, E., Cao, Y., Lau, R.W.H., Nejdl, W. (eds.) ICWL 2011. LNCS, vol. 7048, pp. 41–50. Springer, Heidelberg (2011)
2. Henri, F., Charlier, B., Limpens, F.: Understanding ple as an essential component of the learning process. In: Proceedings of ED-Media 2008 Conference, Vienna, Austria, pp. 3766–3770 (2008)
3. Gillet, D., Law, E.L.C., Chatterjee, A.: Personal learning environments in a global higher engineering education Web 2.0 realm. In: IEEE EDUCON 2010 Conference, Madrid, Spain, pp. 897–906. IEEE (April 2010)
4. Wilson, S., Liber, P.O., Johnson, M., Beauvoir, P., Sharples, P.: Personal learning environments: Challenging the dominant design of educational systems. Journal of e-Learning and Knowledge Society 3(2), 27–28 (2007)
5. Mödritscher, F., Krumay, B., El Helou, S., Gillet, D., Nussbaumer, A., Albert, D., Dahn, I., Ullrich, C.: May I Suggest? Comparing Three PLE Recommender Strategies. Digital Education Review 20, 1–13 (2011)
6. Dabbagh, N., Kitsantas, A.: Supporting Self-Regulation in Student-Centered Web-Based Learning Environments. International Journal on e-Learning 3(1), 40–47 (2004)
7. Berthold, M., Lachmann, P., Nussbaumer, A., Pachtchenko, S., Kiefel, A., Albert, D.: Psycho-pedagogical Mash-Up Design for Personalising the Learning Environment. In: Ardissono, L., Kuflik, T. (eds.) UMAP Workshops 2011. LNCS, vol. 7138, pp. 161–175. Springer, Heidelberg (2012)
8. Fruhmann, K., Nussbaumer, A., Albert, D.: A Psycho-Pedagogical Framework for Self-Regulated Learning in a Responsive Open Learning Environment. In: Hambach, S., Martens, A., Tavangarian, D., Urban, B. (eds.) Proceedings of the International Conference eLearning Baltics Science (eLBa Science 2010), Fraunhofer (2010)
9. Zimmerman, B.J.: Becoming a Self-Regulated Learner: An Overview. Theory Into Practice 41(2), 64–70 (2002)
10. Mandl, H., Friedrich, H.: Handbuch Lernstrategien. Hogrefe, Göttingen (2006)
11. Govaerts, S., Verbert, K., Dahrendorf, D., Ullrich, C., Schmidt, M., Werkle, M., Chatterjee, A., Nussbaumer, A., Renzel, D., Scheffel, M., Friedrich, M., Santos, J.L., Duval, E., Law, E.L.-C.: Towards Responsive Open Learning Environments: The ROLE Interoperability Framework. In: Kloos, C.D., Gillet, D., Crespo García, R.M., Wild, F., Wolpers, M. (eds.) EC-TEL 2011. LNCS, vol. 6964, pp. 125–138. Springer, Heidelberg (2011)

# A Federated Recommender System
# for Online Learning Environments

Lei Zhou[1], Sandy El Helou[2], Laurent Moccozet[3], Laurent Opprecht[3],
Omar Benkacem[3], Christophe Salzmann[2], and Denis Gillet[2]

[1] Tongji University,
200092 Shanghai, China
lake.zhou.sh@gmail.com
[2] Ecole Polytechnique Fédérale de Lausanne (EPFL),
1015 Lausanne, Switzerland
{sandy.elhelou,denis.gillet,christophe.salzmann}@epfl.ch
[3] University of Geneva (UNIGE),
Geneva, Switzerland
{laurent.moccozet,laurent.opprecht,omar.benkacem}@unige.ch

**Abstract.** From e-commerce to social networking sites, recommender systems
are gaining more and more interest. They provide connections, news, resources,
or products of interest. This paper presents a federated recommender system,
which exploits data from different online learning platforms and delivers personalized recommendation. The underlying educational objective is to enable
academic institutions to provide a Web 2.0 dashboard bringing together open
resources from the Cloud and proprietary content from in-house learning management systems. The paper describes the main aspects of the federated recommender system, including its adopted architecture, the common data model
used to harvest the different learning platforms, the recommendation algorithm,
as well as the recommendation display widget.

**Keywords:** Technology-Enhanced Learning, Personal Learning Environments,
Federated Recommender System, Web 2.0.

## 1    Introduction

Recommender systems have let to a shift from the user-active mode in search engines
to the information-active mode in information discovery where interesting items are
channeled to the user without (necessarily) an explicit request [1].

From e-commerce (e.g. Amazon[1]) to social networking sites (e.g. Facebook[2], Lin-
kedIn[3]), recommender systems are gaining more and more popularity whether to recommend connections, news, resources to access, or products to purchase.

---

[1] http://www.amazon.com, 06-06-2012
[2] http://www.facebook.com, 06-06-2012
[3] http://www.linkedin.com, 06-06-2012

E. Popescu et al. (Eds.): ICWL 2012, LNCS 7558, pp. 89–98, 2012.
© Springer-Verlag Berlin Heidelberg 2012

With the development of computer technology, learning is no longer limited to classrooms. Technology-Enhanced Learning (TEL) aims at designing, developing and testing socio-technical innovations to support learning practices at both the individual and the organizational level [2]. It helps the learners to learn anywhere and anytime. More and more online platforms, such as Symbaloo[4] and Graasp[5], enable users to access, share, and organize learning resources of all kinds, and manage their own Personal Learning Environments (PLEs). PLEs give students the opportunity to create, organize, repurpose and package their learning content and tools, increasing by that the learning efficiency and effectiveness [3]. Unlike traditional LMS (Learning Management Systems), PLEs are user-centered rather than teacher or course-centered. The shift from LMS to PLEs regarding educational resources introduces an overflow and a distortion: with course-centered LMSs, students are directly provided with a limited amount of selected and dedicated resources whereas with learner-centered PLEs, students have to face a large amount of resources for which they have to perform their own selection. Recommender systems therefore play a key role in open environments such as PLEs helping learners find what matches their interests from a pool of resources which, far from being preplanned and limited, can be added, augmented, and repurposed at run time [4].

Throughout their studies in Swiss universities, students are often exposed to more than one online learning platform. As a matter of fact, the mobility of students across different universities is rising. At the same time, Swiss universities do not all rely on the same online learning platform, even though they have adopted a common single sign-on mechanism. In addition, within a single university, there could be more than one platform used [5]. It becomes essential to establish a system that integrates resources from different platforms, so that students can construct a richer learning environment and access additional distributed resources.

In this paper, we propose a federated recommender system that relies on people's interaction with distributed resources in order to deliver rich and relevant recommendations. Such recommendations can serve as a central access point for learners, enrich platforms used locally (within one institution) by bringing data from other universities and help create learning networks across Switzerland. The platforms themselves consist of LMS and PLEs serving different learning communities from Swiss Universities and including Graasp, Moodle[6], and Mahara[7].

The rest of the paper is organized as follows. Section 2 discusses related work. Section 3 describes the main components of the federated recommender system. Section 4 concludes the paper and discusses future work.

## 2     Related Work

In this section, we discuss existing research around the two essential aspects of federated search or recommendation in learning contexts: the federation approach and

---

[4] http://www.symbaloo.com, 06-06-2012
[5] http://graasp.epfl.ch, 06-06-2012
[6] http://moodle.unifr.ch, 06-06-2012
[7] https://mahara.org, 06-06-2012

architecture. The federation approach concerns about how to get effective data, filter and merge data, while the federation architecture pays more attention to the structure with which the system can be efficiently implemented.

The study summarized in [6] focuses on ranking and merging search results from different resources. In order to efficiently combine different search results and improve performance, several algorithms are tested and compared on ObjectSpot[8], a vertical federated search engine for academic papers and other learning objects. In [7] search results from different platforms are collected and re-ranked by a federated search service. Ranked search results are sent to a widget and displayed to the user. Re-ranking is performed as follows: the widget sends search result URLs (Uniform Resource Locators) to the recommendation service. This service returns personalized recommendations after analyzing attention metadata stored in the database [7]. Attention metadata consists of recorded users' interaction with the recommended items (i.e. preview, like, dislike) in order to leverage user's interest and rank items' global and local popularity (within the target users' network). By mining this metadata, recommended lists for similar queries is improved in subsequent search requests.

Several papers discuss the architecture adopted for federated search or information retrieval from distributed repositories. The multi-agent based architecture proposed in [8] has a master agent that interacts with users and dispatches search requests to service agents of different repositories. Each of the repositories has a service agent that collects and updates metadata, and processes requests sent by the master agent. Once the service agents return their results, the master agent combines the results and displays them to users. In AIREH (Architecture for Intelligent Recovery of educational content in Heterogeneous Environments) [9], an intermediary communication point is proposed for retrieving learning objects from heterogeneous environments. The intermediary communication point is responsible for sending user requests to different repositories and then merging the returned ranked results. In Ariadne [10], a harvester gets metadata belonging to new resources from different learning repositories regularly and incrementally. The efficiency of processing search requests is improved by checking metadata. The OpenScout system [11] follows the same approach.

Our federated engine also relies on a harvester to gather data across different platforms. However, we not only store metadata related to learning objects (or resources) but also interaction data linking users and learning objects. As a result, the federated can offer a personalized recommendation, where personal interests are inferred from user actions. In addition, recommended items are not limited to learning objects, but also include activity spaces and users.

As in [7], we developed a portable widget in order to display recommendation results. A widget is a small Web application that is embeddable in a Web page and allows easy mashups [11]. This choice leads to a lightweight interoperability and an easy integration of the recommendation display service in the online learning platforms involved. The developed widget allows learners to classify recommended items by type (e.g. resources, users, or activity spaces) and gives an overview of the recommended items, whilst providing a link pointing to its physical location in one of the harvested learning platforms.

---

[8] http://www.objectspot.org, 06-06-2012

# 3    Proposed Federated Recommender System

## 3.1    Common Data Model

The federated recommender system exploits interaction data stored in different online learning platforms. "Considering that data models, naming conventions, and formats vary from user to user and network to network" [12], it becomes crucial to adopt a standard data representation and exchange format across different platforms.

Graasp is one of the online learning and collaboration platforms considered. It was built on top of the 3A interaction model illustrated in Fig. 1. We adopt this lightweight model, as a reference model to exchange data across the different learning platforms involved. The 3A interaction model is based on the following main constructs [13]:

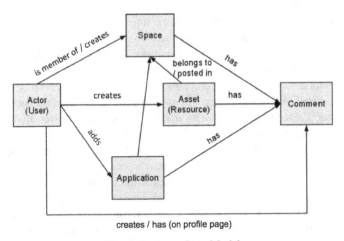

**Fig. 1.** Common Data Model

— Actors: refer to users or people. Initially, the concept of actors integrated also the notion of applications (and more generally any entity capable of initiating an event). Later, a clear separation between human actors and applications was adopted.
— Assets or resources: refer to different kinds of resources or digital artifacts (files, presentations, videos, wikis and etc.) created and shared among actors.
— Activity spaces: refer to online contexts or containers where one or more actors share resources and applications, under the umbrella of an activity space serving an explicitly or implicitly stated purpose. For instance, for every course in a formal learning context, a main activity space can be created to which all students, tutors, and teaching assistants are invited to join. In the same way, a community could create an activity space to which all its members are invited.

Each learning platform involved (e.g. Moodle, Mahara) maps its data into the 3A model and offers REST (Representational State Transfer)[9] APIs that are called by the harvester to get data in XML or JSON (JavaScript Object Notation)[10] formats.

---

[9] https://www.ibm.com/developerworks/webservices/library/ws-restful/, 06-06-2012
[10] http://www.json.org/, 06-06-2012

## 3.2    Architecture

The adopted architecture for the federated recommender system is illustrated in Fig. 2. Its main building blocks are:

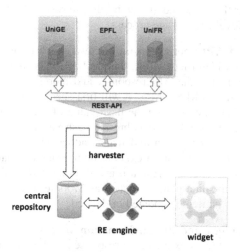

**Fig. 2.** Architecture of the federated recommendation system

— A harvester, which periodically retrieves the metadata from different repositories through REST APIs, parses retrieved data, and stores it in the central repository;
— A recommendation engine (or RE), which runs the recommendation algorithm regularly and then stores the results into the central repository;
— A widget, which queries the central repository using REST APIs and displays recommended items to target users. This widget can be embedded in any platform that implements the adopted REST APIs, such as Graasp, ELGG[11], Liferay[12] or Moodle.

## 3.3    Data Collection: The Harvester

The harvester serves as a middleware between the learning platforms and the central repository. Using the common REST APIs implemented by the learning platforms, the harvester regularly retrieves the metadata, parses it based on the 3A model taxonomy, and updates the central repository. For the sake of privacy, only public and closed items are retrieved. Public items consist of actors, spaces, resources and applications accessible to everyone without any restriction. The content of closed spaces on the other hand, are only accessible to authorized members, while everyone else can only see basic information (e.g. description, title, keywords).

---

[11] http://www.elgg.org, 06-06-2012
[12] http://www.liferay.com, 06-06-2012

During the harvesting operation, two tables are used to store the gathered data.

— An indexing table which stores the URLs of the harvested items;
— A queue table which stores the URLs that are in the waiting list to be harvested;

We describe hereafter the steps undertaken by the harvester and the role of the above tables in the data retrieval and storage process.

**Step 1: Call the REST APIs, get the metadata and check item status.**
Each harvested item is identified with a unique URL. The harvester calculates the hash value of the URL and the API response, and stores them in the index table. When the harvester calls the REST APIs, it will first check if the item's URL exists in the index table. If the URL exists and the hash value of the API response is still the same, nothing is done; if the URL exists but the hash value has changed, the item is updated; otherwise, it is a new item and it gets added into the table. If calling the defined APIs returns 404 errors for an existing item, it means that the item has been deleted from the platform and, as a result, it is also deleted from the index table. This check is important, as in some platforms such as Moodle, it is not possible to query the harvester every time an item is updated or deleted.

**Step 2: Parse the response and store information in central repository.**
For each URL stored in the index table, the response is parsed based on the 3A model taxonomy and the item's metadata (e.g. name, thumbnail image, description) are stored into the central repository.

**Step 3: Check item's child elements.**
Spaces might contain members, resources and subspaces as child elements. Fig. 3 shows the XML response data for a space item containing a subspace, a resource and an actor, including their metadata. For each child element, the URL is stored in the queue table.

**Step 4: Explore items stored in the queue table.**
For each item stored in the queue table, the harvester goes through steps 1 to 3. The top-down recursive process ends when there are no more URLs in the queue table.

```
▼<rdf:RDF xmlns:rdf="http://www.w3.org/1999/02/22-rdf-syntax-ns#"
  xmlns:aaa="http://ple.unige.ch/re/1#"
  xmlns:foaf="http://xmlns.com/foaf/0.1/"
  xmlns:rdfs="http://www.w3.org/2000/01/rdf-schema#"
  xmlns:dc="http://purl.org/dc/elements/1.1/"
  xml:base="http://localhost/mahara/artefact/graaasp/service/data/">
  ▼<rdf:Description rdf:about="36e7e81b9d12dababcbe2febaba8b521-2">
    <aaa:id>36e7e81b9d12dababcbe2febaba8b521-2</aaa:id>
    <aaa:dataset>http://localhost/mahara/</aaa:dataset>
    <aaa:url>http://localhost/mahara/group/view.php?id=2</aaa:url>
    <aaa:name>test for creating space</aaa:name>
    ▶<aaa:description rdf:parseType="Literal">...</aaa:description>
    <aaa:type>space</aaa:type>
    <aaa:spaces rdf:resource="7e14ed175ce447742753df686bdcdaa0-2"/>
    <aaa:assets rdf:resource="63bdeaa8f804a116dd038e61b1452b1c-6"/>
    <aaa:actors rdf:resource="857c9a58e87a91b1a6044fe1e6dbaf26-1"/>
    <aaa:kind>group</aaa:kind>
    <rdf:type rdf:resource="http://ple.unige.ch/re/1#space"/>
    <rdfs:label>test for creating space</rdfs:label>
    ▶<rdfs:comment>...</rdfs:comment>
    ▶<dc:description rdf:parseType="Literal">...</dc:description>
  </rdf:Description>
</rdf:RDF>
```

**Fig. 3.** Example of metadata related to a space

## 3.4    Data Processing: Recommendation Engine

The recommendation engine (or RE) uses the 3A ranking algorithm to compute the relative importance of existing items for a target user. The 3A ranking algorithm is derived from the original pagerank algorithm, which was designed by Page and Brin for ranking hypertext documents for Google [14]. Its main idea can be summarized as follows: if the owner of page j links to a page i, he/she is indicating that page i is important to check. The more incoming links a page has, the more important or authoritative it is. In addition, pages referred to by authoritative pages are considered as more important, and therefore ranked higher than pages linked by non-authoritative ones. Following this idea, item ranks are computed by applying a random walk algorithm on an adjacency graph connecting pages together, with two main parameters: one deciding the probability to choose a random page and the other deciding the probability to follow a page link.

The 3A ranking algorithm follows the same idea except that its graph consists of nodes representing heterogeneous items, connected by edges representing different relation types with equal or different importance weights. For instance, for a space member, an edge having the "membership" weight connects the user node to the space node as a sign of interest of that user in the space. The algorithm's details and probability equation can be found here [15].

In order to apply the algorithm to the harvested data, the RE constructs a graph where each public or closed item fetched is represented with a node. Unidirectional and bidirectional relations between any two items are respectively mapped in the graph by a single edge or two edges in opposite directions connecting the corresponding nodes.

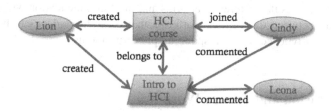

**Fig. 4.** Example for recommendation graph

Fig. 4 illustrates a simple example of a 3A recommendation graph. In the graph, ovals represent user nodes while rectangles represent space nodes and parallelograms represent resources. Arrows represent one way and two-way relationships between items. Since Leona commented on the « Intro to HCI », she is supposed to be interested in HCI. As the author of the resource « Intro to HCI » and the creator of the « HCI course » space, Lion clearly shares the same interests. So does the « HCI course » space member, Cindy. Running the 3A recommendation algorithm with Leona, as the target user, will help her discover spaces and people with shared interests (e.g. Lion, Cindy, and « HCI course ») by following their inter-connections.

### 3.5    Data Visualization: Widget

The widget (open social gadget) is used to display the recommended items and can be applied across different platforms. Its interface is shown in Fig. 5. It is implemented with JavaScript. For each user (student or tutor), the API will return a personalized list of recommendation items, displayed on different rows, according to their type.

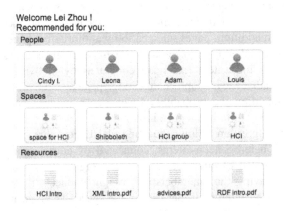

**Fig. 5.** The interface of the widget

When the user clicks on a recommended item, it is the responsibility of the platform where it was actually posted to check whether the user has enough rights to access the item at hand. Swiss universities have implemented Shibboleth [16] as a single sign-on (SSO) mechanism. Shibboleth allows users to login once and have a unique identity across the different platforms and the recommendation widget. Hence, the navigation between the various platforms thanks to the widget can be rendered easy. Once got privileged by the responding platform, the user can do the operations as usual.

## 4    Conclusion and Future Work

This paper presents a relation-based recommender system, which delivers federated recommendation. According to the common data model, the harvester collects and parses metadata from heterogeneous sources. Then, the recommendation engine runs the 3A recommendation algorithm and computes the relative importance of all items based on the metadata stored in the central repository. Each target user gets the recommendation automatically in the widget and is able to access recommended items from the harvested learning platforms.

In the near future, we plan to adopt a hybrid approach for the recommendation engine. For new users, the recommendation engine can hardly provide useful recommendation without sufficient user actions. In the hybrid approach, the 3A relation-based recommendation technique will be combined with content-based analysis, in order to alleviate the cold-start problem. Content-based analysis consists of computing content similarity between items (by comparing different fields such as item title, description and keywords). Then the results of content-based filtering consisting of item-to-item similarity measures are fed into the 3A recommendation algorithm as an extra-relation.

An evaluation with students from different Swiss universities is also planned. The evaluation will focus on the widget's interface usability and the impact of federated search and recommendations as compared to local ones. The usefulness of recommending items from various online platforms used within one university as well as across different universities will be assessed.

**Acknowledgment.** The research work described in this paper is partially funded through the Personal Learning Environment (Phase 3) project of the Swiss AAA/SWITCH program and the ROLE Integrated Project; part of the Seventh Framework Program for Research and Technological Development (FP7) of the European Union in Information and Communication Technologies.

# References

1. Guy, I., Jaimes, A., Agulló, P., Moore, P., Nandy, P., Nastar, C., Schinzel, H.: Will Recommenders Kill Search? Recommender Systems – an Industry Perspective. In: Proceedings of the 4th ACM Conference on Recommender Systems, pp. 7–12 (2010)
2. Manouselis, N., Drachsler, H., Vuorikari, R., Hummel, H., Koper, R.: Recommender Systems in Technology Enhanced Learning. In: Recommender Systems Handbook, Part 2, pp. 387–415 (2011)
3. Dabbagh, N., Kitsantas, A.: Personal Learning Environments, Social Media, and Self Regulated Learning: A Natural Formula for Connecting Formal and Informal Learning. The Internet and Higher Education 15, 3–8 (2012)
4. Tang, T.Y., Mccalla, G.: Smart Recommendation for an Evolving E-Learning System: Architecture and Experiment. International Journal on E-Learning 4, 105–129, http://www.editlib.org/p/5822 (retrieved March 2012)
5. LMS Installations 2010 at Swiss Institutions of Higher Education, http://eduhub.ch/info/lms-installations10.html (retrieved April 2012)
6. Drbálek, Z., Dulík, T., Koblischke, R.: Developing components for distributed search engine ObjectSpot. In: Proceedings of the 8th WSEAS International Conference on Distance Learning and Web Engineering, pp. 82–85 (2008)
7. Govaerts, S., El Helou, S., Duval, E., Gillet, D.: A Federated Search and Social Recommendation Widget. In: Proceedings of the 2nd International Workshop on Social Recommender Systems in conjunction with the 2011 ACM Conference on Computer Supported Cooperative Work, pp. 1–8 (2011)
8. Kaushik, S., Kollipalli, D.: Multi-Agent based Architecture for Querying Disjoint Data Repositories. In: International Conference on Machine and Web Intelligence, pp. 28–34 (2011)
9. Gil, A.B., De la Prieta, F., Rodríguez, S.: Automatic Learning Object Extraction and Classification in Heterogeneous Environments. In: Pérez, J.B., Corchado, J.M., Moreno, M.N., Julián, V., Mathieu, P., Canada-Bago, J., Ortega, A., Caballero, A.F. (eds.) Highlights in Practical Applications of Agents and Multiagent Systems. AISC, vol. 89, pp. 109–116. Springer, Heidelberg (2011)

10. Ternier, S., Verbert, K., Parra, G., Vandeputte, B., Klerkx, J., Duval, E., Ordoez, V., Ochoa, X.: The Ariadne Infrastructure for Managing and Storing Metadata. IEEE Internet Computing 13, 18–25 (2009)
11. Ha, K.-H., Niemann, K., Schwertel, U., Holtkamp, P., Pirkkalainen, H., Boerner, D., Kalz, M., Pitsilis, V., Vidalis, A., Pappa, D., Bick, M., Pawlowski, J., Wolpers, M.: A Novel Approach towards Skill-Based Search and Services of Open Educational Resources. In: García-Barriocanal, E., Cebeci, Z., Okur, M.C., Öztürk, A. (eds.) MTSR 2011. CCIS, vol. 240, pp. 312–323. Springer, Heidelberg (2011)
12. Grewe, L., Pandey, S.: Quantization of Social Data for Friend Advertisement Recommendation System. In: Nagamalai, D. (ed.) PDCTA 2011. CCIS, vol. 203, pp. 596–614. Springer, Heidelberg (2011)
13. El Helou, S., Li, N., Gillet, D.: The 3A interaction model: towards bridging the gap between formal and informal learning. In: Proceedings of the Third International Conferences on Advances in Computer-Human Interactions, pp. 179–184 (2010)
14. Page, L., Brin, S., Motwani, R., Winograd, T.: The PageRank citation ranking: Bringing order to the Web. Technical report. Stanford: Stanford Digital Library Technologies Project (1999)
15. El Helou, S., Salzmann, C., Gillet, D.: The 3A Personalized, Contextual and Relation based Recommender System. Journal of Universal Computer Science 16(16), 2179–2195 (2010)
16. Shibboleth Architecture Technical Overview, http://shibboleth.internet2.edu/docs/draft-mace-shibboleth-tech-overview-latest.pdf (retrieved March 2012)

# Trust and Security Issues
# in Cloud-Based Learning and Management

Birgy Lorenz[1], Kätlin Kalde[1], and Kaido Kikkas[1,2]

[1] Tallinn University, Institute of Informatics, Narva Road 25,
10120 Tallinn, Estonia
[2] Estonian Information Technology College, Raja St 4C, 12616 Tallinn, Estonia
{birgy.Lorenz,katlin.kalde,kaido.kikkas}@tlu.ee

**Abstract.** The goal of our paper is to point out the shortcomings in the cloud-based learning implementations regarding law, policies as well as security threats and awareness. Estonian schools and local authorities are interested in implementing new tools, especially when they are free of charge. Some Tallinn schools are already using systems like edu@live or Google Scholar. We survey and interview schools in Tallinn in order to test their readiness to implement cloud computing. Our results show high interest in using Web 2.0 tools, but also reveal serious lack of knowledge about e-safety as well as little know-how about the responsibilities and limitations in using cloud-based applications to store sensitive data. We also provide recommendations for schools using these tools for both students and teachers.

**Keywords:** cloud-based learning, security, e-safety, cloud management, protection of personal data.

## 1 Introduction

Our study explores the area of cloud-based learning and the management of its implementation at Tallinn schools. The main concerns address the schools' readiness to embrace cloud computing - to understand its ups and downs as well as trustworthiness (who owns the data, can sensitive data be stored etc). A lot of schools have already started to use personal accounts on cloud-based services (Google, Microsoft Live etc), and some schools have clearly forgotten the safety regulations they (as government institutions) should follow.

Our aim was to:

- find out the readiness at Tallinn area schools to implement cloud computing and learning as an educational practice;
- look at the implementation process and its perceived success, best practises at 6 schools – users of live@edu, Google Scholar or services provided by local authorities;
- analyse the safety issues in cloud-based learning and point out things that schools should know and understand before starting to implement cloud-based learning or management systems.

E. Popescu et al. (Eds.): ICWL 2012, LNCS 7558, pp. 99–108, 2012.

We suggest that there should be a test period before any larger implementation, as not all schools are ready. There are some issues with the Estonian law of data protection as well as the Three-Level IT Baseline Security System (ISKE) that should be addressed first on the local authority level.

## 2     Background

In recent years, we have seen keen interest in e-learning ecosystems. The 2001 report by Pew Research Centre "The Digital Revolution and Higher Education" claims that 29% of adult population and 50% of college students consider online courses to be on par with offline ones. Likewise, it has been suggested that the next generation of e-learning will be cloud-based learning (CBL). CBL provides dynamic change in storage resources, sustainability, efficient use and more [3]. Youngsters who are used to have the opportunity to learn anytime and anywhere find it hard to accept that they have a limited access to school – the materials, classrooms and overall learning experience are only available during the school hours, Monday to Friday 8:00-16:00. To address that need there are several different learning systems developed to go beyond just sharing materials, adding blogs, discussions, group work etc. These virtual learning environments also function as personal learning environments and social networks [12, 13, 8].

Among other things, cloud computing allows cutting the expenses on disk space. As Microsoft and Google provide schools with free services capacity building for no extra cost, it is an option schools and local authorities are considering moving to in the near future [7]. CBL provides an option not only to mirror and store data on the Net but also easier user administration and single-password login to different services. CBL is becoming increasingly common worldwide as it is easier and seems to be a perfect solution to bring schools into the new age of teaching and learning [1, 10].

As mobile devices (e.g. tablets) are increasingly used at school, it raises several new issues, e.g. how these tools can be connected to local systems. Sometimes implementing these solutions is either impossible or very costly [19]. New cloud-based learning platforms are considered more flexible and easier to implement as people use similar tools in their everyday life anyway [18]. Some institutions provide private cloud services for their staff and students as well as external people for collaboration purposes [2].

Cloud-based e-learning is also related to mobile learning, as cloud services are usually accessible with mobile devices as well. Thus success stories in both fields are interconnected [11]. A crucial feature in e-learning is the possibility to share learning objects either with the whole Net or between local users. Tagging will be important as well when sharing objects - yet some researchers point our limitations like lack of tagging option and only limited sharing (public, with a link, directly to e-mail) in cloud based systems. On the other hand, traditional e-learning systems provide more numerous options, but are limited to the provider server space [17, 15].

There are alternatives to CBL as well as one of them being browser-based integrated systems that allow cross-usage between different environments. Examples include iGoogle and Netvibes[1], but also educationally oriented projects like Graasp[2] (a system that allows users manage contextual shared spaces rather that manage generic individual network) or ROLE[3], where people can mix and match different apps in their personal learning environment and at the same time be connected to their organisation's virtual learning environment.

## 2.1  Situation in Estonia

Estonian status in e-learning has some distinct features. On the secondary level, the new National Curricula states an obligation for every school to have an e-learning environment [16]. On tertiary level, there are a lot of both open and closed solutions to choose from: Moodle, Blackboard, IVA, LeMill, Wikiversity, WordPress, etc [4]. Some of them (e.g. Moodle) are installed and maintained centrally at dedicated government servers, therefore schools can quickly deploy required learning environment, avoiding technical trouble. In spite of all these promising features, online learning environments tend still to be a kind of Wild West for teachers, yet they may face a need to make a rapid decision about which environment to use.

E-learning as a part of secondary school practice in Estonia is rising, but it is not common yet. Implementing new Web 2.0 tools and solutions in secondary education is not centralized and mandatory as schools can either use the offered systems or decline them. The only mandatory prescriptions are that the school head and secretary must have a contact e-mail and the school must have a web page [14]. The local authority usually provides centralized Internet service; sometimes it also tries to support schools by buying computers. In Tallinn, schools have an option to use a centralized web server, email and domain service [6].

We have also looked at the Estonian Personal Protection Act stating the need to secure data: access can only be granted to relevant persons, changes have to be logged and data can only be processed in the European juridical area - yet some cloud service providers don't specify where the servers are located [9]. At the same time, the Data Protection Inspectorate states that due to the problem being common to the whole Europe (not only Estonia), they will not ban companies from using cloud systems, at least for time being. Estonian government institutions are also required to analyse their services to be in accordance with the IT Baseline Security System (ISKE) [5].

Some schools have already developed their own solutions like using Moodle with Google-based accounts; some use Microsoft Live Services or DropBox. Others try to use the domain service provided by the local authority, but usually end up with problems like limited server space, problematic network architecture, lack of overall knowledge or budget, or limitations on outside access.

The rising interest of using clouds at school is understandable as it provides savings from server costs simplifies maintenance over the Internet and improves usability for teachers and students (they can use it everywhere and any time, both with

---

[1] Social Media Monitoring, Analytics and Alerts Dashboard http://www.netvibes.com
[2] Graasp http://graasp.epfl.ch
[3] Responsive Open Learning Environments (ROLE) http://www.role-project.eu/

computers and mobile devices). The main problems seem to be the possibly conflict-ing level of implementation (national vs local), possible security risks and the danger of re-inventing the wheel' at every school due to the lack of coordination.

## 2.2   Safety in CBL

We consider safety issues in cloud-based learning seriously underestimated at Esto-nian schools. Sometimes, the current implementations outright disregard the personal data protection laws as well as the relevant regulations for government institutions. The main questions often left unanswered are: who owns the data, where are the serv-ers located, are these servers under the legislation of one's country or not, are the access methods secure both for users and administrators, and what would happen if the cloud experienced meltdown or some accounts got compromised [7, 18, 20].

Other issues include: the cloud-based accounts do not allow sufficient logging in case of compromise/break-in depending of a country, there may be no local service provider to contact account administrators cannot see the users' files and folders. Le-gal authorization is needed to investigate an account – a user can store whatever she/he likes (including pornography, illegal software etc) in the system. When a stu-dent's account is compromised, the administrator can only change the password and hope that it will never happen again. In Microsoft's live@edu system, the account cannot even be deleted, it can only be deactivated (it is interesting to note that while similar issues with Facebook have been widely covered, this one has not).

One security hole or misstep in this area can disclose sensitive data to the whole world or give an opportunity for paedophiles to lurk in the school's cloud system - the school likely cannot detect it. And even if they can, they are unable to do anything to protect them. The problem will surface only when something bad has already hap-pened. A bigger issue is that holes in the systems can backfire on using e-learning as a whole, its credibility and trust being seriously undermined. New policies and regula-tions can only limit the use of e-tools at schools.

## 3     Methods

To understand the issue and find solutions, we carried out a 3-step study:

- stage I - we asked two ICT specialists from schools to explain the situation at their schools and why have they implemented live@edu at their schools. It was an open discussion about ideas, problems and trust in the system. The results from the discussion were used as the starting point for the next stage survey questions;
- stage II - we carried out a survey at 28 Tallinn schools (42% of the total num-ber of schools in that area). Of them, 19 use some kind of cloud-based learning environment. We used a web-based questionnaire with 40 questions that were divided into 3 sections for the cloud users: services used, implementation, and background; non-users were asked about prospective implementation and background. We mostly used Likert scale, but also some yes/no answers; a

number of questions were open to allow the schools to explain the issues further. The survey was available to all 66 schools during one week. It was mostly answered by ICT specialists at schools;

- stage III - we chose 6 schools to do a follow-up interview with: 2 schools using Google services, 2 using live@edu and 2 using a solution provided by the local authority. We used structured interview with 21 questions in four sections: current situation, advantages and disadvantages of the system, trust and security of the solution, prospects for future.

We also interviewed a teacher and students at one school who use edu@live and Skype as a distance learning tool (the teacher is based in Canada and students are in Estonia) and the school management who used the same system to store educational and other sensitive data in cloud.

## 4 Results

Analysing results, we found that 61% of the respondents completing the questionnaire said that their school were using cloud-based services and 39% of respondents were not. Some school ICT specialists apparently did not understand the concept of cloud computing at all. Some services were used just by individual users (Picasa, Flickr, SlideShare, blogging, Google or Live or solutions provided by the local authority).

The Top 6 types of services in CBL were Google personal accounting; media file sharing, blogging, picture sharing, other file sharing and MS Live personal accounting. So the main conclusion here is that as a rule, Tallinn schools are not using centralized services provided by Google or Microsoft. All Tallinn school have a possibility to use local clouds and virtual machines provided by the local authority, but these are actually used by 54%

The usage of cloud-based services at schools is shown on Fig. 1 using 5-point Likert scale. The diagram shows the quantity of cloud-based services used by different target groups: school leaders (management), teachers, students and parents. The number of schools means the number of respective answers (e.g. 'parents, very low – 10' shows that 10 schools considered the usage of cloud-based services by parents very low).

94% of the schools we got a response from have only been using the service provider's default settings, 42% have developed some extra rules which usually are difficult to supervise effectively, 26% have used additional settings to increase password security and only one school has written something that might qualify as an official set of rules.

Trust in cloud computing is considered high as 84% of ICT specialists rated it as average or above average. Most respondents suggest that CBL being a new phenomenon at school, no harsh security incidents have happened yet. Most problems are recalled to be related to human errors – e.g. someone has deleted a shared file, someone shared data not supposed to be shared; people don't log out, save their passwords to the public computer or use easy passwords. They mentioned a single case of identity theft. At the same time, all these cases are in fact criminal offences in the sense of the Estonian Penal Code.

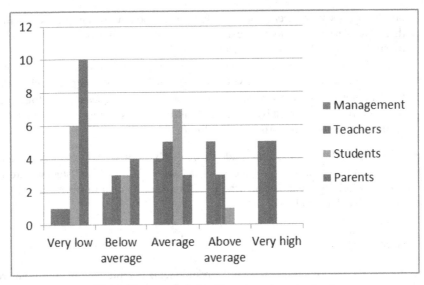

**Fig. 1.** The usage of cloud-based services at school

To secure the system, the only options the schools see are to train the students and staff in proper use, and to use longer and more difficult passwords. Concerning the future, the schools say that the increasing use of clouds might also increase the number of some types of incidents: data leaks, identity theft, break-ins or planting key-loggers to school computers; they also mentioned dependence on the service provider who may shut down the service or start charging excessive fees.

The schools would like to have at least two alternative choices (82%), and 60% would like to receive support from a local service provider. But as for using international or local systems, the school ICT specialists do not mind using either or both solutions. In the centralization sense, the schools strongly disliked the idea of centralizing the service and making it compulsory, 60,7% were against it. But as an option, 68% agreed that the cloud may be a solution for them in the future. 17% said that schools should only use standard solutions without CBL services.

When asked how to implement these services, most schools preferred a step-by-step, voluntary approach, starting with some pilot schools, see fig. 2.

The Stage III respondents identified four types of problems in using CBL: data-related (e.g encryption, backups), training-related (e.g. password security); policy-related (need for common policies) and features-related (the local authority systems have limited support for e.g. IMAP, POP3 or service integration, while cloud-based system often do not allow users to increase security, or in some systems even delete one's account). There were also concerns about the continuity of the system or possible changes of business model resulting in exceedingly high fees.

The teacher and students using Live@edu to communicate between Estonia and Canada said that the system was easy to learn and provides various options. While the respondents mentioned speed as the main shortcoming (some e-mails were delayed), they also expressed uncertainty about the actual privacy of the forums and lists ("or will they end up in Google?").

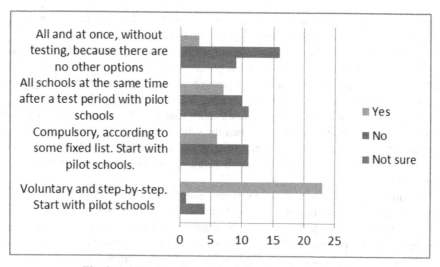

**Fig. 2.** Application of centralized cloud services at schools

To sum it up, the respondents' answers echo lack of actual knowledge about the systems provided – they have not thought about security issues and blindly trust the systems (a recurring explanation being 'we can only use what is offered'). But a the same time, the interest in using CBL is high as 1/3 of the schools expect to start using centralized options during the next school year.

## 5    Discussion

We consider the data about how many schools are moving to use centralized cloud systems and CBL in Tallinn as the most important finding of this study. For now it has largely been an individual effort with no general data available. Some schools have introduced dubious practices like using a single personal account for the whole school - a huge security issue, as when one staff member loses the password or forgets to sign off from a public computer, the whole system is compromised. The problem is even bigger when it happens in a local server or an unencrypted cloud.

The use of educational cloud services provided by Microsoft or Google will provide storage cost reduction as they offer about 10 gigabytes or more of disk space per person free of charge. Even when implementing new services and solutions can be costly at first, the overall cost reduction and benefits from easier management, access and sharing will be greater in the longer run. The only question is if the system can be relied on to being present for the next 5-10 years.

Another concern is the one pointed out by the Data Protection Inspectorate - compliance with the Estonian law. Under European jurisdiction, sensitive data can only be stored in servers or cloud systems. The schools should also have a person responsible for data protection. Access to data should be well-regulated and logged.

We note that schools are still only beginning to incorporate students into the online services that are used by the school. For now, there are several issues waiting to be solved. For example, most schools have asked the students to use their own personal e-mail accounts, instead of providing one by the school.

A peculiar but rather serious issue that cannot be solved by the schools at all is related to the age limits imposed by some popular social networks like Google+ or Facebook. If the school wants to include younger students in projects involving these networks, the students have no other choice but fake their age in order to even get an account registered. At the same time, there is a legal ambiguity - students under 14 are not responsible for their actions even when the school provides them with an account. The parents of the child are not legally responsible for the school either, as they are neither students nor staff members. As a result, no school policy really applies to these children.

The most mentioned security risks were related to human behaviour or system misuse. These issues can be addressed by training, but the lack of supervision is actually 'programmed in the system' as the school administrator cannot legally access user accounts. Another problem is the possibility of incidents remaining hidden for an extended period (e.g. an account is used to store child pornography, either by the user him/herself or somebody who has managed to hijack it) due to the combination of lack of supervision and user incompetence.

We thus recommend the schools to test the CBL systems and find a suitable one, but not to use it exclusively (in case of service discontinuation or fees, a smooth migration path to another service is an absolute must) . Backups should be used whenever possible. Training and raising e-safety awareness among teachers and students is crucial to reduce the number of safety incidents.

The local authorities should be prepared to support schools with help in creating necessary regulations, technical assistance and perhaps even backup solution (for the case of CBL discontinuation). They should also continue providing centralized services and support to at least 1/3 of schools who were not interested in CBL in near future. The best way could be to support the CBL pilot schools that can support others in turn afterwards.

Alternatively, another solution could be to use a radically different solution in the vein of Graasp or ROLE – but the problems seems rather to be related to teaching as well as the values represented by teachers and students than just purely technical choice of systems. The Educational Board of Tallinn has outlined the large variety of solutions (e.g. for e-mail) used by the schools and waiting to be standardized yet. On the other hand, standardization should not result in vendor lock-in.

# 6    Conclusion

The study helped to unveil the legal and trust issues associated to cloud-based learning as well as the management issues of CBL at Estonian schools. A number of online providers offer free for education services which can help schools to cut expenses – however, there are serious implications of security risks that tend to be overlooked. We also stress that schools are institutions where all government regulations apply.

The legal status of CBL in Estonia is somewhat uncertain as seen in example of the Data Protection Inspectorate being unable to say whether and how CBL should be used. Right now, all the legal responsibility lies upon the database owner who sometimes is not even aware of the fact.

Overall lack of knowledge and awareness remains a factor. Many respondents of the study used CBL without any thought of security. There is an urgent need for training, as there has been no training offered on cloud computing -related security.

We warn that serious problems will be likely to rise in case of any wider implementation of new cloud-based services at the current state of things (including but not limited to identity theft, account hijacking etc). So, on the one hand, schools and local authorities should be remarkably more aware of the risks accompanying 'going to the clouds'. On the other hand, CBL does have a potential of notable savings in maintenance costs and data load, as well as other benefits (learn everywhere and any time). But regardless of whether using CBL or local services, awareness and knowledge of e-safety should be promoted to much higher levels.

# References

1. Al-Zoube, M.: E-learning on the Cloud. International Arab Journal of e-Technology 1(2) (June 2009)
2. Doelitzscher, F., Sulistio, A., Reich, C., Kuijs, H., Wolf, D.: Private cloud for collaboration and e-Learning services: from IaaS to SaaS. Computing 91(1), 23–42 (2011), doi:10.1007/s00607-010-0106-z
3. Dong, B., Zheng, Q., Yang, J., Li, H., Qiao, M.: An E-learning Ecosystem Based on Cloud Computing Infrastructure. In: ICALT 2009 Proceedings of the 2009 Ninth IEEE International Conference on Advanced Learning Technologies. IEEE Computer Society, Washington, DC (2009) ISBN: 978-0-7695-3711-5
4. Estonian Information Technology Foundation (EITF), E-LEARNING DEVELOPMENT CENTRE STRATEGY Tallinn (2012)
5. Infosüsteemide turvameetmete süsteem ISKE (2012), http://www.ria.ee/iske/
6. Infotehnoloogia, Tallinna Haridusameti IKT nõukogu protokollid ja arengukava (2012), http://www.tallinn.ee/haridus/otsing?oks=6198
7. Noor, S., Mustafa, G., Chowdhury, S.A., Hossain, M.Z., Jaigirdar, F.T.: A Proposed Architecture of Cloud Computing for Education System in Bangladesh and the Impact on Current Education System. IJCSNS International Journal of Computer Science and Network Security 10(10) (October 2010)
8. Patil, M., Kulkarni, V., Negulur, G., Pashupatimath, A.: CLEM - A Cloud Based Learning Environment for Millennial: Learn – Anytime, Anywhere. In: 2011 International Conference P2P, Parallel, Grid, Cloud and Internet Computing (3PGCIC) (2011) ISBN: 978-1-4577-1448-1
9. Personal Data Protection Act, Directive 95/46/EC of the European Parliament and of the Council (1995)
10. Pocatilu, P., Alecu, F., Vetrici, M.: Measuring the Efficiency of Cloud Computing for E-learning Systems. Vseas Transactions on Computers 1(9) (January 2010) ISSN: 1109-2750
11. Shuai, Q., Ming-quan, Z.: Cloud computing promotes the progress of m-learning. In: 2011 International Conference on Uncertainty Reasoning and Knowledge Engineering, URKE (2011) ISBN: 978-1-4244-9985-4

12. Soumplis, A., Chatzidaki, E., Koulocheri, E., Xenos, M.: Implementing an Open Personal Learning Environment. In: Proceedings of the 2011 15th Panhellenic Conference on Informatics, PCI 2011. IEEE Computer Society, Washington, DC (2011) ISBN: 978-1-61284-962-1

13. Syvänen, A., Muukkonen, J., Sihvonen, M.: Are the open issues of social software-based personal learning environment practices being addressed? In: MindTrek 2009 Proceedings of the 13th International MindTrek Conference: Everyday Life in the Ubiquitous Era. ACM, New York (2009)

14. Tallinna koolide kodulehekülgede vormistamise juhend, Tallinna Haridusameti juhataja 26. veebruar 2009 käskkiri nr 1-2/155 (2009)

15. Tisselli, E.: Thinkflickrthink: a case study on strategic tagging. Communications of the ACM 53(8) (2010)

16. Vabariigi Valitsus, Gümnaasiumi riiklik õppekava (2011), https://www.riigiteataja.ee/akt/114012011002

17. Wang, C-C., Pai, W-C., N. Y. Y.: A sharable e-Learning platform based on Cloud computing. In: 2011 3rd International Conference on Computer Research and Development (ICCRD) (2011) ISBN: 978-1-61284-839-6

18. Wang, Y., Lin, H., Rong, H.: Design of Network Learning Platform Based on Cloud-Computation. Advanced Materials Research (vol. 488 - 489), Key Engineering Materials II (2012)

19. Warschauer, M.: Learning in the Cloud. Technology, Education – Connections (The TEC Series). Teachers College, Columbia University (2011) ISBN 978-0-8077-5250-0

20. Xin, S., Zhao, Y., Li, Y.: Property-Based Remote Attestation Oriented to Cloud Computing. In:2011 Seventh International Conference on Computational Intelligence and Security (CIS) (2011) ISBN: 978-1-4577-2008-6

# Slicepedia: Towards Long Tail Resource Production through Open Corpus Reuse

Killian Levacher, Seamus Lawless, and Vincent Wade

Trinity College Dublin
{killian.levacher,seamus.lawless,vincent.wade}@scss.tcd.ie

**Abstract.** The production of resources supporting the needs of Adaptive Hypermedia Systems (AHS) is labor-intensive. As a result, content production is focused upon meeting the needs of resources with higher demand, which limits the extent upon which long tail content requirement niches of AHS can be met. Open corpus slicing attempts to convert the wealth of information available on the World Wide Web, into customizable information objects. This approach could provide the basis of an open corpus supply service meeting long tail content requirements of AHS. This paper takes a case study approach, focusing on an educational sector of adaptive hypermedia, to test out the effect of using Slicepedia, a service which enables the discovery, reuse and customization of open corpus resources. An architecture and implementation of the system is presented along with a user-trial evaluation suggesting slicing techniques could represent a valid candidate for long tail content production supply of AHS.

## 1   Introduction

Adaptive Hypermedia Systems (AHS) have traditionally attempted to respond to the demand for personalized interactive learning experiences through the support of adaptivity, which sequences re-composable pieces of information into personalized presentations for individual users. While their effectiveness and benefits have been proven in numerous studies [1], the ability of AHS to reach the mainstream audience has been limited [2]. For example, in educational hypermedia systems, this has been in part due to their reliance upon large volumes of one-size-fits-all educational resources available at high production costs [3].

Although extensively studied, solutions proposed so far (section 2) do not address the fundamental problem directly which is the labor-intensive manual production of such resources. As a result, content creation is naturally focused upon addressing the needs of targeted resources in higher demand (area 1 in figure 1). AHS content requirements however, naturally follow a long tail distribution. They require large varieties of unique niche content supplies needed for once-off usages only (area 2), which traditional content production approaches desist due to prohibitive costs. In parallel to these developments, the field of Open Adaptive Hypermedia (OAH) has attempted to leverage the wealth of information, which has now become accessible on the WWW as open corpus

E. Popescu et al. (Eds.): ICWL 2012, LNCS 7558, pp. 109–119, 2012.

information. Open Corpus Slicing (OCS) techniques [4] in particular aim at automatically converting native open corpus resources into customizable content objects meeting various specific AHS content requirement needs (topic covered, style, granularity, delivery format, annotations).

We believe that, in order to serve AHS long tail content requirements, the cost intensive, manual production and/or adaptation of educational resources must be augmented (and if possible replaced) by the automated re-purposing of open corpus content into such resources. A fully-automated, on-demand, content production system based upon an OCS approach could thus theoretically address the long tail content supply paradigm described previously. This paper builds upon previous research in slicing techniques and attempts to provide a first step towards this goal. Educational Hypermedia Systems (EHS) are cited as being the most successful but also most expensive systems to develop content for [5], this paper hence takes a case study approach investigating how educational AHS in particular can be supported by an automated content production service based upon OCS techniques.

**Fig. 1.** The Long Tail of EAH Content Supply

**Contribution:** The rest of this paper presents Slicepedia, a content supply service, based upon slicing techniques, that leverages open corpus resources to produce large volumes of right-fitted information objects. An i) architecture and implementation of the system is presented, followed by ii) a user-trial evaluation, applied in an authentic educational scenario, comparing the suitability of traditional versus slicer based content supply services with respect to user perceived quality and production costs.

## 2   Background and Related Work

The reliance of EHS upon the ability to access large volumes of diverse educational resources has been a problem investigated by many researchers. The reuse and sharing of existing resources, through encapsulation standards such as Learning Objects Metadata(LOM), followed a natural need by the community to reuse previously produced resources, which subsequently led to the creation of many learning object repositories (LOR)[1]. As these repositories grew in size, research focusing upon improving the search and discovery of existing resources [6] naturally emerged as consequence. Tools improving production efficiency [7], by re-purposing existing material already available in LORs into new learning resources, ultimately emerged as both the size and search capabilities of LOR improved. Although these solutions certainly do reduce the production time and costs of learning resources, none of them directly address the fundamental issue which is the initial labor-intensive production of such content. When production efficiency is taken into account, improvements through re-purposing are still carried out manually [5]. This results in a costly content production paradigm with limitations delimited in terms of volume of resources available. OAH attempts to surpass these volume supply limitations through the incorporation of open corpus resources through either manual incorporation [8] techniques, automated [9] and community-based [10] linkage or Information Retrieval (IR) approaches [11]. In contrast with previous solutions, this paradigm offers a much cheaper alternative supply of content, with limitations, in terms of volume of resources available, significantly lower. However even when relevant open web resources are retrieved, IR techniques suffer because they only provide untailored, document level, delivery of results, with limited control over topics, granularity, content format or associated meta-data. Open corpus resources, originally produced for a pre-define purpose, are generally incorporated in their native form, as "one-size-fits-all" documents. This represents a very inadequate match for long tail content niche requirements. As pointed out by Lawless [11], the reuse potential of such resources (complete with original menus, advertisements), are far less adequate than the reuse of selected parts of the article, de-contextualised from their original setting, at various levels of granularity, with associated meta-data and in a delivery format of choice.

**Open EHS Supply Requirements:** In order to clarify what we mean by a long tail content supply scenario, lets consider the following open and user-driven EHS use case scenario. Suppose Alice wishes to improve her grammar skills in Portuguese and decides to use a portal specifically built for this purpose. The system provides e-assessments consisting of traditional gap filling exercises for a given piece of native language text (figure 3a). It provides Alice with a list of various languages $\Lambda$, grammar skills $\Gamma$ and reading level difficulty $\varrho$ to choose from which she selects accordingly to her training needs. So as to sustain learner motivation, the portal additionally provides the ability to select topics of interest, among a large list $\Theta$, which training exercises should also cover. Whenever Alice starts her training, the system searches for resources on the web fulfilling the combined requirements $\Sigma\{\Lambda, \Gamma, \Theta, \varrho\}$ and converts these into grammar e-assessments. The system continuously records the sets of mistakes $\mu$ performed by Alice and includes this additional variable to its content requirement combination $\Sigma$ in order to address the required subset of grammar points of immediate importance. As Alice progresses, the set of requirements $\Sigma$ evolves and so does the content supplied. The portal can supply Alice with as much content as needed for her training.

---

[1] NDLR: www.ndlr.ie, MERLOT: www.merlot.org

As pointed out by Steichen et al. [12], the production of educational resources a-priori of any learner interaction, generally assumes that the type and quantity of resources needed for a particular EHS is known in advance of system deployment. In the use case presented above however, the number of content requests is unknown in advance and the content requirement combination possibilities for $\Sigma$ are very numerous. For this reason, only a handful of deliveries will ever occur for most individual content requests possibilities. This situation portrays a typical long tail distribution (figure 1) scenario which could only be sustained by an automated content production service guaranteeing the on-demand provision of i) large volumes of content, ii) at low production costs, iii) suitable for a large range of potential activities [5]. OCS techniques [4] aim at automatically right-fitting open corpus resources to various content requirements. Open corpus material in its native form is very heterogeneous. It comes in various formats, languages, is generally very coarse-grained and contains unnecessary noise such as navigation bars, advertisements etc. OCS provides the ability to harvest, fragment, annotate and combine relevant open corpus fragments and meta-data in real time. Hence, although the quality of content supplied (with respect to relevance) is important of course, this aspect is addressed by traditional retrieval systems. OCS techniques instead aim at improving the quality, in terms of appropriateness for further AHS consumption, of open corpus resources identified as relevant. It is still unclear, however how the suitability of content generated automatically by such techniques would compare with content manually hand crafted within an educational use case scenario. If such a technique is to be used as a basis for long tail content supply chain services, the suitability of the content produced (requirement iii) from a user's point of view as well as it's production cost (requirement ii) must be examined.

## 3    Slicepedia Anatomy

As depicted in figure 2, a slicer is designed as a pipeline of successive modules, analysing and appending specific layers of meta-data to each document. Large volumes of resources openly available on the WWW, in multiple languages and with unknown page structure, are gathered and then transformed, on demand, into reusable content objects called slices. EHS thus use the slicer as a pluggable content provider service, producing slices which match specific unique content requirements (topic, granularity, annotations, format etc.). The aim of this section is to present the overall architecture and detailed implementation of the slicer used within this experiment. For a more complete description of an OCS pipeline architecture, the reader is referred to the original papers [4].

**Harvester:** The first component of a slicer pipeline acquires and locally caches open corpus resources from the web in their native form. Although standard IR or focused crawling techniques [11] would generally be selected for this phase, this experiment required a tighter control over resources automatically harvested (to allow direct comparisons with manual repurposing approaches see section 4). Thus a simple URL list-harvesting feature was used instead for this component.

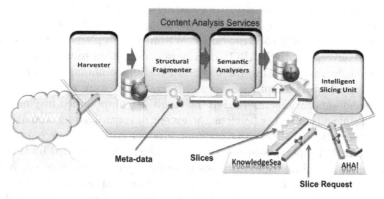

**Fig. 2.** Figure Caption

**Fragmentation:** Once open corpus resources are acquired, each individual document is fragmented into structurally coherent atomic pieces (such as menus, advertisements, main article). The Kohlschutter et. al [13] densitometric approach to fragmentation was selected for the purpose of this experiment as it can process virtually any xml-based document at very high speed.

**Semantic Analyser:** Each fragment is then analysed by a set of annotators. The intention is to produce sufficient discerning meta-data to support the identification and selection of adequate meta-data/fragments combinations matching each EHS content request. Such meta-data might include, writing style, topic covered or the level requirement of content. The set of annotators used for the purpose of this experiment consisted of: i) the AlchemyApi concept tagging service[2], which identifies and associates concepts mentioned within each fragment with Dbpedia instances[3], ii) the open source Flesh annotator[4] determining reading-level difficulties of resources as Flesh Reading scores. iii) Part of speech[5], iv) noun and verb phrases[6], were also identified within fragments and annotated with their relevant linguistic attributes. Finally, fragments were annotated using v) a boilerplate detection algorithm[7], determining to what degree individual page parts are reusable or not. All annotations and fragments were stored as rdf data within a Sesame triple store[8] and available as linked-data.

**Slice Creation:** Once individual fragments and meta-data annotations are available, a slicer is ready to receive slice requests. For each request, a slicing unit combines atomic fragments together, along with relevant meta-data, into customized slices. A slice is defined as: *Customized content generated on-*

---

[2] http://www.alchemyapi.com/api/

[3] http://dbpedia.org/About/

[4] http://flesh.sourceforge.net

[5] Modified version of the Brill Tagger in ANNIE http://gate.ac.uk/

[6] Verb group and noun phrase chunkier in http://gate.ac.uk/

[7] http://code.google.com/p/boilerpipe/

[8] www.openrdf.org

*demand, consisting of fragment(s) (originating from pre-existing document(s)) assembled, combined with appropriate meta-data and right-fitted to the specific content requirements of a slice consumer.* Within this implementation, slice requests were converted into SPARQL queries and submitted to the triple store in order to identify any matching fragment/annotation combinations. Fragments, identified according to adaptation variables requested, were then appended to each other and annotations inserted in the resulting compounded fragment. The array of possible adjustments (such as the extent of control over granularity, formats and annotation) a slicer can offer upon an open corpus resource, is referred to as its Content Adaptation Spectrum (CAS). The CAS provided by this slicer therefore offers 10 adaptation variables (content style, topics covered, reading difficulty, verb chunk tense, number of annotations, paragraph/word number, topic focus, annotation focus, original sources, delivery format) that can be arbitrarily combined to suit various content requirements over any relevant open corpus resources identified. A slice request could hence consist of the following: *slices which have a granularity ranging from 3 sentences up to 3 paragraphs. They should cover the topic of whale migration, should not contain any tables or bullet point lists, should have a Flesh reading score ranging of 45, and contain at least 7 annotations consisting of verbs conjugated at the past perfect continuous.*

## 4   Evaluation and Results

**Aim and Hypothesis:** As discussed in section 2, in order to supply long tail niche requirements, a content production system service should guarantee the provision of i) large volumes of content, iii) at low production costs, iii) suitable for arbitrary activities performed. Although the first condition is necessarily achieved through the selection of an open corpus reuse strategy, the performance of a slicer with respect to the two other conditions is yet to be examined. For this reason, this evaluation focuses, as a first step, upon investigating the suitability and cost of content produced automatically by a slicing system with respect to content manually produced for the same activity. This initial experiment is performed upon a sample of independently selected niche requirements and open corpus resources. Assuming positive results were measured, this would indicate such a technique could also scale for any niche requirement using any open corpus content. Any issues detected at this early stage would only be amplified within a large scale deployment making any scaling pointless. Additionally, since production cost is dependent upon local prices of manual labor as well as individual server specifications, an estimation of production time was considered instead a better proxy for production cost differences. For this reason, the time required to produce content batches was measured for both the educators and slicer. The hypotheses tested within this evaluation are therefore as follows:

- H1: Content manually & automatically produced achieves similar suitability results, from a users point of view.
- H2: Automated slicing offers a reasonable production cost solution for large volumes of content, in contrast with a manual production which is unsustainable

**Evaluation Design:** Since content consumed by EHS is ultimately presented to people, any content production measurement should consider user experience as critical. Furthermore, as the aim consists in evaluating content produced by two different methods, slices should be assessed individually, with interface complexity (figure 3a) and re-composition kept to a minimum in order to avoid any possible interference with the content being evaluated. For this reason, a simplified version of the language e-assessment use-case application presented in section 2 was built specifically for the purpose of this experiment. Within the context of this paper, the purpose of this educational application is to be used only as a "content reuse vehicle" for evaluating the slicer (i.e. not discussing educational aspects).This application represents a well known approach to grammatical teaching, via a Computer Adaptive Testing (CAT) tool, similar in nature to the item response assessment system introduced by Lee et al. [14]. For this reason, it provides a good example of the kind of educational application which could avail of 3rd party content. In this application, users are presented with series of individual open corpus resources (involving no re-composition), repurposed (manually or automatically) as traditional gap filler exercises. Verb chunks items are removed and replaced by gaps, which users must fill according to particular infinitives and tenses specified for each gap. Answers provided are then compared to the original verb chunks and users are assigned a score for each specific grammar point. Slicing open corpus content is known to affect the reading flow and annotation quality of content produced [4]. An evaluation of content performed within the context of a language learning task (by individuals with varying levels of competency in the English language) should hence make participants very sensitive to reading flow properties of content. Moreover, since grammar e-assessment units are created according to verb chunk annotations, any annotation quality issue would provoke major assessment errors, making any training over such content pointless and time consuming to users. Suitability performance, within the context of this use case, hence refers to the ability to correctly assess an individual.

**Content Batch Creation:** The manual content production activity selected for this experiment deliberately involved only the repurposing of existing content (in the spirit of educator repurposing activities described in section ). This decision aspired to replicate a manual content production scenario (used as a baseline) with minimal production time requirements. Our assumption was that any content authoring activities would always depict higher time requirements. Hence, in order to select a truly random set of open corpus pages, a group of five independent English teachers, were asked to arbitrarily select a combined total of 45 pages of their choice from the web. The pages could be selected from any source, according to various combinations of requirements (topics covered, tenses...). They were then asked to select fragments of pages harvested, which they felt were adequate for grammar exercises, and manually annotate tenses encountered within these extract to produce content batch CBM. Fragments could consist of any granularity as long as content, which was not about a specified topic, was discarded. The collection of arbitrarily selected pages, was then harvested from the web in their original form by the slicer. CAS characteristics (including topics) of resources manually produced, were identified and fed into the slicer as independent niche content requirement parameters. The entire set of open corpus content harvested was then sliced with these parameters to produce content batch CBA. Content produced in both batches were subsequently converted into grammar e-assessment pages.

**Evaluation Scenario:** The entire experiment was available online to the public with the interface and questionnaire available in English, Spanish and French. Native and non-native speakers were invited to perform a set of English grammar training exercises using resources randomly selected from each content batch using a latin square design distribution. A unique color was assigned to each content batch and users were unaware which was being presented to them at each task. Users were asked to fill in any blanks encountered (10 gaps on average per page) with the appropriate verb and tense specified for each case (Figure 3a). Following these exercises, they were subsequently asked questions directly, answered using a 10 point Likert scale. Finally, they were asked to order colors, corresponding to each content batch presented, based on their perceived quality.

**Results:** The rest of this section presents a summary of the findings observed throughout this experiment in relation to each hypothesis. A total of 41 users, divided into two groups (Experts (63%) and Trainees (37%)), performed the experiment, most using the English interface (en=66%, non-en=34%).

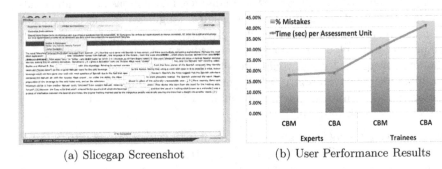

(a) Slicegap Screenshot          (b) User Performance Results

**Fig. 3.** Content Supply Evaluation

**H1:** Statistical t-test analysis, of both the number of mistakes performed by users as well as the time required to perform e-assessments, revealed that any differences measured were statistically insignificant ($p > 0.100$). When trainees were asked whether, for content batch CBA, *"the number of erroneous assessment units presented was tolerable"*, a mean score of 7 out of ten was measured. When asked whether *"Overall, I felt this content was adequate to perform a grammar training exercises"* both content achieved very similar scores (CBM=8.33, CBA=8.57, p=0.536) with t-tests again suggesting any difference observed was insignificant. However, when plotting this data on a graph(Figure 3b. ), a pattern can be observed for both the trainee as well as expert group. In both cases, the number of mistakes and time taken to perform e-assessments, upon content created automatically, appears to be higher than for the content produced manually. This would suggest users do make more errors when using content from the CBA batch. Although automated verb chunk annotation recall accuracies measured outperformed those produced manually (Recall A=0.92, M=0.68), manual annotations precision accuracies were slightly higher than automated ones (Precision M=0.89, A=0.86), which could explain this minor increase in errors observed. Finally, although the difference in errors between content batches was slightly higher for trainees in comparison to experts group, an independent t-test indicated this difference was insignificant (mean dif. E=5.80%, T=7.48%, p=0.891). This indicates that users from the expert group didn't appear to use their language skills to compensate content suitability differences between both batches. Overall, these results suggest that although a pattern of slightly lower performances on assessments automatically generated was observed, this difference was insignificant and didn't appear to affect trainees more than the experts group of users, nor did it appear to decrease the perceived usefulness of the content for the assessment task performed.

**H2:** Because of manual labor production costs being subject to geographical location, an estimation of time required to produce resources was considered a valid proxy for the purpose of these measurements. Since the set of pages used as preliminary resources was purposely manually harvested from the web (section 4), no automated harvesting was performed by the slicer during this experiment. Nevertheless, in order to provide a fair comparison with a manual production approach, an estimation of time required by the slicer to perform this task was necessary. Teachers were asked to only harvest open corpus resources matching specific criteria combinations (such as topics covered, tenses etc...). Hence, an automated harvesting time estimation based upon traditional IR services would have created an unfair advantage towards the slicer, since these techniques only provide keyword searches with little guarantee that harvested resources satisfy these criteria. For these reasons, the OCCS focused crawler [11] was considered a fairer option since it provides the means to specify content to be harvested based upon a wider range of constraints (including topics covered) and also guarantees resources harvested, if any, meet these sets of constraints. Time measurements obtained for this experiment reveal that when no particular content requirement was specified, teachers took an average of 3.75 minutes to harvest open corpus resources and extract arbitrary fragments suitable for grammar exercises. Requesting resources to be on a specific topic, only slightly increased the average time measured (4 min) whereas requesting resources to possess verbs conjugated at particular tenses nearly tripled the time needed (10.5 min). These results follow common sense, since the ability of humans to identify topics covered within resources is much more straight forward than for machines, however the reverse is also true when dealing with specific fine grained requirements such as verb tenses. Teachers on average took 4.25 minutes to annotate fragments (189 words in average, 14 annotations per fragments) leading to a total time ranging from 8 min to 14.75 min to produce these resources. This would be the equivalent of between 1.5 to nearly 3 years of manual labor necessary to produce a hundred thousand of such resources. According to Lawless et al. [11], a time performance of 149,993 valid resources harvested in 43h was measured for the OCCS system (without any cpu parallelization). This is equivalent to $17.2 * 10^{-3}$ minutes of harvesting time necessary per page. Summing extraction, annotation and slice creation time performed on a 2.8GHz machine leads to a total of $5.4 * 10^{-1}$ minutes necessary to produce each page. Assuming no parallelization was used during the slicing process (section 3), this already represents a difference of up to 96% production time increase with respect to it's manual production equivalent. Although automated and manual production time are clearly not directly comparable, one can assume in most cases, server costs per time unit to be much lower than labor costs. Considering the low server production time measured in comparison to the manual tasks, automated content production cost can be inferred to be also much lower than a manual approach and hence more adequate for large number of resources produced.

## 5  Conclusion

Although differences were observed between content automatically produced and manually hand crafted, results presented in this paper indicate that any differences were statistically insignificant. However, when taking into account content batches production costs, automatically generated resources significantly outweighed those manually produced. Hence, in the context of a high speed, low cost production environment, one could easily assume any content produced with unsatisfactory suitability to be discarded and rapidly replaced, which could compensate any decrease in quality. The ability of automated open corpus slicing techniques to produce large volumes of content on-demand, at very low costs and with a suitability comparable to manually produced resources, would thus appear to represent a promising candidate approach to consider for long tail content supply services. As this initial experiment only took into account specific aspects of content quality (i.e. reading flow, annotations...) within a chosen educational content reuse scenario, further empirical research will be required in order to validate this approach within various use cases.

## References

1. Lin, Y.-l., Brusilovsky, P.: Towards Open Corpus Adaptive Hypermedia: A Study of Novelty Detection Approaches. In: Konstan, J.A., Conejo, R., Marzo, J.L., Oliver, N. (eds.) UMAP 2011. LNCS, vol. 6787, pp. 353–358. Springer, Heidelberg (2011)
2. Armani, J.: A Visual Authoring Tool for Adaptive Websites Tailored to Non- Programmer Teachers Jacopo Armani. Educational Technology & Society (2005)
3. Jednoralski, D., Melis, E., Sosnovsky, S., Ullrich, C.: Gap Detection in Web-Based Adaptive Educational Systems. In: Int. Conf. on Web-based Learning (2010)
4. Levacher, K., Wade, V.: Providing Customized Reuse of Open-Web Resources for Adaptive Hypermedia. In: Conf. on Hypertext and Social Media (2012)

5. Meyer, C., Steinmetz, R.: Multigranularity reuse of learning resources. Transactions on Multimedia Computing, Communications, and Applications (2011)
6. Diaz-aviles, E., Fisichella, M., Nejdl, W.: Unsupervised Auto-tagging for Learning Object Enrichment. In: Conf. on Tech. Enhanced Learning (2011)
7. Madjarov, I., Boucelma, O.: Learning Content Adaptation for m-Learning Systems: A Multimodality Approach. In: Luo, X., Spaniol, M., Wang, L., Li, Q., Nejdl, W., Zhang, W. (eds.) ICWL 2010. LNCS, vol. 6483, pp. 190–199. Springer, Heidelberg (2010)
8. Henze, N., Nejdl, W.: Adaptation in Open Corpus Hypermedia. IJAIED 2001: Int. Journal of Artificial Intellligence in Education, 325 – 350 (2001)
9. Zhou, D., Truran, M., Goulding, J.: LLAMA: Automatic Hypertext Generation Utilizing Language Models. In: Conf. on Hypertext and Hypermedia (2007)
10. Brusilovsky, P., Chavan, G., Farzan, R.: Social adaptive navigation support for open corpus electronic textbooks. In: Conf. on Adaptive Hypermedia and Adaptive Web Based Systems (2004)
11. Lawless, S.: Leveraging Content from Open Corpus Sources for Technology Enhanced Learning. PhD thesis, Trinity College Dublin (2009)
12. Steichen, B., Wade, V., Oconnor, A.: Providing personalisation across semantic, social and open-web resources. In: Conf. on Hypertext and Hypermedia (2011)
13. Kohlschütter, C., Nejdl, W.: A Densitometric Approach to Web Page Segmentation. In: Conf. on Information and Knowledge Management (2008)
14. Lee, Y., Cho, J., Han, S., Choi, B.U.: A Personalized Assessment System Based on Item Response Theory. In: Proc. of the Int. Conf. on Web-based Learning (2010)

# Learning Path Construction Based on Association Link Network

Fan Yang[1], Frederick W.B. Li[1], and Rynson W.H. Lau[2]

[1] School of Engineering and Computing Sciences, Durham University, UK
[2] Department of Computer Science, City University of Hong Kong, HK
{fan.yang,frederick.li}@durham.ac.uk, rynson.lau@cityu.edu.hk

**Abstract.** Nowadays the Internet virtually serves as a library for people to quickly retrieve information (Web resources) on what they want to learn. Reusing Web resources to form learning resources offers a way for rapid construction of self-pace or even formal courses. This requires identifying suitable Web resources and organizing such resources into proper sequences for delivery. However, getting these done is challenging, as they need to determine a set of Web resources properties, including the relevance, importance and complexity of Web resources to students as well as the relationships among Web resources, which are not trivial to be done automatically. Particularly each student has different needs. To address the above problems, we present a learning path generation method based on the Association Link Network (ALN), which works out Web resources properties by exploiting the association among Web resources. Our experiments show that the proposed method can generate good quality learning paths and help improve student learning.

**Keywords:** Learning Path, Association Link Network, Learning Resources.

## 1 Introduction

Learning resources (LRs) refer to materials that help students learn and understand certain knowledge. Such LRs can be constructed by different types of media, including text, audio, and video. Typically, producing LRs is very time consuming. With the availability of the Internet, such situation may be improved, as information covering a huge variety of ready-made knowledge, namely Web resources, is made available. Examples of Web resources include materials from Wikipedia, BBC, Reuters, etc. Reusing such resources may help teachers significantly reduce their time on producing LRs and may also facilitate the generation of self-pace courses. However, Web resources may be loosely connected without any well-defined structure or relationship, and may also be redundant. It is not trivial to transform Web resources into LRs, as relationships among LRs are required to be well defined and LRs should be arranged to deliver in a proper order for students to study.

Identifying relevant LRs is essential to learning path [11] generation. Existing work determine such a relevancy by matching student specific requirements, including topics to learn, learning preferences or constraints [4, 3] against the characteristics

E. Popescu et al. (Eds.): ICWL 2012, LNCS 7558, pp. 120–131, 2012.

of LRs, which can be maintained by a list of attributes, such as related topic and difficulty level, or additionally by a structure that defines how LRs are related among each
other [9]. Learning path generation methods aim at arranging selected LRs into a
proper sequence for delivering to students, such that they can learn effectively in
terms of minimizing the cognitive workload. Basic work [4], only considers attributes
associated with each LR, such as its related topic. More advanced works [5, 2] consider the structure among LRs which facilitates them to model the cognitive relationships among LRs. Such relationships are fundamental to learning effectiveness.
However, structures among LRs are not trivial to build. Existing work considers using
pre-defined structures [5] or generating LR structures based on pre-test results [2],
which involves significant human effort.

We present a learning path (LP) generation method based on the Association Link
Network (ALN) [6, 8]. It discovers knowledge structure among Web resources based
on association, allowing teachers to reuse Web resources forming LRs automatically.
Our main contributions include:

1. We apply ALN to transform Web resources into well-structured LRs, where their
   pedagogical attributes, including knowledge domain, importance and complexity,
   can be automatically determined. This allows us to construct a teacher knowledge
   model (TKM) for a course and generate adaptive LP to each student. A student
   knowledge model (SKM) is also included to monitor student learning progress.
2. We model learning paths by a set of three different ALNs, namely LR, topic and
   keyword based ALNs. This modeling allows students to perceive the relationships
   among LRs through different abstraction levels, which can help students minimize
   their cognitive workload during the learning process.

This paper is organized as follows. Section 2 discusses related works. Section 3 and 4
respectively explain the construction of the teacher knowledge model and adaptive
learning paths. Section 5 shows some results and Section 6 concludes this paper.

## 2     Related Work

To support students learning effectively, relevant LRs should be identified and delivered in a proper sequence based on student needs and knowledge background. [4]
proposes using Web resources as LRs without requiring teachers to create LRs. Suitable Web resources are selected based on certain student specific criteria, including
topics to study, learning preferences and learning constraints, e.g. available study
time. [3] also allows students to search LRs for learning. However, the method in
addition performs a query rewriting based on student profiles, which describe student
learning preferences and learning performance (which indicate student knowledge
level), such that students only need to focus on what they want to learn and the system
will take care of the suitability of every LR, which matches the student searching
criteria. [9] proposes a more comprehensive modeling of LRs, where each of them is
designed to associate with a concept, a knowledge type (verbal information or
intellectual skills), and a knowledge level. LRs are connected based on concept

relationships, where teachers manually define prerequisite among concepts. However, such relationships are not fine enough to support arranging individual LRs in a proper sequence for delivery. [1] characterizes LRs based on subjects and organizes LRs by ontology-based subject relations, including part of, prerequisite, and weaker prerequisite relations. They form the basis for both determining the delivery sequence of LRs and selecting suitable LRs according to the student preferred subjects. However, subject information is too coarse that each subject is associated with many LRs, making precise learning path hard to be generated.

Given that LRs are properly modeled, a learning path generation algorithm can be used to deliver LRs for students to learn. [4] allows students to submit queries for selecting suitable LRs. The selected LRs will then be ordered by the topics and the instructional methods that they belong to, respectively. As structures of LRs and relationships among LRs, which are critical to the control of student cognitive workload in learning, are not considered, learning effectiveness cannot be guaranteed. [5] models the structure among LRs based on a hierarchy of topics, which are defined by the ACM Computing Curricula 2001 for Computer Science. The method initially generates all possible learning paths that match the student goal. It then selects the most suitable one for a student to follow by considering the student cognitive characteristics and learning preferences. Although the relationship among LRs is essentially constructed manually, learning effectiveness is better addressed. [2] models the relationships among LRs based on an ontology-based concept map, which is generated by running a genetic algorithm on a set of student pre-test results. The method successfully works out the prior and posterior knowledge relationships of LRs, such that LRs can be delivered based on their difficulty levels and concept relationships to reduce student cognitive workloads during the learning process. However, the results do not necessary reflect the semantic relationships among LRs and may not be applicable to other groups of students who have not taken part in the pre-tests.

## 3    The Teacher Knowledge Model

The Association Link Network (ALN) [6, 8] is designed to automatically establish relations among Web resources, which may be loosely connected without well-defined relations. ALN defines relations among Web resources by analyzing the keywords contained in Web resources. Such relations are referred as associations, which link up Web resources as an ALN to describe the semantic relationships of Web resources, and turn Web resources into LRs. In our work, we further exploit such associations to automatically formulate key attributes of LRs, including their importance and complexity, which are fundamental to learning path (LP) generation. The LPs are exacted from the whole set of 3 different ALNs, namely LR, topic and keyword, to help students perceive LRs together with their multiple levels of relationships. By following such learning paths, the cognitive workload of a student on learning can be greatly reduced. To set up a measure for evaluating student learning progress, we define the set of three ALNs that links up all available LRs of a course as the teacher knowledge model (TKM). We also maintain a student knowledge model (SKM)

(Ref. Section 4) to describe student learning progress. SKM comprises the system recommended LP and the part of the LP that a student has finished studying, together with all relevant LRs. SKM also comprises a student profile, indicating the student's knowledge levels and preferred topics.

Technically, the foundation of ALN is the association of keywords, where there exists an association link between two keywords if these keywords appear in the same paragraph. To facilitate the formulation of LRs and learning paths, we extract the most important keywords identified from a set of LRs as topics, where the association link between two topics are inherited from that between the corresponding keywords. The topics are used as a means to determine whether any two knowledge concepts are related. In contrast to a topic, a keyword only indicates a certain aspect of a piece of knowledge concept. On the other hand, there exists an association link between two LRs if some keywords contained in the two LRs are associated with each other. As an ALN represents a network linking a set of nodes $\{c_1, c_2, \cdots, c_n\}$ by their association, where $n$ is the number of nodes. Mathematically, an ALN is represented by a matrix of association weights $aw_{mn}$, where each formulates the association relation between a cause node $c_m$ and an effect node $c_n$. It is defined as follows:

$$ALN = \begin{pmatrix} aw_{11} & \cdots & aw_{1n} \\ \vdots & \ddots & \vdots \\ aw_{m1} & \cdots & aw_{mn} \end{pmatrix} \tag{1}$$

Particularly, LRs, topics and keywords are all modeled by ALNs. An ALN can be incrementally constructed by adding or removing nodes. When a new node is added to an ALN, we need to check such a node against all existing nodes in the ALN, identifying whether the nodes are relevant and computing the association weights between the newly added node and each of the relevant existing nodes in the ALN. When removing a node, all association links induced by the node will be removed. This incremental property makes adding new Web resources to form new LRs to or removing LRs from a course easily. We now depict the details of the construction of the three different ALNs in our system.

To turn a set of Web resources into LRs, we initially extract their keywords and construct the association links among the keywords by Eq. 2;

$$aw_{ij} = P(k_j|k_i) = (\textstyle\sum_{k=1}^{n} b_{ir})/n \tag{2}$$

where $aw_{ij}$ is the association weight from a cause keyword $k_i$ to an effect keyword $k_j$, $k_i$ is associated to $k_j$ when they appear in the same paragraph [6]. An association weight, which is calculated as $P(k_j|k_i)$, indicates the probability of the occurrence of a cause keyword $k_i$ leads to an effect keyword $k_j$ in the same paragraph at the same time. $b_{ir}$ is the probability of the occurrence of a cause keyword $k_i$ in the $r^{th}$ sentence leads to the occurrence of an effect keyword $k_j$ in the same sentence. $n$ is the number of sentences in the paragraph $p_m$. We apply TFIDF Direct Document Frequency of Domain (TDDF) [7] to extract domain keywords from a set of Web resources, where keywords are texts that appear in a good number of Web resources, i.e. the document frequency is higher than a threshold. The associated relation is determined by $A \xrightarrow{\alpha} B$, meaning that if node $A$ is chosen from an ALN, node $B$ will also be chosen with the probability $\alpha$.

We then extract and link up topics from the LRs. Topics refer to the most important keywords, which have the highest numbers of association links than the other keywords, meaning that they can represent the most important information of a set of LRs. In our experiments, we select the top 20% of keywords forming the topics. Pedagogically, topics model the knowledge concepts covered by the LRs, while keywords are associated to a topic as its key attributes, which help explain why certain knowledge concepts are related to some others. This modeling is much comprehensive than existing work, as they only associate LRs based on topics.

To construct LRs for a course, we follow the knowledge domain (i.e. a set of topics) of the course and select relevant Web resources that match the knowledge domain, turning such resources into LRs. We have conducted experiments on our method using 1085 Web resources about health information from www.reuters.com/news/health. We do not create LRs for similar Web resources in order to avoid students spending time on learning similar content repeatedly. We check Web resource similarity based on their keywords and association links. In the implementation, we pick the first selected item of such Web resources to create a LR and stop creating further LRs for any Web resource that has a high similarity. Fig. 1 shows part of the keyword ALN that we have created, where each node represents a keyword, and each edge, namely an association link, represents the existence of an association between two nodes. The importance of a node is directly proportional to the number of association links connecting to it. Note that the edges showing in the figure do not imply any association weight.

**Fig. 1.** An illustration of a keyword-based ALN

TKM formulates the overall knowledge structure of a course based on topic, keyword and LR ALNs. [10] shows that formulating concepts into a knowledge map, which is a graph having concepts as nodes and they are connected by links that model the relationships between two concepts, can significantly improve student understanding, particularly when comparing with studying through LRs collated by a simple Webpage browse-based structure. Our ALN based knowledge structure is similar to a knowledge map. Instead of having freestyle labeling to formulate the relationship (i.e. the link) between two concepts, we use association weight to model quantifiable relationships among concepts. In addition, we have three different types of ALNs representing different abstraction levels of a set of concepts, i.e. topics, keywords and LR ALNs, where the relationships among such ALNs are also explicitly defined, i.e. given a node in an ALN, the corresponding nodes in the other two ALNs are well-defined. This implies that it is easy to retrieve LRs based on student-preferred topics and the knowledge structure for a set of LRs.

The ALN structure also allows us to automatically compute the complexity and the importance of each LR, avoiding instructors or course designers to manually define such attributes, which is extremely time consuming when there are a massive number of LRs to deal with. More specifically:

- We compute the complexity of a LR, which can be used to match student knowledge level, based on the algebraic complexity of human cognition that associates with the complexity of both keywords and association links of the LR $X$ as follows:

$$\lambda^T = \sum_{K=0}^{D-1} W_k \cdot \lambda_X^k \tag{3}$$

  where $\lambda_X^T$ is the text complexity of LR $X$ in terms of keywords, $D$ is the number of keywords in LR $X$. $\lambda_X^k$ is the number of degree-$k$ association, i.e. the number of keywords having $k$ association links connected to LR $X$, which indicates the complexity of association link. $W_k$ is the number of keywords having degree-$k$ association, which indicates the complexity of keywords. A LR is low in complexity if it has low number of association links while such links are of low degrees.
- The number of association links indicates the number of relationships existing between a node and its connected nodes. The association weight indicates how strong a node is related to another one. We therefore use the association weight and the number of association links to indicate the importance of a node.

## 4    Student Knowledge Model and Personalized Learning Path

Student Knowledge Model (SKM) formulates the student learning progress. It comprises a dynamically generated personalized LP and a set of student characteristics. A personalized LP is technically a subset of the TKM. Student characteristics that we consider include knowledge background, knowledge level, and preferred knowledge concepts, which are learned topics, performance on such learned topics, and topics that a student is interested or can effectively learn, respectively. The algorithm for personalized LP generation is as follows:

1. **Initialization:** Based on the topic ALN of TKM, we determine the starting point of a personalized LP according to the initial knowledge of a student, i.e. the topics learned. If such information does not exist, we consider the topics, where their complexity match the student's knowledge level, and select the most important one as the starting point. This ensures the most suitable and fundamental knowledge is selected for a student to start learning. We compute the complexity of a topic by considering the average complexity of all LRs associated with the topic as follows:

$$D_T(x) = \frac{1}{N}\sum_{p=1}^{n} \lambda^T\left(LR_p\right) \tag{4}$$

where $D_T(x)$ represents the complexity of topic x, and $\lambda^T\left(LR_p\right)$ is the complexity of LR $p$ (ref. Eq. 3).

2. **Incremental LP Generation:** Based on the current node of a LP, we incrementally generate the next node of the LP by identifying a suitable one from the set of direct connected nodes according to the topic ALN of TKM. The selection is based on two criteria: the *complexity* and the *importance* of the topic. The complexity of the topic should match the student's knowledge level. If there are more than one node meeting the complexity criteria, we then select the node with the highest importance $I_{S_i}(x)$, which is formulated by the summation of association weights where student preference on a topic is considered as in Eq. 5:

$$I_{S_i}(x) = \sum_{j=1}^{n} aw_{xj}(x) \cdot P_{S_i}(x) \tag{5}$$

where $I_{S_i}$ represents the importance of topic x for student i, $aw_{xj}(x)$ represents the association weight between topic x and topic j, and $P_{S_i}(x)$ represents student $i$'s preference degree on topic x.

3. **LR Selection:** Based on the LR ALN of TKM, we select a set of LRs, where their associated topics match with the selected topic by step 2. As shown in Eq. 6 and 7, a student specific LR p will be identified by matching the complexity $\lambda^T\left(LR_p\right)$ of the LR with the knowledge level $KL_{S_i}$ of the student.

$$LRs = \left\{p\big|\left\|\lambda^T\left(LR_p\right) - KL_{S_i}\right\| < 0.1KL_{S_i}\right\} \tag{6}$$

$$D_{S_i}(x) = \lambda^T\left(LR_p\right)/P_{S_i}(x) \tag{7}$$

**LP Progression and Alternative LP:** After a student successfully studying a LR, we update the SKM by indicating the student has finished such a LR and the associated keywords. Our system will then go back to step 2 again for incremental LP generation. If a student fails the corresponding assessment, it is likely that the student lacks the knowledge of some aspects of the topic about the LR. To deal with such a learning problem, we adjust the LP by redirecting the student to learn an alternative LR, which is the most important unlearned prerequisite node of the failed LR as defined in the LR ALN of the TKM, before coming back to learn the failed LR. Such an alternation may be carried out repeatedly on the rest of the unlearned prerequisite node of the failed LR if necessary.

4. **Learning Performance:** A student i has finished learning a course when there is no more LR to follow. The student learning performance $D_i$ can be computed by the difference between the real performance $SKM_i$ (i.e. the finished LP) and the expected performance $LP_i$ defined by the recommended LP as stored in the TKM:

$$D_i = \|SKM_i - LP_i\| \tag{8}$$

where $D_i$ evaluates whether the student has a good learning performance at the end his learning. The student has a better learning performance if $SKM_i$ is closer to $LP_i$. Fig. 2 shows an example of a system recommended LP formed by a set of three different ALNs for a student. Fig. 2(a) depicts the topic ALN that comprises 5 topics, forming the topic level of the LP (i.e. project → president → pharmacy → plastic → lead), where the edge thickness indicates the association weight. The corresponding keyword ALN and LR ALN are respectively shown in Fig. 2(b) and 2(c). The highlighted LRs as shown in Fig. 2(c) are the recommended LRs that match the student knowledge level. Since there are associations among LRs through sharing keywords, a student showing interest in a LR may also interest in its associated LR. A student can also gain understanding in a LR through its associated LRs. Our three different ALNs provide such associations and therefore help improve student learning.

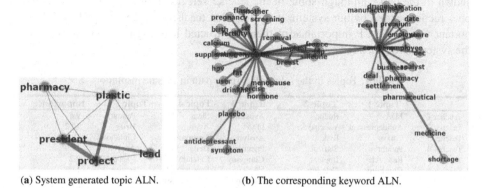

(a) System generated topic ALN.                    (b) The corresponding keyword ALN.

(c) The corresponding LR ALN, representing the system generated LP for a student.

**Fig. 2.** The three different ALN's that constitute the system recommended learning path

## 5    Evaluation

### 5.1    Comparison Based on LP Importance

In this experiment, we compare the quality of manually generated LPs with system recommended ones based on the LP importance, which is evaluated by summing up the importance of the nodes that constitute a LP. Ten teachers are asked to manually construct LPs that comprise 5 nodes (i.e. topics) according to the topic ALN. Such a construction should fulfill two requirements: 1) the selected topics should connect with each other, and 2) should be important to students. Such requirements also govern how the recommended LP generated by our system. Results show that the LP importance of our generated LP is higher than the teacher generated ones. To determine whether the comprehensiveness of the ALN structures will affect the quality of LP generation, we conduct experiments using three different resolutions of the TKM by changing the number of association links constituted the topic ALN. Particularly, we use topic ALNs having 196 links, 271 links and 360 links, which correspond to 20%, 50%, and 80% of the total association links, forming the low, middle and high resolutions of TKM, respectively. Table 1 depicts the details of the LPs constructed by both the teachers and our system based on the middle resolution of TKM. As shown in the table, although some of the teacher selected topics are the same as the ones recommended by our system, indicating that teachers are able to pick some important topics, the LP importance of their constructed learning paths are lower than the system recommended one.

**Table 1.** Topics in the selected learning path in Middle resolution

|  | Topic 1 | Topic 2 | Topic 3 | Topic 4 | Topic 5 | Importance |
|---|---|---|---|---|---|---|
| Teacher 1 | FDA | Roche | **Avastin** | Stent | Patient | 9.6 |
| Teacher 2 | Antidepressant | Vaccine | FDA | Avastin | **Drug** | 15.2 |
| Teacher 3 | Cancer | Risk | Analyst | **Company** | Childhood | 12.8 |
| Teacher 4 | Patient | Staff | Pneumonia | **Drug** | Analyst | 17.0 |
| Teacher 5 | Researcher | Implant | **Company** | Calcium | Cancer | 9.2 |
| Teacher 6 | **Company** | Calcium | HPY | Supplement | France | 11.2 |
| Teacher 7 | FDA | Pneumonia | Dialysis | Antidepressant | Treatment | 12.2 |
| Teacher 8 | Cancer | Implant | Test | Screening | Prostate | 7.2 |
| Teacher 9 | Analyst | **Pharmaceutical** | Medicine | **Company** | Premium | 11.2 |
| Teacher 10 | Antidepressant | Patent | Pneumonia | Analyst | Staff | 15.8 |
| System | Drug | Company | Avastin | Pharmaceutical | Shortage | 27.2 |

Fig. 3 compares the LP importance of the learning paths generated by the teachers and our system when different resolutions of the TKM are made available. In the figure, the left y-axis shows the LP importance and is referred by the histogram, while the right y-axis shows the LP importance ratio of the teacher generated LPs w.r.t. the system recommended one and is referred by the polylines. We group the results by the resolutions of the TKM. It is found that no matter which resolution of the TKM is made available, our system still produces learning paths with a higher LP importance than the teacher generated ones. The upper and the lower polylines respectively show the maximum and the average LP importance ratios of the teacher generated learning paths. They indicate the quality of the learning paths generated by the teachers w.r.t. to the system recommended ones. On the other hand, when the resolution of the TKM increases, the generated LPs both by the teachers and our system also increase in the LP importance. It is because when richer course domain information is made available, i.e. more association links forming the TKM, a better decision can be made on the LP construction. However, as teachers are generally overwhelmed by the massive number of LRs and association links, they tend to construct learning paths based on partial information from the TKM. As a result, their produced learning paths are of lower LP importance.

## 5.2    Comparison on Student Learning Performance

We conducted experiments on comparing student learning performance based on the teacher generated learning paths and the system recommended one. We have invited 10 postgraduate students in computer science to participate the experiments. The students have different learning abilities, which perform differently when studying the same LR. We randomly divide the students into two even groups. The 1st group of students performs learning based on the teacher constructed LPs, while the 2nd group of students learn by the system recommended LP. All students are given 50 minutes for studying the contents (contains 5 LRs) provided the LPs and take the same examination with 25 questions, which assess their understanding. Results show that students using the system generated LP perform better and have more stable performance.

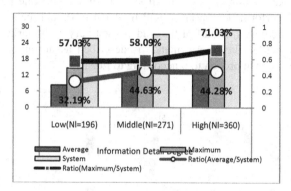

**Fig. 3.** Comparison of the importance of manually selected and system recommended LP in topic layer

**Better performance:** We compare the learning performance between two student groups by one sample t-test based on the differences in their performance variances:

$$t = \frac{\bar{x} - \mu_0}{s/\sqrt{n}} \tag{9}$$

where $\bar{x}$ is the average of the differences in the learning performance variances between the two student groups after studying n LRs, $\mu_0$ is the population mean of the null hypothesis, and s is the standard deviation of the samples. Assume the null hypothesis is that two student groups have the same learning performance on the same LRs. So $\mu_0 = 0$. The t-value is 2.3181 which is larger than the threshold of the t-value 2.1319 when the p-value is set to 0.05. It means the null hypothesis is rejected, i.e. the performance of the two student groups is significantly different. We then compare the detailed learning performance of the two student groups based on each LR. As shown in Fig. 4, students studying using the system recommended LP generally perform better. In average, they got 60.8% in the examination, while the students studying through teacher generated LPs got 51.2% only. Note that y-axis shows the scales of the learning performance, while x-axis shows the indices of individual LRs. Although students using the system recommended LP perform less well in LRs P462 and P193, performance of both student groups in such LRs are still quite similar.

**Stable performance:** We test if the students in each group can have similar learning performance $\sigma_i^2$ on the same LR $i$ by analyzing their performance variances (ref. Eq. 10). The results are shown in Fig. 5, where the y-axis indicates the performance variances.

$$\sigma_i^2 = \frac{1}{m} \cdot \sum_{j=1}^{m}(x_{ij} - \bar{x}_i)^2 \qquad (10)$$

where $\bar{x}_i$ is the average performance on LR i, $x_{ij}$ is the performance on LR j of student $x_j$, and m is the number of students. If different students show similar performance on the same LR, their performance variances will be low. We refer this as stable performance. For instance, if all students have the same performance on the same LR, the performance variance will be equal to 0, and their performance is the most stable. In contrast, if half of the students got very high marks and the other half got very low marks, their performance is described as unstable, where the performance variance can approach to 6 according to Eq. 10.

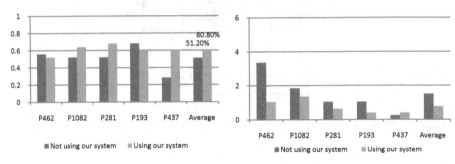

Fig. 4. Learning performance          Fig. 5. Stability of learning performance.

As shown in Fig. 5, although students studying through teacher generated LPs (Group 1) perform slightly better on LRs P462 and P193 than those studying by the system recommended LP (Group 2), the performance of group 1 students is quite unstable, i.e. students perform quite differently in the same LR. Overall, group 2 students generally have more stable performance than group 1 students. However, for LR P437, group 1 student has more stable performance as they have consistently low performance in such a LR. Our experiments indicate that by using the system recommended LP, even student coming with different learning abilities can be trained to perform better in learning. In addition, the entire cohort will have a more stable performance.

# 6    Conclusion and Future Work

In this paper, we have presented an ALN-based LP construction method. We construct multi-level of abstractions of LRs through association, allowing a knowledge map like learning path to be derived. Such a learning path structure can help students learn more effectively. The ALN-based association structure also allows important parameters of LRs, such as their complexity and importance, to be derived. This offers sufficient information for automatic construction of pedagogically meaningful LPs. This feature is particularly critical when a massive amount of Web resources are considered to be transformed as LRs for students to learn. Our experiments show that our method offers better and much stable student learning performance. In practice, as Web resources obtained from different providers may have very different presentations and inconsistent contents. As a future work, we will investigate methods to address such presentation and consistency problems to allow students to learn more smoothly with Web resources constructed learning materials.

# References

1. Acampora, G., Gaeta, M., Loia, V.: Hierarchical optimization of personalized experiences for e-Learning systems through evolutionary models. Neural Comput. & Applic. 20, 641–657 (2011)
2. Chen, C.: Ontology-based Concept Map for Planning a Personalised Learning Path. British Journal of Educational Technology 40(6), 1028–1058 (2009)
3. Dolog, P., Simon, B., Nejdl, W., Klobucar, T.: Personalizing Access to Learning Networks. ACM Trans. on Internet Technology 8(2) (2008)
4. Farrell, R., Liburd, S.D., Thomas, J.: Dynamic Assembly of Learning Objects. In: World Wide Web Conference on Alternate Track, pp. 162–169 (2004)
5. Karampiperis, P., Sampson, D.: Adaptive Learning Resources Sequencing in Educational Hypermedia Systems. Educational Technology & Society 8(4), 128–147 (2005)
6. Luo, X., Fang, N., Hu, B., Yan, K., Xiao, H.: Semantic representation of scientific documents for the e-science Knowledge Grid. Concurrency Computat.: Pract. Exper. 20, 839–862 (2008)
7. Luo, X., Fang, N., Yu, S., Yan, K., Xiao, H.Z.: Experimental Study on the Extraction and Distribution of Textual Domain Keywords. Concurrency Computat.: Pract. Exper. 20, 1917–1932 (2008)
8. Luo, X., Xu, Z., Yu, J., Chen, X.: Building Association Link Network for Semantic Link on Learning resources. IEEE Trans. on Automation Science and Engineering 8(3), 482–494 (2011)
9. Melia, M., Pahl, C.: Constraint-Based Validation of Adaptive e-Learning Courseware. IEEE Trans. on Learning Technologies 2(1), 37–49 (2009)
10. Shaw, R.: A study of learning performance of e-learning materials design with knowledge maps. Computers & Education 54, 253–264 (2010)
11. Yang, F., Li, F.W.B., Lau, R.W.H.: An Open Model for Learning Path Construction. In: Luo, X., Spaniol, M., Wang, L., Li, Q., Nejdl, W., Zhang, W. (eds.) ICWL 2010. LNCS, vol. 6483, pp. 318–328. Springer, Heidelberg (2010)

# Discovering Hierarchical Relationships
# in Educational Content

Marián Šimko and Mária Bieliková

Institute of Informatics and Software Engineering, Faculty of Informatics
and Information Technologies, Slovak University of Technology in Bratislava,
Ilkovičova 3, 842 16 Bratislava
{simko,bielik}@fiit.stuba.sk

**Abstract.** Adaptive educational hypermedia necessitate semantic description of a domain, which is used by an adaptive engine to perform adaptation to a learner. The bottleneck of adaptive hypermedia is manual authoring of such semantic description performed by a domain expert mainly due to the amount of descriptions to be created. In this paper we present a method for automated discovery of is-a relationship, one of the most important relationships of conceptual structures. The method leverages specifics of educational content. The evaluation shows reasonable accuracy of discovered relationships reflecting in reduced domain expert's efforts in domain model creation.

**Keywords:** adaptive hypermedia, domain model, semantics discovery, automatic relationship discovery, natural language processing.

## 1 Introduction and Related Work

In order to enable adaptation during learning within an educational web-based system, a subject domain has to be properly semantically described. An adaptive engine utilizes *domain model* – a representation of a domain conceptually describing resources to be a subject for adaptation.

Domain representation among different educational systems varies from conceptual maps to complex domain ontologies [8]. In most cases, core domain model consists of domain knowledge elements (concepts represented by relevant domain terms) and relationships between them. There are typically dozens of concepts and hundreds of relationships of various kinds in a domain model making manual creation and maintenance of such structure a demanding and very difficult task. It is important to seek for methods that facilitate domain model creation and reduce a teacher's (or an instructional designer's) efforts.

Automated domain model creation is possible by processing underlying textual content and/or a structure of a course. Much research has been devoted to text mining, however, to our best knowledge, only a small number of approaches focus on *educational* text mining, while considering its *specifics* such as domain specificity of vocabulary (it is natural to introduce new terms) or explanatory nature of language used (learning objects are richer in explanatory phrases).

E. Popescu et al. (Eds.): ICWL 2012, LNCS 7558, pp. 132–141, 2012.
© Springer-Verlag Berlin Heidelberg 2012

There exist few approaches to automatic relationship acquisition in adaptive learning. The authors of adaptive system My Online Teacher developed a method for computing similarity between concepts by calculating correspondence weights computation between concepts attributes [5]. The idea is based on co-occurrence comparison of keywords and overall attributes' contents of concepts. Sosnovsky et al. aim at automated prerequisite and outcome relationships identification [10]. Based on predefined concept pattern detection, they extract concepts from learning objects on C programming language. An interesting example of automated metadata acquisition was performed in the case of adaptive vocabulary acquisition system ELDIT [2], where methods and techniques of natural language processing were employment in order to create relationships between vocabulary entries and their examples. In our previous work we devised a method for relevant domain terms relatedness computation based on statistical and graph processing of the domain model [12]. Zouaq and Nkambou present a two-step method for domain ontology learning from educational text, including concept relationships [16]. The method is based on pattern-based semantic analysis and linguistic processing of educational content. A semi-automatic approach to domain model building is presented by Šaloun et al. [11].

Despite small number of approaches in the domain of adaptive learning, there is a lot of work in taxonomical relationship extraction in the field of ontology learning. The approaches can be according to Cimiano [3] divided into the three groups: lexico-syntactic patterns matching (e.g., [7]), leveraging distributional hypothesis (e.g., [1]), and co-occurrence analysis (e.g., [6]). These approaches form a solid basis for further adoption to educational domain to utilize the potential of educational text specifics.

In this paper we present a method for automated relationship discovery in educational content. We extend our previous research in the area of automated domain model acquisition [13] and we focus on hierarchy (is-a) relationship between relevant domain terms. It constitutes one of the most important types of relationships as it forms a skeleton of a domain representation. We present three techniques, each covering different linguistic aspect of educational content.

## 2   Method for Is-a Relationship Discovery

Our method for is-a relationship discovery combines statistics- and linguistics-based approaches to data mining. It builds on preceding learning objects preprocessing and relevant domain terms identification steps, which are based on analysis of learning content [13].

The method incorporates three techniques, each consisting of different steps:

- Explanation phrase processing,
  - explanation phrase lookup,
  - relevant domain term overlap computation,
  - distance of overlapping tokens computation;
- Determination phrase processing,
  - determination phrase lookup,

- relevant domain term overlap computation;
- Relevant domain term lexical analysis,
    - relevant domain term lexical overlap computation.

The final step of each technique is is-a relationship generation, where relationships are generated and a confidence for each relationship is derived. While focusing on a different language aspect, each technique yields its own set of is-a relationships. These sets are filtered and combined with respect to a relevance of particular technique in order to produce a single set of is-a relationships[1].

### 2.1 Explanation Phrase Processing

This technique is based on lexico-syntactic analysis of underlying text content. Our aim is to find explanation phrases in sentences and extract *explanation candidates* for is-a relation.

The main idea is to search for patterns, which indicate is-a relationship between relevant domain terms. Patterns are inspired by a seminal work of Hearst, where she proposed a set of general patterns for hyponymy relationship acquisition from unstructured text [7]. We adopt such patterns for an educational domain by incorporating lexical and syntactical constructions that are used with the intent to teach, explain or clarify (hence they involve a potential is-a relationship). Learning objects typically are represented by resources, which aim to introduce and expound certain phenomena related to subject domain. For instance, the pattern:

$$\text{Understand } \{something\} \text{ to be/mean } \{something\}$$

in a learning object may indicate is-a relationship. It is more likely to indicate is-a relationship in a learning object than in an ordinary text. In lexico-syntactic patterns definition we particularly focus on verb forms that indicate an effort of cognitive organization of objects in the sentence, e.g., to be, to understand, to constitute, to name, to represent, to divide, to belong to, to fall into, etc.

When matching patterns, not only word forms but also their morphological tags are matched reflecting into increased accuracy of match. For example, applying a rule consisting of explanation verb form "is termed as" bound with all nouns and adjectives in nominative case will match the sentence *"Biologically our species is termed as Homo sapiens"* indicating is-a relationship: *is-a*(Homo sapiens, species).

Explanation phrase processing is divided into the following steps:

1. *Explanation phrase lookup.* In this step we use predefined rules to match patterns adopted for educational text with learning objects content and extract so called explanation phrase candidates, which contain tokens satisfying morphological criteria defined by the rules.

---

[1] In fact, the final step of our method covers relationship combination, duplicates removal, and loop resolution. Since we aim to explore the three techniques, detailed description of these steps is beyond the scope of the paper.

2. *Relevant domain term overlap computation.* The goal of this step is to check if extracted explanation phrases contain relevant domain terms. We compare explanation phrase candidate tokens with relevant domain terms and compute lexical overlap between their word forms. Basically, more overlapping words, the higher overlap.

3. *Distance of overlapping tokens computation.* We recognize distance of a token as a measure representing how tight the token is bound to an explanation verb. The closer a token is, the more likely it is paradigmatically related to explanation head, which indicates is-a relationship.

4. *Is-a relationship generation.* We generate is-a relationship and compute confidence of relationship correctness based on (i) lexical overlap with available relevant domain terms, and (ii) distance obtained in previous steps.

## 2.2  Determination Phrase Processing

A characteristic of an explanatory text is that it expounds new topic and extends a vocabulary by introducing new terms. The main idea of this technique is based on an observation that newly defined relevant domain terms are relatively often accompanied by a term that clarifies or classifies relevant domain terms' meaning. Accompanying terms are nouns or noun phrases, as they are main holders of the meaning (in contrast with other lexical categories such as adjectives or adverbs, which qualify nouns). For example, from the sentence *"Here is an example which uses the predicate listp to check for a list."* we deduce that *is-a*(listp, predicate). In this work we refer to such relation between two terms to as determination. A phrase composed of two (or more) such terms, i.e., nouns or noun phrases that collocate, we refer to as *determination phrase*. Determination phrases are typically bound with rather technical terms, which have roots in a language (natural or artificial) different from the language of a subject domain.

Is-a relationships indicated by determination phrases more likely refer to the concepts from lower parts of taxonomy as they connect a more specific term with a term of any level of specificity. We assume that there is reduced intent of a teacher to explicitly determine a more general term by accompanying it with another more general term.

Determination phrase processing consists of the following steps:

1. *Determination phrase lookup.* In the first step we look up all determination phrases in learning objects by matching the syntactical pattern:

$$NP_0 \ NP_1 \ [, NP_2 \ \ldots \ [\text{and/or}] \ NP_n]$$

representing subsequently collocated noun phrases. $NP_0$ is supersumed and $NP_{1..n}$ are subsumed noun phrases. Further restrictions related to noun phrases' grammatical categories (e.g., number, case) are language-specific and may reflect different morphological and word-formation rules.

2. *Relevant domain terms overlap computation.* Similarly to the preceding part of the method, we check after matching the pattern if extracted determination phrases contain relevant domain terms. For each determination phrase

token we compute lexical overlap with relevant domain terms. Distance discrimination factor is not relevant here as the distance is constant for all overlapping relevant domain terms.

3. *Is-a relationship generation.* In this step we generate is-a relationship candidates by traversing all determination phrases in each document and computing is-a relationship confidence. We consider in computation the overlap with relevant domain terms and also the count of determination phrase occurrences. It is due to the fact that determination phrases occur more frequently across the whole text corpora. The number of occurrences of such phrases is directly proportional to the number of occurrences of technical (relevant domain) terms (since determination phrases more likely cover sequences of noun phrases containing technical terms).

### 2.3 Relevant Domain Term Lexical Analysis

This technique's basis follows from an observation that basic word forms of relevant domain terms, which form is-a relationship, often overlap lexically (e.g., data type vs. atomic data type). Based on an assumption that a longer form is a specification of a shorter form, we examine the extent to which two relevant domain terms overlap lexically.

Relevant domain term lexical analysis consists of the following steps:

1. *Relevant domain terms lexical overlap computation.* In this step we match lexical forms of relevant domain term representations. We compute lexical overlap between each pair of relevant domain terms in a course as follows:

$$overlap(rdt_i, rdt_j) = \frac{|L(rdt_i) \cap L(rdt_j)|}{|L(rdt_i) \cup L(rdt_j)|} \tag{1}$$

where $rdt_i$ is a relevant domain term and $L(rdt_i)$ is a set of token lemmas of $rdt_i$. For the example above holds: $overlap(data\ type;\ atomic\ data\ type) = 0.6\bar{6}$. Lexical overlap is directly proportional to the number of tokens common for both relevant domain terms. Overlap is equal to 0 for lexically different terms and for equal ones it is 1.

2. *Is-a relationship generation.* We compute confidence of relationships based on relevant domain terms lexical overlap. We believe even a small overlap can indicate relatively reliable presence of is-a relationship between two relevant domain terms.

The proposed method for is-a relationship generation is based on comprehensive linguistic analysis of learning objects. It particularly considers specifics of educational content and the explanatory nature of learning material. It is based on an assumption that learning objects contain explanatory phrases (indicated by selected explanatory verbs) and determination phrases (a specific form of collocation of nouns or noun phrases). In addition, it utilizes lexical analysis of multiword relevant domain terms.

Although being language independent, the method's accuracy is strongly connected with language-specific patterns and lexico-syntactical matching rules that are used by a particular technique.

# 3   Evaluation

We evaluated our method in the domain of learning programming in a course of Functional programming lectured at the Slovak University of Technology in Bratislava.

## 3.1   Data and Method Application

The official learning material for functional programming consists of 79 explanatory learning objects on the functional programming paradigm and programming techniques in the Lisp language. The material is hierarchically organized into chapters and sections according to a printed textbook for the course. All learning materials are in Slovak. The course is available online in our adaptive educational system ALEF [14].

As the Functional programming course has already been involved in adaptive learning as a part of our previous research [12,14], learning objects have assigned relevant domain terms defined by domain experts.

Before evaluating partial techniques for domain model acquisition, we preprocessed all 79 learning objects following the natural language processing pipeline consisting of tokenization, POS tagging, lemmatization and sentence-based segmentation. Then we applied our method for is-a relationship discovery. By applying all three techniques for is-a relationship extraction (explanation phrase processing, determination phrase processing, relevant domain term lexical analysis), we extracted 84, 92 and 55 is-a relationships, respectively. By making union from all is-a relationships we obtained a final set of 206 unique relationships, which were a subject of evaluation.

## 3.2   Results and Discussion

We performed two-step evaluation of our method: a posteriori evaluation and comparison against the gold standard. In a posteriori evaluation we involved four domain experts to assess correctness of acquired relationships in order to set relevancies of the techniques accordingly. We achieved the best results for determination phrase processing, followed by relevant domain term analysis. Relationships acquired by explanation phrase processing ranked third, mainly due to the highest complexity of natural language processing. We used the information about technique correctness to update overall relationship confidences and to create a combined sorted list of is-a relationships. Providing more details on a posteriori evaluation is beyond the scope of this paper.

We evaluated the updated set of is-a relationships against the gold standard represented by a functional programming domain model created manually by a group of several domain experts independently of our method. The manually created domain model is employed in adaptive learning portal ALEF [14] as a part of educational activities at the Slovak University of Technology in Bratislava.

The gold standard consists of 162 relevant domain terms and 256 relationships in between. 128 of them are is-a relationships, 135 relevant domain terms are involved in is-a relationship (at least one incident edge is is-a relationship). It is important to note that the relevant domain terms from the gold standard correspond to relevant domain terms utilized by our method.

In order to evaluate the validity of generated is-a relationships, we borrowed from the work of Mädche and Staab [9]. In their work they proposed two layers of taxonomy comparison: lexical and conceptual. At lexical comparison level the terminological overlap between two taxonomies is computed. At the conceptual comparison level semantic structures of taxonomies are compared.

As the relevant domain term sets are intentionally identical, lexical comparison level is not relevant here. We assess the structure of the generated is-a relationships only. We follow their approach and adopt the definition of semantic cotopy of concept in taxonomy and slightly change it for our purpose:

$$SC(rdt, DM) = rdt_j \in DM : isa_{DM}(rdt, rdt_j) \vee isa_{DM}(rdt_j, rdt) \qquad (2)$$

where $SC$ is semantic cotopy of relevant domain term $rdt$ in the domain model $DM$. $isa_{DM}$ is is-a relationship in domain model $DM$. Semantic cotopy of a relevant domain term $rdt$ represents a set of all subsumed and supersumed relevant domain terms of $rdt$ in a given domain model $DM$.

We utilize the notion of semantic cotopy and we define taxonomic precision and taxonomic recall measures as follows:

$$P_T(DM_{retr}, DM_{rel}) = \frac{\sum\limits_{rdt \in DM_{uni}} |SC(rdt, DM_{retr}) \cap SC(rdt, DM_{rel})|}{\sum\limits_{rdt \in DM_{uni}} |SC(rdt, DM_{retr})|} \qquad (3)$$

$$R_T(DM_{retr}, DM_{rel}) = \frac{\sum\limits_{rdt \in DM_{uni}} |SC(rdt, DM_{retr}) \cap SC(rdt, DM_{rel})|}{\sum\limits_{rdt \in DM_{uni}} |SC(rdt, DM_{rel})|} \qquad (4)$$

where $P_T$ and $R_T$ are taxonomic precision and recall of domain model $DM_{retr}$ with respect of domain model $DM_{rel}$, respectively. $DM_{retr}$ represents domain model containing is-a relationships generated by our method ("retrieved") and $DM_{rel}$ represents the gold standard ("relevant"). $DM_{uni} = DM_{rel} \cup DM_{retr}$.

These are one of the strictest measures for quantitative comparison of two taxonomical structures as they fully consider transitivity of is-a relationship. If some erroneous is-a relationship occurs in the center of taxonomy, it affects not only incident relevant domain terms, but also all subsumed and supersumed relevant domain terms in a hierarchy.

Beside comparison of taxonomical structures, we further want to assess the method we proposed. Data that are used, i.e., learning object corpus that was processed, are an important factor of the method success rate. The method we proposed relies on the already defined set of relevant domain terms and it assumes that they occur within the text. However, we found out that some relevant domain terms as defined by the gold standard creators did not occurred in the learning objects in the form we were able to process (e.g., they occur in non-processable content such as pictures, or contain special symbols not properly recognized during preprocessing step). As a result, such relevant domain terms cannot be involved in any relationship. Thus, we computed taxonomic precision and recall considering both (i) the gold standard, and (ii) the gold standard without relevant domain terms that could not be found in the learning objects. The results depicting precision and recall measures together with F-measure (denoted as $P_T$, $R_T$, $F_T$ for (i) and $P'_T$, $R'_T$, $F'_T$ for (ii)) are presented in Fig. 1.

We consider the obtained results of the evaluation very reasonable. Precision of the generated is-a relationship is very promising, recall is a bit lower than expected. Deeper insight into the results revealed that recall is to a certain extent affected also by underlying text corpora that is a source for processing.

We identified several reasons that could have a negative impact on the results of evaluation:

– language - Slovak language is inflective language containing considerable number of exceptions in morphology, word formation and also in phrasing. Our method could benefit from more precise preprocessing including constituent identification and anaphora resolution. The language issue reflects into pattern detection and reduces number of correctly matched patterns. However, since the proposed method is language-independent (albeit different patterns for distinct languages need to be defined), we anticipate much better results for less complicated languages such as English. As the explanation phrases processing yielded less satisfactory results, we may also focus on patterns refinement by creating stricter matching criteria.

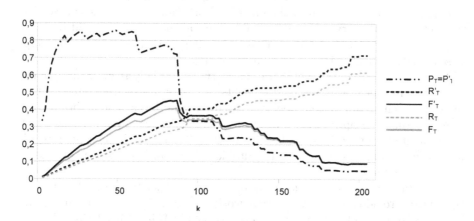

**Fig. 1.** Precision, recall and F-measure for top $k$ generated is-a relationships when compared against the gold standard. We considered two gold standard variants: containing all relevant domain terms from the domain model ($P_T$,$R_T$,$F_T$) and only relevant domain terms that were recognized in the text ($P'_T$,$R'_T$,$F'_T$).

- size of text corpora - size of functional programming learning objects corpora is much smaller than corpora, where similar tasks from related fields such as ontology learning were applied. The less content, the lower the chance to extract is-a relationships. This drawback can be potentially reduced by processing additional, student generated content created during learning. When considering collaborative learning web-based environments, external learning resources assigned by students may be processed. As a result, new relationships may be extracted that can enrich or enhance existing set.
- the gold standard accuracy - unlike other approaches, we could not compare the results against extensively used gold standards such as WordNet. In order to be objective, we need to admit that accuracy of the gold standard we used is not perfect. Although the precision of the manually created domain model (in comparison with an non-existent perfect domain model) most probably cannot be doubted, the recall may be disputable. As the gold standard is a result of small group of domain experts, it may consider some valid relationships to be incorrect (or disputable - other domain experts opinions could be not uniform), it may reflect into decreased precision, recall and F-measure of automatically generated is-a relationships.

## 4    Conclusions

Automated metadata discovery is very important for adaptive web-based educational systems since necessary semantic descriptions of underlying resources are very hard to create and maintain manually. By devising our method for hierarchical relationship discovery in educational texts we extend the state-of-the-art in the educational text processing and educational metadata acquisition. We built on the preceding research in lexico-syntactical analysis of text while adopting to and leveraging specifics of educational content.

Evaluation of the method in the functional programming course showed that the method yields very promising results that can be used as a solid basis for supporting content and metadata authors by offering them sets of relationships to select from while designing an adaptive course.

The issue of automated metadata discovery is especially relevant in dynamically changing social learning environments [14,15] with user-generated content (tags, comments, annotations) being created on daily basis. The ability to provide necessary descriptions in such environments is reduced even more and with no automated support for metadata creation they cannot fully benefit from advanced functionality such as recommendation or personalized search over user-generated content.

In our future work we will focus on discovery of other types of relationships. We aim to provide an integrated framework for educational content mining by following up the results of our previous works [12,13]. While considering adaptive web-based learning 2.0, we will also research how user-generated content can supplement content provided by teachers and to what extent user-generated content (and which forms) could facilitate and improve metadata discovery from text content that it is assigned to.

**Acknowledgments.** This work was supported by grants No. VG1/0675/11, VG1/ 0971/11 and it is a partial result of the Research and Development Operational Program for the projects SMART, ITMS 26240120005 and SMART II, ITMS 26240120029, co-funded by ERDF.

# References

1. Bisson, G., Nedellec, C., Canamero, L.: Designing clustering methods for ontology building: The Mo'K Workbench. In: Proc. of the First Workshop on Ontology Learning, OL 2000. CEUR-WS, vol. 31, pp. 13–19 (2000)
2. Brusilovsky, P., Knapp, J., Gamper, J.: Supporting teachers as content authors in intelligent educational systems. Int. Journal of Knowledge and Learning 2(3/4), 191–215 (2006)
3. Cimiano, P.: Ontology Learning and Population from Text: Algorithms, Evaluation and Applications. Springer (2006) ISBN: 978-0-387-30632-2
4. Cimiano, P., Hotho, A., Staab, S.: Learning concept hierarchies from text corpora using formal concept analysis. J. of Artificial Intelligence Research. 24, 305–339 (2005)
5. Cristea, A.I., de Mooij, A.: Designer Adaptation in Adaptive Hypermedia Authoring. In: Proc. of the Int. Conf. on Information Technology: Computers and Communications ITCC 2003, pp. 444–448. IEEE (2003)
6. Fotzo, H.N., Gallinari, P.: Learning generalization/specialization relations between concepts: application for automatically building thematic document hierarchies. In: Proc. of the 7th Conf. on Computer-Assisted Inf. Retr., CID, pp. 143–155 (2004)
7. Hearst, M.: Automatic acquisition of hyponyms from large text corpora. In: Proc. of the 14th Int. Conf. on Computational Linguistics, pp. 539–545. ACL (1992)
8. Henze, N., Nejdl, W.: A Logical Characterization of Adaptive Educational Hypermedia. New Review of Hypermedia and Multimedia 10(1), 77–113 (2004)
9. Maedche, A., Staab, S.: Measuring Similarity between Ontologies. In: Gómez-Pérez, A., Benjamins, V.R. (eds.) EKAW 2002. LNCS (LNAI), vol. 2473, pp. 251–263. Springer, Heidelberg (2002)
10. Sosnovsky, S., Brusilovsky, P., Yudelson, M.: Supporting Adaptive Hypermedia Authors with Automated Content Indexing. In: Proc. of 2nd Int. Workshop on Authoring of Adaptive and Adaptable Educ. Hypermedia, pp. 380–389 (2004)
11. Šaloun, P., Velart, Z., Klimanek, P.: Semiautomatic domain model building from text-data. In: Proc. of Sixth Int. Workshop on Semantic Media Adaptation and Personalization SMAP 2011, pp. 15–20. IEEE Computer Society (2011)
12. Šimko, M., Bieliková, M.: Automatic Concept Relationships Discovery for an Adaptive E-course. In: Barnes, T., Desmarais, M., Romero, C., Ventura, S. (eds.) Proc. of 2nd Int. Conf. on Educational Data Mining, EDM 2009, pp. 171–179 (2009)
13. Šimko, M., Bieliková, M.: Automated Educational Course Metadata Generation Based on Semantics Discovery. In: Cress, U., Dimitrova, V., Specht, M. (eds.) EC-TEL 2009. LNCS, vol. 5794, pp. 99–105. Springer, Heidelberg (2009)
14. Šimko, M., Barla, M., Bieliková, M.: ALEF: A Framework for Adaptive Web-Based Learning 2.0. In: Reynolds, N., Turcsányi-Szabó, M. (eds.) KCKS 2010. IFIP AICT, vol. 324, pp. 367–378. Springer, Heidelberg (2010)
15. Tvarožek, J.: Bootstrapping a Socially Intelligent Tutoring. Information Sciences and Technologies Bulletin of the ACM Slovakia 3(1), 33–41 (2011)
16. Zouaq, A., Nkambou, R.: Building Domain Ontologies from Text for Educational Purposes. IEEE Trans. Learn. Technol. 1(1), 49–62 (2008)

# An Evaluation Methodology for C-FOAM Applied to Web-Based Learning

Ioana Ciuciu and Yan Tang Demey

Vrije Universiteit Brussel, Brussels, Belgium
{iciuciu,yan.tang}@vub.ac.be

**Abstract.** C-FOAM (Controlled Fully Automated Ontology-based Matching Strategy) is one of the seven matching strategies of the Ontology-based Data Matching Framework (ODMF). As a composition of the matching algorithms at the levels of string, lexical and graph, C-FOAM interprets and compares the user input against the ontology graph, and produces a matching score. Based on this score, C-FOAM (1) provides the similarity score between the user knowledge and the knowledge stored in the knowledge base, which can be used to evaluate a learner; and (2) retrieves and recommends similar patterns (learning materials) from the knowledge base to the learner. This paper presents a generic evaluation methodology and discusses the evaluation results while using C-FOAM in a Web-based personalized, collaborative and intelligent learning tool in the medical domain.

**Keywords:** ontology-based data matching, ontology, evaluation methodology, recommender, web-based learning.

## 1 Introduction and Motivation

C-FOAM (Controlled Fully Automated Ontology-based Matching Strategy) was designed and implemented under the Ontology-based Data Matching Framework (ODMF). It is the most hybrid of all the ODMF strategies, combining different other ODMF algorithms and strategies, summing up their complexities but also their advantages. The initial goal of ODMF was to serve as a tool to calculate competency gaps between learning materials, a person profile (e.g. CV) and a job or a task description in the domain of human resource management (HRM), in the context of the EC FP6 Prolix project. Later on, C-FOAM was applied in a collaborative eLearning setting in the medical domain in order to evaluate medical prentices and to recommend personalized learning materials to them, according to their knowledge and gaps. This was done in the context of EC FP6 3D Anatomical Human (3DAH) project.

The focus of this paper is the evaluation of C-FOAM and the evaluation results. The rest of the paper is organized as follows: Section 2 presents the related work of the paper. Section 3 is the paper background. Section 4 illustrates the case study of this paper. The evaluation methodology is described in Section 5. Section 6 discusses the evaluation results. We conclude and present the future work in Section 7.

E. Popescu et al. (Eds.): ICWL 2012, LNCS 7558, pp. 142–151, 2012.
© Springer-Verlag Berlin Heidelberg 2012

## 2    Related Work

The related work of this paper refers to the evaluation methodologies (particularly of ontology-based data matching) on the one hand and on the other hand it refers to eLearning techniques applied to the medical (anatomical) domain in a collaborative setting. Let us discuss the two aspects in the following paragraphs.

*Evaluation Methodology.* A generic evaluation methodology does not exist. They are often application specific. Program evaluation methodologies [1,2] are often used to systematically collect information about the activities/processes, characteristics and outcomes of programs in order to make a justification on a program or a process, improve its effectiveness, and draw decisions for future programing.

Utilization-focused evaluation [3] is used to executing evaluations that are practical, ethical and accurate. For example, the evaluation methods in [4] contain activities on using non-experimental methods to evaluate social programs.

More specifically, purpose oriented evaluation methodologies [5], which contain the methodologies of formative evaluation, pertaining evaluation and summative evaluation, are used respectively on evaluating process, the value before the implementation, and the outcome of a method/system.

Our evaluation method adapts the principles in the methodologies for program evaluation and purpose oriented evaluation in order to evaluate ontology-based matching strategies (C-FOAM in the case of this study).

*Collaborative Web-based Learning.* This has been a hot topic at the level of worldwide[1] and European[2,3] initiatives during the past few years.

The SIMPEL[4] project developed guidelines [6] for sustainable eLearning in SMEs. Among the phases of the vocational training proposed by SIMPEL representing an eLearning strategy there is the 'Evaluation and improvement' phase. This phase is researched in our paper with a focus of one of the open questions mentioned in the SIMPEL guidelines regarding the benefits of the Semantic Web to creating personal learning environments. The need for an evaluation strategy is also reported by the MENON[5] network in [7]. Hamburg [8] proposes a set of eLearning practices for SMEs based on communities of practice.

The ELQ-SME[6] project reports on the insufficient knowledge and adaptation to real needs and expectations of the trainees [9]. The European Commission

---

[1] http://www.theglobeandmail.com/report-on-business/
how-to-bake-innovation-into-the-corporate-dna/article1574586/
(Accessed 3 July 2012).
[2] http://ec.europa.eu/enterprise/initiatives/ipr/training/
index_en.htm (Accessed 3 July 2012).
[3] http://esf-mam.net/moodle2/ (Accessed 3 July 2012).
[4] http://www.ier-nl.net/IER-SIMPEL-GuidelinesHTMLpage.htm
(Accessed 3 July 2012).
[5] http://www.menon.org/index.php?option=com_content&task=
view&id=14&Itemid=12 (Accessed 3 July 2012).
[6] http://nettskolen.nki.no/in_english/elq-sme/index.html (Accessed 3
July 2012).

recommendations regarding eLearning in SMEs [10] encourage partnership, shared knowledge, learning materials reuse, creation of learning communities and a common language for the purpose of learning.

The PC Med Learner introduced in this article addresses all the above mentioned recommendations by providing an eLearning system that is: (1) intuitive; (2) based on collaborative knowledge sharing; (3) based on the communities of practice and Semantic Web[7] technologies; (4) ontology-based; and (5) user-oriented.

A number of works have been done lately in the field of personalized delivery of learning materials for eLearning. They mainly focus on capturing the user context in order to be able to recommend the right content, in the right form, to the right learner. Examples are as follow, just to name a few:

Baloian et al. [11] proposed a recommender system, which suggests multimedia learning material based on the learner's background preferences and available software/hardware. This approach faces the inconvenient of information overloading. Schmidt [12] proposes an approach for capturing the context of the learner based on the semantic modeling of the learner's environment. Yu [13] proposes a method for context-aware learning content provisioning for ubiquitous learning.

The approach presented in this paper goes beyond the state of the art, in that it focuses on capturing and evaluating the user knowledge, rather than context and environment. Regarding the evaluation methodology and the delivery of the learning materials, they are based on the ontology-based data matching methodology, which contributes from the community (e.g. members multiple organizations, which share a common goal) knowledge.

## 3    Background

The *knowledge* in this study (e.g., learning materials) is grounded in natural language, following the paradigm of Developing Ontology Grounded Methodology and Applications (DOGMA) [14,15]. In DOGMA, the ontology is two-layered, in order to make the reuse of facts easier. It is separated into 1) a *lexon* base layer (binary facts represented in a semi-natural language) and 2) a *commitment* layer (defining constraints on the committed lexons). For example, the following lexon ⟨*human anatomy, lower limb, has part, part of, muscle* ⟩ means the fact that "in the context of human anatomy, the lower limb has as part the muscle and muscle is a part of the lower limb". A commitment (constraint) on this lexon can be, e.g. "every muscle belongs to at most one lower limb". The commitment language is specified in a language such as OWL[8] or SDRule [16].

The learner's knowledge is matched against the knowledge stored in the knowledge base using an *ontology-based data matching strategy*. The ontology-based data matching framework (ODMF, [17]) contains matching algorithms originally for: 1)

---

[7] http://www.w3.org/2001/sw/ (Accessed 3 July 2012).

[8] Web Ontology Language (OWL), http://www.w3.org/TR/owl-ref/ (Accessed 3 July 2012).

matching strings; 2) matching lexical information, such as using WordNet and 3) matching concepts in an ontology graph. There are several ontology-based data matching strategies in ODMF. Each strategy contains at least one graph algorithm.

In this study the C-FOAM matching strategy is applied in order to mine the user knowledge for accurate retrieval of learning materials. C-FOAM is described below.

*C-FOAM.* The C-FOAM strategy starts with combining two character strings representing context-object pairs. If the two character strings of the contexts are the same, data objects that belong to the same object type will be compared. To resolve the actual data objects stored in the ontology, the combination of both the context term and the object term is used.

In case the data object is denoted by several terms, a lexical lookup is done taking synonyms into account. If a given object term could not be found in the ontology and lexicon, the best fitting data object is returned from the ontology using fuzzy matching based on string similarity (e.g. using JaroWinklerTFIDF algorithm [18,19]). The distance (similarity) between the given data object and the most similar data object in the ontology should be above a certain threshold, which is set in the application configuration of our tool. If the data object is found based on fuzzy matching, then a penalty percentage will be used on the confidence value for the matching score. A penalty is a weight that is used to reduce a score. Its value varies from 0 to 1. Suppose we want to use 0.5 as a penalty value for adjusting a score of 0.8, and we use multiplication as the means of reduction. We will then get a score of 0.4 at the end.

C-FOAM is based on two main modules: (1) the *Interpreter* module and (2) the *Comparator* module, as shown in Fig. 1. The interpreter module makes use of the lexical dictionary, WordNet [20], a domain ontology and a string matching algorithm to interpret end users' input. Given a term that denotes either (a) a concept in the domain ontology, or (b) an instance in the ontology, the interpreter will return the correct concept(s) defined in the ontology or lexical dictionary, and an annotation set. The comparator can use any combination of the different graph algorithms to produce a composite score.

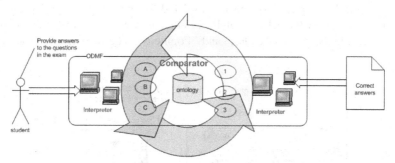

**Fig. 1.** C-FOAM

Users may select the matching algorithms of string, lexical and graph for C-FOAM. Let us select JaroWinklerTFIDF as the string matching algorithm, Word-Net synonym finder as the lexical matching algorithm and LeMaSt (lexon matching algorithm, [17]) as the graph matching algorithm to run our use case.

## 4    Case Study

We illustrate and evaluate C-FOAM in the context of a Web-based tool for collaborative learning in the medical domain [21]. The tool is a computer-aided learning system called Personal and Collaborative Medical Learner (PC Med Learner). PC Med Learner evaluates employees of a medical enterprise and recommends personalized learning materials for competency improvement based on the learners' knowledge (competencies) and a competency ontology. The medical domain was selected as proof of concept, but the approach can be adapted to any domain.

PC Med Learner is based on three pillars: (1) a collaborative knowledge base (KB), storing different parts of knowledge from the domain experts and the learning materials (e.g. images, videos, text) annotated with the competency ontology (expressed both in natural language (lexons) and RDF(S)); (2) a 3D interactive anatomy browser, for visualization; and (3) an ontology-based data matching strategy (C-FOAM), which mines and examines the user knowledge by computing the similarity scores.

We have tested our approach on a learning scenario, as follows:

- Step 1) the computer   shows a highlighted zone in the anatomy browser;
- Step 2) the student gives text input - the anatomical structure he considers to be highlighted;
- Step 3) the matching engine finds the similarity scores (between student input and the KB);
- Step 4) PC Med Learner calculates the matching score;
- Step 5) repeat Step 1, 2 and 3 as many times as wanted;
- Step 6) PC Med Learner calculates the final score;
- Step 7) PC Med Learner shows the correct answers for the answers with final score ≠ 100%;
- Step 8) the computer finds and suggests the learning materials to the student, based on the annotations in the KB. The eight steps are illustrated in Fig. 2.

Five anatomical structures have been considered for the test, with the corresponding learning materials in the KB: "Patella", "Gluteus Medius", "Acetabular Labrum", "Extensor Hallucis Longus Tendon" and "Popliteus". The learning materials for the

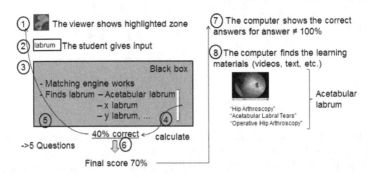

**Fig. 2.** Web-based collaborative learning scenario

five anatomical structures consist of scientific publications and books, images and videos. The annotations corresponding to the learning materials are transformed into lexons (299 lexons in total in the lexon base) in order to be processed by the C-FOAM algorithms. The final goal is to find the final score and to suggest learning materials.

A test was simulated composed of five questions with correct and wrong answers to analyze the behavior of the system when evaluating a student. In order to test PC Med Learner, the user answers range from correct ("patella"),    typo error ("patela"), synonym ("kneecap"), partially correct ("labrum"), partially wrong ("plantaris", "disease"). The typo error case is solved using the string matching algorithm in C-FOAM. The case concerning synonyms uses the lexical matching algorithm in C-FOAM. For the last two questions, the answer was supposed to be wrong, that means 0% matching. However, the results found by C-FOAM are different from 0% (we obtained 0.30% for "plantaris" and 0.11% for disease). This is because C-FOAM finds semantic links between these concepts in the ontology graph, although these two concepts are different. Actually, "plantaris" and "popliteus" are both muscles of the "Posterior Compartment of the Lower Leg". Whilst for "disease", there are many annotated learning materials related to the diseases of the "popliteus", therefore, even if the concepts do not match, the score should be different from zero.

## 5    Evaluation Methodology

Our evaluation method adapts the principles in the methodologies for program evaluation [1] and purpose oriented evaluation [5] in order to evaluate ontology-based matching strategies (C-FOAM in the case of this study).

The basic principle in the program evaluation methodologies is that the evaluation methodology needs to help PC Med Learner to improve its services and/or functions, and, also help to ensure that it is delivering the right services and/or functions. The evaluation method needs to help PC Med Learner to improve the matching results, and to ensure that it is delivering the correct list of recommended learning materials.

The principles in the purpose oriented evaluation methodologies are as follows:

- It must be able to determine what information exists in the process of PC Med Learner, which is important so that the engineers can analyze the processing information;
- We need to use it to test and collect continuous feedback in order to revise the process, which is also important;
- It must have precondition analysis and post-condition analysis of the evaluated systems;
- End users must be able to judge the outcome of a system based on the evaluation methodology.

Accordingly, we have developed an evaluation method that can be used to evaluate any of the matching strategies from ODMF (see Fig. 3).

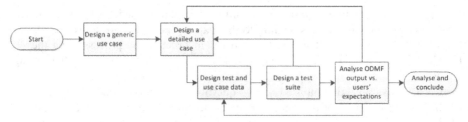

**Fig. 3.** A generic ODMF matching strategy evaluation method

The steps of designing a generic use case and design a detailed use case are the preparation steps. We scope the problem in the step of designing a generic use case and initialize clear requirements for a viable use case. Terms and tests are gathered and analyzed from the test beds' materials. The output of this step is a report containing a generic use case. The problem is specified in the step of designing a detailed use case. We specify the design terms from the previous step by specifying types of information (e.g. process information) used by PC Med Learner. We also analyze preconditions and post-conditions of the use case. The output of this step is a report containing a detailed use case.

In the step of design test and evaluation data, we design the test data that are used by PC Med Learner (not by end users). The output of this step is a report containing a list of test and evaluation data. In the step of design a user test suite, a knowledge engineer designs a user test suite, the data of which need to be provided by an expert.

The output of this step is a report analyzing PC Med Learner outputs vs. experts' expectations, a comparison, which can be a figure or a data sheet. In the step of analyze and conclude, we analyze the comparison report that is produced in step 5 and draw valuable conclusions.

## 6    Evaluation Results

In what follows, we evaluate the results of PC Med Learner against experts' expectations. Note that, in our problem setting, there is only one expert. In the future, we will study how to involve multiple experts in the evaluation cycle. We use the satisfactory rate in order to evaluate PC Med Learner. This rate is calculated based on the similarity scores generated by PC Med Learner and the experts' expected relevance levels in the test suite. The relevance levels provided by the experts need to be correctly interpreted in order to calculate the satisfactory rate. The average score provided by PC Med Learner is 0.5, the maximum score is 1 and the minimum score is 0. Therefore, the scale of the similarity scores is [0, 0.2]. We equally split it as follows: Relevance Level 5 – similarity score > 0.8; Relevance level 4 – similarity score > 0.6 and <= 0.8; Relevance level 3 – similarity score > 0.4 and <= 0.6; Relevance level 2 – similarity score > 0.2 and <= 0.4; Relevance level 1 – similarity score <= 0.2.

If a similarity score falls in the range, then we say that the similarity score is "completely satisfied". If it does not fall in the range, then we need to calculate the bias. The bias of this evaluation set is calculated as the minimum value of low boundary bias and high boundary bias, which are calculated as shown below:

```
IF (Similarity Score < Low Boundary)
    THEN Low Boundary Bias = Low Boundary - Similarity Score
    ELSE Low Boundary Bias = Similarity Score - Low Boundary
IF (Similarity Score < High Boundary)
    THEN High Boundary Bias = High Boundary - Similarity
Score
    ELSE High Boundary Bias = Similarity Score - High
Boundary
```

For instance, if the similarity score for relevance level 3 is 0.41, then the low boundary bias is $0.41 - 0.4 = 0.01$ and the high boundary bias is $0.6 - 0.41 = 0.19$. The bias is the smallest value in $\{0.01, 0.19\}$, therefore 0.01. If the bias is less than 0.2 (one interval), then we say that this similarity score is "satisfied". If it is more than 0.2 and less than 0.4 (two intervals), then we say it its "not really satisfied". All the remaining scores are considered "completely unsatisfied".

**Table 1.** Conclusion of evaluating C-FOAM

| PC Med Learner Using C-FOAM |
| --- |
| **1. Difficulty of managing the required knowledge resource** |
| C-FOAM is the most difficult of all the ODMF strategies because it is the composition of matching algorithms and/or other matching strategies (e.g. LeMaSt & JaroWinkler). |
| **2. Difficulty of using the strategy** |
| Usage level-basic to professional. Knowledge engineers need to know how to configure the penalty scores and understand the meaning of these scores. |
| **3. Satisfactory rate** |
| Satisfactory rate is 78% (completely satisfied and satisfied, see Fig. 4). |
| **What affects the matching score** |
| Any factors that affect the selected algorithms are counted as the factors that affect the similarity scores. In addition, the two penalty values are the factors that affect the final scores. |
| **Advantage** |
| C-FOAM contains the advantages of all the combined algorithms and strategies. |

For the particular use case described in this paper, the results showing the PC Med Learner similarity scores versus experts' expected scores (see Fig. 4) are as follows: out of nine questions, three similarity scores completely satisfy the experts' expectations (out of which there is one similarity score that is perfect match); four scores satisfy the users' expectation; only two scores do not really satisfy the experts' expectation. There are zero completely unsatisfied similarity scores.

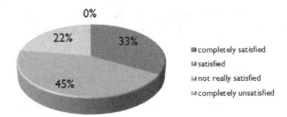

**Fig. 4.** C-FOAM similarity scores vs. expert expected scores

The satisfactory rate is 78%: 33% completely satisfied + 45% satisfied. The evaluation results are recorded in Table 1.

We show the satisfactory score to the evaluator as a conclusion. It is important that we also show the process information and reasoning, for instance, which score for which question is satisfied and why it is satisfied. Based on the information and the generated reasons, the evaluator can provide valuable suggestions to the system provider or the knowledge manager in order to enhance the strategies in the future. The satisfactory score internal process is not completely visualized here due to page limitations.

## 7    Conclusion and Future Work

In this paper, we have presented the evaluation methodology for the C-FOAM ontology-based data matching algorithm. The evaluation methodology shows a satisfactory rate of 78% when comparing the results of the Web-based learning tool (C-FOAM based) with the experts' expectations. The evaluation results depend on the expertise level of the expert who is responsible for providing the expectations. Different experts may lead to different judgments on the outcome of the Web-based learning tool. The outcome may be changed when its knowledge base (i.e. lexons) is updated. The quality is therefore dependent on the domain expert responsible of the management of the knowledge base.

These aspects, a verification on the user improvement and different statistics capturing the learner's individual characteristics and learning behavior will be taken into account during the recommendation phase in the future work of this research.

Our goal of using the approach of using C-FOAM for eLearning is to demonstrate the usefulness of the matching strategies in ODMF. Those strategies have been applied in different domains, such as human resource management and smart environment applications. In the future, we will work on a use case of matching images in the OSCB project using C-FOAM.

**Acknowledgements.** This study was partly supported by the Open Semantic Cloud for Brussels (OSCB) project. The authors would like to thank all the EC FP6 Prolix project and EC FP6 3D Anatomical Human project partners for their contribution.

# References

1. Patton, M.Q.: Qualitative Research and Evaluation Methods, 3rd edn. Sage Publications, London (2002) ISBN 0-7619-1971-6
2. CDC: Developing Process Evaluation Questions, At the National Center for Chronic Disease Prevention and Health Promotion, Healthy Youth, Program Eval. Resources (2009)
3. Stufflebeam, D.L., Madaus, G.F., Kellaghan, T.: Utilization-Focused Evaluation, Evaluation in Education and Human Services, vol, vol. 49, pp. 425–438. Springer, Heidelberg (2006)
4. Blundell, R., Costa Dias, M.: Evaluation methods for non-experimental data. Fiscal Studies 21( 4), 427–468 (2000)
5. Bhola, H.S.: Evaluating "Literacy for development" projects, programs and campaigns: Evaluation planning, design and implementation, and utilization of evaluation results. UNESCO Institute for Education, Hamburg, Germany (1990)
6. Hall, T., et al.: Strategies, Models, Guidelines to use eLearning in SMEs. The SIMPEL project's position on the development of sustainable eLearning in SMEs (2008)
7. Aceto, S., et al.: Benchmarking Policies and Initiatives in support of e-learning for Enterprises in Europe. Final benchmarking report. MENON Network (2007)
8. Hamburg, I., Engert, S., Anke, P., Marin, M.: Improving e-learning 2.0-based training strategies of SMEs through communities of practice. In: WBE 2008, Innsbruck, Austria, pp. 200–205 (2008) ISBN: 978-0-88986-724-6
9. Paulsen, M.F.: Successful E-learning in Small and Medium-sized Enterprises. The Norwegian School of Information Technology (2009)
10. Daelen, M., et al.: E-learning in Continuing Vocational Training, particularly at the workplace, with emphasis on Small and Medium Enterprises. Final Report (EAC-REP-003). European Commission, Directorate General for Education and Culture (2005)
11. Baloian, N., Galdames, P., Collazos, C.A., Guerrero, L.A.: A Model for a Collaborative Recommender System for Multimedia Learning Material. In: de Vreede, G.-J., Guerrero, L.A., Marín Raventós, G. (eds.) CRIWG 2004. LNCS, vol. 3198, pp. 281–288. Springer, Heidelberg (2004)
12. Schmidt, A., Winterhalter, C.: User Context Aware Delivery of E-learning Material: Approach and Architecture. J. of Universal Comp. Sc. 10(1), 28–36 (2004)
13. Yu, Z., Nakamura, Y., Zhang, D., Kajita, S., Mase, K.: Content Provisioning for Ubiquitous Learning. IEEE Pervasive Computing 7(4), 62–70 (2008)
14. Meersman, R.: Ontologies and Databases: More than a Fleeting Resemblance. In: ISMIS 1999 (1999)
15. Spyns, P., Tang, Y.: An ontology engineering methodology for DOGMA. J. of Applied Ontology 3(1-2), 13–39 (2008)
16. Tang, Y., Meersman, R.: SDRule Markup Language: Towards Modeling and Interchanging Ontological Commitments for Semantic Decision Making. In: Handbook of Research on Emerging Rule-based Languages and Technologies: Open Solutions and Approaches. IGI Publishing, USA (2009) ISBN: 1-60566-402-2
17. Tang, Y., et al.: Towards Evaluating Ontology Based Data Matching Strategies. In: RCIS 2009, pp. 137–146 (2010)
18. Jaro, M.A.: Probabilistic linkage of large public health data files. Statistics in Medicine 14, 491–498 (1995)
19. Winkler, W.E.: The state of record linkage and current research problems. Statistics of Income Division, Bureau of Census, Washington DC, USA (1999)
20. Fellbaum, C.: WordNet: an electronic lexical database. MIT Press, Cambridge (1998)
21. Ciuciu, I., Tang, Y.: A Personalized and Collaborative eLearning Materials Recommendation Scenario Using Ontology-Based Data Matching Strategies. In: Meersman, R., Dillon, T., Herrero, P. (eds.) OTM 2010. LNCS, vol. 6428, pp. 575–584. Springer, Heidelberg (2010)

# Modeling the Knowledge Domain of the Java Programming Language as an Ontology

Aggeliki Kouneli[1], Georgia Solomou[1], Christos Pierrakeas[1,2], and Achilles Kameas[1]

[1] Educational Content, Methodology and Technology Laboratory (e-CoMeT Lab),
Hellenic Open University (HOU), Greece
[2] Dept. of Computer Science in Administration and Economy
Technological Educational Institute (TEI) of Patras, Greece
{kouneli,solomou,pierrakeas,kameas}@eap.gr

**Abstract.** Java is a very popular programming language and many study programs in Informatics worldwide include courses particularly designed for its learning. It is considered as the best paradigm for introducing students with object-oriented programming and concepts. Considering Java's popularity, we initially make an attempt to model this language by using a quite expressing and rich knowledge representation structure, like is ontology. Our aim is to capture the semantics of Java concepts in a way that would render them utilizable by intelligent e-learning applications. Because the construction of an ontology is not an easy task, we follow very specific steps when building the Java ontology. We then take advantage of an already implemented model describing the structure of learning outcomes and combine it with our ontology, with a view to offer a more effective way in organizing the course of Java in the Hellenic Open University.

**Keywords:** ontologies, java, programming languages, distance education, learning outcomes.

## 1 Introduction

In distance education, the delivery of knowledge is accomplished through learning management systems or other similar in scope applications and mechanisms. The extension of these systems with semantic-aware technologies could benefit both learners' and tutors, by providing them with intelligent applications and tools.

Ontologies are a very popular knowledge representation technique that provides applications with the ability to process semantics. They enable knowledge reuse and sharing across applications and groups of people and appear with many applications in various fields. Especially in the field of education, ontologies have been used for representing knowledge domains, teaching strategies, student profiles, as well as for competence and learning goal's modeling [1]. Besides, as stated by Mizoguchi et al. in [6], ontologies render education systems smart and reflective, deliver explicit knowledge, standardize the vocabulary of a knowledge domain, and make communication easier and knowledge reusable.

E. Popescu et al. (Eds.): ICWL 2012, LNCS 7558, pp. 152–159, 2012.

Having these in mind, through this work, we make an attempt to create an ontology with the view to capture all knowledge delivered by a distance learning course. Our goal is to incorporate the resulting model in an appropriately designed intelligent mechanism able to process education-specific ontologies. Such a mechanism, capable of combining and inferring knowledge, could provide both learners and tutors with alternative and more effective paths in learning.

In section 2 we make reference to the ontologies' exact definition and to a methodology for building ontological representations. Section 3 gives an outline of all concepts and relationships used for modeling the Java programming language. In section 4 we apply this ontology in order to create and organize the learning outcomes for the course of Java. Conclusions follow, in Section 5.

# 2    About Ontologies

In this section we propose a methodology, for creating well-structured ontological representations.

## 2.1    Definition and Structure

The computer and information science borrows the word 'ontology' from Philosophy and assigns to it a more specific and technical definition. Gruber in [3] defines an ontology as *"an explicit specification of a conceptualization"* and outlines its utilization as a means to represent a specific domain of knowledge or discourse in a more typical way.

Ontologies, representing the knowledge and capturing a particular domain's semantics, constitute a formalism for perceiving and processing information, sharing knowledge, allowing its reuse and thus enabling communication between heterogeneous and distributed systems.

The basic structural elements of an ontology are a) *classes*, representing the concepts related to a specific domain of knowledge, b) *properties*, expressing types of interactions among the domain concepts and further divided into *object properties* and *datatype properties*, c) *instances*, representing specific entities that are members of a class and d) *axioms* that express true facts about the ontology entities.

## 2.2    A Methodology for Building Ontologies

The task of building an ontology requires significant effort and collaboration between ontology engineers and domain experts. Many different methodologies, describing the process of developing an ontology have been proposed in literature, albeit none of them has been standardized yet. Some well-known methodologies that mainly apply to the development of domain ontologies are proposed in [2], [7] and [8].

Based mostly on the quite popular approach of Noy and McGuinness, described in [7], we adopt the following five phases for building our domain ontology (see Fig. 1):

1. *Specification*: This is the starting phase where all necessary knowledge needs to be specified by experts of the knowledge domain based on various characteristics about the resulting ontology, like the level of formality, its purpose and scope, the intended end-users, etc.

2. *Conceptualization*: During this phase the important terms of the knowledge domain are enumerated, finally leading to the design of the domain's concept map.

3. *Implementation*: Includes the transformation of the previously created conceptual model into a formal computable model, by utilizing a typical language, like OWL.

4. *Evaluation*: The phase of evaluation implies the ontology's check in terms of clarity, consistency and reusability.

5. *Documentation and maintenance*: The last phase, where it is necessary to document all implemented concepts and relations in the ontology for future reference and maintenance reasons.

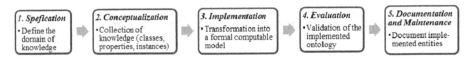

**Fig. 1.** The five steps in the ontology building methodology

# 3    The Java Ontology

By following our ontology building methodology, we constructed an ontological model for the knowledge domain of the Java Programming Language. The ontology was constructed by the aid of Protégé and we were based on the most recent version of the Web Ontology Language and W3C standard, OWL 2[1].

## 3.1    Concepts in Java

As a first step, we collected the main concepts of Java based on the formal guide of the Java programming language, known as the *The Java Tutorial*, and provided by the Oracle Corporation[2].The main top concept, derived from this conceptual analysis, is captured by the *JavaElement* class, whereas other top concepts are ii) *Keyword* and iii) *LiteralValue*.

As is shown in Fig. 1, the *JavaElement* class is divided into twelve different subclasses, each one describing key elements and concepts met in the vocabulary and syntax of the Java programming language. More specifically, the *DataType* class encompasses the notion of data types in Java, such as *primitive* data types and *non-primitive (reference)* data types an consists of the respective classes. The latter is further divided into all possible structures for expressing a reference data type in Java, that is *Array*, *Class* and *Interface*.

---

[1] http://www.w3.org/TR/owl-primer/
[2] http://docs.oracle.com/javase/tutorial/

**Fig. 2.** Part of the class hierarchy of the implemented ontology about the Java programming language.

Operators constitute another basic element, met not only in Java, but also in any other programming language, and so a class with this name was included in our model. Operators were grouped into the following categories (transformed into classes) and set under the *Operator* class: *ArithmeticOperator*, BitwiseOperator,

*AssignmentOperator*, *ConditionalOperator*, *ShiftOperator*, *UnaryOperator* and *RelationalOperator*.

Variables are another essential element in a programming language and its notion in Java has been expressed via a separate class (*Variable*). Since Java contains four types of variables, i.e. *instance* variables, *class* variables, *local* variables and *parameters*, we took consideration for all these by setting respective classes in our model (*ClassVariable, InstanceVariable, LocalVariable* and *Parameter*) and placed them as children of the main *Variable* class.

The class *Statement* represents the smallest standalone element of a Java program. Under this class, three subclasses were created (*ControlFlowStatement, DeclarationStatement, Expression*) reflecting the various types of statements that a programmer may use in order to write source code in Java. The *ControlFlowStatement* class is further refined in a number of more specific types, each represented by a subclass and populated with a set of individuals corresponding to keywords used for their declaration.

As far as the Java methods are concerned, they are captured by the *Method* class that contains the following subclasses: *AbstractMethod, FinalMethod, ClassMethod* and *InstanceMethod*. Furthermore, provision for all object-oriented concepts, such as *object, constructor, interface, class* and *packages* has been made in our ontology.

The *Exception* class stands for a specific element in Java, which expresses problematic and erroneous situations when compiling or running a Java program. All exceptions that cannot be caught are considered members of the *UncheckedException* class. This is further divided into *RunTimeException* and *Error* classes. A runtime exception aims to capture all those exceptions that are internal to the application, in contrast to an external error case, which is included in the the *Error* class. Any other exception belongs to the *CheckedException* class which is sibling of *UncheckedException*.

Finally, one of the top classes in the Java ontology is *Keyword*, expressing reserved words with a special use within a program. Those keywords can be visibility modifiers (members of the *Modifier* class) or even terms that control the access privileges of various Java elements (members of the *AccessControlModifier* class). On the other hand, *LiteralValue* is a top class containing literals that have a special meaning for the Java compiler.

### 3.2     Description of Properties

The various types of interaction among ontology concepts are expressed through respective relations, known as *properties*. Properties are divided into *datatype properties* which link an individual to a particular value and *object properties* that are relationships between individuals.

We have defined 7 properties. More specifically, the pair-wise inverse properties *isSubclassOf* and *isSuperclassOf* are used to declare a parent-child relation between two Java classes. They are irreflexive, meaning that no individual can be related to itself via such a property. *hasMember* and *isMemberOf* are also inverse properties and used for relating Java interfaces, methods or packages. The *instance* property connects a Java class with its members, whilst the *hasModifier* property correlates any individual with a certain modifier. Finally, to determine the particular relation of a Java concept with a reserved keyword, the *isDefinedByKeyword* property is used.

## 4     The Role of the Java Ontology in Defining Learning Outcomes

All courses of the Hellenic Open University (HOU), which is an educational institution in Greece, specialized in lifelong learning, have been designed according distance learning principles. This means that each piece of its provided educational material has been directly related to learning outcomes. Learning outcomes play an important role in the instructional design process and especially in when organizing a distance learning course. According to [5], learning outcomes are statements that show *"what a learner is expected to know, understand and be able to demonstrate after completion of a learning process"* and should accompany any educational material serving the purposes of a study program offered from distance.

The knowledge domain of the Java programming language is covered by the HOU's course module, of 'Software Engineering', which is offered as part of the HOU's study program in Informatics.

In a previous work, described in [4], an ontological model has been introduced for representing learning outcomes' structure and classification. This model has been successfully applied for the reconstruction of 32 learning outcomes referring to Java *Operators*, *Arrays* and *Statements*.

Through this work, we took advantage of the aforementioned model and augmented it so as to include our proposed ontology about Java. Our aim was to enhance this mixed schema with the possibility to process, organize and correlate learning outcomes according to their subject and thus lead to the creation of effective learning paths.

For expressing the subject of a learning outcome (i.e., the particular concept of the knowledge domain to which this learning outcome refers) the datatype property *subject* was used in the previous introduced model. Consequently, any request for classifying or correlating learning outcomes according their subject, was actually based on a string match process. By augmenting this model with the Java ontology, *subject* was transformed into an object property. Consequently, each reference to a Java concept in the combined schema was replaced by its corresponding entity in the Java ontology. As a result, a richer network of relationships among learning outcomes was produced, being thus possible to retrieve and infer more semantically enriched results.

To determine the possibilities of this new, enhanced ontological model we run some semantic queries against it, through the DL query tab of Protégé. For example, if we want to obtain all learning outcomes concerning *Statements* in Java, we need to run the following query: `subject some Statement`. This query, expressed in the Manchester OWL Syntax, returns 9 results (see Fig. 3), each one being an instance of the *LearningOutcome* class. A more careful look, though, reveals that none of the retrieved individuals explicitly refers to Java *Statements* but to narrower in meaning concepts. For example, individual PA_PLH24_E2_24 refers to *Control Flow Statements* (see Fig. 3). Nevertheless, the retrieval of this particular individual becomes possible because *Control Flow Statement* has been declared as a subclass of the *Statement* class. The same holds for all other obtained results.

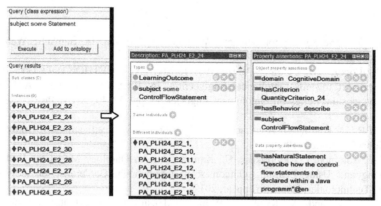

**Fig. 3.** Searching for learning outcomes concerning Java *Statements* (*left*). Ontological representation of instance PA_PLH24_E2_24 in Protégé (*right*).

# 5    Conclusions and Future Work

What we presented here was an ontology representing the most important notions in the Java programming language. To this end, we had in mind both the official Java Tutorial and the extent to which this domain is covered by the introductory Java course offered by the study program in Informatics of HOU.

This representation was implemented by following very specific steps (methodology). The resulting model captures the most important aspects of Java as classes and correlates them through a number of relationships. The aim of this approach was to produce a semantically enriched representation about a so popular knowledge domain in the field of Informatics, with a view to further exploit it within intelligent e-learning applications. For the time being, and in order to examine our ontology's added value in deploying intelligent applications, we combined it with an already implemented ontological schema describing learning outcomes. As a result, we managed to enhance this model in terms of learning outcomes discovery and retrieval.

Our future goal is to feed this combined schema in an appropriately designed e-learning application, able to handle semantics. By this way, we could probably enhance and alleviate the process of designing a course, by allowing ontology-based systems to process knowledge and lead to more effective decisions.

**Acknowledgement.** The research described in this paper was partly funded by the National Strategic Reference Framework programme 2007-2013, project MIS 296121 "Hellenic Open University".

# References

1. Devedžić, V.: The Setting for Semantic Web-based Education. In: Semantic Web and Education. Springer, New York (2006)
2. Fernandez-Lopez, M., Gomez-Perez, A., Juristo, N.: METHONTOLOGY: from Ontological Art towards Ontological Engineering. In: Proceedings of the AAAI 1997 Spring Symposium Series on Ontological Engineering, pp. 33–40. AAAI Press, Stanford (1997)
3. Gruber, T.R.: A Translation Approach to Portable Ontology Specifications. J. Knowledge Acquisition 5, 199–220 (1993)
4. Kalou, A., Solomou, G., Pierrakeas, C., Kameas, A.: An Onotlgy Model for Building, Classifying and Using Learning Outcomes: In International Conference on Advanced Learning Technologies, Rome (to appear, 2012)
5. Kennedy, D., Hyland, A., Ryan, N.: Writing and using Learning Outcomes. Bologna Handbook, Implementing Bologna in your Institution, C3. 4-1, 1–30 (2006)
6. Mizoguchi, R., Ikeda, M., Sinitsa, K.: Roles of Shared Ontology in AI-ED Research: Intelligence, Conceptualization, Standardization and Reusability. In: International Conference on Artificial Intelligence in Education, pp. 537–544 (1997)

7. Noy, N., McGuinness, D.: Ontology Development 101: A Guide to Creating Your First Ontology. Stanford Knowledge Systems Laboratory Technical Report KSL-01-05 and Stanford Medical Informatics Technical Report SMI-2001-0880 (2001)
8. Uschold, M., King, M.: Towards a Methodology for Building Ontologies. In: Proc. Of Workshop on Basic Ontological Issues in Knowledge Sharing in Conjuction with International Joint Conference on Artificial Intelligence, Montreal, Canada (1995)

# Towards Universal Game Development in Education

## Automatic and Semiautomatic Methodologies

Javier Torrente[1], Ángel del Blanco[1], Ángel Serrano-Laguna[1],
José Ángel Vallejo-Pinto[2], Pablo Moreno-Ger[1], and Baltasar Fernández-Manjón[1]

[1] Department of Software Engineering and Artificial Intelligence,
Complutense University of Madrid,
C/ Profesor José García Santesmases sn, 28040 Madrid, Spain
{jtorrente,angel.dba,pablom,balta}@fdi.ucm.es
aserrano@e-ucm.es
[2] Department of Computer Science, University of Oviedo, Asturias, Spain
vallejo@uniovi.es

**Abstract.** Serious games are increasingly being used in education to support the development of skills that future professionals and citizens require. However, the inclusion of games in the curricula can threaten the universal right to education for students with disabilities if they are not designed to be accessible. In this paper we discuss the need for tools that assist educators and educational content providers in producing games that are equally accessible for all. The goal is to minimize the cost and effort needed for introducing accessibility in serious games. We discuss to what extent the process of making a serious game accessible can be automated and supported by software tools that minimize human intervention. We conclude that there is a set of common accessibility barriers, especially those related to interaction and physical disabilities, that can be addressed systematically in a high proportion and therefore could be dealt with by software. Other problems, especially those more close to structure, storyboard and design, still need direct intervention from the game authors, but could be facilitated with appropriate methodologies and auditing tools.

**Keywords:** accessibility, educational games, serious games, universal design.

## 1 Introduction

Education is a universal right, and this adds an imperative to consider accessibility as a high priority requirement whenever new technologies are brought into the educational process. Otherwise we may be threatening the equality of opportunities for all students. This should be the case of educational games (a.k.a. serious games), which are rapidly gaining acceptance, and will probably become a relevant educational tool for enthusiastic teachers in the next few years [1]. But actual level of accessibility in videogames (both commercial and educational) is still low compared to other kind of technologies and digital static contents like the web [2].

E. Popescu et al. (Eds.): ICWL 2012, LNCS 7558, pp. 160–169, 2012.
© Springer-Verlag Berlin Heidelberg 2012

One of the main arguments to explain the few attention that accessibility receives in games is that it means an extra burden for the developers and an increase factor of the investments. Firstly, design complexity increases. Games are intricate, heterogeneous and highly interactive applications that provide unique experiences depending on who is playing and what title is being played [3]. Designing an engaging, appealing and meaningful game for a wide number of users is an art that requires loads of expertise and creativity. When designers have also to cope with the special needs of users with disabilities the difficulty of the job increases substantially. And secondly, developers are faced with extra implementation challenges. Dealing with accessibility usually requires integrating (or even developing) complex and expensive technologies, such as text-to-speech or voice recognition. And it may even require producing special hardware (e.g. adapted game controllers).

All these overheads may be affordable for large entertainment game development projects, and even then most entertainment games tend to ignore accessibility concerns. However, educational games do not typically have large budgets, with many initiatives being led by enthusiastic educators and organizations with little resources. To avoid leaving accessibility concerns out of these projects, making accessible game-based educational content should be as seamless and cost-effective as possible. To accomplish this goal, we advocate for making the process as automated and straightforward as possible, limiting human intervention when possible in order to alleviate the cost overhead. To achieve the objective, it would be necessary to integrate accessibility tools and technologies in educational games development software, thus facilitating the implementation of accessibility features. This would facilitate design by providing game authors (i.e. educators) with reusable components and interfaces that are ready to use, resulting in significant savings.

This paper aims to answer the question of to what extent the introduction of accessibility in educational games can be automated. We build on our previous experiences developing accessibility solutions for educational games that we have tried to integrate in the eAdventure game platform.

## 2    Related Work

### 2.1    Approaches to Accessibility in Games

Traditionally, accessibility in games has been addressed individually in most of the cases, either adapting a specific title to meet the needs of a particular user profile [4–6], or developing games for a specific community of users with disabilities [7–9]. Audio games, for example, are designed for users with a visual disability [10]. However, other approaches have adopted a more general and holistic perspective, proposing frameworks and methodologies that consider the needs of different profiles of users that could also be applied to different types of games [11].

For example, in [12] the authors propose Unified User Interface Design, a methodology for designing universally accessible games where game tasks are devised without considering a specific modality or interaction device. In further design phases, alternative interaction methods are designed for each task depending on the needs of the target audience. Therefore the game design is extensible, facilitating the subsequent inclusion of accessibility features to cater for the needs of other users.

## 2.2   The eAdventure Educational Game Platform

eAdventure [13] (formerly <e-Adventure>) is a game authoring platform especially oriented to education[1] [14]. Although eAdventure's capabilities support the creation of a variety of 2D games, it was originally focused on point-and-click adventure games. This decision was driven by the consideration that these are the most appropriate genres for education because of their strong narrative underpinnings and predominance of reflection over action [15]. From an accessibility perspective, this genre does not pose barriers such as time pressure or fast-paced action, although a variety of barriers related to modality remains (they are highly visual, require moving a mouse for identifying objects, etc.).

There are two components in eAdventure: a game editor used to create the games and a game engine, used to run them. The typical workflow is to create and test the games with the editor, and then use editor's exportation features to produce a distributable package bundling all the assets that the game engine needs to process the games, which are a set of XML documents that describe the game and art resources (images, sounds, videos, etc.). The game editor includes education-oriented features and tries to simplify the game creation process as much as possible.

The game universe in eAdventure games is defined by composing elements of different types: characters, items, active areas, and the game scenarios (a.k.a. scenes), which are composed by a 2D background image and a set of interactive elements.

## 3     Experiences Developing Accessible Interfaces with eAdventure

We have used eAdventure to explore the automatic generation of accessible interfaces for two games that we present in this section as case studies. Upon the eAdventure source code, we built components that adapted the user interface depending on a given user profile. In this section we will elaborate on the level of automation achieved in each case. For each case, we have evaluated the usability from the end user's perspective, by asking different users to interact with each type of resulting accessible interface. Further technical details on the implementation of these interfaces can be found on previous publications [17, 18].

The official eAdventure distribution complies out-of-the-box with a certain level of accessibility for users with hearing disabilities, as all the information provided by audio can also be displayed with text. It is also accessible for users with a cognitive disability as it integrates an adaptation engine that allows game authors to tailor the game experience to each user capabilities (e.g. alternative contents or puzzles or skipping complex parts). For that reason, our work has focused more on improving accessibility for users with visual and motor disabilities.

---

[1] `http://e-adventure.e-ucm-es`

### 3.1    Fully Automatic Adaptation of Interfaces - The case of 1492

In a previous work we have described a prototype built upon eAdventure v1.0 [18] that supported alternative modalities through a combination of input and output modules. Two user profiles were considered: blind users and users with a motor disability. Among the wide variety of levels of visual impairments, we characterized the blind user profile as users that needed the aid of screen reading software to use a computer. We considered users with a motor disability as those needed of using voice recognition software to interact with a computer due to reduced or lack of mobility. Both user profiles encounter barriers when interacting with point-and-click applications as they are not able to use the mouse.

The game author was only allowed to enable or disable the modules during the exportation process. All the adaptation to the user profile was performed automatically by analyzing the game description XML files and art resources (see Fig. 1).

The results were two new modalities which had common inner workings. The interaction was performed through short commands formulated in natural language (e.g. "grab the notebook" or "talk to the character"). An interpreter received the commands, executed them if they were correct, and provided feedback about the results using the appropriate channel for the active user profile (auditory for the blind user through a built-in text-to-speech engine, text for the user with a motor disability). Blind users introduced the commands using the keyboard, while users with a motor disability used speech.

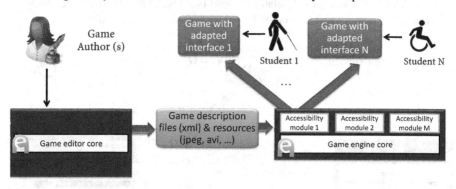

**Fig. 1.** Basic accessibility architecture. Accessibility was provided by specific input/output modules integrated with the engine, which are activated when the game was exported.

Command processing was directed by a regular grammar combined with a fixed list of synonyms for relevant verbs (actions) and nouns (interactive elements). The regular grammar was automatically generated from the description of the game, taking the actions defined for the interactive elements available in each game scenario. During game play, the number of actions and interactive elements available in eAdventure games is susceptible to change at any time as they depend on the value of a number of variables that vary dynamically according to the rules the game author specifies (this is the mechanism that eAdventure provides to define the game structure and flow). To deal with this issue the grammar was rebuilt each time an internal variable changed and also each time the scenario was reloaded.

This approach was applied to the 1492 game (available from the eAdventure website). It was evaluated by two users, one of each profile. Users were able to interact with and complete the accessible version of the game in the experiment (around 20 minutes of game play), but the system presented several usability flaws. The most important was that the user's vocabulary did not always match the system's vocabulary, defined by a list of synonyms that included at least 4 equivalent words for each keyword. As a result, command recognition accuracy was low, having little chances of succeeding if the game had taken longer to complete. Natural language processing techniques, combined with a well-defined ontology containing a wider vocabulary may overcome this type of issues. Such ontology could effectively cover most of the vocabulary related to actions, as these are common for most eAdventure games (e.g. grab, use, talk, examine, etc.). However, the nouns used for the game items cannot be anticipated as these are user-defined, requiring the game author to provide additional synonyms. Other usability problems found may be solved by improving the implementation of the system (e.g. delays in the auditory feedback generated).

### 3.2    Semiautomatic Adaptation - The Case of "My first day at work"

Building upon the experience of the 1492 game, we conducted another experiment which resulted in the game "My first day at work", developed in collaboration with Technosite, a company of the ONCE (National Organization for the Blind in Spain) group. We refined the process to address the limitations found (see Fig. 2) by improving flexibility of the accessibility features that now could be configured with the game editor.

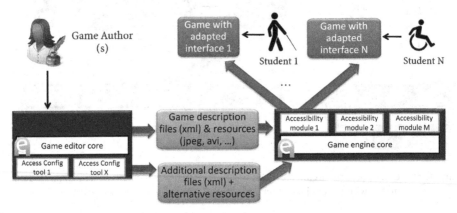

**Fig. 2.** Improved architecture and workflow. The accessibility features are now configurable from the editor to match different user profiles. The editor also produces automatically additional description files and resources.

In addition to the blind and motor disability profiles, a new user profile was considered: users with low vision. Colleagues from Technosite identified the adaptations this profile needed, which included screen and text magnification and use of a high contrast color scheme. Low vision users were expected to have problems to inspect the game scenes and find interactive elements as for them shapes and images blur with the background of the scene or with other elements.

We tried to keep the human work needed to accommodate the needs of these users to a minimum. The approach followed was to develop a low vision mode in the game engine. We started by developing an alternative rendering mode that improved the contrast of the interactive elements over the background of the game scenarios. This kind of technique has been applied to improve the accessibility of other games in the past [9], although focus has been placed on a single title instead of trying to build a generic and reusable system. This kind of adaptation introduced the novelty of modifying the rendering pipeline (i.e. how the game is painted), in contrast to blind users and users with a motor disability that required adapting the modality. The game engine automatically applied a light green filter to the interactive elements which increased their brightness and a dark purple filter to decrease the brightness of other areas, facilitating the identification of those interactive elements. Font sizes and colors used for cursors, buttons and menus were also automatically adapted.

However further adaptations were needed. Through early prototypes we found out that some scenes could not be adapted by automatically applying a filter, like those using images with text embedded. In these cases, authors should produce alternative graphic resources and include them in the game manually.

Although "My first day at work" was focused on meeting the needs of the three bespoke profiles (blind, motor disability and low vision), we also tried to make it accessible to users with cognitive disabilities (e.g. Down and Asperger syndromes). We wanted to explore the kind of adaptations these users require, who usually experience difficulties to understand complex language, memorize large pieces of information or present attention deficit disorders.

Dealing with these problems is much more complicated and there is little room for automation. The eAdventure adaptation engine was used to provide alternative paths in the game with different levels of difficulty, or alternative versions of text intensive components such as conversations.

The game was evaluated by 10 users with a disability (3 blind users, 4 with low vision and 3 with reduced mobility). Apart from minor usability problems that could be solved by researchers during the experience, all users were able to complete the game (around 60 minutes of game play).

## 4    Discussion

In the case studies presented the kind of adaptations that were required to meet users' needs varied across profiles. These adaptations affected diverse aspects of the game and were achieved with different levels of automation.

### 4.1    Level of Automatic and Semi-automatic Adaptation

Table 1 shows a summary of the adaptations performed. Adaptations related to the modality, how the user interacts with the game or perceives the game feedback are prone to be automated (e.g. interfaces for blind users and users with reduced mobility). This does not mean that solutions are straightforward, but that current state-of-the-art in technologies like text-to-speech or voice recognition allows building interfaces that can be used by a high number of users. Once these interfaces have been built, they can be reused across different games with little extra work.

**Table 1.** Summary of adaptations performed for each profile. Table reflects what aspect of the game were affected and the level of automation achieved.

| Profile | Aspect | Adaptation (s) | Automation |
|---|---|---|---|
| Blind | Interaction / modality | New interaction and adapted return of information | High |
| Motor disability | Interaction / modality | New interaction | High |
| Low vision | Interface / rendering pipeline | High contrast rendering filters, magnification, alternative images and color schemes | Medium |
| Cognitive disability | Game design and content | Lessened difficulty of puzzles, alternative version of texts | Low |

Other types of disability require adapting how the game is rendered (e.g. users with low vision). The process can be automated to some extent, as the rendering pipeline in game engines can be configured to apply transformations over specific elements, like applying filters, using alternative color schemes (for example to deal with color blindness) enlarging images or providing a magnifier. However, there is a point where alternative versions of art resources may be needed, having a greater impact on the cost of the game. In the case of the game "My First day at work", it was necessary to produce 647 art resources in first instance, including images, animations for characters, videos and sounds. To make it accessible for users with low vision it was needed to produce alternative versions of 53 art resources, an increase of 7,57%. Although this value is not very high it could increase exponentially if more profiles were considered (e.g. users with color blindness), so it is important to keep the number of manually crafted alternative resources as low as possible.

### 4.2    Non-automatic Adaptations and Auditing Tools

Other accessibility profiles (e.g. those related to cognitive disabilities) may not be subject to automatic adaptation and therefore are harder to address. The adaptations they require are related to the design of the game, which is difficult to analyze and modify without requiring the intervention of the game author. Some AI techniques could be explored to solve some of the problems, like using automatic text analysis to simplify the language used if the user has a cognitive disability, but it is unlikely to achieve similar levels of automation to those previously described in section 3.

In these cases other approaches could be followed. Game authors could be provided with tools to perform accessibility auditing over the games, following the guidelines of the W3C ATAG recommendation [19]. These tools would work as accessibility evaluation tools for the web, searching the game structure for potential accessibility barriers (e.g. complex language, too many interactions available in a game scene, use of time pressure, etc.).

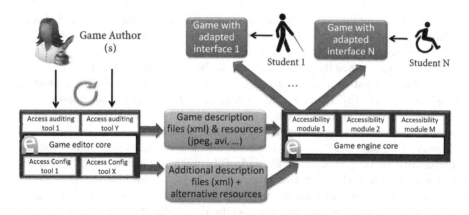

**Fig. 3.** Final architecture and workflow. Auditing and feedback tools are added, forming an iterative process of accessibility improvement.

An additional benefit of inspection and auditing tools is that they are educational, as they can recommend solutions to the game author and give further details about why problems encountered may endanger access for users with disabilities. The results of the auditing process could be presented in a human readable report, but could also be displayed in their context while the game runs to maximize the educational value. However, developing auditing tools is only feasible if the structure of the game is explicitly defined, as it is in eAdventure and most game authoring software, but not in game engines or frameworks where the game structure emerges or is implicitly defined. The final diagram of editing and running accessible games would look like the one Fig. 3 shows.

## 5    Conclusions and Future Work

Educational games should be as accessible as possible to avoid a potential digital divide when they are brought into the classroom. To achieve this it is necessary to reduce the overhead needed to make the games accessible, especially in education where budgets are usually limited. Cost reduction can be reached by integrating accessibility tools in game development software. In this paper we have gathered different previous experiences creating accessible games with reusable tools, analyzing the strengths and limitations of each technical approach.

Based on these experiences, we have summarized the lessons learned during the process, ending up in the proposal of an architecture and workflow for the creation of accessible educational games. The focus of the study has been to identify what kind of accessibility adaptations can be performed automatically or semi-automatically, as these are the ideal approaches to keep the cost down.

We conclude that there are adaptations that can be performed mostly automatically, (e.g. generation of alternative interfaces) and have a significant impact in the accessibility of the games. Other adaptations can be performed semi-automatically, like having the tool try to create automatically alternative graphic resources (using filters and special rendering effects), and having a human provide alternative resources only in those cases when the automatic process was not enough.

On the contrary, when these processes cannot be automated, or when there is need for additional insight on the performance of the automated processes, we propose developing accessibility auditing tools to educate, detect barriers and propose solutions to improve the process of introducing accessibility. Nonetheless this is just a proposal that we expect to develop further in future research.

Finally, it should be noted that these automatic adaptations were designed specifically for educational games, where the tradeoff between cost and accessibility is critical, and accessibility should not be ignored. We consider that entertainment games may also benefit from this type of automatic and semi-automatic approaches, even though the game industry tends to favor specific developments for each game, due to the rapidly changing technology required to be competitive in that space.

**Acknowledgments.** We acknowledge the next organizations that have partially supported this work: the Spanish Ministry of Science and Innovation (grant no. TIN2010-21735-C02-02); the European Commission, through the Lifelong Learning Programme (projects "SEGAN Network of Excellence in Serious Games" - 519332-LLP-1-2011-1-PT-KA3-KA3NW and "CHERMUG" - 519023-LLP-1-2011-1-UK-KA3-KA3MP) and the 7th Framework Programme (project "GALA - Network of Excellence in Serious Games" - FP7-ICT-2009-5-258169); the Complutense University of Madrid (research group number GR35/10-A-921340) and the Regional Government of Madrid (eMadrid Network - S2009/TIC-1650).

# References

1. Johnson, L., Adams, S., Cummins, M.: NMC Horizon Report: 2012 Higher Education Edition. The New Media Consortium, Austin (2012)
2. Bierre, K., Chetwynd, J., Ellis, B., Hinn, D.M., Ludi, S., Westin, T.: Game Not Over: Accessibility Issues in Video Games. In: 11th International Conference on Human-Computer Interaction (HCII 2005). Lawrence Erlbaum Associates, Inc. (2005)
3. Gee, J.: Good Video Games and Good Learning: Collected Essays on Video Games, Learning and Literacy (New Literacies and Digital Epistemologies). Peter Lang Publishing (2007)
4. Atkinson, M.T., Lawrence, A.E.: Making the mainstream accessible: redefining the game. In: Sandbox Symposium 2006, ACM SIGGRAPH Symposium on Videogames, Boston, Massachusetts, pp. 21–28 (2006)
5. Allman, T., Dhillon, R.K., Landau, M.A.E., Kurniawan, S.H.: Rock Vibe: Rock Band® computer games for people with no or limited vision. In: Proceedings of the 11th International ACM SIGACCESS Conference on Computers and Accessibility, pp. 51–58. ACM (2009)
6. Yuan, B., Folmer, E.: Blind hero: enabling guitar hero for the visually impaired. In: Proceedings of the 10th International ACM SIGACCESS Conference on Computers and Accessibility, pp. 169–176. ACM (2008)

7.  Savidis, A., Stamou, A., Stephanidis, C.: An Accessible Multimodal Pong Game Space. In: Stephanidis, C., Pieper, M. (eds.) ERCIM UI4ALL Ws 2006. LNCS, vol. 4397, pp. 405–418. Springer, Heidelberg (2007)

8.  Gutschmidt, R., Schiewe, M., Zinke, F.: Haptic Emulation of Games: Haptic Sudoku for the Blind. In: PETRA 2010 Proceedings of the 3rd International Conference on PErvasive Technologies Related to Assistive Environments, Samos, Greece (2010)

9.  Westin, T.: Game accessibility case study: Terraformers – a real-time 3D graphic game. Presented at the (2004)

10. Friberg, J., Gärdenfors, D.: Audio Games: New perspectives on game audio. In: ACM SIGCHI International Conference 2004, Singapore (2004)

11. Westin, T., Bierre, K., Gramenos, D., Hinn, M.: Advances in Game Accessibility from 2005 to 2010. In: Stephanidis, C. (ed.) HCII 2011 and UAHCI 2011, Part II. LNCS, vol. 6766, pp. 400–409. Springer, Heidelberg (2011)

12. Savidis, C., Stephanidis, A.: Unified User Interface Design: Designing Universally Accessible Interactions. International Journal of Interacting with Computers 16, 243–270 (2004)

13. Torrente, J., Del Blanco, Á., Marchiori, E.J., Moreno-Ger, P., Fernández-Manjón, B.: <e-Adventure>: Introducing Educational Games in the Learning Process. In: IEEE Education Engineering (EDUCON) 2010 Conference, pp. 1121–1126. IEEE, Madrid (2010)

14. Moreno-Ger, P., Burgos, D., Sierra, J.L., Fernández-Manjón, B.: Educational Game Design for Online Education. Computers in Human Behavior 24, 2530–2540 (2008)

15. Dickey, M.D.: Game Design Narrative for Learning: Appropriating Adventure Game Design Narrative Devices and Techniques for the Design of Interactive Learning Environments. Educational Technology Research and Development 54, 245–263 (2006)

16. Torrente, J., Moreno-Ger, P., Fernández-Manjón, B., Sierra, J.L.: Instructor-oriented Authoring Tools for Educational Videogames. In: 8th IEEE International Conference on Advanced Learning Technologies (ICALT 2008), pp. 516–518. IEEE, Santander (2008)

17. Torrente, J., Vallejo-Pinto, J.Á., Moreno-Ger, P., Fernández-Manjón, B.: Introducing Accessibility Features in an Educational Game Authoring Tool: The Experience. In: 11th IEEE International Conference on Advanced Learning Technologies ICALT 2011, pp. 341–343. IEEE (2011)

18. Torrente, J., Del Blanco, Á., Moreno-Ger, P., Martínez-Ortiz, I., Fernández-Manjón, B.: Implementing Accessibility in Educational Videogames with <e-Adventure>. In: First ACM International Workshop on Multimedia Technologies for Distance Learning, MTDL 2009, pp. 55–67. ACM Press, Beijing (2009)

19. W3C: Authoring Tool Accessibility Guidelines, 2.0 (2012), http://www.w3.org/TR/ATAG20/

# Towards Social Learning Games

Élise Lavoué

Université de Lyon, CNRS
Université Jean Moulin Lyon 3, MAGELLAN, LIRIS, UMR5205
Elise.Lavoue@univ-lyon3.fr

**Abstract.** In this paper, we focus on a new type of emerging learning games: Social Learning Games (SLG). We define SLG as games that enhance learning by offering educational contents according to a learning scenario and by supporting a community that offers condition for social learning. Leaning upon this analysis, we propose a model of SLG, which relies on five components: decision-making, contextual discussions, social capital, educational feedback and dashboard. We highlight the learning possibilities offered by this design approach, such as stimulating learners throughout decision-making process and cultivating learners' engagement in the game. This theoretical contribution has been integrated into a Social Learning Game called CIBUS dedicated to the field of entrepreneurship. We present the specific structure of the learning scenario that allows the regulation of the progress of the learners in the game, by giving freedom in the participation in the community. Finally, we explain how the design approaches we propose allow supporting three levels of learning involved in the game: individual, within the group, and within the community.

**Keywords:** Social Learning Game, Game-based Learning, Design approach.

## 1 Introduction

This paper focuses on a new type of games, called Social Learning Games (SLG). This term has emerged in recent years but is not yet well defined. Some works refer to Multiplayer Learning Games (MLG), others to Massively Multiplayer Online Role-Playing Games (MMORPG), and others to Social Games (SG). So it is still unclear what are Social Learning Game (SLG) and what are their interests in the educational domain. Our approach relies on the initiative to combine two ways of learning: game-based learning and social learning. These two types of learning can be interconnected and involve each other, so as to enhance the learning of both pedagogical content and collaborative skills.

The first part of this paper is dedicated to the study of MLG and MMORPG, to identify their strengths and weaknesses. This study allows us to identify the characteristics of SLG. In the second part, we propose a model of SLG based on five components. We show their interests for learning purposes. This approach is illustrated by a SLG called CIBUS, which has been developed to learn the basis of the field of entrepreneurship. We highlight the challenges to take up for designing such a game, principally the regulation of the progress of the players. We detail the specific structure of scenario we have developed. We finally detail the three levels of learning that have to be considered (individual, group and community) and the way our approach allows it.

E. Popescu et al. (Eds.): ICWL 2012, LNCS 7558, pp. 170–179, 2012.
© Springer-Verlag Berlin Heidelberg 2012

# 2    Learning in MLG and Social Interaction in MMORPG

## 2.1    Multiplayers Learning Games (MLG)

Michael and Chen [1] define serious games as "*games that do not have entertainment, enjoyment, or fun as their primary purpose*". Serious games can be applied to a broad spectrum of application areas, e.g. military, government, educational, corporate, healthcare [2]. According to Squire and Jenkins [3] "*What we do know is that games, simulated environments and systems, etc., allow learners to experience situations that are impossible in the real world for reasons of safety, cost, time, etc.*". Learning Game (LG) is a specific type of serious games that has learning as main objective, unlike political or advertising games. Game-Based Learning (GBL) has the potential of improving training activities and initiatives thanks to its engagement, motivation, role-playing, and repeatability (failed strategies can be modified and tried again). These games have proven to be useful to provide learners with pedagogical content in a ludic or/and realistic way [3].

However most of LG are played individually and learners evolve in the game making right or wrong decisions, without interaction with "real" learners. One way to enhance learning and engagement in the game is to allow collaboration by proposing a multiplayer environment. Actually, we observe the emergence and success of online multiplayer games in the world [4] and even in education [5]. Multiplayer Learning Games (MLG) usually immerse the players in a virtual 2D or 3D environment and propose collaborative activities [6]. This type of game can support development of a number of various skills: strategic thinking, planning, communication, collaboration, group decision-making and negotiating skills [7, 8]. Players learn not only from the game, but from each other [5].

But these games allow collaboration only within a limited number of students inside the virtual world. Furthermore, collaboration occurs according to a predefined learning scenario, often regulated by a teacher. Learners so lack freedom of choice and of possibility of interaction with other learners. We think that it is one of the main reasons why students tend to consider Computer-Based Learning Environments as unexciting [9]. We think that the participation in a large learning community can arouse the learners' engagement. That is why we were interested in studying Massively Multiplayer Online Role-Playing Games (MMORPG) that are nowadays predominantly played by digital natives.

## 2.2    Massively Multiplayer Online Role-Playing Game (MMORPG)

Massively Multiplayer Online Games (MMOG) are games that are played online by hundreds of players simultaneously. Educational MMOG often works as tournaments and are based on competition between groups of students like in [10]. The most popular type of MMOG, and the sub-genre that pioneered the category, is the Massively Multiplayer Online Role-Playing Game (MMORPG). An MMORPG is "*an immersive 3D worlds where hundreds or thousands of players connect simultaneously from all over the world in order to meet each other in a simulated reality*" [11]. Many

MMORPGs offer support for in-game guilds or clans, that are groups of players coming together to share knowledge, resources, manpower to reach common goals. For example, World of Warcraft [11] is a MMORPG set in a fantasy world (like The Lords of the Rings). The aim of the game is to conduct a series of missions, so-called quests, with progressive levels of difficulty.

There is much international scientific research in the sociological and psychological field that clearly demonstrates how this kind of game changes significant characteristics of the players; for example, the ability to be a group, to take on leadership, to manage roles and to interact in order to achieve a common goal [12, 13]. We agree with Egenfeldt-Nielsen [14] that, "*in a socio-cultural perspective, video games are the tools for constructing a viable learning experience, but not the learning experience per se. Video games mediate discussion, reflection, facts, and analysis facilitated by the surrounding classroom culture and the student's identity. In other words, video games are interesting not for their content but for the way new explorations initiate negotiations, constructions, and journeys into knowledge*". We can think interaction in a MMORPG as a condition for social learning [15]. In fact, social learning is based on the mutual aid between players like in any other online community [16, 17]. Players exchange ideas, solve problems and create relationships, by the way of technologies like chat or forum. Online social networks have proven that people can be highly motivated to become part of a community activity, participate in group activities and form committed behavior patterns [18]. Social Games (SG) like Zynga's Farmville and others are surpassing traditional gaming in terms of ongoing participation.

So MMORPG help to learn collaborative skills, foster learners' engagement in the game and create dynamic learning opportunities due to the community. Role-playing incite players to help each other to solve problems, by using their different knowledge and capabilities. But their use is rather limited in the educational domain, since they do not propose educational content and are not based on a learning scenario.

# 3    A model of Social Learning Game

In this section, we propose a generic model of Social learning Games (SLG) that answers the following issue: how to combine social and educational aspects in a same game? This model aims to encourage learners to participate in the learning community in a relevant manner, i.e. related to the educational content of the learning game.

## 3.1    A generic Model of SLG

We define Social Learning Games (SLG) as games that enhance learning by offering educational contents according to a learning scenario and by supporting a community that offers condition for social learning. We propose on Fig. 1 a model of SLG based on five main components that connect the learning community to the learning game. We think that decision-making is the main component that makes the link between the two aspects of SLG. The other components help the process of decision-making.

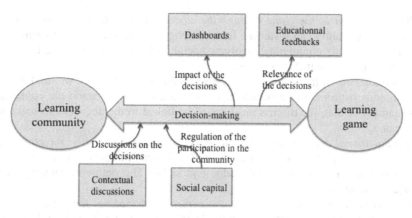

**Fig. 1.** Components of a Social Learning Game (SLG): the elements are presented according to their proximity with the extremities of the double arrow

— *Decision-making*: According to Steven Johnson, the basic feature of videogames is that they force us to make decisions [20]. In a SLG, decisions are made in a social context and the discussions between learners within the community can help them to make the decisions in the game.
— *Contextual discussions*: the players have to be able to have contextual discussions so as to progress in the game, for example to make a decision, or to exchange on knowledge to acquire.
— *Social capital*: it is based both on the level of participation in the community and on the relevance of this participation according to the decisions made in the learning game. It is the most important indicator associated with a player and has to work like a reward system.
— *Educational feedbacks*: it is very important to present to learners information on the relevance of the decisions they made, so that they can learn from their errors and acquire the knowledge of the game.
— *Dashboards*: dashboards have to present indicators that give information to learners both on their participation in the community and on the impact of their decisions at different levels: at the individual level, at the level of the players that have the same role and at the level of all the community. They so support and enhance a monitoring and a reflexivity process for learners [19] involved in collaborative and social activities.

## 3.2   Learning through Our Model of SLG

There is a reciprocity link between the game and the community: on the one hand, playing the game incites learners to participate in the community to discuss on the educational contents, to make decisions in the game and to share their knowledge; on the other hand, participating in the community helps learners to progress in the scenario of the game and to learn the associated knowledge. These characteristics involve different ways to enhance learning in SLG, among which we highlight:

- *The engagement in the game through the community*: we think that the participation in a community can foster the learners' engagement in the learning game. The interactions in the community involve a social dynamic that can incite learners to play the game, even if it is "serious".
- *The mutual help in the community to make decisions in the game*: we think that the discussions within the community can help learners to understand the contents of the game. For that, the discussions have to be linked to the decisions to make into the game.
- *The educational contents to initiate discussions in the community*: the contents of the game, more particularly the decisions to make, can initiate discussions between learners that have different knowledge and skills. The online community is the place for these discussions.
- *The freedom in the community and the control in the game*: the learners benefit from both the controlled progress in the learning scenario and the free discussions in the community. The association of these two components offers an adequate level of regulation.

## 4     An Example of SLG: CIBUS

The model of SLG proposed in the previous section has been integrated into a Social Learning Game called CIBUS. CIBUS is based on the mechanisms of entrepreneurship and distinguishes four roles: investors, shareholders, company managers and politicians. We first illustrate our model with this game. We then show the design choices that have been made to answer the following issues: how to regulate the progress of the learners in the predefined learning scenario, while the participation in the community is free? How to support the individual learner, the groups of learners within collaborative activities and the learning community in a same game?

### 4.1     General Presentation of CIBUS

As illustrated on Fig. 2, the interface of CIBUS presents the game (learning scenario and decisions), the collaboration functionalities and the dashboards at once. In order to achieve a clear and functional interface for the players, the interface has been decomposed into these three thematic frames. It is very easy to navigate from one to another via a slider, which allows keeping game data loaded and ready to display. We present the three frames of the CIBUS game according to our model of SLG:

- *Scenario/Decisions*: it is composed of three main elements: (1) the learning *scenario* displays the progress of the simulation and the learners have to make decisions according to different types of modules (see part 4.2); (2) the *social capital* is calculated on the number of events created, the number of messages per discussion, the rating of the messages, the influence of the individual decision of a collective decision; (3) *educational feedbacks* on the decisions are given at different levels, according to the structure of the learning scenario detailed in part 4.2 (feedbacks on one or several decisions inside a phase, global feedbacks after a phase, a final feedback on the way the game was conducted by all the players).

— *Collaboration*: at any time learners can create an event to start a contextual discussion in a forum. The invited learners can participate by indicating the aim of their message so as to make it contextual: introduction to the discussion, question, affirmative answer, negative answer, neutral, idea proposal, intention of decision or a search for information. This aims to provoke a reflection when posting a message and the others can better understand the message. Furthermore, learners can rate the messages written by the others (with a like or a dislike).

— *Dashboards*: there are three dashboards: a *decision dashboard* (summary of the impact of the decisions made: e.g. number of decisions made by phase, number of decisions that made the indicators increase or decrease), a *collaboration dashboard* (summary and statistics on the collaboration: e.g. number of messages, number of rates) and a *general dashboard* (summary and general statistics of the game).

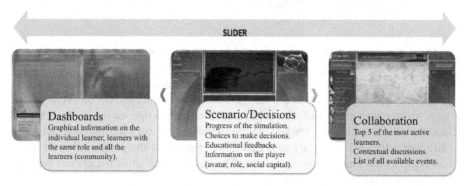

**Fig. 2.** The three interfaces of the Social Learning Game CIBUS

## 4.2    The Players Regulation in CIBUS

In this part, we describe the structure of the learning scenario chosen for the CIBUS game to regulate the progress of the learners in the simulation, taking into account the free participation in the community. In fact, some players may progress more slowly if they participate more in the community. The structure of the scenario is composed of four elements: phases, buffer states, modules and allocation of roles and phases.

— *Phase*: a phase corresponds to a set of knowledge the learners have to acquire. A phase can be dedicated to a role, to several roles or to all players. According to the phase, the learners are asked to collaborate with the learners of their team (e.g. the board meeting of a company), of their role (e.g. all the company managers), or with learners that have other roles. For example in Fig 3, the phases 1, 2 and 8 are carried out in parallel by all the learners, in order to learn the basic notions on the role: Phase 1 has two roles is common (investors and shareholders), whereas Phases 2 and 8 are dedicated to a single role (respectively company managers and politicians). Then, Phase 3 is common to all players. They are finally separated into several parallel phases (4, 5, 6, 7); each role is represented in each phase. The learners can collaborate, collect information from other roles, negotiate and exchange the knowledge they have acquired during the first phases of the scenario.

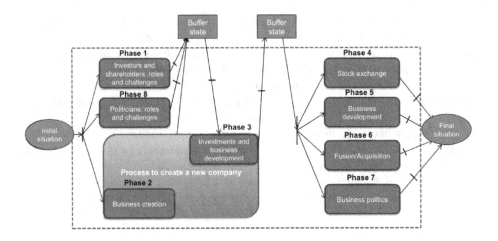

**Fig. 3.** Structure of the learning scenario in the CIBUS Social Learning Game (SLG)

— *Buffer state*: at the end of a phase, the learners are directed in a buffer state where they have additional information on the educational concepts via different media (e.g. videos, web sites) and are asked some questions to deepen these concepts. As some modules inside the phases require collaboration between players that have different roles, it is necessary to regulate the progress in the game so that all players begin a new phase at the same time. The buffer states allow the players waiting for the others and continue playing.

— *Allocation of roles and phases*: the learners do not always collaborate with the same people. At the initial phase and after a buffer state, the learners can choose a role and phases based on a limited number of players per role and per phase. When the maximum number is reached, we allocate automatically a role (only at the initial phase) or a phase. For example on Fig. 3, the learners can choose one of the four phases (4, 5, 6 and 7) but a phase is automatically closed when the maximum number of participants is reached.

— *Modules*: the phases are composed of different types of modules, allowing regulation within the phases. The different types of modules are:

  • Free module: the learners answer individually a series of questions. The learners can create events to debate on a decision, since the decisions made by a learner can influence the progress of the scenario for the others (for example, if the majority of the investors do not want to invest in an industrial sector, the concerned companies risk to go bankrupt). Finally learners make their own decision.

  • Critical module: learners involved in a same phase have to reach an agreement on one or several decisions. If only one player do not agree, a message appears to warn all the participants. This type of module is used for important decisions (and associated concepts) of the learning scenario. The aim is to lead the learners to collaborate with the other players involved in a given phase.

  • Sliding module: at any moment of the learning scenario, a critical event can occur and all the learners have to discuss to make a collective decision by a referendum. The final decision is made automatically according to the rule: « majority is right ». This type of module aims to give the opportunity for all players to discuss. For example in the scenario of CIBUS, we inform the players of a hurricane and its consequences on the stock market. They have to make a decision for all the community.

### 4.3    Individual, Collaborative and Community Levels

In SLG, we have to consider and support both the individual player and the whole community, and a middle level of the players who have the same goals. In fact, we think that different kinds of learning processes can occur [21]: reflective learning when learners are conscious of the impact of their actions (like in learning games); collaborative learning when learners collaborate for the same goal (like in multi-player games, for example for a quest); and social learning when learners have interaction within the community with learners who do not necessarily have the same objectives but that may have useful information and provide help (like in a MMORPG). As mentioned in previous parts, this distinction appears in several elements of CIBUS:

— The dashboard: it presents several indicators at the three levels we distinguish. On a same interface, learners can visualize their own indicators (that evolve according to individual decisions), the indicators of the learners that have the same role (that evolve according to individual and collective decisions) and the indicators of the whole community (that evolve according to individual and community decisions). It can enhance a reflexivity process, by comparing the level of their indicators with the others and help them to situate within the group and the community.
— The different types of module: according to the type of module, the decisions are made at different levels: at an individual level in free modules, at a collective level in a critical module and at the community level in the sliding module.
— The contextual discussions: when starting a discussion, learners can invite the players and the roles that they want, so creating discussion within one role, several roles or the whole community (all the players). These discussions can be started at any moment of the scenario, not necessarily only when intended.

## 5    Conclusion and Future Works

As a conclusion, we have contributed to specify the characteristics of a new type of games that emerges: Social Learning Games (SLG). SLG offer educational contents according to a learning scenario like Learning Games and learners participate in a learning community that can help them to solve problems, exchange ideas and be more engaged in the game like MMORPG or Social Games. We proposed a generic model of SLG based on five components: decision-making, contextual discussions, social capital, educational feedback and dashboard. We highlighted the possibilities offered by this design approach of SLG, like the stimulation of the learners for decision-making, reinforcement of the learners' engagement in the game, and conditions for social learning based on the educational contents provided in the game.

We then illustrated our model of SLG with the CIBUS game. The structure of the learning scenario is based on specific elements (phases, modules, buffer states, allocation of roles and phases) that allow the regulation of the progress of the learners in the game, by giving freedom in the participation in the community. The design approach we propose allow taking into account and support three levels of learning involved in the game: individual, within the group, and within the community.

At present, we are preparing an experiment to evaluate the learning effects when playing the CIBUS game, according to the different types of learning expected. This experiment will take place on a large scale, so as to be able to evaluate the impact of the community on the processes involved and the learners' behavior in the game and the community (e.g. engagement, participation, motivation). In a short-term perspective, we also plan to transpose the game in another domain, so as to test the genericity of the approach and the effects of the domain on the results observed.

**Acknowledgement.** The author would like to thank the students of the CIBUS team and their tutors for the development of the game.

# References

1. Michael, D., Chen, S.: Serious Games: Games That Educate, Train, and Inform. Course Technology PTR (2005)
2. Susi, T., Johannesson, M., Backlund, P.: Serious games – An overview. School of Humanities and Informatics, University of Skövde, Sweden (2007)
3. Flynn, R., McKinnon, L., Bacon, E., Webb, J.: Maritime City: Using Games Technology to Train Social Workers – Some Initial Results. In: Anacleto, J.C., Fels, S., Graham, N., Kapralos, B., Saif El-Nasr, M., Stanley, K. (eds.) ICEC 2011. LNCS, vol. 6972, pp. 415–418. Springer, Heidelberg (2011)
4. Rosenbloom, A.: Interactive immersion in 3D graphics. Communications of the ACM 47, 28–31 (2004)
5. Purdy, J.A.: Serious Games: Getting Serious About Digital Games in Learning. Corporate University Journal 1, 3–6 (2007)
6. Marty, J.-C., Carron, T.: Observation of Collaborative Activities in a Game-Based Learning Platform. IEEE Transactions on Learning Technologies 4, 98–110 (2011)
7. Squire, K., Jenkins, H.: Harnessing the power of games in education. Insight 3, 5–33 (2003)
8. Kirriemuir, J., McFarlane, A.: Literature Review in Games and Learning. Futurelab, Bristol (2004)
9. Bodin, M., Marty, J.-C., Carron, T.: Specifying Collaborative Tools in Game-Based Learning Environments: Clues from the trenches. In: European Conference on Game Based Learning 2011, pp. 46–56. Academic Publishing International, Athenes (2011)
10. Araya, R., Jiménez, A., Bahamondez, M., Dartnell, P., Soto-Andrade, J., González, P., Calfucura, P.: Strategies Used by Students on a Massively Multiplayer Online Mathematics Game. In: Leung, H., Popescu, E., Cao, Y., Lau, R.W.H., Nejdl, W. (eds.) ICWL 2011. LNCS, vol. 7048, pp. 1–10. Springer, Heidelberg (2011)

11. Benassi, A., Orlandi, C., Cantamesse, M., Galimberti, C., Giacoma, G.: World of Warcraft in the Classroom: A Research Study on Social Interaction Empowerment in Secondary Schools. In: European Conference on Game Based Learning 2011, pp. 35–45. Academic Publishing International, Athenes (2011)

12. Jang, Y., Ryu, S.: Exploring game experiences and game leadership in massively multiplayer online role-playing games. British Journal of Educational Technology 42, 616–623 (2011)

13. Johnson, N., Xu, C., Zhao, Z., Ducheneaut, N., Yee, N., Tita, G., Hui, P.: Human group formation in online guilds and offline gangs driven by a common team dynamic. Physical Review E 79 (2009)

14. Egenfeldt-Nielsen, S.: Overview of research on the educational use of video games. Digital Kompetanse 1, 184–213 (2006)

15. Wenger, E.: Communities of practice: learning as a social system. The Systems Thinker 9, 5 (1998)

16. Preece, J.: Sociability and usability in online communities: Determining and measuring success. Behavior and Information Technology 20(5), 347–356 (2001)

17. Garrot, E., George, S., Prévôt, P.: Supporting a Virtual Community of Tutors in Experience Capitalizing. International Journal of Web Based Communities (IJWBC) 5(3), 407–427 (2009)

18. Kamal, N., Fels, S., Ho, K.: Online social networks for personal informatics to promote positive health behavior. In: Proceedings of Second ACM SIGMM Workshop on Social Media, pp. 47–52. ACM, New York (2010)

19. Michel, C., Lavoué, E.: KM and Web 2.0 Methods for Project-Based Learning. In: Ifenthaler, D., Isaias, P., Spector, J.M., Kinshuk, S.D. (eds.) MEShaT: a Monitoring and Experience Sharing Tool. Multiple Perspectives on Problem Solving and Learning in the Digital Age, pp. 49–66. Springer, Heidelberg (2011)

20. Johnson, S.: Everything Bad Is Good for You: How Today's Popular Culture Is Actually Making Us Smarter. Riverhead Hardcover (2005)

21. Lavoué, É.: Social Tagging to Enhance Collaborative Learning. In: Leung, H., Popescu, E., Cao, Y., Lau, R.W.H., Nejdl, W. (eds.) ICWL 2011. LNCS, vol. 7048, pp. 92–101. Springer, Heidelberg (2011)

# Computer Games and English Language Learning

Sabina-Nadina Cehan and Dana-Anca Cehan

"Al. I. Cuza" University of Iaşi, Romania

**Abstract.** School lore has it that young learners acquire foreign languages easily by playing computer games. In an attempt to investigate this claim, a study was conducted involving 228 lower and upper secondary school Romanian students. The investigation probed for age and gender differences in the students' attitudes towards learning English from computer games, as well as for specific instances of language learning. The language remembered from playing reveals which game elements and properties appear most conducive to language learning. The frequency of a word or phrase, its bearing in the logic of the game, and the game capacity to present contextualized language, simultaneously seen and heard, are important factors. Nevertheless, there is ample evidence of significant limitations. The analysis shows strengths and weaknesses that may be relevant for foreign language learning game design.

**Keywords:** learning English as a foreign language, computer games, incidental learning, language acquisition, game design.

## 1    Introduction

Traditionally, learning a foreign language takes place in the classroom, a controlled environment where new information is introduced sequentially. The target language is practised, remembered and used in oral and written exercises and activities and both the teacher and the mother tongue represent aids in comprehension. Nevertheless, learners may find alternative avenues of acquisition through exposure to television programmes, movies, books, self-study materials, the Internet and computer games in the target language. This is the case for a sizeable proportion of Romanian students of English, as they have little difficulty in coming across such alternative resources. It is not uncommon to hear reports from both Romanian teachers and learners of English stating that computer games have had a positive impact on the acquisition of English.

Even without any focus on the actual learning of a foreign language, computer games seem to enhance the player's competence in the target language. The most obvious reasons are, first, that mere exposure to the target language provides the opportunity for repetition and recall of learnt language in new contexts. Second, games in the foreign language need to be understood in order to be played properly. Thus, especially with more complex games, where the linguistic input is extensive, comprehension plays an important part. Not everything can be learnt by trial and error or by just observing how the game develops. Some rules or explanations given in the target language have to be decoded by the player from the very beginning. Moreover, the

E. Popescu et al. (Eds.): ICWL 2012, LNCS 7558, pp. 180–189, 2012.

logic of the computer game often constitutes feedback as to the correctness of the decoding. Third, computer games contextualize language: it is common for words or sentences to appear in computer games in their written and spoken forms concurrently with relevant images. Thus, it appears that computer games have the right ingredients to foster foreign language learning.

In order to assess the validity of such a claim and the importance of sources for learning English outside the classroom, research was carried out among 228 students of English enrolled in several secondary schools, mainly in Iaşi. The inquiry aimed to shed light on the relationship between gender and age and the English language learnt from sources outside the classroom as named in the questionnaires or identified by the participants in the study. These were (not in any particular order): television programmes, movies, cartoons, books, self-study materials, computer games, tutoring, family, and the Internet. The evidence given in terms of the students' intake was also taken into consideration. The focus of this article is on the role that computer games in English seem to play in the students' acquisition of English as a foreign language.

## 2    Research Questions, Instruments and Methodology

The questions that stood at the basis of the investigation were the following. First, to what extent are learners aware that they learn English from sources outside the classroom? Specifically, are computer games in the target language perceived as (comprehensible) input or as noise by learners? Second, what language is linked directly to these outside sources? More to the point, can learners offer specific examples of words, phrases or sentences in English that they remember having learned from computer games? Finally, are there differences in their answers that seem to be linked to age or gender?

In order to answer these questions, a questionnaire was conceived to assess the learners' openness to non-traditional, outside-the-classroom sources of learning English. It was written in English, as it was expected that most pupils had sufficient knowledge of the target language. The questionnaire was divided into two parts. The first set of questions required factual information about the respondents (e.g., grade, age and gender). These were followed by a series of ten "Yes/No" questions relating to their English learning habits and their opinions on learning from outside sources. Two types of questions were asked for each of these sources, the first regarding the usage of the source and the second asking whether the respondents felt that it was conducive to learning English. Specifically, regarding computer games, the respondents were asked "Do you play computer games in English?" and "Do you think you learn English by playing computer games?".

The second part of the questionnaire consisted of a table in which the respondents freely wrote what they remembered to have learned from the different sources. To help them, the sources were restated and a column was provided for the names/titles of computer games, TV programmes, movies, books, or web-sites used. It was reasoned that in asking the respondents to first think about specific instances, another step was taken to facilitate their access to the language linked directly to the sources. In other words, remembrance was facilitated by providing an intermediate step.

The respondents were enrolled in the fifth, sixth, eleventh and twelfth grades. Their ages ranged from ten to twenty-one. As no pupil in the sixth grade was older than fourteen and none of the pupils in the eleventh grade was younger than fifteen, the fifth and sixth-graders were generically called the under-fifteen or the younger group, while the eleventh and twelfth graders were referred to as the over-fifteen or the older group. Thus, in the under-fifteen group were 124 pupils, out of which 63 were boys and 61 girls, while in the over-fifteen group were 104 pupils, out of which 46 were boys and 58 were girls.

# 3    Data Analysis

The information from the questionnaires was analyzed quantitatively by introducing the respondents' age-group, gender and individual answers to questions one to ten into an Excel file. Based on the compiled data, graphs were created evincing the percentages of learners who gave positive answers. However, the number of respondents was not considered large enough to be representative from a statistical point of view, and the results are shown in graphs in percentages and are considered to indicate trends by default.

## 3.1    Preliminary Observations

When the questionnaires were administered, some learners asked how certain words – that they knew how to pronounce – were written. These occurrences constitute evidence in themselves that learners do not acquire the pronunciation and the spelling of a word at the same time. This means that (for English, at least) the acquisition of the phonetic and the written image of a word requires different types of practice. For this reason, it needs to be emphasized that the questionnaires show *what the learners think they know how to write*. From this perspective, the very written nature of the questionnaire limits the respondents' ability to answer. Their answers may have been different, had there been a recorded interview part.

The second part of the questionnaire allowed the respondents to write as much or as little as they chose. Hence, some questionnaires were left blank while others had a few titles written in, but no specific examples of language were given. A fair number of respondents were able to give many examples, while a few found there was not enough space for what they felt they could write. For instance, one sixth-grader chose to fill the entire free examples rubric with an impressive total of fifty-eight extremely diverse words. However, none of these words was directly linked to a definite source. Some of the words given were common and easy enough (such as names of colours) and very likely to have been learnt in the classroom, while other words were probably learnt from outside sources. This was by no means a singular case.

Various explanations are possible for the range of individual reports. Thus, if a respondent did not write anything in the questionnaire in the free examples part, s/he may simply not have remembered any relevant instances at that moment. Another possibility is that s/he may have recalled how to pronounce the word(s), but did not know the spelling, or s/he may indeed have felt that no target language had been acquired outside the classroom. Moreover, for most of the acquired target language items, the learner may not have remembered where they were first encountered or at what exact moment fully understood. In other words, the learner may have lost the connection between the source and the language item.

Before discussing the results, one more clarification is necessary: the research takes into account any computer game that the respondent might have ever played, which means in the Romanian context, mostly commercial games. In 2009, based on an analysis of the titles given by the respondents, the most popular games were: *Need for Speed, FIFA, Grand Theft Auto, Counter Strike, The Sims, Age of Empires, World of Warcraft, Metin, Call of Duty, Diablo.* One twelfth-grader mentioned "Discworld MUD (a text-based online multiplayer game; very complex, requires constant use of English)". Children and teenagers usually played these games at home, on their personal computers, or in special computer "cafés". To the authors' knowledge, special educational games are a rarity in the Romanian educational context in general and in the English classroom in particular.

## 3.2    Results and Discussion

Questions two and three referred directly to computer games and checked for the learners' habits and whether they felt that they acquired English while playing (see Fig. 1). In the answers provided there is a visible change across age. As they grow older, young people seem to abandon playing computer games. Moreover, they no longer feel that they gain target language from computer games to the same extent. A closer look at possible gender differences reveals interesting facts. The under-fifteen group is highly homogeneous, with both genders playing computer games just as much and finding the experience similar in terms of language learning. However, the over-fifteen group paints a different picture. Although older boys and girls play computer games in the same proportion, fewer older girls find playing computer games facilitating for learning English in comparison with the older boys. Of the latter, all those who do play find some learning value in computer games.

Explanations for these differences probably reside in both the groups' respective language levels and the types of games preferred by boys and girls of different ages. Thus, having a more limited understanding of the target language, the under-fifteen

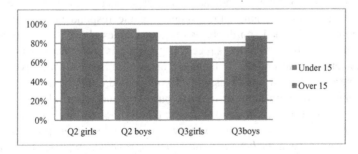

**Fig. 1.** Percentages of positive answers to questions 2 and 3 comparing girls and boys from the two age groups. Q2: "Do you play computer games in English?". Q3: "Do you think you learn English by playing computer games?"

group may find computer games a rich source of exposure to old and new language, irrespective of gender. In the older group, however, the gender difference might be explained by game preferences, with a good portion of the girls favouring less linguistically complex or challenging games.

The type of language items that younger learners retain from computer games include words, phrases and short sentences. Below are some examples gathered from the free report section.

**Table 1.** Examples of language retained from computer games given by the under-fifteen group

| Words in isolation | Nouns | blood; bone; boy; capsule; car; clothes; coach; computer; curse; dog; employee; explosive; federation; fish; freedom; game(s); gems; girl; goal; instructions; inventory; items; kingdom; llama; magazine; man; manager; milk; mouse; movie; ninja; noble; oil; options; penguin; pet; pimps; player; pulsar; queen; rainbow; rank; recipe; ring; robbers; salt; settings; shot; silk; spider; sugar; sword; team; tournament; war; wedding; witch; world |
|---|---|---|
| | Adjectives | crazy; Dutch; good; wonderful |
| | Adverbs | now |
| | Verbs: bare infinitive | finish; have; pass; play; quit; ride; start; talk; tackle; wear; yawn |
| | Verbs: long infinitive | to capture; to graduate; to marry; to trade |
| | Verbs: past participle | born; graduated |
| | Verbs: present participle | playing |
| Phrases | Noun phrases | a new manager; stolen treasure; game over; Muscle Cars; employment office; the end |
| | Verb phrases | to have something repaired; to play a trick; to win a contest; to take part; |
| Sentences / Utterances | Come for me! | Fire! |
| | Play tutorial; | So what? |
| | play again | Your skills are not yet complete |
| | Run, Donkey, run | Fire in the hole |
| | Leave me alone | Begin the tournament |
| | Kill the cop | |
| Examples with mistakes | backpak; excelent; inventori; setings; Folow me!; I'm a beck!; Come one!; I'm positions!; Play Campaing; Newe Game; to acomplish; You've been atacked; A friend in need is a friend indeed | |

The examples above clearly indicate that younger learners acquire target language while playing computer games, thus supporting the respondents' intuitive claims. Several points can be made on the basis of the examples above. First, a large portion is made up of words in isolation, suggesting that at this stage learners notice, understand and retain small chunks of language at a time. Some of the given examples could be part of different word classes (i.e. *noble* could either be a noun or an adjective, or *yawn* could be a noun or a verb), but it was not clear whether the learners were aware of the different morpho-semantic possibilities for one and the same word. The bulk of the examples are a large variety of nouns, either in the plural or the singular. Some words, such as *boy, car, dog, fish, girl, man, milk, mouse, movie, pet, queen, now, finish, play* are extremely common and it is very likely that the learners encountered them at school as well. That the respondents linked these to computer games may indicate that the games provide a linguistic and situational environment where the learners are frequently exposed to these words, hence the learners' association of these vocabulary items with the game situation rather than with the lessons. Other examples, such as *blood, curse, federation, pulsar, sword, tournament, war, witch* are less common and less likely to have been introduced in their regular lessons, given their age and general level of English. Computer games are the more likely source, with some respondents indicating the exact title of the game from which they learnt a particular word.

In terms of word classes, the fact that nouns and verbs dominate in comparison to adjectives and adverbs seems to indicate that learners make mostly one-to-one connections between linguistic items and their referents. Computer games provide sufficient contextual clues for such connections to be readily made. For instance, it is not uncommon for the player to give commands to a game character and then observe the character perform the action, or for the image of an item, such as a *sword*, to be accompanied by both the written and spoken word forms. However, it is much more difficult to subtract the meaning of adjectives and adverbs. For example, in order to deduct what *crazy, wonderful*, or *now* mean, it is necessary to create appropriate complex contexts for such manner, quality or time orientation to become evident.

Some of the verbs were given in non-finite forms, that is the long infinitive (i.e. *to marry, to trade*), the present participle (i.e. *playing*) and the past participle (i.e. *graduated, born*). This may suggest that these forms have not been analyzed morphologically or syntactically yet. That is, it is not clear for the learner that *to + verb, verb + -ed*, or *verb + -ing* each constitute a form which has certain rule-governed functions. Nevertheless, the absence of any third person present simple forms (*verb + -s*) may be interpreted as an indication that the present simple tense has been acquired by this stage and the *-s* is recognized as a separate tense marker. It is probable that this rule was acquired in school, but playing computer games does not seem to aid in acquiring the grammatical rules of the language.

A second interesting point relates to the phrases and utterances that the respondents wrote down. With only two notable exceptions, they are short, no longer than three words. The noun phrases seem to refer to a specific item (e.g. *stolen treasure*) or a moment in the game (e.g. *the end, game over*). Of the verb phrases, two refer to a specific activity (*to play a trick, to win a contest*). This would suggest that the learners have not yet analyzed the phrases into their components and have not come to any rule generalisation. Nevertheless, at least one learner has shown awareness of generalisation possibilities when s/he gave the example of *to have something repaired.*

Almost all the utterances found are in the form of instructions and have the verb in the imperative. These instructions initiate a reaction or a change in the game (*play tutorial, begin the tournament*) or they may be given by a game character to another and implicitly to the player (*Kill the cop; Run, Donkey, run*). However, learners seem to also specifically retain game messages that probably count as positive (*A friend in need is a friend in deed* (sic!)) or negative feedback (*Your skills are not yet complete*). Thus, the respondents' answers show that what they notice and retain are language chunks of importance to the task-driven environment of the games.

The third and final point has to do with the mistakes that have been found in the given examples. On the whole, there are remarkably few misspelled words in comparison with the amount of target language written correctly. Most mistakes seem to be related to pronunciation and spelling transfer problems. Thus, in *excelent or *settings failure to double the *l* and the *t*, respectively, may have been caused by the learners' transferring the rule of letter-sound correspondence from Romanian. The same is probable for *backpak: the missing *c* may be a victim of the one-to-one correspondence between the letter *k* and the sound /k/. Another spelling problem originating in phonological transfer is evident in *I'm posiţions!* (sic!) where the learner apparently felt the need to represent the sound /ʃ/ by writing ţ, a letter that does not exist in English. In the same example the absence of *in* is also noticeable and may lead to the supposition that the learner only heard something in the game, but did not see it written.

Since the data analysis has indicated that function of age group the percentages of learners who play computer games are very close, it may be worthwhile to see what examples the older respondents gave. These are shown below.

**Table 2.** Examples of language retained from computer games given by the over-fifteen group

| Words in isolation | Nouns | axe; blight; craft; fight; hermit; hunter; instance; larder; might; ogre; priest; shaman; sword; warrior |
|---|---|---|
| | Verbs | call |
| Phrases | noun phrases | too much weight on the pass through; game over |
| | verb phrases | invite out; |
| Sentences / Utterances | hire a nanny; propose engagement; visit neighbours; Do you need a ride?; | start game; You win; In order to start playing L2, you need to create a cha-racter |
| Examples with mistakes | The rogues are safe, for the moment. | |

The over-fifteen group gave fewer examples of language they felt they learnt playing computer games. The main reason for this may be that they have reached a language level at which little of the language they encounter in games is new. Similar to the other group, the older learners gave examples of language frequently encountered in computer games, or directly linked to the tasks that the player needs to fulfill so as to progress in the game. Examples include: *start game, game over, You win* or *In order to start playing L2, you need to create a character*. Sentences lacking subjects, such as *hire a nanny, propose engagement* or *visit neighbours* seem to be instructions that the player can give to a game character, again probably linked to the progression of the game. Furthermore, a look at the 'Words in isolation' category reveals that, with the exception of *call*, it is void of any common vocabulary, suggesting that older learners automatically perceive and understand this part of the lexis. What they appear to retain from the games are words that may refer to particular characters (*hunter, hermit, shaman*), objects (*axe, sword*) or activities in the game (*fight*).

Apparently, the main difference between the two groups resides in the type of language that they acquire from playing computer games and in the quality of the acquisition. On the one hand, for the younger group both the more common and the more advanced vocabulary items that are found in computer games are new and worth retaining. Moreover, for most young learners the limited target language proficiency impedes their remembering phrases and sentences longer than a few words. On the other hand, the older group's examples suggest that in their case only strong contextualization helps language to be retained. The difference in language proficiency between the two groups is also evident in the instances found in the 'Examples with mistakes' category. The younger learners are obviously still struggling with English spelling, while in the older group's examples there is only one mistake.

### 3.3    Considerations on the Present Research and Further Possible Improvements

The present research could be called tentative at best. It is in fact part of a larger project which considered various alternative resources for learning English, of which computer games represent one option. It provides a general and somewhat superficial overview of the English learning potential through computer games for Romanian pupils. Nevertheless, it proves that learning does take place and it points to the complexity of the issue at hand.

A more valid and relevant research would require in depth, controlled and extended testing. For instance, one could envisage a one-month study on a pool of minimum ten subjects whose exposure to computer games in English and the benefits thereof would be analysed. First, one would need to ascertain that there are not any significant differences in the respondents' level of English and that they are all familiar with computer games to the same extent at the beginning of the study. Second, their daily exposure to English in the classroom and outside should be monitored so as to identify any language that is repeated. The hours spent playing would also need to be the same for all participants in the study. Ideally, all subjects should play the same computer game, be it educational or commercial. A linguistic analysis of this game could also prove useful, if, for instance, one were to compute the frequency of words and grammatical structures found in the language content. These frequencies could then be corroborated with the language that subjects report to have learned. Finally, there are several possible ways in which language learned by subjects could be identified, and it is advisable to combine research techniques for the sake of validity. For instance, subjects could be asked to keep journals of their learning experience while at the same time monitoring their gaming performance and periodically testing them orally and in writing on the language found in the game. Theoretically, such a complex research project is bound to result in valuable data about learning a foreign language in general and the roles of consciousness and memory therein.

## 4    Computer Games: Characteristics, Strengths and Potential

The learning potential of games in general, and that of computer games, in particular, cannot be denied. Yet, what and how games teach seem difficult questions to answer. The language that students remembered from playing computer games already indicates the general content of the games. Thus, the gamers become familiar with the soccer industry, players and tactics, they delve into fantasy worlds populated by exotic characters, engage in combat and simulate real life. Can any of the skills acquired while playing be transferred to real-life situations? Whichever the answer, it must be emphasized that the incidental learning of some foreign language is an unexpected boon. It follows that computer games must have elements or characteristics that favour language acquisition. If these could be correctly identified, they could be transferred to future computer games focusing explicitly on language learning.

Crawford's definition of game as a "closed formal system that subjectively represents a subset of reality" (p 7) seems suitable for a start in this endeavor. It highlights that games have limits in the number of rules and the rigid conditions under which they operate. This provides not only for a feeling of safety, but also for a fair amount of purposeful repetition. It is not accidental that learners remembered to write *Your skills are not yet complete* or *game over*, language which is directly related to the game's inherent rules of play. Likewise, the elements with which a game operates and which make up the reality subset are limited (e.g., *warrior*, *shaman*, *priest*, etc. are characters in the game, but not *accountant*).

Another important characteristic of some computer games is their "replayability". This feature directly relates to the already mentioned idea of repetition, but also to the player's individualised experience of the game and its potential for creativity. A game's final purpose is to finish or win within the given framework, but the player is free to experiment, choose and combine elements and movements. Like a game of chess, a computer game can be brought to an end in an almost infinite number of ways due to the combination of possible moves. In other words "a game presents a branching tree of sequences and allows the player to create his own story by making choices at each branching point" (Crawford: 10). Language is similar to some degree because of its paradigmatic and syntagmatic dimensions. A lot can be said with twenty nouns, an indefinite article, five verbs and the present simple.

Language learning computer games need to offer more than what can already be done in the classroom with pen and paper. A colourful activity in which you match a written word with its referent on the screen is not a computer game just because it is designed by a programmer and played on a laptop. The already existing design frameworks of role-playing, simulation, and strategy games seem capable enough to carry language learning along, which indicates that they represent a valid starting point for developing language learning games. Moreover, the goal of learning a (foreign) language is the ability to effectively use it in appropriate contexts. Therefore, learners/players need to be given the possibility or even be required to produce language in a language learning game. Evidence from the inquiry in what target language students retain from computer games also indicated differences of age and proficiency which need to be taken into account so as to maintain an appropriate balance between the competence of the learner/player and the linguistic challenge of the game.

## 5   Conclusions

To conclude, the present research has shown that a large number of Romanian students feel that they learn English from playing computer games and are able to prove it. The examples of learnt language given by the respondents are overwhelmingly isolated vocabulary items and whole sentences, suggesting that grammar rules and patterns are either learned implicitly or never consciously noticed. Furthermore, age and gender seem to play a part in the language that is retained. As an alternative, additional resource to the traditional classroom context, computer games favour the incidental learning of new language due to the high level of contextualisation through images and sounds and its purposeful presence. Thus, existing computer game design frameworks could be adapted to suit language-learning educational games.

# References

1. Al-Hejin, B.: Attention and Awareness: Evidence from Cognitive and Second Language Acquisition Research. Teachers College, Columbia University Working Papers in TESOL & Applied Linguistics, vol. 4(1) (2004), http://journals.tc-library.org/index.php/tesol/article/view/43/50 (accessed December 20, 2011)
2. Crawford, C.: The Art of Computer Game Design. Electronic Version
3. Franciosi, S.J.: A Comparison of Computer Game and Language-Learning Task Design Using Flow Theory. CALL-EJ 12(1), 11–25 (2011), http://callej.org/journal/12-1/Franciosi_2011.pdf (accessed May 4th 2012)
4. Gass, S.M.: Input, Interaction, and the Second Language Learner. Lawrence Erlbaum Associates, Publishers, New Jersey (1997)
5. Koster, R.: A Theory of Fun for Game Design. Paraglyph Press, Scottsdale (2005)
6. Lightbown, P.M., Spada, N.: How Languages are Learned, 2nd edn. Oxford University Press, Oxford (1999)
7. Park, E.S.: On Three Potential Sources of Comprehensible Input for Second Language Acquisition (2005), http://journals.tc-library.org/index.php/tesol/article/download/5/6 (accessed December 10, 2011)
8. Salazar, P.: Comprehensible Input and Learning Outcomes. Jornades de Foment de la Investigació (2011), http://www.uji.es/bin/publ/edicions/jfi2/compren.pdf (accessed November 28, 2011)
9. Schmidt, R.W.: The Role of Consciousness in Second Language Learning. Applied Linguistics 11(2) (1990), http://www.corpus4u.org/forum/upload/forum/2006062200592293.pdf (accessed December 15, 2011)

# AMASE: A Framework for Composing Adaptive and Personalised Learning Activities on the Web

Athanasios Staikopoulos, Ian O'Keeffe, Rachael Rafter, Eddie Walsh,
Bilal Yousuf, Owen Conlan and Vincent Wade

Knowledge and Data Engineering Group, School of Computer Science and Statistics,
Trinity College Dublin, Ireland
{Athanasios.Staikopoulos,Ian.OKeeffe,Rachael.Rafter,Eddie.Walsh,
yousufbi,Owen.Conlan,Vincent.Wade}@scss.tcd.ie

**Abstract.** Personalised Web information systems have in recent years been evolving to provide richer and more tailored experiences for users than ever before. In order to provide even more interactive experiences as well as to address new opportunities, the next generation of Personalised Web information systems needs to be capable of dynamically personalising not just web media but web services as well. In particular, eLearning provides an example of an application domain where learning activities and personalisation are of significant importance for engaging and enhancing the learning experience of a learner. This paper presents a novel approach and technical framework called AMASE to support the dynamic generation and enactment of *Personalised Learning Activities*, which uniquely entails the personalisation of media content and the personalisation of services in a unified manner. In doing so, AMASE combines state of the art techniques from both adaptive web and adaptive workflow systems.

**Keywords:** Adaptive Framework, Personalised Learning, Learning Activities, Adaptive Services and Workflow.

## 1 Introduction

The Internet is increasingly being seen as a replacement for the desktop environment providing an integrated platform in which users interact with rich media content and services to carry out complex tasks. In order to further enhance the user's experience of the web, personalisation techniques need to be applied to web content, services and the workflow coordination of those services and content. Personalisation aims to ensure that media content and services are selected and tailored according to the user's personal needs, preferences, goals and context [1].

In order to enhance and improve the interactivity of the user experience, the next generation of Personalised Web information systems needs to be capable of dynamically personalising web media, services and workflow in a unified manner [2]. Typically most existing approaches to personalisation on the web have focused on tailoring only multimedia content, which is restricted to adaptive content, selection

E. Popescu et al. (Eds.): ICWL 2012, LNCS 7558, pp. 190–199, 2012.

and navigation but have as yet omitted to consider adaptive workflow and adaptive services. In the AMAS project[1] we aim to develop innovative techniques and technologies to address this challenge and to support the dynamic and integrated personalisation of web media and services in the domain of eLearning.

eLearning is an inherently web-based domain where personalisation is of major importance. In eLearning, learning activities have been widely accepted as a means of providing greater engagement and enhancement of the learning experience [3]. Learning activities can be considered as specialised workflows, coordinating learning/educational content and tasks. In this case typical participants of the workflow are the learner and the educator. Many research projects such as LADiE [4] and successful learning activity environments such as LAMS [3] have investigated the pedagogic benefits of learning activities, such as for example, a peer review[2]. Personalised Learning Activities provide all the opportunities of learning activities but with the significant advantages of content, services (tools) and workflow being dynamically adapted to benefit individual learners. This customisation can be based on different "dimensions" of the learning occurrence such as the learner's preferences, prior knowledge, competences and context [5]. In AMAS we define the notion of a Personalised Learning Activity as a learning experience that involves the integration and personalisation of the selection, sequencing and presentation of both content and services.

This paper presents AMASE, a core technical framework of the AMAS project, which implements our approach for the dynamic generation and enactment of Personalised Learning Activities on the Web. AMASE combines the complimentary power of state-of-the-art techniques from the domains of both adaptive web and adaptive workflow systems. The actual adaptation process is a hybrid approach, utilising the capabilities of abstracted workflow and rule-based systems. In order to evaluate our approach and technical framework we have implemented an authentic case study involving undergraduate students of an SQL course.

The remainder of the paper is structured as follows: Section 2 presents the AMASE approach and framework. Section 3 describes the case study we have used to evaluate our approach and framework. Section 4 outlines the initial results of our evaluation. Section 5 presents a state-of-the-art review of related work. Finally, Section 6 summarises the main contributions of our approach.

## 2    AMASE Technical Framework

The AMASE framework supports the generation of Personalised Learning Activities, combining media content and (user centric) services in a unified manner. The framework is based on a number of interconnected components that generate, execute and support the user's interaction with a personalised activity. Fig. 1 portrays the AMASE architecture.

---

[1] AMAS SFI project, please refer to http://kdeg.cs.tcd.ie/amas
[2] In a peer review activity the learner reviews the work of one or more of his/her peers.

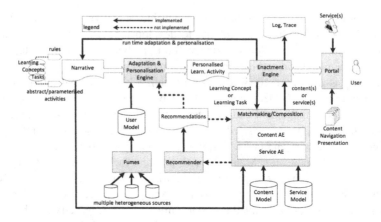

**Fig. 1.** AMASE Architecture Overview

Consider an educator (learning designer) who is designing a new course about Databases and SQL. Initially, he/she uses an authoring tool such as GRAPPLE [6] to conceptually design the course (Fig. 1 does not show the authoring phase of AMASE, rather the end product of that authoring). The design includes three key elements: the concepts and tasks from the learning domain (e.g. SQL commands and triggers), one or more abstracted or parameterised learning activities based on these concepts/tasks (e.g. SQL activity), and finally a set of adaptation rules that govern how the concepts and tasks should be adapted in different contexts (e.g. for novel/expert learners).

Three different types of adaptation rules are supported. Rules implemented with a concrete rule language such as Drools. These rules are stored within a repository, in this case the Drools Guvnor. Graph rules provide a more general and flexible mechanism in which learning designers can specify their own complex adaptation rules graphically. They are defined by a *when* clause (defining the triggering condition), a *before_pattern* (specifying the pattern to find in an activity graph) and an *after_pattern* (specifying the replace pattern). These rules are implemented similarly to the Graph Transformations rules defining the *pre* and *post* conditions on graphs [7]. Finally, there are Relationship rules that specify relationships among *Concepts* and learning *Activities* and which trigger adaptations. Based on these rules we have specified a number of predefined relationships that are available to a learning designer and which modify and compose an activity. For example, a *replaceWith* rule replaces one concept or activity with another and a *hasPrerequisite* rule applies a learning concept/activity before another.

Next, a Narrative contains the rules that are to be evaluated and used by the Adaptation and Personalisation Engine in order to create an executable Personalised Learning Activity.

A User Model stores the preferences, competencies, learning objectives and goals for each learner. User Models themselves are stored in a repository, such as an eXist database. In order to extract and combine information about a user from different sources such as their personalised learning environment (e.g. Sakai, Moodle) or social media, we use FUMES [8], a Federated User Model Exchange Service that implements a mapping-based approach to handle heterogeneity across different user models.

In AMASE we endorse a hybrid adaptation approach, combining the advantages and capabilities of workflow and rule-based systems. Rules are used to specify and evaluate the adaptation conditions as well as to trigger adaptations, while workflows are used to support the composition and coordinated execution of learning tasks. The adaptation process is depicted in Fig. 2. As inputs the Adaptation and Personalisation Engine receives: (i) an optional abstracted learning activity defining partial and parameterised workflows, (ii) a set of adaptation definitions, (iii) adaptation instances to generate in the first case rules to be evaluated and in the second case facts that will be inserted in the engine, (iv) a User Model to parameterise the adaptation with the preferences, competencies and objectives of a learner, and (v) a domain model defining the learning concepts and relations. In a case where an abstracted learning activity is not provided, the Personalised Learning Activity is constructed from scratch, exclusively by the adaptation rules. Finally, if a User Model is not provided then the adaptation process continues and generates a learning activity that applies to all users.

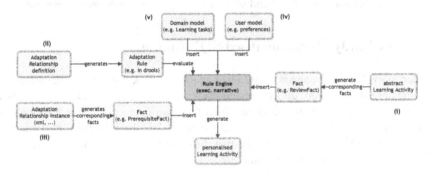

**Fig. 2.** Adaptation Process

As a result of the adaptation process, a Personalised Learning Activity is generated as a Business Process Model and Notation (BPMN) workflow specification, ready for execution. At this stage the activity has been personalised but remains abstract, as the appropriate content and services have not yet been selected in order to instantiate the tasks. The next step is to deploy the personalised activity to the Enactment Engine, so that it can be executed and made available to the learner. The Enactment Engine is a jBPM based workflow engine that supports the concurrent execution of multiple learning activities (BPMN workflows) assigned to individual as well as collaborating users. Learning activities are also stored in a repository so they can be reused and further customised for different domains and contexts. The current state of an executing learning activity is persistent and stored in a database. This enables us to support long-lived activities as they are dynamically loaded from a database. As the Enactment Engine provides the execution environment for learning activities, it interacts with the Narrative, to get adaptation rules that are to be evaluated at run time and accordingly trigger the dynamic adaptation of executing learning activities. The monitoring/logging mechanism monitors the instantiation and initiation of activities.

A learner interacts with the personalised activity through the web-based learning Portal (see Fig. 1). The Portal provides the learner with an environment in which both the content and services that make up the activity are available in an integrated manner. As the learner interacts with the Portal, requests are sent to the Enactment Engine in order to retrieve the appropriate content and services for the learner. At this point requests are passed to the matchmaking/composition service, which selects and composes if necessary, the appropriate content and services on a "just in time" basis. The service provides an interface for querying and composing available resources (content and services) based on the metadata descriptions that are stored in the corresponding content and service repositories. If the result of a query returns a set of results, the service will either compose content and services (based on a template) or select the most appropriate one (based on specific selection criteria). The decision to compose or select a service is based on the operating semantics of the service. As part of the matchmaking/composition mechanism, the Narrative is also used to provide rules that can influence the personalised selection and sequencing of both content and services. Similarly, we plan to use a Recommender system that will allow more serendipitous suggestions of content and services (or tools) based on user behaviour.

## 3    Case Study: A Personalised SQL Course

In order to evaluate our approach and technical framework we have implemented an authentic case study, where undergraduate students access an "SQL Database" course for a period of three months and from which they can interact with the Personalised Learning Activity that has been generated for them. We describe how the Personalised Learning Activity is generated for two different types of student in Section 3.1, and how they interact with it in Section 3.2.

### 3.1    Personalisation of the Learning Activity

In general, as part of the course users have to initially practice their SQL skills with a database sandbox environment and then to perform a Web Quest in which they must find and bookmark relevant material from the open web. This is followed by three parallel tasks: that of getting an assignment, designing a database with a design tool and implementing a database. Once users have completed all three activities they continue with the submission of their project. While users perform these tasks, they can participate in an online discussion forum and study specific assigned SQL topics.

In order to illustrate the personalisation of the course we consider two different learners: an expert (user01) and a novice (user02) who have individual learning preferences and prior knowledge. Fig. 3 provides screen captures of the Personalised SQL Course that is produced for user01 and user02. Due to their different competencies the adaptation process will assign a Practice Database for user02 but not for user01. In particular for user02 the matchmaker will associate that task with an Oracle database tool, due to his/her SQL preference for Oracle (over MySql). Next, for user02 the general Web Quest task will be replaced by a Questionnaire task, due to his/her learning preference to learn through examples (Constructivism). For user01 the matchmaker will resolve the Web Quest task to a combination of two services, the Search and Bookmarking. Both learners are assigned the Suggested Reading task. For user01 the Study SQL task is parameterised with a few SQL topics that are related to advanced and expert users, whereas for user02 the task is parameterised with more topics that are related to novice users. Next user01, due to his/her prior knowledge of information retrieval, will receive an assignment to implement a meta-search engine, whereas user02 due to his/her background in e-commerce, will have to build an air-ways reservation system. Both users are provided with the design database, imple-ment database, and forum tasks. Next assuming that for user02, the submission period has expired, the submit task is changed into a late submission task. Finally, the review task will only be assigned to user01.

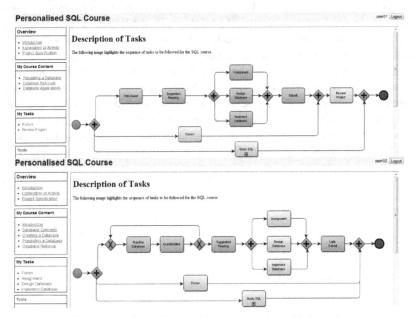

**Fig. 3.** Case Study for user01 (above) and user02 (below)

## 3.2    Personalised Learning Portal

Learners interact with the Personalised Learning Activity via a web Portal. The Portal interface (see Fig. 3) is divided into two main areas, the navigation menu on the left hand side of the screen providing access to general information about the course, the tools to be used, the assigned content and tasks, and the content panel on the right hand side. As shown in Fig. 4-left, once a topic is selected the content panel displays the content with the appropriate navigation options (submenu, buttons). Similarly, once a task is selected the content panel displays the appropriate services with which users can interact (see Fig. 4-right).

In order to realise the different tasks of the Personalised Learning Activity, the services need to be registered with the system. The metadata for the services are stored in a service repository describing the services/tools in terms of a service location (URI), type (e.g., SOAP, REST, Portlet), key-value pairs characterising the service, inputs, outputs, pre-conditions and post-conditions. Both services and tools offered by external and internal providers can be registered. Similarly, metadata about the attributes and characteristics of media content are stored in a content repository. In this case, most of the services are developed as Java portlets, which are deployed in a Liferay Portal server.

In this case study the services used are: 1) a Practice SQL Sandbox Service allowing students to try different SQL commands. 2) a Forum Service allowing for inter-student and tutor-student discussions, 3) a Search Service allowing students to perform web searches based on Microsoft Bing 4) a Bookmarking Service allowing students to keep track of their bookmarked links and submit them as part of the activity 5) a Submission Service allowing students to upload their project reports 6) a Late Submission Service replacing the submission service after a deadline is reached and penalising students for late submissions 7) a Review Service providing students with access to a set of reports that have been randomly allocated to them for review 8) a Recommender Service suggesting selected further reading based on the relevant resources that each student bookmarked 9) a Notification Service notifying students and educators with an email about their allocated tasks and 10) a Questionnaire service that randomly selects SQL questions to test the command skills of some learners.

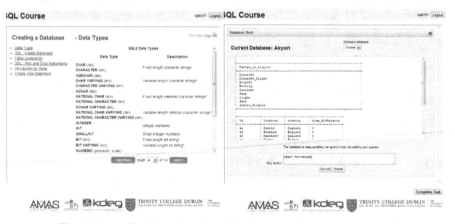

**Fig. 4.** Personalised Learning Portal for content (left) and services (right)

# 4    Evaluation

We have evaluated our approach and technical framework through the case study described in Section 3 during the 2011/12 academic year. The course involved ninety undergraduate students from 3rd and 4th year. In particular, we examined our system under three criteria: the students' perception of the usability of the system, the effectiveness of the system and its performance. Students' perception was evaluated via a questionnaire and elicited learner opinions about the quality of the experience in using the learning activities and web Portal. Overall the students' perception of the system was positive. For example 90% of students felt that the course (Personalised Learning Activity) generated for them reflected the answers they gave via a self-evaluation instrument about their database skills and knowledge. 84% of students felt the course was easy to navigate. 71% of students said the course generated did not appear disjoint, and 83% of students found the flow between the tasks appropriate. In terms of performance, given that this is the first version of the system, the system performed within acceptable time boundaries. For example, the time for building a Personalised Learning Activity was between [2942, 3335] milliseconds, the time each piece of content/task took to build and load was minimal, while the system could easily escalate to many concurrent users (e.g., 100) with no problem. Also upon analysis of the system log files we found that 93% of students completed all of the tasks assigned. In addition, we find that on average each piece of content (273 in total) provided was visited 44 times by each student over the 3 month period the course was given. As a result, we would argue that both these results support the fact that students found the course both usable and engaging. In the future we intend to further evaluate our system in terms of effectiveness. This will be based on a comparative analysis of the questionnaires and assignments that the students completed this year, and in previous years when Personalised Learning Activities were not used. For brevities sake we have not included the full experimental results but these are available online from our website[3].

## 5    Related Work and Discussion

Current integrated learning environments such as Blackboard, Sakai and Moodle provide the delivery of content and services. However, such environments do not go far enough in addressing the particular needs of a learner via personalisation and suffer from the "one size fits all" problem. Furthermore, despite their support for services, they do not provide any means by which a learning designer can control the sequencing of the services included in their activity. Another common limitation of such learning environments is their closed nature [9], limiting educators to only use services provided by the system. On the other hand, specialised adaptive hypermedia systems such as GALE [10] and ADAPT2 [11] handle content adaptivity but fail to address the requirement for services, (ADAPT2 provides limited support for services, treating them as a special type of content allowing very limited capabilities with respect to the type of control flow that can be used to sequence the services). The IMS Learning Design (LD) specification [12] can be used to describe pedagogically driven learning activities using a platform independent language. However, the specification itself provides only basic support for adaptivity and use of services, supporting only three types of services, namely: an email, a discussion and a search service. Additional services can be added, however the actual implementation of these services is

---

[3] http://kdeg.cs.tcd.ie/amas/initial_evaluation.pdf

left up to the platform. Where LD-based systems have been extended to support the "adaptive selection" of external services, as is the case with the GSI [13] and the Gridcole [14], their support is limited to the instantiation of abstract service definitions and manual selections, not taking into account the learner's needs.

From the perspective of adaptive services and workflow, eFlow [15] provides an approach for the dynamic composition, enactment and management of composite services. ADEPT [16] also supports the modification of processes during execution, both at definition and instance level. YAWL supports the dynamic selection of worklets [17] at runtime based on a set of rules that are written by the workflow designer. AgentWork [18] provides the ability to modify process instances by dropping or adding individual tasks based on events and rules. In addition, CAWE [19] is an adaptive workflow system that supports adaptation based on the individual user, the contextual properties and the device they are using. Finally, C-BPEL [20] supports the adaptive selection of services to instantiate the activities in a workflow at runtime. However, most of the workflow approaches outlined do not perform adaptations upon an abstracted and standard workflow language as BPMN, but rather upon concrete implementations that are tied to specific technologies such as for YAWL and WS-BPEL. That means educational designers need to be experts in these languages in order to design a complete and executable learning activity. Services and exchanged data are also hard bound to the workflow, therefore not allowing the dynamic resolution of tasks to services based on their descriptions. There are also even less approaches allowing the dynamic adaptation of workflow instances based on the just in time evaluation of rules. In addition most of these systems they do not consider adaptation from a personalisation and customisation perspective. As a result a user model is not captured and it does not play a significant role in the adaptation process. Finally, there are even less approaches considering the domain specific characteristics and design principles of learning activities.

# 6    Conclusions

In this paper we have presented AMASE, a novel approach and technical framework providing a personalised and interactive learning experience for learners. AMASE supports the dynamic generation and enactment of Personalised Learning Activities, consisting of both media content and (user centric) services in a unified manner that are personalised to suit different learners.

AMASE is based on a number of distinctive characteristics and provides several advantages over other state of the art offerings. In particular it has the ability to combine both media and services, which can be personalised both in their enactment and in their sequencing via a workflow. This combination of all of these techniques together in a unified system is something that has not been done before, and which we feel is particularly suitable for advancing both the interactivity and suitability of web-based systems, in particular web-based learning systems.

**Acknowledgement.** This work was funded by Science Foundation Ireland via grant 08/IN.1/I2103.

# References

1. Brusilovsky, P.: Adaptive Navigation Support. In: Brusilovsky, P., Kobsa, A., Nejdl, W. (eds.) Adaptive Web 2007. LNCS, vol. 4321, pp. 263–290. Springer, Heidelberg (2007)
2. De Bra, P., Aroyo, L., Chepegin, V.: The next big thing: Adaptive web-based systems. Journal of Digital Information 5 (2006)
3. Dalziel, J.: Implementing Learning Design: The Learning Activity Management System (LAMS). In: Crisp, G., Thiele, D., Scholten, I., Barker, S., Baron, J. (eds.) Learning, pp. 593–596 (2003)
4. Jeffery, A., Conole, G., Falconer, I.: LADiE Project Final Report, http://misc.jisc.ac.uk/refmodels/LADIE/www.elframework.org/refmodels/ladie.html
5. Wade, V.: Challenges for the Multi-dimensional Personalised Web (2009)
6. Dagger, D., Harrigan, M., Kamari, G., Wade, V.: GRAPPLE and Graph Drawing (2008)
7. Baresi, L., Heckel, R.: Tutorial Introduction to Graph Transformation: A Software Engineering Perspective. In: Ehrig, H., Engels, G., Parisi-Presicce, F., Rozenberg, G. (eds.) ICGT 2004. LNCS, vol. 3256, pp. 431–433. Springer, Heidelberg (2004)
8. Walsh, E., O'Connor, A., Wade, V.: Supporting Learner Model Exchange in Educational Web Systems. In: 7th International Conference on Web Information Systems and Technologies (2011)
9. Dagger, D., O'Connor, A., Lawless, S., Walsh, E., Wade, V.P.: Service-oriented e-learning platforms: From monolithic systems to flexible services. IEEE Internet Computing 11, 28–35 (2007)
10. Smits, D., De Bra, P.: GALE: a highly extensible adaptive hypermedia engine. In: Hypertext 2011, pp. 63–72 (2011)
11. Brusilovsky, P., Sosnovsky, S., Yudelson, M.V.: Ontology-based Framework for User Model Interoperability in Distributed Learning Environments. Exchange Organizational Behavior Teaching Journal, 2851–2855 (2005)
12. Consortium, I.M.S.G.L.: IMS Learning Design Specification (2003)
13. De la Fuente Valentín, L., Pardo, A., Kloos, C.D.: Generic Service Integration in Adaptive Learning Experiences using IMS Learning Design. Computers & Education 57, 1160–1170 (2011)
14. Bote Lorenzo, M.L., Gómez Sánchez, E., Vega Gorgojo, G., Dimitriadis, Y.A., Asensio Pérez, J.I., Jorrín Abellán, I.M.: Gridcole: A tailorable grid service based system that supports scripted collaborative learning. Computers & Education 51, 155–172 (2008)
15. Casati, F., Ilnicki, S., Jin, L., Krishnamoorthy, V., Shan, M.-C.: Adaptive and Dynamic Service Composition in eFlow. In: Wangler, B., Bergman, L.D. (eds.) CAiSE 2000. LNCS, vol. 1789, pp. 13–31. Springer, Heidelberg (2000)
16. Dadam, P., Reichert, M.: The ADEPT project: a decade of research and development for robust and flexible process support. Computer Science Research and Development 23, 81–97 (2009)
17. Adams, M., ter Hofstede, A.H.M., Edmond, D., van der Aalst, W.M.P.: Worklets: A Service-Oriented Implementation of Dynamic Flexibility in Workflows. In: Meersman, R., Tari, Z. (eds.) OTM 2006. LNCS, vol. 4275, pp. 291–308. Springer, Heidelberg (2006)
18. Robert, M., Ulrike, G., Erhard, R.: AgentWork: A Workflow System Supporting Rule-based Workflow Adaptation. Data & Knowledge Engineering 51, 223–256 (2004)
19. Denko, M., Ardissono, L., Furnari, R., Goy, A., Petrone, G., Segnan, M.: The Context Aware Workflow Execution Framework, Citeseer, pp. 1–21 (2007)
20. Ghedira, C., Mezni, H.: Through Personalized Web Service Composition Specification: From BPEL to C-BPEL. Electronic Notes in Theoretical Computer Science 146, 117–132 (2006)

# Learning Activity Sharing
# and Individualized Recommendation
# Based on Dynamical Correlation Discovery

Xiaokang Zhou[1], Jian Chen[1], Qun Jin[1], and Timothy K. Shih[2]

[1] Graduate School of Human Sciences, Waseda University,
Tokorozawa, Japan
[2] Dept. of Computer Science & Information Engineering,
National Central University, Taoyuan, Taiwan
{xkzhou@ruri,wecan_chen@fuji,jin@}waseda.jp,
timothykshih@gmail.com

**Abstract.** In this study, we concentrate on learning activity sharing and individualized recommendation based on dynamical user correlations, in order to support and facilitate the web-based learning process integrated with social streams. A user correlation-based learning activity model is built to demonstrate the relations among user, learning task and learning activity. Based on these, an integrated method is proposed to provide a target user with the possible learning activity as the next learning step, which is expected to enhance the learning efficiency. Finally, design of a Moodle-based prototype system is discussed.

**Keywords:** Social Learning, Social Stream, Learning Activity, Social Media, Learning Activity Sharing.

## 1 Introduction

Traditional e-learning usually has a pre-defined curriculum with certain knowledge. Users always have to follow the defined instruction and assessment procedure to conduct a learning process, which may not suit for the personal requirement. The idea of social learning, considering that people can learn from one another, including such concepts as observational learning, imitation, and modeling [1], focuses on learning that occurs within a social context. That is, people can learn by observing the behavior of others and the outcomes of those behaviors [2]. Differing from conventional learning, social learning means people are no longer learning only from instructors or by themselves, but learning through interactions and collaborations in a community or across a social network.

In our previous study, a set of metaphors [3] have been introduced and defined to represent a variety of so-called social stream data including different aspects of people's information behaviors and social activities with a hierarchical structure. After that, two other metaphors, Heuristic Stone and Associative Ripple, are further defined to assist users' information seeking which can best fit users' current interests

E. Popescu et al. (Eds.): ICWL 2012, LNCS 7558, pp. 200–206, 2012.
© Springer-Verlag Berlin Heidelberg 2012

and needs with two improved algorithms [4]. Based on these, the so-called Dynamical Socialized User Networking Model (DSUN) [5] has been designed for the description of users' potential profiling and dynamical relationships.

In this study, we try to integrate the social streams into the web-based learning system, in order to provide users with the individualized recommendations in the learning activity sharing process. In details, for a target user, the user correlations, which are analyzed from the DSUN model, along with the learning patterns, which are used to describe users' learning behaviors, are employed in our integrated approach to infer the possible next learning activity according to his/her current learning activity.

The rest of this paper is organized as follows. We give a brief overview on the related work in Section 2. In Section 3, following the introducing of the DSUN model, a user correlation-based learning activity model is addressed to demonstrate the relations among user, learning task and learning activity. Based on these, in Section 4, we develop an integrated method to figure out the certain learning activity for the personalized recommendation, and further show the architecture of the prototype system. We conclude this study and give promising perspectives on future works in Section 5.

## 2 Related Work

Numerous applications of social streams in SNS have been addressed in recent years. For example, Signorini Alessio et al. show that twitter can be used as a measure of public interest or concern about health-related events by examining the twitter streams to track rapidly-evolving public sentiment and activity [6]. Analysis of twitter communications in [7] showed the experimental evidence that twitter can be used as an educational tool to help engage students and to mobilize faculty into a more active and participatory role. A study addressed in [8] examined the impact of posting social, scholarly, or a combination of social and scholarly information to twitter on the perceived credibility of the instructor, which may have implications for both teaching and learning.

As for the information and knowledge sharing aspects, [9] has pointed out the fundamental issue of social learning relies on the delivery of right information to appropriate social groups in favor of the stated perspectives. Evidences have revealed in [10] and [11] that the wiki-based forum system can prompt learners to share information and raise their interests in examining the discussion series. [12] indicates that the analysis of weblog can enhance the cognition construction in a specific domain with the statistical results on a 30-participant experiment.

In the information recommendation field, the web mining approaches have been extensively used for information recommendation [13]. As an additional area, the semantic web mining was proposed [14]. A new document representation model was presented in [15], which is based on users' implicit feedback to achieve better results in organizing web documents, such as clustering and labeling. Identifying relevant web sites from user activities is another attempt of organizing web pages [16].

LinkSelector [17] is a web mining approach focusing on structure and usage. By this approach, hyperlinks-structural relationships were extracted from existing web sites and theirs access logs.

# 3    Modeling of Learning Activity Based on User Correlation

## 3.1    Dynamical User Correlation Discovery

A Dynamically Socialized User Networking (DSUN) model has been constructed based on the analysis of social streams in our previous study [5], in order to discover and represent users' potential profiling and dynamical correlation. It can be defined and expressed as:

$$G_{DSUN}(V, E, W)$$

where

$V = \{v_1, v_2, v_3, ..., v_n\}$: a non-empty set of vertexes in the network, each of which indicates a user in the system.

$E = \{e_{ij}: <v_i, v_j> \mid$ if correlation exists between $v_i$ and $v_j\}$: a collection of edges that connect the vertex in V, which represent all the relationships among every vertex in the network.

$W = \{w_{ij} \mid if \exists e_{ij} \in E\}$: the weight $w_{ij}$, appending on the corresponding edge, is developed to identify the strength of specific relation between two users. This value is also employed to dynamically construct the model.

Based on these discussed above, the value of $w_{ij}$ between vertex $v_i$ and $v_j$ with a specific threshold will be used to determine whether the relation exists between these two users. Furthermore, the DSUN model will be constructed timely and dynamically based on users' current interests and individual needs. Besides, these relations appending on each edge within the DSUN model can be employed in the user correlation analysis, which is expected to further benefit the learning activity recommendation process.

## 3.2    A Hierarchical Model for Learning Activity with User Correlation

Following the discussion above, a hierarchical model is addressed to interpret the structure and relations in a learning course shown in Fig. 1.

A learning course may be divided into several learning tasks with a certain sequence to complete a learning purpose. In each task, a series of learning activities are assigned to users in order to guide them to realize the task. For example, to a specific English learner, it can remind him/her to memorize new words in early morning, to learn English grammar in the morning, and to do exercise in the afternoon. For the users in a learning course, a learning task may be assigned to a group of users. To pursue the similar learning purpose, these users may generate an amount of interactions. All these posts and interactions, which could be viewed as parts of social streams, can further be utilized to analyze user correlations according to a specific learning task during a specific period. Moreover, based on these dynamical correlations, the similar learning activity, especially those successful sequences of learning actions, can be shared between them. And the learning experience can also be diffused one by one among all the users in this learning course.

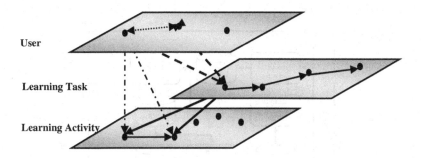

**Fig. 1.** A hierarchical model for learning activity with user correlation

# 4 Learning Activity Sharing and Recommendation

## 4.1 Sharing and Recommendation Mechanism

Both user correlations and learning patterns are taken account into the recommendation of learning activity. That is, user correlations indicate the interaction factor among a group of users in a learning course, while learning patterns represent the learning behavior factor that has been recorded in the log data. In details, as discussed above, the DSUN model can be constructed to present users' potential profiling and dynamical relationships in accordance with the organized social streams, in which the specific correlations between the target user and others can be further extracted. Meanwhile, the learning patterns, which are used to describe the commonness of users' learning behaviors, can also be categorized with our proposed algorithm [18] in order to divide the whole user group into a series of sub-groups with the certain characteristic. Based on these, these two important factors are further employed in order to calculate the weight of a set of learning actions, which are selected from the users in those sub-groups and inferred as the possible next learning action according to the target user's current learning action. The formula can be expressed in Eq. 1.

$$W_{Act} = \sum_{i=1}^{k} \frac{Wp_i * \sum CoD(Act, \ v_j)}{m_i} \tag{1}$$

where, $Wp_i$ is the weight of each learning pattern, the value of which is depended on the similarity between each pattern and the target user. $m_i$ denotes the amount of users assigned in each sub-group according to learning patterns. $CoD(Act, v_j)$ denotes the contribution degree of those users who conduct this action and are connected with the target user in the DSUN model. Thus, the learning actions with higher weight will be recommended to the target user as the next learning action.

## 4.2     Architecture of a Prototype System

The architecture of a prototype system for the individualized learning activity recommendation is shown in Fig.5.

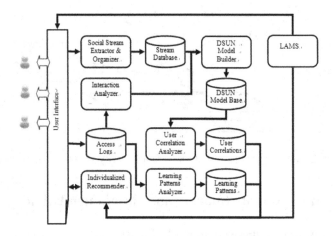

**Fig. 2.** Architecture of the prototype system for learning activity recommendation

In details, the Social Stream Extractor & Organizer is employed to extract the social streams posted by users and further organize them in the Stream Database. The DSUN Model Builder is used to construct the DSUN model based on the organized social streams saved in Stream Database and user interactions analyzed by Interaction Analyzer. As to User Correlation Analyzer, the correlation among the target user and other users can be figured out. Likewise, the Learning Patterns Analyzer contributes on categorizing Learning Patterns according to learning behaviors saved in Access Logs. Finally, the Individualized Recommender is responsible for calculating the weight of a list of potential learning activities and sending the most possible next learning activity as the feedback to the target user.

## 5     Conclusion

In this study, we have proposed a unified method to integrate social media into a web-based learning system, and further concentrated on the individualized recommendation of learning activities based on the user correlations in a social learning environment.

We first introduced a learning activity model based on user correlation to demonstrate the relations among the user, learning task and learning activity. Based on these, an integrated method was proposed to calculate the most possible next learning activity for the personalized recommendation. Besides, the design of the prototype system has also been discussed.

As for the future work, we will implement and evaluate this prototype system. We will also compare our proposed method with other related personalized learning systems and go further to evaluate the recommended information of learning activities.

# References

1. Ormrod, J.E.: Human learning, 3rd edn. Prentice-Hall, Upper Saddle River (1999)
2. Social Learning Theory,
   `http://teachnet.edb.utexas.edu/~Lynda_abbot/Social.html`
3. Chen, H., Zhou, X.K., Man, H.F., Wu, Y., Ahmed, A.U., Jin, Q.: A Framework of Organic Streams: Integrating Dynamically Diversified Contents into Ubiquitous Personal Study. In: Proc. 2nd International Symposium on Multidisciplinary Emerging Networks and Systems, Xi'an (2010)
4. Zhou, X.K., Chen, H., Jin, Q., Yong, J.M.: Generating Associative Ripples of Relevant Information from a Variety of Data Streams by Throwing a Heuristic Stone. In: Proc. ACM ICUIMC 2011 5th International Conference on Ubiquitous Information Management and Communication, Seoul, Korea (2011)
5. Zhou, X., Jin, Q.: Dynamical User Networking and Profiling Based on Activity Streams for Enhanced Social Learning. In: Leung, H., Popescu, E., Cao, Y., Lau, R.W.H., Nejdl, W. (eds.) ICWL 2011. LNCS, vol. 7048, pp. 219–225. Springer, Heidelberg (2011)
6. Signorini, A., Segre, A.M., Polgreen, P.M.: The Use of Twitter to Track Levels of Disease Activity and Public Concern in the US during the Influenza A H1N1 Pandemic. PLOS ONE 6(5) (2011)
7. Junco, R., Heiberger, G., Loken, E.: The effect of Twitter on college student engagement and grades. Journal of Computer Assisted Learning 27(2), 119–132 (2011)
8. Johnson, K.A.: The effect of Twitter posts on students' perceptions of instructor credibility. Learning Mediaand Technology 36(1), 21–38 (2011)
9. Vassileva, J.: Toward Social Learning Environment. IEEE Trans. Learning Technologies 1(4), 199–214 (2008)
10. Tsai, W.T., Li, W., Elston, J., Chen, Y.: Collaborative Learning Using Wiki Web Sites for Computer Science Undergraduate Education: A Case Study. IEEE Trans. Education 54(1), 114–124 (2011)
11. Hwang, Y., Kim, D.J.: Understanding Affective Commitment, Collectivist Culture, and Social Influence in Relation to Knowledge Sharing in Technology Mediated Learning. IEEE Trans. Professional Communication 50(3), 232–248 (2007)
12. Du, H.S., Wagner, C.: Learning With Weblogs: Enhancing Cognitive and Social Knowledge Construction. IEEE Trans. Professional Communication 50(1), 1–16 (2007)
13. Srivastava, J., Cooley, R., Deshpande, M., Tan, P.-N.: Web Usage Mining: Discovery and Applications of Usage Patterns from Web Data. ACM SIGKDD 1(2), 12–23 (2000)
14. Stumme, G., Hotho, A., Berendt, B.: Semantic Web Mining State of the Art and Future Directions. In: Web Semantics: Science, Services and Agents on the World Wide Web, vol. 4(2), pp. 124–143 (2006)
15. Poblete, B., Baeza-Yates, R.: Query-Sets: Using Implicit Feedback and Query Patterns to Organize Web Documents. In: Proc. WWW 2008, Beijing, pp. 41–48 (2008)

16. Bilenko, M., White, R.W.: Mining the Search Trails of Surfing Crowds: Identifying Relevant Websites From User Activity. In: Proc. WWW 2008, Beijing, pp. 51–60 (2008)
17. Fang, X., Liu Sheng, O.R.: LinkSelector: A Web Mining Approach to Hyperlink Selection for Web Portals. ACM Transactions on Internet Technology 4(2), 209–237 (2004)
18. Chen, J., Jin, Q., Huang, R.H.: Goal-Driven Process Navigation for Individualized Learning Activities in Ubiquitous Networking and IoT Environments. Journal of Universal Computer Science (to appear)

# Designer - Supporting Teachers Experience in Learning Management Systems

Silvia Baldiris[1], Sabine Graf[2], Jorge Hernandez[1],
Ramon Fabregat[1], and Nestor Duque[3]

[1] Institute of Informatics and Aplications (IIiA) University of Girona, Girona, Spain
{baldiris,ramon,jehernan}@eia.udg.es
[2] School of Computing and Information Systems, Athabasca University, Canada
sabineg@athabascau.ca
[3] National University of Colombia, Campus Manizales, Manizales, Colombia
ndduqueme@unal.edu.co

**Abstract.** In the lifelong learning context, the efficiency of learning is measured according to the users' achievement of the target competences. However, in a virtual learning environment supporting the competence development process ends up being an elusive and time-consuming task for teachers or instructional designers. In this paper, we introduce Designer, an approach for teachers to help them in designing courses via a semi-automatic design process based on dynamic user modeling and adaptive learning design generation. A qualitative and quantitative evaluation demonstrated the effectiveness of Designer in supporting teachers to create adaptive courses.

**Keywords:** Learning design generation, standards, adaptation, user modeling, planning.

## 1 Introduction

The generation of learning designs adjusted to user characteristics (i.e., learning styles and competences) [1],[2],[3] is not an easy problem, in particular for the teachers. Actually, this problem implies that teachers need to know the different instructional theories to support the design generation. They also need to control the different user variables to consider in the learning design construction such as users' learning styles and competences, among others. Furthermore, teachers need to know how to develop standardized learning designs for the specific learning platform they use.

In this paper, we introduce Designer, an approach for teachers to help them in designing courses via a semi-automatic design process based on competence definitions, user modelling and adaptation task. The main elements of our approach include: 1) the generation of a standardized and conditional learning design adjusted to IMS Learning Design specification; 2) the dynamic modelling of users' competences and learning styles and 3) the automatic generation of learning designs based on planning techniques that consider the users' competences and learning

E. Popescu et al. (Eds.): ICWL 2012, LNCS 7558, pp. 207–214, 2012.

styles. The aim of Designer is therefore to enable teachers to easily create standardized and adaptive learning designs by using a semi-automatic approach.

The paper is structured as follows. The second section introduces an analysis of the state of the art about the learning design generation process. In the third section, the general framework of our approach is introduced. The fourth section describes the two different planning problems for generating the learning design. The fifth and sixth sections describe some implementation details and the evaluation of the proposed semi-automatic learning design generation process respectively and finally the seventh section presents some concluding remarks and proposals for future work.

## 2     State of the Art about Learning Design Generation Process

A well-accepted definition for a learning design process is the following: the process that should be followed by teachers in order to plan and to prepare the instruction [4]. This process could be developed: 1) manually where teacher develop the design completely, 2) semi-automatically, with only a few inputs from the teachers or 3) automatically without teacher's intervention.

With the purpose to facilitate teachers the task of creating learning design manually, different solutions have been proposed, among them: Recourse [5], CopperAuthor [6], Reload[7], Collage[8], MOT+[9] and LAMS[10], ASK-LDT [11].

Semi- automatic and automatic learning design generation have been faced througt different points of view. In [3], [12] Karampiperis and Sampson proposed an approach based on a knowledge ontology, learning object metadata and competences which uses a weighted shortest path algorithms to generate an optimum learning path.

Duque et al. [13] proposed a multi-agent system for planning and execution of virtual personalized courses. Castillo et al. [14], using the SIADEX planner, addressed the problem to dynamically generate the planning domain based on the learning objects' metadata. Morales et al. [15] introduced a new approach that extends their previous work where they propose a multi-plan generation approach based on the user performance in different tests not using conditional planning. Ullrich and Melis [16] proposed a courseware generation framework based on HTN planning, PAIGOS, which generates structured courses that are adapted to a variety of learning goals and to learners' competencies.

In the state of the art, some researchers mention that the dynamic learning style modelling process is an interesting issue to research [17], [18], [19]. However, this dynamic process is not addressed until now in the learning design generation process. This means that it is not specified how this dynamic process affects the generated designs in the execution time. This paper addresses the dynamic process in the learning design and is based on our investigations in previous work about dynamic user modeling based on learning styles [20].

On the other hand, the big effort developed for international organization of standardizations has not been considered in the teacher's normal activities. Many teachers do not know the specifications and it is common when teachers are faced to use the standards they feel the standards are difficult to use.

In our research, we aim at alleviating the workload for teachers of creating adaptive courses by reducing the complexity involved in authoring standardized and adaptive learning designs adjusted to their students' characteristics (competences and learning styles), which are inferred through a dynamic user modelling approach. In the next section, we show the general elements of our framework.

# 3    General Framework for Learning Design Generation

Figure 1 shows the general elements of our framework. The Competence Definition permits to define appropriate performances that should be demonstrated by a person on a specific context. The competence definition consists of: Competence General Information, Competence Elements which are smaller learning purposes, Didactical Guidelines and the Competence Context. Competence Elements in turn describe the Essential Knowledge and Competence Evidence.

The User Model Initialization identifies and stores the initial state of the user model variables using the Learner Information Profile (LIP) Specification [21] schema. The Local Learning Objects and Activity Metadata Definition is referred to label the learning objects develop by teachers (internal objects) with metadata. Distributed Learning Objects Metadata Searching is a mechanism supported by agent technologies and its main purpose is to consider external learning objects the learning designs generation process.

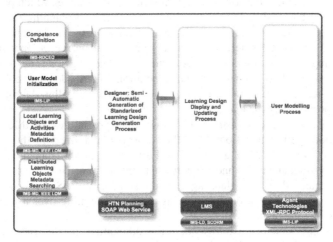

**Fig. 1.** Proposed framework for learning design generation

**Designer:** Semi–Automatic Standardized Learning Design Generation Process, is in charge of designing adapted teaching-learning experience (i.e. the creation of adaptive learning paths) adjusted to the IMS-LD level B [22]. The generated design can be displayed and updated later according to the performance and characteristics of the students, captured through the user modelling process.

The Learning Design Display and Updating Process is the process in charge for presenting and maintaining learning design execution according to the user model.
The User Modelling Process aims at creating and maintaining an up-to-date user model. We consider two user characteristics, competences and learning styles.

For addressing the overall adaptation process we consider two perspectives: design time (when the course is created and composed in the LMS) and run time (when learners are learning in the course). At the design time, the necessary information for the Designer (agent who generates the course) is developed and constructed and the execution time, the generated learning design is displayed in the LMS [23] and the user behaviour is monitoring.

## 4    Planning Learning Design Generation

As was mentioned before the Designer is in charge of designing adapted teaching-learning experience. We have modelled the problem of learning design generation as a planning problem, using HTN planning as a generation mechanism. HTN planning [24] was selected because the course domain is constructed from the competence definition, which has a hierarchical structure.

HTN planning or actually any planning paradigm imply to face the domain and problem generation which are inputs for the planners. The planning domain describes all actions needed to achieve one or more goals expressed in the planning problem.

The planning problem describes the initial state of all variables which participate in the problem and the goals. Then, we consider two different planning problems. The first one for generating a learning design based only on the competence definition provided by teachers, considering the initial state of the users' competence. In the second planning problem, we consider both the users' learning styles and competence.

The core of the first scenario is the generation of an adequate course for all students registered to a class that take into account only the definition of the competence provided by the teacher.

The initial state is constructed using the procedures getMetadata and getOrganization. getOrganization takes the information defined in the competence definition and converts it in a term list. Furthermore, getMetadata analyses the learning objects metadata files and converts them in a term list.

The main method in the planning domain is generateIMSLD, which uses the information provided by the organization list structure iterating over it recursively in order to construct the plan.

In the second scenario, we extended the adaptation in the first scenario by additionally considering students' learning styles in the adaptation process. The core of the adaptation process based on learning styles is to select the best order to present learning resource types according to the learning style information, as suggested for example in [25]. Results of this study [25] indicated that students are more satisfied with their learning experiences and need less time for learning if they receive learning objects ordered according with their learning style preferences. In order to include the adaptation based on learning styles we have created another method called GetPreferences for obtaining the information related to the students' learning style preferences and include it in the initial state of the user model [20].

## 5     Integration upon dotLRN

In order to integrate our proposals upon OpenACS/.LRN, the following implementations were developed: 1) Designer Service v1.0, implements a planning web service based on SOAP, which listens user's requests and sends as a reply an IMS-LD unit of learning. 2) Designer Client v1.0 Package: implements a web service client upon dotLRN in order to send planning requests to the Designer Service and process its responses. The parameters that the Planner Clients sends in its requests are the IMS-RDCEO of a course generated by the Competences Package, the list of learning content metadata URLs associated to the course and the users' preferences. The Planner Engine responds with an adapted course, which the planner client automatically loads and deploys as an adapted learners' unit of learning using Grail [23]. For users it is not necessary the technical management of any specification because we have created users interfaces.

## 6     Evaluation

The main purpose of the evaluation is to verify the teachers' satisfaction with our solution offered for generating adapted learning designs based on students' competences and learning styles. The principal actor in this evaluation is the teacher who evaluated the approach considering three dimensions:

- The main elements of the learning and teaching process description (Competence definition, metadata specification and the link between both).
- The semi-automatic generation process.
- The adaptation process.

Six teachers from Universitat of Gerona participated in this study. The teachers were from different fields including pedagogy, economy, law, psychology, tourism and administration science. Teachers have different levels of experience in online learning in particular in the use of virtual learning environments.

Quantitative analysis was used to get data about teachers' perception on how important the proposed dimensions (described at the beginning of this section) are and how our solution satisfies their expectation about them. All teachers were asked to fill out a survey, created according to a Gap Service Quality Model [26]. Gap Service Quality Model have been strongly validated in different domains to measure users satisfaction reporting good results [27]. The survey consisted of fifteen questions, including five questions for each of the three proposed dimensions in order to obtain feedback from the teachers about their perception of each dimension.

Figure 2 shows the results of the Gap analysis. In general, all teachers have assigned a high score to the importance and satisfaction for each dimension. The difference between importance and satisfaction (gap) for the proposed solutions is very small (least than 1 point out of 10). It means the proposed solution seems to meet the expectations of the teachers who participated in this study.

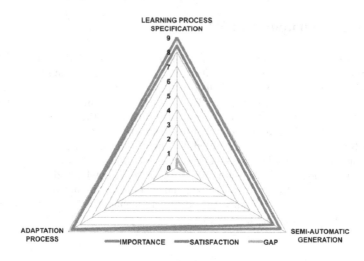

**Fig. 2.** Gap Model Results

## 7    Conclusions and Future Works

Developing adaptive and standardized courses is very time-consuming for teachers. In this paper, we introduce an approach for reducing teachers' workload for generating standardized and adaptive learning designs. Designer: Semi–Automatic Standardized Learning Design Generator was introduced and evaluated.

Our evaluation showed that the participating teachers found our approach useful, especially for the possibility to easily create an IMS-LD and also for the possibility of providing learning paths adapted to the students' learning styles and competences. However, they also complained that the production of learning resources and virtual activities and its semantic relations through metadata requires an initial extra effort. But they also agreed that in subsequent opportunities, this effort decreases as the possibility of reutilization grows.

Future works will be oriented to take into account other students' features such as special needs and also teachers' preferred methodologies for learning design creation.

## References

1. Graf, S., Kinshuk, D.: Providing Adaptive Courses in Learning Management Systems with Respect to Learning Styles. In: Richards, G. (ed.) Proceedings of the World Conference on E-Learning in Corporate, Government, Healthcare, and Higher Education (e-Learn), pp. 2576–2583. AACE Press, Chesapeake (2007)
2. Popescu, E.: Evaluating the Impact of Adaptation to Learning Styles in a Web-Based Educational System. In: Spaniol, M., Li, Q., Klamma, R., Lau, R.W.H. (eds.) ICWL 2009. LNCS, vol. 5686, pp. 343–352. Springer, Heidelberg (2009)

3. Karampiperis, P., Sampson, D.: Adaptive Learning Objects Sequencing for Competence-Based Learning. In: 6th IEEE International Conference on Advanced Learning Technologies. IEEE Computer Society Press (2006)
4. Reigeluth, C.M.: Instructional Design Theories and Models, a new paradigm of instructional theory. Laurence Erlbaum Associates (1999)
5. TENCompetence: Recourse, http://tencompetence-project.bolton.ac.uk/ldauthor/
6. Open Universiteit Nederland: CopperCore, http://coppercore.sourceforge.net/
7. Bolton, U.: Of: Reusable eLearning Object Authoring & Delivery (RELOAD)
8. Hernández-leo, D., Villasclaras-fernández, E.D., Asensio-pérez, J.I., Jorrín-abellán, I.M., Ruiz-requies, I., Rubia-avi, B.: COLLAGE☐: A collaborative Learning Design editor based on patterns. Learning 9, 58–71 (2006)
9. Paquette, G., De La Teja, I., Leonard, M., Lundgren-Cayrol, K., Marino, O.: An Instructional Engineering Method and Tool for the Design of Units of Learning. In: Koper Rob, T.C. (ed.) A Handbook on Modelling and Delivering Networked Education and Training, pp. 161–184 (2005)
10. LAMS: Learning Activity Management System, http://www.lamsinternational.com/
11. Sampson, D., Karampiperis, P., Zervas, P.: ASK-LDT: A Web-Based Learning Scenarios Authoring Environment Based on IMS Learning Design. Advanced Technology for Learning (Discontinued) 2 (2005)
12. Karampiperis, P., Sampson, D.: Adaptive Learning Object Selection in Intelligent Learning Systems. Journal of Interactive Learning Research 15, 389–407 (2004)
13. Duque Méndez, N.D., Ovalle Carranza, D.A., Jiménez Builes, J.A.: Artificial Intelligence For Automatic Generation Of Customized Courses. In: Bohman, E.P.P. (ed.) World Conference on Educational Multimedia, Hypermedia and Telecommunications, pp. 2693–2698 (2002)
14. Castillo, L., Morales, L., González-Ferrer, A., Fdez-Olivares, J., Borrajo, D., Onaindía, E.: Automatic generation of temporal planning domains for e-learning problems. Journal of Scheduling 13, 347–362 (2009)
15. Morales, L., Castillo, L., Fernández-Olivares, J.: Planning for Conditional Learning Routes. In: Aguirre, A.H., Borja, R.M., Garciá, C.A.R. (eds.) MICAI 2009. LNCS, vol. 5845, pp. 384–396. Springer, Heidelberg (2009)
16. Ullrich, C., Melis, E.: Pedagogically founded courseware generation based on HTN-planning. Expert Systems with Applications 36, 9319–9332 (2009)
17. Graf, S., Liu, T.-C.: Supporting Teachers in Identifying Students Learning Styles in Learning Management Systems: An Automatic Student Modelling Approach. Educational Technology & Society 12, 3–14 (2009)
18. Ortigosa, A., Paredes, P., Rodriguez, P.: AH-questionnaire☐: An adaptive hierarchical questionnaire for learning styles. Computers & Education 54, 999–1005 (2010)
19. Carmona Márquez, C., Castillo Jordán, G., Valldeperas, E.M.: Modelo Bayesiano del Alumno basado en el Estilo de Aprendizaje y las Preferencias. IEEE-RITA Revista Iberoamericana de Tecnologías del Aprendizaje 4, 139–146 (2009)
20. Baldiris, S., Graf, S., Fabregat, R.: Dynamic User Modeling and Adaptation based on Learning Styles for Supporting Semi-Automatic Generation of IMS Learning Design. In: The 11th IEEE International Conference on Advanced Learning Technologies, Athens, Georgia, USA (2011)
21. IMS: IMS Learner Information Package Specification (2001)
22. IMS: IMS Learning Design. Version 1.0. Final Specification (2003)

23. Escobedo Del Cid, J.P., Valentín De La Fuente, L., Gutiérrez, S., Pardo, A., Delgado Kloos, C.: Implementation of a Learning Design Run-Time Environment for the .LRN Learning Management System. JIME Special Issue: Adaptation and IMS Learning Design, 1–16 (2007)
24. Erol, K., James, H., Dana, N.: HTN planning: Complexity and expressivity. In: Twelfth National Conference on Artificial Intelligence (AAAI 1994), pp. 1123–1128. AAAI Press/MIT Press, Seattle, Washington (1994)
25. Popescu, E., Badica, C.: Providing Personalized Courses in a Web-Supported Learning Environment. In: IEEE/WIC/ACM International Conference on Web Intelligence and Intelligent Agent Technology - Workshops (2009)
26. Parasuraman, A., Zeithaml, V., Berry, L.: SERVQUAL- A Multiple-Item Scale for Measuring Consumer Perceptions of Service Quality 64, 12–40 (1998)
27. Landrum, H., Prybutok, V., Zhang, X., Peak, D.: Measuring IS System Service Quality with SERVQUAL: Users Perceptions of Relative Importance of the Five SERVPERF Dimensions. International Journal of an Emerging Transdiscipline 12, 18–35 (2009)

# Broadening the Use of E-Learning Standards for Adaptive Learning

Anna Mavroudi[1] and Thanasis Hadzilacos[1,2]

[1] Open University of Cyprus, Cyprus
anna.mavroudi@st.ouc.ac.cy
[2] Computer Technology Institute and Press "Diophantus", Greece
thh@ouc.ac.cy

**Abstract.** This paper presents two specific educational applications that make use of the IMS-Learning Design specification as the basis for adaptive web-based learning. Specifically, learner profiling and personalization is achieved in adaptive courseware compliant with the specification and including a diagnostic learning style test and an educational recommender system. These components make use of the learning style and prior knowledge respectively, in order to adapt the presentation of the learning material and the feedback given to the learner.

**Keywords:** IMS-LD, IMS-QTI, adaptive learning, learning style test, educational recommender system.

## 1 Introduction

The work described in this paper is motivated by the fact that an opportunity is being shadowed by a problem: adaptive learning can be managed effectively by the IMS-LD specification (the opportunity) which has been criticized as being too technical (the problem). Indeed, the IMS-LD specification has been frequently used for adaptive, web-based learning (see for example [1]), but it has been criticized for being too difficult for non-technical users (see for example [2]). This restricts the development of IMS-LD compliant courseware to these sub-groups of stakeholders (researchers, teachers, instructional designers) that have a fairly good technical background. An interesting research challenge is to describe potential uses of this e-learning standard for adaptive courseware that do not require much technical knowledge and furthermore, to design, develop and evaluate the courseware.

Learner's prior knowledge and their learning style are two parameters often referenced in the recent literature being used for adaptation. In a preliminary study reported here that was conducted among ten teachers and instructional designers, it seems that indeed they try to augment the learning experience (both face-to-face and e-learning) using these parameters at a great extent. This paper describes two adaptive components: a diagnostic learning style quiz and an educational recommender system, which are based on the learning style and prior knowledge of the learners, respectively. The IMS-LD specification is being used as the basis of the adaptive method.

E. Popescu et al. (Eds.): ICWL 2012, LNCS 7558, pp. 215–221, 2012.

The remainder of the paper is structured as follows: the research methodology is being discussed, starting from the choice of Design-Based Research as the appropriate methodological framework. Implementation issues follow for both the diagnostic quiz and the recommender system. In conclusion, the promise of IMS-LD use on adaptive learning is discussed and future plans concerning the integration with mobile learning and SCORM are outlined.

Of course, compliance with an e-learning standard does not guarantee achievement of the desired educational goals. Rather, standards mostly provide mechanisms for promoting interoperability, re-usability, accessibility and other 'good utilities' of learning objects or learning activities. Thus, they can be considered as mechanisms that promote quality in e-learning, though not necessarily in learning. As far as IMS Learning Design (IMS-LD) [3] is concerned, it is a pedagogically neutral specification in the sense that it provides a formalization of the teaching-learning process through the metaphor of the theatrical play [4], leaving all the pedagogically vital decisions, such as teaching strategies, learning objectives etc, up to the instructional designer. Finally, the IMS Question & Test Interoperability (QTI) specification [5] describes a data model for the representation of questions, tests and their result reports. It enables sharing of test items and result data among authoring tools, learning systems, e-portfolios, e-assessment systems etc. Additional related information, such as outcomes, grades and associated metadata can be also transferred among compliant systems.

## 2     Research methodology

### 2.1     Design-Based research

According to the Design-Based Methodology (DBR), the design of educational intervention starts with the definition of a meaningful problem for the practitioners and requires their collaboration in order to produce: domain theories or a design framework or design methodologies [6]. This paper acknowledges the problem of having a mechanism –the IMS-LD specification for web-based learning- which may be optimal for adaptive learning but, on the other hand, is cumbersome for non-technical users. For this purpose, it proposes design methodologies i.e. practical guidelines on "how to implement a set of designs, what kind of expertise is required and who should provide the expertise" [6].

### 2.2     The Preliminary Survey

The table below shows the answers of ten participants who answered, through an online questionnaire in a 5-point Likert scale, the extent to which they adapt their teaching practices according to certain parameters (1 meaning "totally disagree" to 5 meaning "totally agree" with the statement "I adapt my teaching practices according to these parameters"). The participants' occupations (6 from Greece, 1 from Portugal, 1 from Malaysia, 1 from Cyprus and 1 from USA) were either instructional designers and/or educators teaching in schools. All answers but one (who gave grade 2) ranked learning style as an important or extremely important parameter (gave grades 4 or 5).

Table 1. Adaptive learning parameters

| Descriptive Statistics | | | |
|---|---|---|---|
| | N | Mean | Std. Dev |
| Prior knowledge | 10 | 3.90 | 1.197 |
| Learning style | 10 | 4.00 | .816 |
| Learning strategy | 10 | 4.30 | .949 |
| Time availability | 10 | 4.00 | .943 |
| Learning objectives | 10 | 4.10 | .994 |
| Valid N (listwise) | 10 . | | |

A follow up discussion through a semi-structured interview aiming to elaborate on the answers of the questionnaire revealed that this educator would also like to incorporate learning style as a defining parameter for his teaching practices, if suitable tools were available. In conclusion, it seems that learning style is a determining parameter. As one participant mentioned during the follow-up discussions :"I think that the teaching process is not far away from a successful theatrical play. You can't play every day the exact same performance for a different audience. You must check the audience response, have a great variety in the repertoire and adapt according to your audience. Repeating the exact same play again and again is not theatre, it is called cinema."

Being itself a metaphor of the theatrical play and providing through this metaphor a formalization of the teaching-learning process, the IMS-LD specification can sustain effectively strategies for adaptive learning.

## 3    Our Adaptive Learning Scenario

The learning scenario that was implemented with the use of the IMS-LD specification consisted of five phases, each containing numerous learning tasks:

1. Diagnostic evaluation concerning prior knowledge and learning style
2. Presentation of the new knowledge
3. Test new knowledge
4. Synthesize knowledge and reflect
5. Apply knowledge

The diagnostic learning style quiz was implemented in the first phase and the educational recommender system in the third phase, for the development of which no technical knowledge is required, since the needed work is graphically represented and designed at an abstract level. The detailed description of the learning scenario is out of the scope of this paper. In brief, in this specific learning scenario, the learning process follows a deductive-inquisitory approach since it presents information to the learners and then the learners themselves produce complete examples of work as assignments. The learning scenario uses various categories of adaptation (adaptive learning flow/content, adaptive grouping, adaptive feedback and adaptive evaluation) that were needed in order to support the learning goals. Web2.0 tools were also used to support collaboration and reciprocity and SCORM compliant learning objects to present the learning materials.

## 4    Development and Implementation of the Diagnostic Learning Style Quiz

The development of this test follows a well-known and widely-accepted VARK (visual-auditory-read/write-kinaesthetic) quiz, which consists of a set of 16 multiple response questions ([7]). For each question the learner may choose one or more options and even omit a question. When the test terminates, the learner is presented with the results and the tutor can also be informed. This may enhance the learner' metacognition as well as help the tutor to provide more personalized instruction. The above scenario may also be used as part of a wider scenario that exploits the results with the use of adaptive content: for example, the same learning resource, with or without audio narrative. Technically this is possible through the use of 'div classes' in XHMTL documents that show or hide elements (like an audio recording or an image) on a conditional basis ([1], [8]).

A research question that needs to be taken into account in this point of the learning design is related to the balance between using information and media in a way that makes most sense to the learner so as to provide differentiated learning on the one hand, and, on the other, according to the theory of multiple intelligences ([9]), engaging all the learners with a variety of methods and media. This decision would inform the next stage of the learning design that involves the presentation of the new knowledge.

As mentioned, the IMS-LD specification leaves all the important decisions up to the instructional designer. The authors decided to provide adaptive presentation of information (e.g. show/hide an image or an audio narrative etc) only if there is clear indication concerning the dominant learning preference. Otherwise, the learning materials are presented 'as-are' along with all their media elements. The VARK test provides an algorithm to reveal whether a learner has one clear preference or she is a multimodal learner. The test that was implemented simulates this algorithm through the combined use of properties and conditions, as defined by the IMS-LD specification. Thus, the first module of the Unit of Learning is comprised by the VARK test, following by the presentation of the new knowledge in an adaptive (in case of a single preference) or a non-adaptive mode (in case of a multimodal learner).

## 5    The Educational Recommender System

Moving to the second phase of the learning scenario, the learners are presented with a number of learning activities (ranging from 0 to 8, depending on the level of their prior knowledge and experience) in the use of a specific e-learning authoring tool. First, they evaluate themselves on their prior knowledge in a 5- point Likert scale and the tutor is informed about it as well. The learning activities are basically a set of "How-To's" presenting the key functionality of the tool that the course is about. The final goal is to synthesize their knowledge and implement a showcase (i.e. a complex task) using the authoring tool. Prior to that, the instructional designer has created as part of the learning strategy a 'relevancy matrix' between the pool of the "How-To's" and the pool of the "Showcases". Between the phase of the presentation of the prerequisite knowledge (i.e. "How-To's") and the synthesis of the showcase on behalf of the learners, there is an extra phase which consists of a quiz. The goal of the quiz is to conclude on the learners' actual prior knowledge. Thus, in the lesson plan, there exists another matrix that relates the questions with the "How-To's". So literally, the "How-to's", the questions and the "Showcases" are interrelated. The recommender system, using properties and conditions of the IMS-LD specification (Level B), combines these relations, calculates a 'contiguity grade' for each "Showcase" based on the learner's answers and proposes to the learner specific "Showcases". Subsequently, the learner may discuss this suggestion with her tutor and decide whether she should follow it or pick another "Showcase" instead. Figure 1 depicts the idea of recommending the proper "Showcase" after calculating the "contiguity grade" mentioned above. All the needed work is based on the process of setting properties and rules through a graphic user interface, so no technical knowledge (like scripting or XML knowledge etc) is needed, irrespectively of the IMS-LD compliant editor being used.

**Fig. 1.** The use of IMS-LD rules

# 6    Overall learning Strategy for Adaptive Learning and Evaluation Framework

For the scope of this work, the evaluation framework aims at gauging the effectiveness of the learning strategy for the design of adaptive learning, which is being summarized at the table below and shows how the learning preference informs the design of learning activities:

**Table 2.** Mappings between learning preferences and the design of learning activities

| Learning preference | Learning activities with: |
|---|---|
| Auditory | Recordings, audio narratives |
| Visual | Diagrams, pictures, flowcharts, slides |
| Read/Write | Web 2.0 tools (forum, chat, wiki), open ended questions, lists, essays |
| Kinaesthetic | Mobile learning, real-life learning experiences |
| Multimodal | All the above |

The learning strategy was inspired by the guidelines of N. Fleming (the creator of the VARK test), but also by current trends in educational technology that have already proved in the wider educational industry their positive effects in the learning process (Web 2.0 tools, mobile learning). It further tries to combine these two strands so that: the selection of the media should not only be in accordance with the learning preferences, but also, in a second level should avoid cognitive load and related effects, like the split attention effect. What remains yet, is to test the effectiveness of this learning strategy. For this purpose, the evaluation framework would provide a 360-degree feedback by taking into account evaluation parameters in each of the three levels: 'traditional' (classroom-based) learning, e-learning, and mobile learning. Through the analysis of the interviews, the interplay of these levels was depicted as shown in the figure below. E-learning is conceptualized as an augmentation of 'traditional' learning in which the use of technology plays a decisive role and mobile learning is conceptualized as an augmentation of e-learning where context conditions (basically the "where", the "who" and the "why", as mentioned in [10]) and mobile devices also play a decisive role in the teaching-learning process.

# 7    Conclusions and Future Plans

In the learning design strategy, the kinesthetic addition may not be very useful for the 'traditional' desktop e-learning or for the face- to-face, classroom-based learning, but it might be useful when it comes to mobile learning, something that it is included in future plans. As mentioned in [7], the kinesthetic type is in favor of field trips and training with real-life examples, which are very much aligned with the philosophy of mobile learning. Exploring the possibilities of the IMS-LD specification for adaptive and mobile learning is an interesting opportunity for future research [11]. Moreover, future plans involve the integration of four specific SCORM (v1.2) metadata elements that may be also used for adaptive learning: "cmi.student_preference.audio", "cmi.student_preference.text", "cmi.student_preference.speed", "cmi.core.session_time" and "cmi.student_preference.language". The mechanism for combining SCORM with IMS-LD is already in place, as described in [12]. Finally, the reusable Units of Learning (literally .zip files that are comprised by the learning recourses and their metadata, and a file that contains the structure of the lesson) that contain the implementations of the diagnostic quiz, the recommender system and the wider adaptive learning scenario can be downloaded from the project website [13].

**Acknowledgements.** The VARK test is licensed under copyright, Version 7.1 (2011) held by Neil D. Fleming, Christchurch, New Zealand. Permission by the creator of the VARK questionnaire (N. Fleming) should be provided in order to be able to use any VARK copyrighted material.

# References

1. Burgos, D., Tattersall, C., Koper, E.J.R.: Representing adaptive and adaptable Units of Learning. How to model personalized eLearning in IMS Learning Design. In: Computers and Education: E-learning - from Theory to Practice. Kluwer, Germany (2007)
2. Gómez, S., Mejía, C., Huerva, D., Fabregat, R.: Context-Aware Adaptation Process to Build Units of Learning Based on IMS-LD Standard. In: Int. Conf. on Education and New Learning Technologies (EDULEARN 2009) Conference, Barcelona, España (2009)
3. Learning Design Specification, http://www.imsglobal.org/learningdesign/
4. Jeffery, A., Currier, S.: What Is...IMS Learning Design? CETIS (2005), http://publications.cetis.ac.uk/wp-content/uploads/2011/10/WhatIsLD2_web.pdf
5. IMS Question & Test Interoperability Specification, http://www.imsglobal.org/question/
6. What is Design-based Research?, http://projects.coe.uga.edu/dbr/explain01.htm#method
7. Fleming, N.: VARK Questionnaire, http://www.vark-learn.com/english/index.asp
8. Santos, S.G., Pardo, A., Kloos, C.D.: Authoring Courses with Rich Adaptive Sequencing for IMS Learning Design. J. UCS, 2819–2839 (2008)
9. Gardner, H.: Frames of Mind: The Theory of Multiple Intelligences. Basic Books, New York (1983)
10. Sariola, J., Sampson, J., Vuorinen, R., Kynäslahti, H.: Promoting mLearning by the Uni-iWap project within higher education. In: International Conference on Technology and Education, Florida State University, Tallahassee (2001)
11. Specht, M., Burgos, D.: Implementing Adaptive Educational Methods with IMS Learning Design. In: Proceedings of Adaptive Hypermedia, Dublin, Ireland (2006), http://dspace.learningnetworks.org (retrieved June 30, 2006)
12. Tattersall, C., Burgos, D., Vogten, H., Martens, H., Koper, R.: How to use ims learning design and scorm 2004 together. In: Proc. of the International Conference on SCORM 2004. Tamkang University, Taipei (2006)
13. OpenSOA project website, http://opensoa.ouc.ac.cy

# RECALL – Location Based Services
# for Excluded Communities

Camelia Popescu[1], David Brown[2], and Nick Shopland[2]

[1] Centre for Professional Training in Culture, Bucharest, Romania
camelia.popescu@cppc.ro
[2] Computing and Technology Team, Nottingham Trent University,
Professor in Interactive Systems for Social Inclusion, Nottingham, UK
{david.brown,nicholas.shopland}@ntu.ac.uk

**Abstract.** RECALL is a European Transversal project developing location based services in assistive technologies to allow people with learning disabilities and sensory and physical impairments to plan and independently carry out their route to work and community activities, helping them to overcome physical and psychological barriers to independent travel and community inclusion.

The Route Mate application is being designed for the Android System and will be available in English, Bulgarian, Greek and Romanian lan-guages. Three modes of Route Mate have been implemented and tested which allow users to plan and practice their routes to different community opportuni-ties. The Plan mode promotes User Created Content and allows RECALL to be personalized to users' needs. The Usage mode offers self directed learning op-portunities by allowing users to practice the routes they have created in the Plan Mode. Challenge Mode is based on games based learning to reinforce route learning in an engaging way.

**Keywords:** m-learning, social inclusion, adult education, route planning, memory and concentration.

## 1 Preliminary Issues

### 1.1 Recall Project

On leaving compulsory education, people with learning disabilities, who have previously been provided with transport to allow them to access community activity, suddenly become excluded from lifelong learning and community activity because of their lack of independent travel skills [10]. One of the core skills required for leading an independent life, social inclusion and accessing the world of work is the gaining of independent travel skills and having the confidence to learn and travel new routes [3].

RECALL is a project (504970-LLP-1-2009-1-UK-KA3-KA3MP) financed by European Union. This project develops location based services in assistive technologies to allow people with disabilities to plan and independently carry out their route to work and community activities. This reconnection to work and community and

E. Popescu et al. (Eds.): ICWL 2012, LNCS 7558, pp. 222–227, 2012.
© Springer-Verlag Berlin Heidelberg 2012

reengagement in active citizenship will significantly increase the personal fulfilment in a multiply disadvantaged and excluded group.

## 1.2    Route Mate Concept

Route Mate is an application developed in this project for the Android System and it is specified in English, Bulgarian, Greek and Romanian languages. Three modes of Route Mate allow the end users to plan, rehearse and then actually reconnect with learning, employment and other community opportunities. This approach combines location based services with game based learning approaches [1].

Route Mate will develop lifelong learning skills of: route planning; memory and concentration; stress management; time-management; understanding targets and deadlines.

The following target groups can take advantage from this application: people with learning disabilities; people with sensory impairments; people with mobility impairments; trainers and carers; parents, friends and relatives of disabled people; social Service providers; organizations of/for disabled people; travel networks.

## 1.3    Cognitive Maps

Route Mate is intended to aid the development of cognitive maps which, after development, can be used to gain skills which enable individuals to travel independently. The application makes use of GPS technology commonly found in modern smart phones and Google Maps to provide the mapping service which is displayed on the devices screen.

Cognitive maps are formed when individuals repeatedly navigate a specific environment [4]. After construction, cognitive maps are later used to aid subsequent navigation to a location. An individual's inability to form cognitive maps can lead to disorientation, confusion and anxiety and is a significant reason why people with intellectual disabilities suffer from difficulties in social integration. A human's navigation ability relies on two strategies, egocentric tasks and allocentric tasks. An egocentric strategy is the use of information learned in a sequential manner from a route and the landmarks on that route to effectively reach the target. An allocentric strategy is the use of a mental representation or cognitive map that includes the direction and distance between points, landscapes and targets [9].

Route Mate uses a number of strategies (Plan, Use & Challenge) to encourage cognitive map formation.

## 1.4    Location Based Services

A location based service offers real time support should route divergence occur or some other error be made. Should users get lost, Route Mate can automatically text the user's GPS position with a street name to a nominated other's mobile device, or call a nominated helper to help them conversationally to navigate to safety. Unlike the mobile route guidance systems used by vehicle drivers the system is less likely to suppress the development of cognitive or mental maps[5].

## 1.5     Game Based Learning Approach

Games engage the learner voluntarily in sufficient repetitions of the activities to ensure learning takes place [7]. They provide immediate feedback so that an activity is easily linked with a learning outcome [7]. They can also be structured with different levels of challenge to scaffold the planning of new routes and the first instances of travelling these new routes. The scaffolding can also be structured to support collaboration with peers or teachers, and then be programmed to offer less intervention as the user develops the confidence and skills to, ultimately, travel these routes independently.

# 2     Project Methodology

## 2.1     Preliminary Testing

The project started with a research phase in order to understand the problems that target groups are facing. USERfit methodology [8] was used to assist in the identification of the relevant design issues and convert them to design requirements that can then be incorporated into the first and subsequent prototypes or versions.

To achieve the project's objectives, project partners were asked to carry out two activities.

The first was to document information on:

- The profile of their testing group
- What teaching instruments and materials are normally used in independent travel training, if such training is provided, and who normally provides it.
- The attitudes of the beneficiaries, their trainers and their carers towards developing their ability to travel independently.
- The initial attitudes of the beneficiaries, their trainers and their carers towards the use of Route Mate as a means of independent travel training.

The second was to collect feedback from users on their experience of using the preliminary version of Route Mate application. This required partners to tabulate three sets of information.

- Stakeholder Overview: For each stakeholder category, a design implication was identified and the resulting action for the redesign stated.
- Stakeholder Attributes to establish the functional implications and desired product characteristics based on the stakeholder attributes revealed by the stakeholder overview.
- Requirements Summary: this prioritises the requirements. For each desired product characteristic, any possible conflicts with other desired characteristics were considered. For each requirement the priority for it being met was rated high, medium or low.

This research resulted in 33 desired product characteristics for people with a cogni-tive, sensory or physical impairment and 16 for their carers or trainers. Each characteristic was rated by the group as either of high, medium or low priority for development.

Carers and trainers agreed that the following characteristics were of high priority for the next phase of development: full & detailed user manual; alerts user when approaching a dangerous situation; remind user of key road safety issues; allow real time monitoring; panic button easily accessible; send map reference; offline route management; remote tracking of user.

On the other hand people with cognitive/physical disabilities identified as important the following characteristics: game based learning approach; interactions with the application should be mistake tolerant; all information & interaction can be presented in multiple modes; tutorial/review of the main features of the application.

## 2.2    Iterative Testing

During the next phase these new design requirements were added and accessibility features designed and embedded for Android OS. Through iterative testing, experts from the project measured performance against agreed indicators to ensure that we meet the objectives of increasing independence and inclusion for the target groups and of reconnecting excluded learners back to their communities and lifelong learning opportunities. For bug fixing an Issue Tracking software application was used.

For iterative testing the methodology proposed some specific steps and tools to be used:

- Testing will be conducted in teams: one and one evaluator.
- Relatively quiet and short roads will be chosen.
- Two testing sessions will be conducted with every user.
- Tools to be used: test scripts to guide users through each mode, observation sheets to record any usability issues, template to collect the data.

## 3    Description of the Application

Route Mate has three modes of use: Plan, Use and Challenge. Plan mode gives the user the option to create a new route, or load and modify an existing route with the help of a parent, carer or trainer. They can enter the start point using selection on a map and can also enter the start time of their journey, set daily alarms and end address of their new route (fig 1).

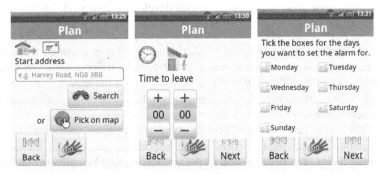

**Fig. 1.** Planning a route

An emergency contact can be specified and points of interest can also be set between the start and end points using the phone's camera to break the journey up into a num-ber of smaller routes connected by key landmarks and more effectively scaffold its learning.

The initial design only allowed route creation on the device itself, and required users to enter location data while walking the route. Further the application was extended to allow route preparation via a desktop browser, enabling access to a larger screen area and easier interaction methods. This added flexibility and the availability of additional resources is intended to enhance the opportunity for transition between egocentric and allocentric viewpoints,

Implementation of the Route Mate application has followed an iterative development method:

- v1.0 - Original Route Mate application as it stood at the start of the project.
- v1.1 - Use Mode - allowing identification and incorporation of refinements and bug fixes.
- v1.2 - Plan Mode - includes the console that enables management, planning and editing of routes on the phone using a PC.
- v1.3 - Challenge Mode. This is where gamification will be applied.
- v1.4 - Final version. This will be a consolidated version for piloting and will be the version that the project publishes for wider use.

## 4     Future Development

For the last phase of product development - Challenge Mode, the framework developed for Plan and Use modes will be augmented with entertaining and amusing additions that make planning and following a route more meaningful and engaging, as well assisting the user's progress from egocentric to allocentric understanding of context. The approaches under consideration seek to reflect the Plan, Use and (recursively) Challenge modes already outlined:

- Treasure hunt (sequential) - associate with route planning and creation activities
- Find as many items as possible - associate with using route
- Find fires and put them out - associate with developing independence / confidence (on a particular route)

However the gamification is implemented, the application is intended to assist and extend a travel training curriculum, and so must provide trainers with adequate support, and give them confidence that it can be used within the training curriculum, as well as providing additional, flexible approaches for developing individual users' learning opportunities.

From valorisation point of view, project plans will facilitate wider mainstreaming and exploitation of the final version of the application at regional, national and inter-national levels. The final version of the application will be uploaded on Android Market.

# References

1. Brown, D.J., McHugh, D., Standen, P., et al.: Designing Location-Based Learning Experiences for People with Intellectual Disabilities and Additional Sensory Impairments. Comput. Educ. 56, 11–20 (2011)
2. Burnett, G.E., Lee, K.: The Effect of Vehicle Navigation Systems on the Formation of Cognitive Maps. Traffic and Transport Psychology: Theory and Application, 407–418 (2005)
3. Department of Health: Valuing People: A New Strategy for Learning Disability for the 21st Century: A White Paper (2001)
4. Jheng, S., Pai, M.: Cognitive Map in Patients with Mild Alzheimer's Disease: A Computer-Generated Arena Study. Behav. Brain Res. 200, 42–47 (2009)
5. Lindstrom, J.: Safe navigation with wireless technology. In: Roe, P.R.W. (ed.) Towards an Inclusive Future: Impact and Wider Potential of Information and Communication Technologies, pp. 9–23. COST, Brussels (2007)
6. MacKeith, J.: The Development of the Outcomes Star: A Participatory Approach to Assessment and Outcome Measurement Housing. Care and Support 14, 98–106 (2011)
7. Pivec, M.: Editorial: Play and Learn: Potentials of Game-Based Learning. British Journal of Educational Technology 38, 387–393 (2007)
8. Poulson, D., Ashby, M., Richardson, S.: USERfit: A practical handbook on user-centred design for assistive technology. In: ECSC-EC-EAEC, Brussels-Luxembourg (1996)
9. Tolman, E.C.: Cognitive Maps in Rats and Men. Psychol. Rev. 55, 189–208 (1948)
10. Walker, A.: Unqualified and underemployed: Handicapped young people and the labour market. Macmillan, London (1982)

# BlueFix: Using Crowd-Sourced Feedback to Support Programming Students in Error Diagnosis and Repair

Christopher Watson, Frederick W.B. Li, and Jamie L. Godwin

School of Engineering and Computing Sciences, University of Durham, United Kingdom
{christopher.watson,frederick.li,j.l.godwin}@durham.ac.uk

**Abstract.** Feedback is regarded as one of the most important influences on student learning and motivation. But standard compiler feedback is designed for experts - not novice programming students, who can find it difficult to interpret and understand. In this paper we present BlueFix, an online tool currently integrated into the BlueJ IDE which is designed to assist programming students with error diagnosis and repair. Unlike existing approaches, BlueFix proposes a feedback algorithm based upon frameworks combined from the HCI and Pedagogical domains, which can provide different students with dynamic levels of support based upon their compilation behaviour. An evaluation revealed that students' viewed our tool positively and that our methodology could identify appropriate fixes for uncompilable source code with a significantly higher rate of speed and precision over related techniques in the literature.

**Keywords:** Programming Education, Feedback, Compiler Errors, Crowd Fixes.

## 1    Introduction

Feedback is regarded as one of the most important influences on learning and motivation [2][3]. To satisfy learning outcomes in an introductory programming course, a student has to develop a range of programming knowledge: syntactic, semantic, schematic, and strategic [18]. When learning to program students' are guided on the correctness of their syntax by compiler feedback. However standard compiler feedback is designed for experts - not novices, and often fails to match their current level of conceptual knowledge, making it difficult to understand. [9] considers the effect poor quality compiler feedback can have on programmers from a HCI perspective. They conclude that although programmers can often encounter cryptic messages which are difficult to resolve, most related disciplines have not paid much attention to this aspect, because it is felt that programmers should adapt to compilers. In contrast most pedagogical theory places a strong emphasis on adaption to the individual to make instruction most effective. Clarity and elaboration are fundamental principles of good feedback from both a HCI [9] and pedagogical perspective [2][3], yet most standard compiler messages fail to adhere to this [10]. Additionally due to parsing limitations, compilers often present the same feedback for a range of distinct errors [8][9][10]. This ambiguity poses a problem considering that novice programmers lack

E. Popescu et al. (Eds.): ICWL 2012, LNCS 7558, pp. 228–239, 2012.

the experience and expertise to identify the actual fault in their syntax [8]. Unsurprisingly it is not uncommon to observe novices applying almost random strategies to resolve compiler feedback which they struggle to comprehend [11], possibly blindly acting on the feedback provided with the belief that the computer is always right [9]. In this paper we present BlueFix, an online tool currently integrated into the BlueJ IDE which is designed to assist programming students with error diagnosis and repair. Our contributions include:

- Unlike [10][17], BlueFix proposes a feedback algorithm based upon frameworks combined from the HCI and Pedagogical domains, which can provide different students with dynamic levels of support based upon their compilation behaviour.
- Unlike standard compilers, BlueFix also provides combined feedback measures, supporting a learner with appropriate levels of elaborative feedback, rather than simply assuming a one size fits all approach.
- Also unlike standard compilers, BlueFix places an emphasis on teaching programming students how to resolve errors by example, and therefore suggests methods to resolve syntax errors using a database of crowd-sourced error fixes.
- BlueFix also shows a substantial improvement in performance of existing solutions, both in terms of the time taken to identify appropriate feedback and code fixes [10] and precision [17].

The remainder of this paper is organised as follows. Section 2 discusses related work. Section 3 presents the BlueFix architecture. Section 4 discusses initial findings on novice compilation behaviour and further motivations for the work in this paper. Section 5 presents an evaluation of BlueFix. Finally, Section 6 concludes the paper.

## 2    Related Work

Prior research has demonstrated that poor quality compiler feedback can have a negative effect on learning performance. [1] propose an algorithm to quantify the extent to which a student struggles to resolve syntax errors during a programming session. Using compiler data gathered from students taking an introductory Java course, [1] identified a significant relation between a student's mean *error quotient* and their overall course mark. Implying that students who struggle to resolve syntax errors perform worse on assessments than those who do not. In a related study [7] found that programming students experienced syntax issues regardless of their ability. However, the students who performed less well on a programming course were more likely to have been unable to produce syntactically correct code for programming exercises.

In general, two main approaches can be used to make compiler feedback more appropriate for novices [9]. The first approach consists of enhancing and/or rewriting standard feedback in laymans terms, and/or adding additional elaborations to clarify the feedback provided [3]. [6] developed a pre-compiler for Java based upon this approach. Although the system was not formally tested, instructors reported they were spending less time explaining compiler feedback to students over the duration of a course. A similar approach was used by [14]. However, elaborative feedback was only provided after a student had made the same error multiple times - thereby reducing the likelihood they would become reliant on the support and fail to develop a "feel for syntax" [9]. In contrast, [4] found additional elaborations did not necessarily help novices to resolve errors more quickly or correctly. However the authors question the validity of their own study, as it used students who had programming experience. The weakness of these techniques is that they do not address the possible inaccuracy of the reported error message. Even with additional elaborations, it is possible that a student will fail to understand the feedback provided, as it fails to align with their current level of programming knowledge [9]. Also the elaboration provided is usually generic, which is substantially less effective than response-contingent feedback [3].

The second approach involves directly tailoring the feedback provided based upon a static analysis of a student's uncompilable source code. Approaches such as [12][13] provide implicit feedback [3][10] to students, by spell-checking identifiers. Whilst this technique can provide Knowledge of Correct Response (KCR) feedback [2], it can only be applied on a limited subset of error types. An alternative approach, which has been gaining momentum in recent years, builds upon the observation that novices will often seek debugging help from online forums. However, standard search algorithms are based upon string literals rather than code semantics - making it more difficult for novices to identify relevant error fixes. A solution to this problem is to identify and provide a student with examples of how other programmers have resolved similar errors in the past [15]. By comparing the similarity of a student's code against a database of crowd-sourced error fixes [10][16][17], standard compiler feedback could be substantially enhanced with elaborative feedback [5] - effectively demonstrating to a student how to fix an error. This technique also addresses the issue of possible message inaccuracy - as even if the compiler feedback was inaccurate, fix suggestions could demonstrate how to transform damaged code into compliable code.

## 3    BlueFix: Methodology and Implementation

BlueFix is aimed at supporting a programming student in acquiring fundamental syntactic and semantic [18] Java knowledge, by demonstrating how syntactic errors can be corrected through two forms of elaborative feedback: enhanced error messages and crowd-sourced example error fixes. Unlike prior work [10][17], the BlueFix approach (Fig. 1) has been developed by combining sound feedback principles from both a HCI [9] and pedagogical perspective [3] (Table. 1). The originality of BlueFix is to combine these frameworks by proposing a set of techniques which provide a student with a progressively increasing level of elaborative compiler feedback, based upon the extent to which they struggle to resolve a particular error. In contrast, prior solutions [10][17] simply provide the student with all available elaborative feedback simultaneously - which is unlikely to be processed effectively by a novice and risks cognitive overload [3]. Instead the approach of BlueFix is to first encourage a student to resolve an error themselves, and then to dynamically adjust the level and type of elaborative feedback provided if they fail to do so. We believe this approach will support students' in developing debugging expertise - therefore allowing them to focus upon program logic and developing schematic knowledge [18] rather than syntax issues.

**Fig. 1.** Flow chart of the BlueFix process. Interventions are based on a student's error state

From a HCI perspective, [9] suggests that in order to be most effective, compiler feedback should be divided into three increasing levels of elaboration:

1. Provide the programmer with a short message of the problem.
2. Provide brief explanations or generic examples.
3. Provide a further level of support based upon potential corrective actions.

These principles along with pedagogical feedback principles [3] (Table. 1) are tightly integrated into the BlueFix approach (Fig. 1). BlueFix initially provides a student with the standard compiler error - even though it may be inaccurate. This is an intentional choice; so that a student can develop a "feel for syntax" [9] and recognise errors in different environments without BlueFix support. If the student is unable to resolve an error on the second attempt (where resolve is defined as obtain either a different message or compiled code), then in line with [3][9] the level of elaborative feedback is increased to either implicit KCR [2] feedback or additional elaborations based upon the type of error message. If the error still persists on a third successive compilation, then the student is supplied with concept notes and crowd-sourced error fixes to demonstrate how others have resolved a similar syntactic problem in the past.

**Table 1.** Selection of pedagogical feedback principles [3] applied in BlueFix

| # | Principle | BlueFix Application |
|---|---|---|
| 1 | Provide elaborated feedback to enhance learning. | BlueFix provides elaborated feedback in the form of error message explanations and fix suggestions. |
| 2 | Present elaborated feedback in manageable units. | BlueFix increases the amount of feedback supplied gradually responding to a sequence of student errors. |
| 3 | Keep feedback as simple as possible, but no simpler | Students are supplied with increasing levels of feedback abstraction when they fail to resolve errors. |
| 4 | Provide feedback after students have attempted a solution. | BlueFix provides feedback each time the student attempts compilation. |
| 5 | For difficult tasks, use immediate feedback. | As programming is a higher order cognitive task, BlueFix provides feedback immediately on compilation. |
| 6 | For low-achieving students, use correct response and elaboration. | Supplies the student with more elaborations to aid understanding in response to increasing compile fails. |

An initial database of fixes was constructed using the compiler logs gathered (see Section 4) from students on the Introduction to Programming course at our university. BlueFix also allows additional fixes to be collected and added to its database during a lab session, by using additional classes which we have integrated into the BlueJ IDE. If BlueFix determines that the student requires an error fix, a list of fixes are queried and retrieved from an online MySQL database based upon a generalised error message (no identifiers), ranked, and presented to the student within a JFrame (Fig. 2).

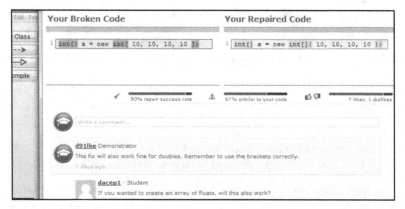

**Fig. 2.** BlueFix interface, showing a sample fix and student-demonstrator discussion

Unlike [10], BlueFix also includes social media aspects. Students can rate fixes using 'like' buttons, allowing the better fixes to be more prominently ranked and displayed. Additionally, students are able to engage in anonymous discussions about particular error fixes with their peers and instructors - providing students who are usually reluctant to ask for assistance an opportunity to clarify issues and collaborate [5] (Fig. 2).

### 3.1    BlueFix Process: Determining Relevant Feedbacks at Each Stage

In this sub-section, we outline the process and techniques BlueFix uses to determine the most appropriate feedback mechanisms at each stage of execution (Fig. 1).

**Stage: Supply Implicit Feedback.** The most likely cause of a "cannot find symbol" error is the misspelling of a variable, method, class, or package identifier. For this type of error, suggesting a fix which has been applied in the past is not appropriate. User defined types and naming within the Java language mean that although two classes or methods may share the same name, they may not share the same semantics. It is worth noting that in the case of our current dataset, these techniques can be applied to a substantial percentage of errors recorded (27%). Unlike [17] we therefore have constructed special handlers for the following unknowns.

1. *Unknown class.* This error is usually caused by either misspelling a class name or failing to import a required class from the API or a local package. BlueFix contains

a Map of all Java SE6 and Java SE7 packages indexed on the class name. When this error is reported, BlueFix first recursively scans the students BlueJ project and extracts the packages and classes within. The unrecognised class name is extracted from the compiler message, and compared against each of the names classes in the project, along with API classes. This comparison is performed using String matching techniques (Jaro-Winkler algorithm [19]). If a match is found (score >0.90), then it is added to an internal list of possible matches. The list is then sorted on score, and the closest match returned. If an import statement is missing from the project, this is also returned to the student. An example is shown in (Fig. 3).

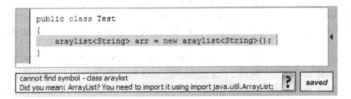

**Fig. 3.** BlueFix correcting an identifier misspelling and providing the required import line

2. *Unknown package.* Essentially the same approach as unknown class, however attempts to suggest a package path using the last word on the import line as the class.
3. *Unknown method.* The internal parse tree of BlueJ is used to first determine the type of object calling a method and the class containing the method call. Through the internal debugger and reflection, lists of method signatures for the object type (and its super-classes) are retrieved and each name is compared against the name of the unknown method. As with unknown class handler, Jaro-Winkler is used and the closest match suggested to the student as a possible fix.
4. *Unknown variable.* The internal parse tree is used to extract the names of all identifiers within a class between the error line location and the closest method signature before it. Field names of the class are then added to a list of identifiers and Jaro-Winkler similarity computed.

**Stage: Supply Elaborated Error Message.** If either the initial error type was not an unknown identifier, or if BlueFix was unable to determine suitable implicit feedback, then the next level of elaborative feedback is generated. Although prior solutions [6][14] have supplied elaborative feedbacks in the form of supplementary error explanations, these explanations lacked grounding in pedagogical or HCI principles - therefore increasing the risk that a student would still not be able to comprehend the cause of an error from the feedback provided. Another criticism of this approach is that it fails to address the lack of locality or specificity of standard messages, thereby supplying the student with additional feedback regardless as to whether the underlying message (or feedback) is correct or not. The resulting student confusion from inaccurate elaborations can clearly have a negative effect on the learning process [2][3]. To address this issue, [9] presented a set of eight principles of effective compiler message design: clarity, specificity, context-insensitivity, locality, proper phrasing, consistency, suitable visual design, and extensible help. To enhance the effectiveness of standard compiler feedback, BlueFix contains a database of 92 distinct compiler error messages and rewritten versions that conform to the sub-principles of clarity and proper phrasing: using positive tone, providing constructive guidance and reducing jargon. Future enhancements will attempt to address the specificity, context-insensitivity and locality principles by performing additional parsing checks to tailor the feedback supplied based directly to the student's damaged source code.

**Stage: Supply Concept Notes and Fix Suggestion.** If the elaborated error messages fail to assist a student in resolving an error, then BlueFix will attempt to locate and present a code fix. This is a stored piece of code which is similar to the student's uncompilable source code (and the same error message). A fix is defined as the changes made on the stored uncompilable code, to transform it into the stored fixed code.

*Construction of a Database of Fixes.* The compiler events in our dataset (Section 4) were processed on a per-week, per-student, and per-filename basis. For each week, the successive $n$ compiler events that a student performed, were classified into a set of tuples $\{\{c_1, c_2\},.., \{c_{n-1}, c_n\}\}$, so that the errors the student fixed during a session could be identified. Unlike existing solutions [10][17] which consider all tuples to be a valid fix if the compile success status of $\{c_i, c_j\}$, $i$ = false, and $j$ = true, we only consider such events to be a *possible* fix. In our solution, we first assess the quality of a possible fix before adding it to our database. We believe this will help to improve the quality of available fixes. For example, a student could resolve an error by simply deleting or commenting out blocks of code. Although this can transform the code into a compliable state, it is unlikely to resolve the underlying error. Therefore unlikely to show a student how to resolve an error which they are struggling with. To detect deletion fixes we compute the diff ratio (ignoring whitespace) between the source code of each $c_i$ and $c_j$. If the number of insertions and changes = 0, and the deletes > 0, we classify the fix as a deletion fix. Commented fixes are detected by using a regex expression on the error line. However we are currently experimenting with performing additional comment checks by using the patches (text differences between the two files) generated by a diff algorithm. Analysis on the precise metrics is still required.

*Identifying Appropriate Fixes.* The first step used to determine fixes for the student's uncompilable source code is to retrieve all possible fix tuples from the database, which have the same generalised error message (no identifiers) as the student has.

However not all of these retrieved fixes can be applied to the student's code. We therefore need a measure of similarity between a student's uncompilable source code and the uncompilable source code in a fix tuple. That way we can determine the changes that were performed on a similar piece of code, to make it compliable. Previous work [10] proposed using a structure-based similarity technique, where the parse tree of a student's uncompilable source code was generated, then compared against the parse trees of possible fixes. Whilst this approach benefits from high precision, performing node-by-node comparison of multiple parse trees incurs a substantial time cost; making the technique unfeasible for larger databases or longer code fragments. As with [17] we therefore chose to compute similarity by using a string matching algorithm. These methods in general have the advantage of a low time cost. A range of measures were considered: Levenshtein, Dice Coefficient and Needleman-Wunsch. However, we found the best performance in terms of balancing speed and accuracy came from calculating the Jaro-Winkler distance [19] between the source files.

The problem is that edit distance algorithms can over penalise for different method, variable, or class identifiers. We therefore use the BlueJ lexical analyser to first tokenize both the students uncompilable source code, and the uncompilable source code of each of the fix tuples retrieved so far. As with [17] we then compute the line similarity between the error line of the student's uncompilable code against the error line of each fix tuples uncompilable code. However unlike [17] and due to our preliminary findings on location inaccuracy (Section 4), we also incorporate region similarity into an overall appropriateness measure. This is calculated in the same was as line similarity, but includes lines up to 4 lines behind the reported error location and 4 lines after.

As BlueFix allows a student to rate fixes using a simple like/dislike system we also include student ranking in our appropriateness measure, to allow more 'stable' or 'popular' fixes to be higher ranked than fixes have not been successful in the past. BlueFix takes all this information into account in its scoring function. The appropriateness of each fix is scored as:

$$\text{Fix Appropriateness} = (5L + 2R + 1T) / 8 \qquad (1)$$

where $L$ is the Jaro-Winkler similarity between the tokenized error line in the student's code against the error line in the candidate fix; $R$ is the Jaro-Winkler similarity between the tokenized error region of the student's code and candidate fix; $T$ is the % of student 'likes' of a fix. The exact coefficients have been derived through trial and error. We wanted to place a greater emphasis on an individual line match rather than region, as a region may contain many irrelevant lines. The possible fixes are then ranked using a Comparator based upon fix score and the fixes with a score higher than a threshold (currently set at 0.8) are presented to the student. Future work will include reassessing the coefficients and threshold, as the size of the fix database increases.

*Substituting Fixes.* Before presenting a fix to a student, as with [17][10] we apply a token-based substitution of variable names and values in the selected fix for those in the student's original code. This ensures that the elaborative feedback in the form of a fix suggestion is tailored to the student's coding context, thereby increasing the likelihood of understanding [2][3]. The student can directly request BlueFix to apply the fix to their code by using the 'apply fix' button. After this, BlueFix will invoke the java compiler to determine whether or not the fix has resulted in compliable code or not, and update a successful substitution counter in the database accordingly. This function is currently restricted to single line fixes.

## 4     Further Motivations for Work

To explore aspects of novice compilation behaviour we used a sample of students who studied the 2011/2012 Introduction to Programming course at our university.

The course was designed to teach Java to student's of varying abilities and assumed no prior programming experience. Lectures were supported by a weekly practical session where students would practice programming problems using the BlueJ IDE. We decided to directly gather information on student compilation behaviour by creating an extension to BlueJ. Each time the student compiled their code on a university PC, the extension would log a snapshot of their program source code along with information on the result, timestamp, error message and line number. A total of 39 students' provided us written consent to use their logged data. In terms of prior programming experience, we note that 10 students indicated they had prior experience; however when asked the size of the largest program they had written, the majority indicated a small program (<1000 lines). 6 of these students indicated they had previously used Java, but on average had less than a year's experience. Although we collected logs for 15 practical sessions (teaching weeks 4-19), we restrict our analysis to only 11 of these sessions due to student examination and assignment work.

During the 11 logged practical sessions, our plugin recorded a total of 22,993 distinct compiler events of which 11,412 (49.6%) were compiler errors. As 2,937 distinct messages were recorded, we classified errors into a hierarchy based upon message abstraction level and type. This yielded eight top level groupings (Table. 2). We found that 85% of the errors that students encountered came from three categories: identifiers (38%), syntax (26%) and computation (24%).

**Table 2.** Classification of Java Compile Time Errors

| Group | Description | Example Subgroup |
|-------|-------------|------------------|
| Syntax | Violate the fundamental syntax rules of Java | ; expected |
| Computation | Program logic definition, flow control. | illegal operations |
| Identifiers | Unknown, re-declaring variables / methods | unknown method |
| Scope | Access violations: public, private, packages | method is private |
| Exceptions | Error handling, try-catch keywords | try without a catch |
| Inheritance | Method / variable overriding, super | super-type not called |
| Abstract | Misuse of abstract keyword | cannot have body |
| Static | Relate to use of class and object types | cannot be referenced |

**Syntax Errors as a Predictor of Student Performance.** To analyse a possible link between syntax errors and student performance we applied the error quotient algorithm proposed by [1] to our data set. As our students had not yet completed their final exam, we compute an interim ability score as a function of five completed assessment components. These are the total marks (%) that the student gained on: (A) weekly exercises, (B) fault injection report, (C) multiple choice concepts exam, (D) paper based programming exam, (E) computer based programming exam. Each task is weighted in terms of the amount of programming involved and the module weighting. An ability score is computed as: $(1A + 1.5B + 2C + 2.5D + 2.5E)$, normalized into the range 0-100. Applying this function to the 39 participants of our study yielded a normal distribution of ability scores (Shapiro-Wilk's $p > .05$) ranging from 22.69 to 84.91. Consistent with the findings of [1], a linear regression revealed that a student's mean error quotient could statistically significantly predict their ability score, $F(1, 37)$

= 8.695, $p$ < .005 and the student's mean error quotient accounted for 16.8% of the explained variability in ability scores (adjusted $r^2$ = .168) - a medium effect.

**Accuracy of Error Messages and Location.** The fault injection assignment required students to inject 30 random faults (change variable, delete line / character) into a small Java project (~600 lines) and evaluate the hypothesis: "it is difficult for compilers to identify which programming errors have been made, and the location of the problem". Out of the 39 students who participated in this study, 22 (56%) believed it was difficult for a compiler to identify which programming errors had been made, and 23 (59%) believed it was difficult for the compiler to isolate the location of the error. The average distance between reported error location and actual error location was 4.02 lines ($SD$ = 1.19), however students found this distance varied considerably depending upon the type of error. The average number of reported messages that the students thought were inaccurate was higher than anticipated, with a mean of 29.5% ($SD$ = 14.83). Concluding opinions by the students were mixed. Some students commented that they had "*no issues*" with the error messages as they "just get used to them". Other students were more critical, stating that "*the advice it* (the compiler) *gives often ends up breaking the programs even more. As such, it is best not to rely on it too much*". Nevertheless these findings indicate that over half of our students were not satisfied with the lack of appropriate guidance from standard compiler feedback.

# 5    Evaluation of BlueFix

## 5.1    Student Feedback

We have conducted an evaluation of a prototype system using a focus group of 11 students from the Introduction to Programming Course at our university. Students were provided with a demonstration and discussion of prototype BlueFix functionality, and asked to complete a short questionnaire. All students viewed the enhanced error messages and fix suggestion capabilities of BlueFix as a useful aid to help with error resolution. 63% viewed fix suggestions as the most useful form of support, and 37% viewed enhanced error messages as the most useful. 81% of the students perceived value of including a social aspect which would allow them to discuss particular fixes with peers and instructors. The interesting finding of our evaluation is that 72% of the students believed that error fixes should be tailored to their broken code; however the fixes should not be able to be directly applied, for example, by clicking "apply this fix". This is possibly due to the opinion that applying a fix may damage the code further, or transform it to the point where the student no longer comprehends it.

## 5.2    BlueFix Precision Compared to HelpMeOut

To evaluate the precision of our approach, we chose to run BlueFix on 20 test cases for each of the error groups in Table 2. Faults such as renaming a variable, deleting a random line, switching parameters, and removing a random character were performed on a small Java project consisting of 7 Java classes and approximately 6,000 lines of code. The project was not part of the BlueFix database of fixes. At the time of running, BlueFix contained 7,645 distinct error fixes, covering 842 distinct error types. To compare BlueFix to related work, we have implemented the methodology presented in [17]. Fixes were returned to an expert programmer who would determine whether or not they provided an example of how to repair the mutation. Findings on the precision and recall of both techniques are shown in Table 3.

**Table 3.** Comparing BlueFix precision, recall and $F_1$ to HelpMeOut [17]

| | | BlueFix | | | HelpMeOut | | |
|---|---|---|---|---|---|---|---|
| Error Group | Cases | Precision | Recall | $F_1$ | Precision | Recall | $F_1$ |
| Syntax | 20 | 51.98 | 25.49 | 27.67 | 34.60 | 31.36 | 28.33 |
| Computation | 20 | 47.37 | 10.25 | 13.51 | 35.42 | 13.57 | 13.99 |
| Identifiers | 20 | 86.84 | 0.70 | 1.38 | 5.21 | 22.18 | 2.67 |
| Scope | 20 | 46.93 | 45.20 | 34.00 | 36.67 | 50.86 | 31.93 |
| Exceptions | 20 | 38.52 | 36.38 | 19.60 | 27.92 | 24.39 | 17.86 |
| Inheritance | 20 | 32.46 | 36.36 | 24.88 | 28.21 | 42.63 | 26.04 |
| Abstract | 20 | 40.35 | 27.81 | 23.73 | 28.75 | 33.25 | 20.85 |
| Static | 20 | 40.70 | 84.21 | 51.64 | 32.22 | 88.33 | 41.60 |
| Overall $M$ | | 48.14 | 33.34 | 24.55 | 28.62 | 39.32 | 22.91 |
| Overall $SD$ | | 16.77 | 25.18 | 14.72 | 10.06 | 23.35 | 11.88 |

A Wilcoxon Signed-Rank test was performed to determine if there were any differences in the precision of fixes suggested by BlueFix and HelpMeOut [17]. We found a statistically significant difference in the precision rate of BlueFix ($Mdn = 50.0$) compared to HelpMeOut ($Mdn = 33.4$), z = 6.29, p < .0005. Out of 160 test cases, BlueFix had a higher precision on 82 cases (51.3%), a worse precision rate on 11 cases (6.8%) and no difference on 67 cases (41.9%).

## 6     Conclusion and Future Work

In this paper we have presented BlueFix: an online tool integrated into the BlueJ IDE which is designed to assist programming students with error diagnosis and repair. The original contribution of BlueFix is to propose an algorithm and methodology to supply individual students with dynamic levels of feedback support, based upon combining feedback frameworks taken from both the HCI and Pedagogical domains. We have also added to the growing body of knowledge on novice compilation behaviour by presenting preliminary findings from analysing quantitative compiler data gathered over a one year Java programming course. We have conducted an evaluation of BlueFix, which revealed that students viewed the tool positively, and an initial evaluation of BlueFix precision suggests an improvement of 19.52% over a previous technique [17]. Future work will consist of evaluating BlueFix accuracy on a larger data set, and possibly expanding the tool to provide advice on runtime errors through analysing stack traces. Additionally we plan to evaluate the effectiveness of BlueFix by deploying it during the 2012/2013 academic year and comparing its effects on learning and compilation behaviour [1] to the 2011/2012 cohort.

# References

1. Jadud, M.C.: Methods and Tools for Exploring Novice Compilation Behaviour. In: Proc. ICER, pp. 1–5 (2006)
2. Jaehnig, W., Miller, M.A.: Feedback types in programmed instruction, a systematic review. The Psychological Record 57(2), 219–232 (2007)
3. Shute, V.J.: Focus on Formative Feedback. Review of Educational Research 78(1), 153–189 (2008)
4. Nienaltowsi, M., Pedroni, M., Meyer, B.: Compiler error messages: what can help novices? In: Proc. SIGCSE, pp. 168–172 (2008)
5. Sykes, E.R., Franek, F.: Presenting JECA: A Java Error Correcting Algorithm for the Java Intelligent Tutoring System. In: Proc. IASTED, pp. 151–156 (2004)
6. Flowers, T., Carver, C.A., Jackson, J.: Empowering students and building confidence in novice programmers through Gauntlet. In: Proc. FIE, pp. T3H/10–T3H-13 (2004)
7. Denny, P., et al.: Understanding the Syntax Barrier for Novices. In: Proc. ITiCSE, pp. 208–212 (2011)
8. Marcrau, G., Fisler, K., Krishmanurthi, S.: Measuring the Effectiveness of Error Messages Designed for Novice Programmers. In: Proc. SIGCSE, pp. 499–504 (2011)
9. Traver, V.J.: On Compiler Error Messages: What They Say, and What They Mean. Advances in Human Computer Interaction (1) (2010)
10. Watson, C., Li, F.W.B., Lau, R.W.H.: Learning Programming Languages through Corrective Feedback and Concept Visualisation. In: Leung, H., Popescu, E., Cao, Y., Lau, R.W.H., Nejdl, W. (eds.) ICWL 2011. LNCS, vol. 7048, pp. 11–20. Springer, Heidelberg (2011)
11. Kummerfeld, S.K., Kay, J.: The Neglected Battle Fields of Syntax Errors. In: Proc. ACE, pp. 105–111 (2003)
12. Burrel, C., Melchert, M., Mann, S., Bridgeman, N.: Augmenting Compiler Error Reporting in the Karel++ Microworld. In: Proc. NACCQ, pp. 41–46 (2007)
13. Sykes, L.: Process Model for the Java Intelligent Tutoring System. Journal of Interactive Learning Research 18(3), 399–410 (2007)
14. Murphy, C., Kaiser, G.E., Loveland, K., Hasan, S.: Retina: Helping Students and Instructors Based on Observed Programming Activities. In: Proc. SIGCSE, pp. 178–182 (2009)
15. Brandt, J., et al.: Example-Centric Programming: Integrating Web Search into the Development Environment. In: Proc. CHI, pp. 513–522 (2010)
16. Mujumdar, D., et al.: Crowdsourcing Suggestions to Programming Problems for Dynamic Web Development Languages. In: Proc. CHI EA, pp. 53–56 (2011)
17. Hartmann, B., MacDougall, D., Brandt, J., Klemmer, S.R.: What would other programmers do? Suggesting Solutions to Error Messages. In: Proc. CHI, pp. 1019–1028 (2010)
18. Meyer, R.E.: From Novice to Expert. In: Handbook of Human-Computer Interaction, pp. 781–795. Prentice-Hall (1997)
19. Cohen, W.W., Ravikumar, P., Fienberg, S.E.: A comparison of string distance metrics for name-matching tasks. In: Proc. IIWeb, pp. 73–78 (2003)

# Dealing with Open-Answer Questions in a Peer-Assessment Environment

Andrea Sterbini[1] and Marco Temperini[2]

[1] Computer Science, Sapienza University of Rome,
Via Salaria. 113, 00198 Rome, Italy
[2] Dept. Computer, Control, and Management Engineering, Sapienza University of Rome,
Via Ariosto. 25, 00185 Rome, Italy
sterbini@di.uniroma1.it, marte@dis.uniroma1.it

**Abstract.** Correction of open answers questions is an heavy task as, in principle, all the students answers have to be graded. In this paper we give evidence of the possibility to reduce the teacher's workload on open questions questionnaires, by a module managing a rough constraint-based model of the students' decisions, involved in a peer-assessment task. By modeling students decisions we relate their competences on the topic (K) to their ability to judge (J) others' work and to the correctness (C) of their own (open) answer. The network of constraints and relations established among the above variables through the students' choices, allows us to constraint the set of possible values of the answers' correctness (C). Our system suggests what subset of the answers the teacher should correct, in order to narrow the set of hypotheses and produce a complete set of grades. The model is quite simple, yet sufficient to show that the number of required corrections is as small as half of the initial answers. In order to show this result, we report on an extensive set of simulated experiments which answer to three research questions: 1) is the method described able to deduce the whole set of grades with few corrections? 2) what set of parameters is best to run actual experiments? 3) is the model "robust" respect to simulations with high probability of random data?

**Keywords:** Open answers questions, peer-assessment, social-collaborative learning.

## 1 Introduction and Motivations

Collaborative and social learning are important approaches of web-based e-learning; they allow to exploit the attitude of students towards social network interaction. In social-collaborative e-learning students are part of a community, which supports collaborative experiences as social activities, exchange of mutual help, and peer-evaluation (1,2). Students can participate to a social-collaborative e-learning system in many ways (posting to forum, submitting homework, exchanging peer-activities and some more). From the teachers' point of view, however, the most challenging and time-consuming task is the correction of (open) answers to open questions. Thus the teacher might

E. Popescu et al. (Eds.): ICWL 2012, LNCS 7558, pp. 240–248, 2012.
© Springer-Verlag Berlin Heidelberg 2012

become a bottleneck, if s/he is overwhelmed by such duties. So it is reasonable to look for methods to reduce teacher's workload related to grading open answers.

Several authors approach this problem, using data mining techniques, where different ways of analyzing a texts' corpus are used, to classify them and unveil new relations among them (3,4). Such approaches (such as text clustering, self-organizing mapping, analysis of word associations co-occurring in answers) are mostly used to support business decisions on products (5). On the other hand, we deal with the problem of grading open answers, in a didactic and social-collaborative setting, in which peer-evaluation is supported (6). Peer assessment is normally analyzed by comparing the peer's grades to the teacher's ones (7,8,9). In this work, instead, we try to leverage the information and the constraints hidden in the peers' network of choices to produce a complete picture of the grades through the correction (by the teacher) of only a small set of answers.

The OpenAnswers system is designed to be a 2-components web-application: the interface/database, which allows delivering open questions and storing (open) answers; it allows the students to peer-evaluate each other's answers and the teacher to manage questionnaires and the grading process; peer-evaluation from the students is done by selecting the best answer to a given question, among a small subset of the given answers. The second component is a Prolog module using Constraint Logic Programming (CLP), that supports both the generation of hypotheses of correctness for the answers (based on the students' peer-evaluation) and narrowing the set of hypotheses (by exploiting the subset of graded answers). In particular the CLP engine proposes to the teacher the next most useful answer to be graded, selected in such a way that the set of remaining hypotheses progressively reduces to a singleton.

In this paper we present an extensive experimentation of the system. The primary research questions, here are: 1) whether this very simple model is able to deduce a single hypothesis through the correction of only a reasonably small set of answers, and 2) which one works better, among several strategies and sets of parameters, and under what conditions. A third research question concerns the "robustness" of the deduction model in these simulated experiments. I.e., with respect to high probability of forbidden combinations of variables in the generated experiments. We think that the experimentation results are encouraging, we plan to test the model on real data, and, from the formal point of view, to extend the model to capture other behaviors such as cheating, plagiarism, lack of interest/motivation.

## 2    Representation of Students' Decisions

The CLP module represents students as triples of finite-domain variables <K,C,J>: K represents students' Knowledge about the question's topic; C is Correctness of their (open) answer; J is their ability to Judge another peer's answer. For the sake of simplicity (and of computational performance in the present prototyping phase), the chosen domains of variables' values are minimal:

− **K**: {good, enough, bad}
− **C**: {correct, wrong}
− **J**: {good, educated guess, bad}

Not all combinations of the above make sense, thus we introduce the following constraints:

| | | | |
|---|---|---|---|
| — *K = bad* | => | *C = wrong* | (open answers are not guessable) |
| — *K = bad* | => | *J = bad* | (assessment needs knowledge) |
| — *C = wrong* | => | *K in {enough, bad}* | |

Notice that, for the moment, we are ruling out behaviors like "plagiarism from external resources", which is detectable by similarity tests and Google queries.

In particular, the second constraint is inspired by the Bloom's taxonomy of cognitive activities (10), in which Judgment is at a higher cognitive level than Recall or Apply knowledge; so we "constraint" the student to be a bad judge if s/he has low knowledge.

### 2.1    Behavior Constraints

Students have to answer to questions before they move to the peer assessment phase, to avoid plagiarism from peers, then they peer evaluate others' answers. This is done by proposing each student with a (sub)set of answers (related to the same question) and by asking to select the best one. The students' behaviors are modeled through constraints describing the relations among a student's representation and her peer-evaluation of others' answers. Constraints are defined by the following notation:

- S        the set of answers to choose from
- X        the chosen answer
- S\X      the remaining choices
- C(X)     the correctness of the chosen X answer
- W(S)     the subset of wrong S answers

Depending on the student's ability to judge, J, we model 3 types of behaviors:

- a good judge always selects one of the best answers;
- an average judge applies an "educated guess" strategy, by first ruling out wrong answers and then choosing randomly among the remaining options;
- a bad judge chooses completely randomly.

We use the student's Judgment to constraint the possible values of correctness of the assessed answers:

- *J = good*     => *C(X) = max C(S)*    (a good judge chooses a good answer)
- *J = edu_guess* => *C(X) > max C(W(S))* (a so-so judge rules-out wrong answers)
- *J = bad*      => *C(X) = any*    (a bad judge chooses at random)

From which we can infer that:

- *C(X) < max C(W(S))* => *J = bad*    (a wrong answer is chosen only by a bad judge)

The constraints are used both ways, to constrain C when J is known, and vice-versa.

## 2.2   Finding the Correct Answers

Once OpenAnswers has gathered all the peer-assessment choices, the constraints connecting all J, K and C variables are built and the set of all possible explanations (assignments of the Correctness variables) that satisfy such constraints is computed. Then the actual explanation of the answers should be searched among the hypotheses, through the correction of some answers, done by the teacher. As the teacher's time is a scarce resource, we try to optimize the correction phase, by suggesting the minimum set of corrections required to pin down one hypothesis explaining the peer-assessment data. The set of hypotheses is analyzed to suggest a correction strategy with a minimum number of corrections, by means of a greedy strategy, where the system repeatedly suggests the next most useful answer to correct, and then filters-out all the hypotheses with a different correctness value for that answer, until a single hypothesis remains.

To select the next "most useful" answer to correct, two strategies are available:

— **min_diff:** the answer is selected such that the difference between the number of hypotheses where it is marked "wrong", and the number of hypotheses where it is marked "correct" is minimal. In this way, after each correction we get rid of a good deal of hypotheses.
— **max_wrong:** the answer marked in most hypotheses as "wrong" is selected. While this may lead to a longer sequence of corrections, it would rule out a lot of hypotheses, should the answer be actually "correct". This strategy is suggested by the fact that students will never accept a "deduced fail" grade, and therefore the teacher should always correct all answers marked "wrong".

# 3   Simulated Experiments

We want to leverage peer-assessment to help the teacher grading a set of open-answer questions by correcting a minimum set of answers. Our goal is to streamline the teacher's workflow and to spread the use of open-answer questions for student assessment. Because of delays in the implementation of the web-based interface, we have run simulated experiments to assess the model validity and to determine the best set of parameters to run real-data experimentation.

## 3.1   Methodology

The research questions underlying the following experimentation are:

• We want to know whether the above bare-bone model is able to deduce a single hypothesis through the correction of only a reasonably small set of answers.
• Which particular set of parameter values and strategies works better.
• We wish to test the robustness of the deduction model respect to experiments generated with bigger or smaller "slackness", i.e. with higher or lower probability that a forbidden combination of <K,J,C> is generated.

## 3.2    Experimental Setting

The experiments have been designed ranging over the following parameters:

- input parameters:
  - **Students**: number of students (two cases, with 10 and 20 students)
  - **Options**: how many answers is a student expected to peer-evaluate (from 2 to 5)
  - **Distribution**: probability distribution of knowledgeable students (good/average/bad) generated in each experiment:
    - o  1% / 30% / 69% (very few actually show knowledge);
    - o  10% / 50% / 40% (something better, yet very few are "good");
    - o  30% / 50% / 20% (the topic has been studied)
    - o  69% / 30% / 1% (the topic is known quite satisfactorily)
  - **Slackness**: probability of forbidden combinations in generated triples (a way to measure robustness of the system: 1%, 50%)
  - **Strategy**: selection of the best next answer to correct (min_diff, max_wrong)
- output values:
  - **L**: average length of a correction
  - **FP**: avg. false positives (wrong answers deduced correct by the system)
  - **FN**: avg. false negatives (correct answers deduced wrong by the system).

For each set of possible input parameters, we have run 30 experiments and for each experiment we have computed all the possible sequences of corrections a teacher could be facing for that set of (generated) peer-assessment choices. Minimum, maximum, average and stdev of the Length, FP and FN values have been collected.

# 4    Results

The tables below show how much the correction length, false positives and false negatives depend on the choice of the parameters.

Table 1 shows, for each number of students (10 or 20), what percentage of the answers should be corrected to deduce a single hypothesis, depending on the correction strategy (min_diff or max_wrong) and on the distribution of the students' knowledge (K). Green highlights the best third of corrections, yellow the mid third, and orange the worst third. From the table we can see that:

- both for 10 and 20 students, the shortest corrections are obtained when the students are proposed 4 or 5 options to judge.
- when students are knowledgeable (leftmost columns) the corrections are shorter
- the max_wrong strategy tend to find shorter corrections
- all in all we gather that 50% of answers to correct by the teacher are enough to obtain a complete correction.

Table 3 shows the False Positives percentages, highlighting (for each number of students) with green (orange) the lowest (highest) values. From the table we gather that the best strategy in this case to minimize false positives is min_diff,

**Table 1.** Average correction length (% of the total answers)

| Average correction Length/% | | | slack | P(bad) | P(avg) | P(good) | |
|---|---|---|---|---|---|---|---|
| | | | 1 | | | | |
| | | | 1 | 20 | 40 | 69 | P(bad) |
| | | | 30 | 50 | 50 | 30 | P(avg) |
| #students | #options | strategy | 69 | 30 | 10 | 1 | P(good) |
| 10 | 2 | max_wrong | 48 | 64 | 79 | 91 | |
| | | min_diff | 77 | 79 | 81 | 86 | |
| | 3 | max_wrong | 46 | 51 | 68 | 82 | |
| | | min_diff | 68 | 68 | 67 | 74 | |
| | 4 | max_wrong | 41 | 47 | 70 | 90 | |
| | | min_diff | 61 | 65 | 61 | 61 | |
| | 5 | max_wrong | 45 | 49 | 51 | 78 | |
| | | min_diff | 54 | 56 | 62 | 69 | |
| 20 | 2 | max_wrong | 44 | 69 | 84 | 97 | |
| | | min_diff | 77 | 77 | 81 | 84 | |
| | 3 | max_wrong | 42 | 53 | 72 | 90 | |
| | | min_diff | 65 | 69 | 70 | 76 | |
| | 4 | max_wrong | 40 | 47 | 47 | 84 | |
| | | min_diff | 59 | 58 | 62 | 70 | |
| | 5 | max_wrong | 43 | 44 | 57 | 86 | |
| | | min_diff | 55 | 57 | 61 | 64 | |

**Legend**

lower third for this number of students
middle third for this number of students
higher third for this number of students

**Table 2.** Average False Negatives (correct answers deduced wrong)

| Average False Negatives (%) | | | slack | P(bad) | P(avg) | P(good) | |
|---|---|---|---|---|---|---|---|
| | | | 1 | | | | |
| | | | 1 | 20 | 40 | 69 | P(bad) |
| | | | 30 | 50 | 50 | 30 | P(avg) |
| #students | #options | strategy | 69 | 30 | 10 | 1 | P(good) |
| 10 | 2 | max_wrong | 0 | 1 | 0 | 0 | |
| | | min_diff | 2 | 10 | 3 | 2 | |
| | 3 | max_wrong | 0 | 0 | 0 | 1 | |
| | | min_diff | 8 | 7 | 8 | 4 | |
| | 4 | max_wrong | 0 | 0 | 0 | 0 | |
| | | min_diff | 4 | 8 | 11 | 2 | |
| | 5 | max_wrong | 0 | 0 | 0 | 0 | |
| | | min_diff | 3 | 5 | 8 | | |
| 20 | 2 | max_wrong | 0 | 0 | 0 | 0 | |
| | | min_diff | 4 | 6 | 7 | 2 | |
| | 3 | max_wrong | 0 | 0 | 0 | 0 | |
| | | min_diff | 3 | 13 | 10 | 4 | |
| | 4 | max_wrong | 0 | 0 | 0 | 0 | |
| | | min_diff | 2 | 15 | 15 | 3 | |
| | 5 | max_wrong | 0 | 0 | 0 | 0 | |
| | | min_diff | 12 | 14 | 8 | 1 | |

**Legend**

MIN for this number of students
MAX for this number of students

**Table 3.** Average False Positives (wrong answers deduced correct)

| Average False Positives (%) | | | slack | P(bad) | P(avg) | P(good) | |
|---|---|---|---|---|---|---|---|
| | | | 1 | | | | |
| | | | 1 | 20 | 40 | 69 | P(bad) |
| | | | 30 | 50 | 50 | 30 | P(avg) |
| #students | #options | strategy | 69 | 30 | 10 | 1 | P(good) |
| 10 | 2 | max_wrong | 6 | 13 | 12 | 3 | |
| | | min_diff | 1 | 1 | 1 | 3 | |
| | 3 | max_wrong | 9 | 15 | 13 | 7 | |
| | | min_diff | 3 | 7 | 4 | 0 | |
| | 4 | max_wrong | 8 | 19 | 14 | 7 | |
| | | min_diff | 4 | 6 | 4 | 4 | |
| | 5 | max_wrong | 11 | 19 | 22 | 14 | |
| | | min_diff | 10 | 13 | 8 | 0 | |
| 20 | 2 | max_wrong | 7 | 7 | 7 | 2 | |
| | | min_diff | 2 | 4 | 1 | 1 | |
| | 3 | max_wrong | 6 | 14 | 12 | 6 | |
| | | min_diff | 4 | 6 | 2 | 0 | |
| | 4 | max_wrong | 8 | 13 | 27 | 12 | |
| | | min_diff | 8 | 5 | 2 | 0 | |
| | 5 | max_wrong | 6 | 20 | 17 | 9 | |
| | | min_diff | 6 | 11 | 9 | 6 | |

**Legend**

MIN for this number of students
MAX for this number of students

**Table 4.** Sum of lenght, false positives and false negatives

| Average - L+FP+FN | | | slack | P(bad) | P(avg) | P(good) | |
|---|---|---|---|---|---|---|---|
| | | | 1 | | | | |
| | | | 1 | 20 | 40 | 69 | P(bad) |
| | | | 30 | 50 | 50 | 30 | P(avg) |
| #students | #options | strategy | 69 | 30 | 10 | 1 | P(good) |
| 10 | 2 | max_wrong | 55 | 78 | 91 | 94 | |
| | | min_diff | 80 | 90 | 88 | 90 | |
| | 3 | max_wrong | 55 | 66 | 81 | 90 | |
| | | min_diff | 79 | 82 | 79 | 78 | |
| | 4 | max_wrong | 48 | 66 | 84 | 97 | |
| | | min_diff | 68 | 79 | 76 | 67 | |
| | 5 | max_wrong | 56 | 68 | 73 | 92 | |
| | | min_diff | 67 | 74 | 78 | 68 | |
| 20 | 2 | max_wrong | 51 | 76 | 91 | 98 | |
| | | min_diff | 83 | 87 | 88 | 87 | |
| | 3 | max_wrong | 48 | 67 | 84 | 96 | |
| | | min_diff | 72 | 88 | 82 | 80 | |
| | 4 | max_wrong | 48 | 60 | 74 | 96 | |
| | | min_diff | 68 | 78 | 79 | 73 | |
| | 5 | max_wrong | 49 | 64 | 74 | 96 | |
| | | min_diff | 73 | 82 | 78 | 71 | |

**Legend**

MIN for this number of students
MAX for this number of students

Table 4 allows us to examine the trade-off among the correction length (L), number of false positives (FP) and of false negatives (FN): each cell shows the sum of the three contributions. We gather that, for both cases of 10/20 students:

- the best minimizing strategy is max_wrong
- the best number of answers to peer-evaluate (options) is 4

- with more knowledgeable students (leftmost columns) the correction is shorter;
- the minimal value for L+FP+FN is between 50% and 75%.

Now, what about the robustness of the deduction model? By increasing the "slack" (i.e. with higher probability of generating forbidden combinations of <K, J, C>) we see in Table 5 that with 50% slackness (rather than the 1% used so far):

- the quality of the correction degrades, yet not dramatically, since the minimal value for L+FP+FN is between 65% and 77%.

**Table 5.** Average L+FP+FN when slack = 50%

| Average - L+FP+FN | | | slack 50 1 30 69 | P(bad) 20 50 30 | P(avg) 40 50 10 | P(good) 69 30 1 | |
|---|---|---|---|---|---|---|---|
| #students | #options | strategy | | | | | |
| 10 | 2 | max_wrong | 92 | 86 | 70 | 87 | P(bad) |
| | | min_diff | 89 | 86 | 88 | 86 | P(avg) |
| | 3 | max_wrong | 73 | 70 | 76 | 77 | P(good) |
| | | min_diff | 86 | 80 | 80 | 79 | |
| | 4 | max_wrong | 71 | 74 | 67 | 79 | |
| | | min_diff | 78 | 82 | 75 | 80 | |
| | 5 | max_wrong | 71 | 69 | 66 | 80 | |
| | | min_diff | 75 | 77 | 80 | 78 | |
| 20 | 2 | max_wrong | 81 | 84 | 78 | 77 | |
| | | min_diff | 87 | 86 | 91 | 91 | |
| | 3 | max_wrong | 69 | 71 | 79 | 79 | |
| | | min_diff | 84 | 86 | 80 | 83 | |
| | 4 | max_wrong | 71 | 73 | 64 | 68 | |
| | | min_diff | 79 | 82 | 80 | 80 | |
| | 5 | max_wrong | 77 | 67 | 64 | 73 | |
| | | min_diff | 77 | 79 | 75 | 79 | |

**Legend**

MIN for this number of students
MAX for this number of students

# 5    Conclusions

The experiments discussed in Section 4 allow us to conclude that the approach proposed in this paper is viable, and can help teachers in a semi-automated correction of open-answers. When the number of students increases the max_wrong strategy works better, and comes to deduce a complete set of grades by marking less than half the answers. This suggests that a mixed strategy could exist, producing shorter corrections than the min_diff one, but with less mistakes (FP+FN) than max_diff.

However, it is clear that our experimentation is "synthetic", in that it uses <K,J,C> triples that were randomly generated in the system itself. We are eager to check the deduction model on real data. To this aim, we are implementing a web-based interface to deliver, correct, and peer-assess open-answer questionnaires.

We should say the model does not capture (yet) other important behaviors:

- cheating/plagiarism (CP): the students copy their answer from external resources
- lack of interest (LI): the student is not willing to properly assess his peers' answers

- lack of anonymity (LA): the students flag their answer to make it recognizable by others

Which suggest us to expand the student model by adding:

- new (finite domain) variables to model the above cases
- new constraint rules to model the student's decisions depending on the CP, LI, LA values

Moreover, to improve computation times, to be able to introduce soft constraints and probability, and to learn the model's parameters from experimental data, we are working on translating the above CLP model to Bayesian Networks (12).

## References

1. Cheng, Y., Ku, H.: An investigation of the effects of reciprocal peer tutoring. Computers in Human Behavior 25 (2009)
2. Kreijns, K., Kirschner, P.A., Jochems, W.: Identifying the pitfalls for social interaction in computer supported collaborative learning environments: a review of the research. Computers in Human Behavior 19, 335–353 (2003)
3. Li, H., Yamanishi, K.: Mining from open answers in questionnaire data. In: Proc. KDD 2001, pp. 443–449. ACM, USA (2001)
4. Rosell, M., Velupillai, S.: Revealing Relations between Open and Closed Answers in Questionnaires through Text Clustering Evaluation. In: Proc. LREC 2008, Eur. Language Resources Ass. (2008)
5. Yamanishi, K., Li, H.: Mining Open Answers in Questionnaire data. IEEE Intelligent Systems, 58–63 (September/October 2002)
6. Sterbini, A., Temperini, M.: Good students help each other: improving knowledge sharing through reputation systems. In: Proc. 8th International Conference on Information Technology Based Higher Education and Training (ITHET), Kumamoto, Japan (2007)
7. Falchikov, N., Goldfinch, J.: Student Peer Assessment in Higher Education: A Meta-Analysis Comparing Peer and Teacher Marks. Review of Educational Research 70(3), 287–322 (2000)
8. iPeer, http://ipeer.ctlt.ubc.ca
9. PEAR, http://www.uoguelph.ca/peartool/
10. Bloom, B.S. (ed.): Taxonomy of Educational Objectives. David McKay Company Inc., New York (1964)
11. Sterbini, A., Temperini, M.: Supporting Assessment of Open Answers in a Didactic Setting. In: Social and Personal Computing for Web-Supported Learning Communities (SPEL 2012), ICALT 2012, Rome, Italy (2012)
12. Sterbini, A., Temperini, M.: Correcting open-answer questionnaires through a Bayesian-network model of peer-based assessment. In: International Conference on Information Technology Based Higher Education and Training (ITHET 2012), Istanbul, Turkey, June 21-23 (2012)

# Slide Test Maker
# An Educational Software Tool
# for Test Composition

Salvatore Cuomo[1], Vittorio Fuccella[2], and Aniello Murano[1]

[1] Dipartimento di Scienze Fisiche, Università di Napoli Federico II,
Via Cinthia 26, 80137 Napoli, Italy
[2] Dipartimento di Informatica, Università di Salerno,
Via Ponte Don Melillo, 84084 Fisciano(SA), Italy
salcuomo@unina.it, vfuccella@unisa.it, murano@na.infn.it

**Abstract.** In every day life education, tests play a key role. They represent a standard vehicle for assessing proficiency, measuring aptitude or determining skill and knowledge in any teaching field. In this paper, we present Slide Test Maker (STM), a software tool based on Java, whose main objective is to help teachers in a quick composition of online tests. Starting from a generic lesson in slide-show format, STM allows the user to easily *tag* the contents (texts, sounds, images, video, etc.) in the presentation, in order to construct the test, in a very easy and intuitive way. The composed test can then be saved and exported in PDF format and as a Learning Object in a standard format.

## 1 Introduction

Nowadays the assessment is a fundamental part of the instructional learning process. The summative assessment programs are used for grading and accountability purposes while the formative assessments are adopted to diagnose and modify the conditions of learning and instruction. The formative use of assessment occurs during the learning process, gives information on the learning state of the class, and allows the teacher to decide the most suitable learning path [15]. Software tools enable the support of many data collections, complex analysis, individualized feedback and scaffolding features needed for the formative use of assessment [10], [18], [14]. Online testing methodologies are used in several international assessment programs. For example, in 2009 the Programme for International Student Assessment (PISA) has included the electronic texts to test reading, and in 2006 PISA experimented an innovative computer-based assessment program in the science disciplines. Companies and non-profit organizations offer service for developing on line tests able to select skills and ability of the students. For example, in 2008 Educational Testing Service (ETS), a U.S. nonprofit educational institution, published a report in which it is observed that 4 million people will take ETS-developed tests on computer. Software tools, that implement *Computerized Adaptive Testing* (CAT), have been repeatedly shown to significantly benefit student achievement.

E. Popescu et al. (Eds.): ICWL 2012, LNCS 7558, pp. 249–257, 2012.

In the last decade, many software tools for online testing have been fruitfully developed. Among the others, we recall here *Xerte*, *eXelearning*, *Ispring*, *Flypaper*, *Docebo*, *Moodle*, *eLearning Place*, *CADATS*, and *SIETTE* (see [4], [7], [2], [8], [3], [11]).

As reported in a survey [13], online assessment has recently been used in several application areas, such as CAT, automatic question generation, analysis of log data, *m-learning* and *educational gaming*.

Online tests are often packaged in Learning Management System (LMS). A LMS is aimed at managing an e-learning environment, establishing the organization and delivery of content, administrating resources and tracking learning activities and results [9]. Unfortunately, several LMSs are designed in a general purpose way and it is possible to observe that there is an unnatural separation between the teaching and the assessment phases. Usually, teachers have to refer to two or more tools for addressing both aspects. Also, tests are often built from scratch, without taking any advantage from the digital material produced during the previous teaching phase. Most of the research carried out so far has taken into account the fully automatic generation of questions from an input text [19,12,17] and the generation of tests through the selection of items from an existing question repository [20,16]. Nevertheless, the systems for automatic question generation are still far from giving satisfactory results. In fact, after the generation, the human intervention is anyhow necessary for verifying the good sense of the items before using them in a test [13]. Thus, if a user wants to create a test based on his/her syllabus, s/he has to perform the tedious process of copying the content from the teaching material (slide presentations, in most cases) and pasting it to the form-based interfaces used to compose tests.

The above motivations led us to design an educational software tool, named *Slide Test Maker* (STM), aimed at assisting teachers in producing tests in a semi-automatic way, starting from multimedia data stored in Power Point or Impress presentations. The tool allows the user to easily *tag* the material in the presentation, in order to quickly paste it in the form-based interface used to compose the test. The interaction paradigm used to tag the content allows the teacher to avoid the tedious sequence of copy-and-paste interactions needed to fill the test composition form.

Furthermore, STM can produce the tests as Learning Objects (LOs) in a standard format, which can be executed in any standard compliant LMS environment.

It is worth noting that STM, being a tool that produces online tests, retains all positive aspects of similar tools developed in this field. Moreover, STM takes into account an important aspect for the students: the exercise and the self-assessment. In *formative assessment* [14], at the end of each lesson, the student practices on a test based on the lesson itself. During the test, the feedback given on each question has an important role. STM integrates in teacher's feedback precise references to the slides from which the question is based. This way, a student can investigate any matters over which it has gaps without having to spend too much time looking for them in the teaching material.

The tool has been evaluated with pilot users. Interviews with them allowed us to enhance its design and to demonstrate that their level of satisfaction with the tool's usability and efficiency is high.

The rest of the paper is organized as follows: the next section describes the STM tool in details. In Section 3, we report the results of an informal evaluation of the software tool with pilot users. Lastly, Section 4 offers our conclusions and outlines the future work.

## 2   The STM Software Tool

Slide Test Maker (STM) is a software tool based on Java, whose aim is twofold: on one hand, it helps teachers to quickly compose online tests; on the other hand, it enables the packaging of tests and the educational material on which the test is based in a single standard LO.

Starting from a lesson in a slide-show format, STM allows the teacher to tag all contents (texts, sounds, images, video, etc.) slide by slide. The tagged content can be pasted to the test through a very easy and intuitive interaction paradigm.

The tool provides a graphical interface that assists the teacher to produce the online tests under the form of PDF (pencil and paper) or LOs. Therefore, the teachers can design new quizzes according to students study schedule and integrate the course material in it.

Through the main menu of the application, the user can execute the following main operations:

1. Creating/editing a test;
2. Creating questions from a slide show;
3. Exporting the test in a standard format.

### 2.1   Creating/Editing a Test

The interface to create and edit a test is simple and intuitive. A new test can be created (or an existing one opened) using the menu or the toolbar. The application interface is vertically divided into two views, each taking approximately half the application window. The *Test View* is on the left hand side, while the *Question View* is on the right hand side, as shown in Figure 1.

The *Test View* represents the current state of the test composition, reporting a summary of the main test information, including the number and the type of the questions currently inserted in the test. From the toolbar located above the view it is possible to save and export the test, and edit the test by adding a new question or deleting an existing one.

The *Question View* contains a simple form through which a new question can be created or an existing one edited. Two types of questions are supported at present: *multiple choice* and *true/false*. A *multiple choice* item is composed of a *stem* and a list of *options*. The *stem* is the text that states the question. The only correct option is called the *key*. *True/false* items are a variation of multiple choice items where the stem contains a statement and only two options (*true* and *false*) are provided.

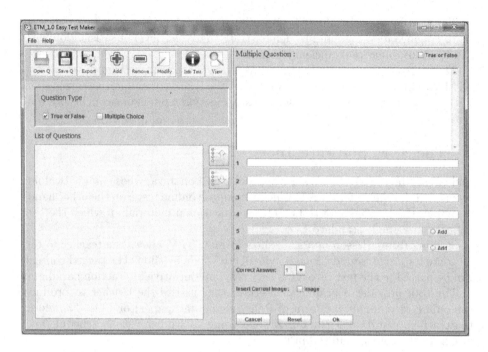

**Fig. 1.** The *STM* interface

## 2.2   Creating Questions from a Slide Show

At any point during the editing of a test, the teacher can import a slide-show lesson, by means of the command *Open Slide Show*. As soon as this operation is performed, a pop-up window is opened. This view, called *Slide Show View*, allows the teacher to browse the slides of the presentation (see Figure 2): by using the toolbar buttons on the top of the new window, it is possible to move through the slides one by one or five by five.

The view shows a preview of the current slide. The slide elements, including text and multimedia content, can be interactively selected and used for the currently edited question of the test by directly *tagging* them. In particular, we adopted the following interaction design:

- *Element Selection.* Any element can be selected in the classic way: a mouse left-button click allows to select an element while the text can be selected by clicking and dragging the mouse pointer.
- *Composition of the question stem.* A mouse left-button double-click pastes the selected element to the form field representing the *stem* of the currently edited question in the *Question View*. A single multimedia element can be used in a stem.
- *Composition of the question options.* The creation of an option can be done through the mouse or through a keyboard shortcut: a mouse right-button click opens a pop-up toolbar allowing the user to choose the index of the

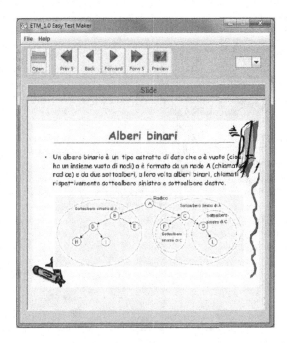

**Fig. 2.** The *Slide Show View*

option; pressing a number key on the keyboard, while a selection is active, is a shortcut to create an option: the number associated to the pressed key corresponds to the index of the option.

It is worth noting that the multimedia can be easily added to a stem as it is done with the text. This is different and much easier than classic test making software tools, where a multimedia is usually loaded by browsing the file system. This feature saves considerable time and effort for making a test.

The *Slide Show View* is shown in superposition to the *Test View*. In this way, the user can observe both the slides and the currently edited question in the *Question View*, at the same time. An example of execution of the tool where a text segment is pasted from the presentation to the text field of an option is shown in Figure 3.

### 2.3  Exporting the Test

Once all questions have been composed, the teacher can shuffle them in the desired order.

During the composition of a test, by means of the command *Save Questions*, the teacher can save the test produced so far. Finally, by means of the commands *Create PDF* and *Export to LO* it is possible to export a created test in PDF or in a standard LO format.

In particular, an LO is produced in compliance to SCORM 2004 [1]. The presentation files used to compose the test can optionally be packaged in the

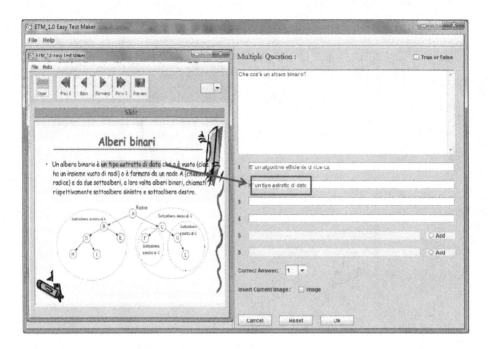

**Fig. 3.** Screenshot of the tool showing a text segment pasted from the *Slide Show View*

LO together with the test. The test is exported in the *IMS Question and Test Interoperability* (QTI) [6] standard format. During the production of the test, STM records the association of every single item to the slides of the presentation on which the question is based. Thus, using the *feedback* feature embedded in the QTI format, the slides can be referenced during the execution of the test by a student. This way, the student can deepen those topics where s/he has weaknesses without having to spend too much time looking for them in the teaching material.

STM also provides an environment in which the produced quizzes can be quickly tested. A screenshot of a test executed in such an environment is shown in Figure 4. At the end of the execution, a score is provided by STM. It is worth noting that if a question contains multimedia objects, only a thumbnail of it is attached to the question. The object can be viewed in full size or launched in an external player through a simple mouse click.

Further features supported (not reported in detail here) in STM are a detailed help tutorial and a digital and "pencil and paper" test output format.

## 3   Evaluation

STM has been evaluated with 5 (4 male, 1 female) pilot users, all of them being university professors (three computer scientists). The participants were asked to use the tool and then their judgment was gathered in an interview with

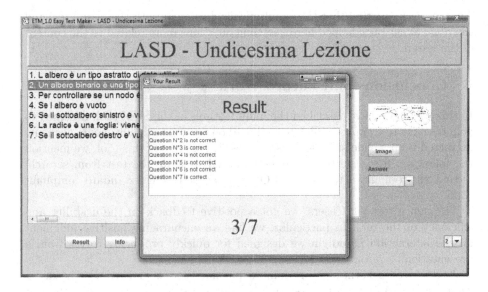

**Fig. 4.** The *STM* results

the authors. As a main result, we were interested in assessing the interaction paradigm presented in Section 2.2 to test if it gives a significant advantage to the teacher in quickly producing a test from a presentation.

The evaluation was carried out in two rounds. The first round was aimed at obtaining feedback from users and modify the tool accordingly. The second round, instead, was aimed at validating the changes performed after the first round.

In the first round the users were invited to freely test the tool, with the only required task of creating a test from a presentation of their choice from the learning material of their course syllabus. According to the opinions expressed in interviews, we obtained a good level of satisfaction, with all the users being favorable to use STM in their daily teaching activities. The critical issues raised by users were mainly related to the arrangement of the interface widgets. Furthermore, the users requested the development of an online help and the production of a short video demonstration showing the salient features of the tool.

In the second round, the users were provided with a short presentation and were instructed to create a small test composed of five questions. The users were invited to study the presentation for a while and write down on a paper the questions they felt most relevant to the lesson. After that, they were invited to compose the test with both STM and their favorite software tool. It is interesting to note that three users out of five used the same test making tool ( *QuizFaber* v.2 [5]). The users confirmed the positive impression they had after the first round and noticed the greater efficiency of STM, compared to the other classic tools.

As a further interesting feedback obtained through the test with users, we report that a user appreciated the *Test View* interface, saying that it gave a better summary of the test information than analogous interfaces of other tools.

Another user reported that the simultaneous display of both the *Test View* and the *Slide Show View* helped her in settling questions more related to the content of the lesson.

# 4  Conclusions and Future Work

In this paper, we have described the main features of the STM tool, designed to help teachers to compose online tests, based on textual and multimedia elements extracted from a slide-show lessons. As positive aspects of this tool, we mention the following: first, the teacher does not need to write the test from scratch; second, the tool allows to produce LOs that can be run in a standard compliant LMS.

Through a test with users, we got a positive feedback on the usability and efficiency of the tool. In particular, we had an encouraging positive judgment on the interaction paradigm we designed for quickly producing a test from a presentation.

As a future work, the support of more question types is planned. Furthermore, we are going to develop the tool as a production software and to distribute it under an open source license. Lastly, we are designing a client-server run time environment where the tests can be deployed and taken by the students.

**Acknowledgments.** We thank Christian Alfano for his help in the implementation of the STM software.

This research paper is partially supported by F.A.R.O. Project, founded by University of Naples Federico II and Compagnia di San Paolo Fundation.

# References

1. Adl scorm, http://www.imsglobal.org/
2. Docebo, http://www.docebo.com/
3. elearning place, http://education.qld.gov.au/learningplace/
4. exelearning, http://www.exelearning.it/
5. QUIZ Faber, http://www.lucagalli.net/
6. Ims question and test interoperability, http://www.imsglobal.org/
7. Ispring, http://ispring.com/
8. Moodle, http://moodle.org/
9. Britain, S., Liber, O.: A framework for the pedagogical evaluation of elearning environments. Technical report (February 2004)
10. Brown, J., Hinze, S., Pellegrino, J.W.: Technology and formative assessment. In: Good, T. (ed.) 21st Century Education. Technology, vol. 2, pp. 245–255. Sage, Thousand Oaks (2008)
11. Conejo, R., Guzmán, E., Millán, E., Trella, M., Pérez-De-La-Cruz, J.L., Ríos, A.: Siette: A web-based tool for adaptive testing. Int. J. Artif. Intell. Ed. 14(1), 29–61 (2004)
12. Costagliola, G., Ferrucci, F., Fuccella, V., Oliveto, R.: eworkbook: a computer aided assessment system. International Journal of Distance Education Technologies 5(3), 24–41 (2007)

13. Costagliola, G., Fuccella, V.: Online testing, current issues and future trends. Journal of e-Learning and Knowledge Society (Je-LKS) 5(3), 83–93 (2009)
14. Cuomo, S., Fuccella, V., Murano, A.: Full formative assessment based on educational video games. In: Proceedings of DMS 2010 (DET Workshop) - The 16th International Conference on Distributed Multimedia Systems, Oak Brook, Illinois, USA, October 14-16, pp. 228–231 (2010)
15. Frignani, P., Bonazza, V.: Le prove oggettive di profitto. Strumenti docimologici per l'insegnante, Carocci (2003)
16. Hoshino, A., Nakagawa, H.: A Cloze Test Authoring System and Its Automation. In: Leung, H., Li, F., Lau, R., Li, Q. (eds.) ICWL 2007. LNCS, vol. 4823, pp. 252–263. Springer, Heidelberg (2008)
17. Hwang, G.-J., Chu, H.-C., Yin, P.-Y., Lin, J.-Y.: An innovative parallel test sheet composition approach to meet multiple assessment criteria for national tests. Computers and Education 51(3), 1058–1072 (2008)
18. Lalos, P., Lazarinis, F., Kanellopoulos, D.: E-snakes and ladders; a hypermedia educational environment for portable devices. Int. J. Mob. Learn. Organ. 3(2), 107–127 (2009)
19. Lee, C.-L., Huang, C.-H., Lin, C.-J.: Test-Sheet Composition Using Immune Algorithm for E-Learning Application. In: Okuno, H.G., Ali, M. (eds.) IEA/AIE 2007. LNCS (LNAI), vol. 4570, pp. 823–833. Springer, Heidelberg (2007)
20. Mitkov, R., Ha, L.A.: Computer-aided generation of multiple-choice tests. In: Proceedings of the HLT-NAACL 2003 Workshop on Building Educational Applications Using Natural Language Processing, HLT-NAACL-EDUC 2003, Stroudsburg, PA, USA, pp. 17–22. Association for Computational Linguistics (2003)

# Learning Analytics for Learning Blogospheres

Manh Cuong Pham, Michael Derntl, Yiwei Cao, and Ralf Klamma

RWTH Aachen University
Advanced Community Information Systems (ACIS),
Informatik 5, Ahornstr. 55, 52056 Aachen, Germany
{pham,derntl,cao,klamma}@dbis.rwth-aachen.de

**Abstract.** In blogospheres the learning process is characterized by evolving roles of bloggers and dynamic change of content. Existing approaches for learning blogospheres do not provide a comprehensive solution to dealing with these dynamics. In this paper, we propose a learning analytics approach for learning blogospheres unifying two complementary perspectives: (1) structural analysis of the blogosphere to identify learners' social capital; and (2) content analysis to capture dynamics in blog content over time. To support both types of analysis, social network analysis methods are applied as a fundamental approach to analyzing and visualizing knowledge sharing on learning blogospheres. We exemplify the learning analytics approach using two real-world learning blogospheres: the Mediabase – a large blog collection for technology enhanced learning, and the European eTwinning Network – a lifelong learning blogsphere. Results show that both analytics perspectives in combination advocate an advanced learning analytics approach to understanding and assessing learning processes in learning blogospheres.

**Keywords:** learning analytics, content analysis, Web 2.0, social network analysis, social capital.

## 1 Introduction

From company blogs and newspaper blogs to personal blogs, blogs are bringing online users a new media channel to share knowledge with dynamics and flexibility. Various blogs and the links among them are shaping diverse *blogospheres*. Blog-based learning activities take place in the blogosphere for informal and lifelong learning [10,15]. These activities enable learners to collect learning material, to develop ideas, and to share with and get feedback from others in learning communities. Through blogging activities, bloggers are able to enrich their domain knowledge or improve their professional skills.

In blogospheres the learning process is characterized by evolving roles of bloggers and the permanent change of content and topic focus. The evolving roles are developed through learners' blogging activities. Bloggers are able to develop their emerging ideas during their blogging [10]. Comments from others may help bloggers complete "half-baked" ideas, which can be seen as a social learning process as well [9]. During such a process social capital is accumulated and the

E. Popescu et al. (Eds.): ICWL 2012, LNCS 7558, pp. 258–267, 2012.

individual learners' roles in the blogosphere emerge gradually. The blogosphere content changes and matures accordingly and these dynamics reflect the bloggers' change in blogging skills, knowledge and influence. Thus, the blogging processes in learning blogospheres are genuinely self-regulated through knowledge sharing in communities of practice [12, 20].

Analyzing and exposing these dynamics in learning blogospheres can be facilitated by different visual and analytic approaches. Visual representations are well established tools to enable users to see, explore, and understand large amounts of data and thus provide an intuitive method of acquiring and assimilating information [17]. More recently, learning analytics has gained popularity as a method for interpreting a wide range of data produced by and gathered on behalf of students in order to assess learning progress, predict future performance, and spot potential issues [7]. Several blogosphere analytics tools exist and can be embedded into the blog site. Blog reading and writing statistics show detailed information about the quality, updating frequency, and popularity in the blogospheres. For example, Google Analytics[1] provides a set of analytics services including real-time reporting, custom reports, visualization, dashboards, and sharing. While these analytics tools produce valuable interactive reports, they do not consider or expose learning processes, development of social capital, emerging learner communities, or evolving learning content within blogospheres.

In this paper we aim to overcome these shortcomings by advocating a learning analytics approach for learning blogospheres that integrates the structural analysis perspective with the content analysis perspective. Social network analysis is applied for the learning analytics approach. Based on previous research on blogs' contributions in knowledge sharing [10], we specifically address these research questions:

– How can social network analysis be conducted in learning blogospheres to identify social capital and learner communities?
– How can content analysis be conducted to identify topic bursts and shifts in blogosphere content?
– How can these two analytic perspectives be integrated to produce a comprehensive learning analytics approach for learning blogospheres?

Addressing these questions, we outline social network analysis methods to observe bloggers' development and to assess bloggers' social capital, and content analysis methods to identify and expose blog content dynamics (Section 2). In two case studies in Section 3, we demonstrate these methods on two different learning blogospheres. One is a blog collection for technology enhanced learning (the Mediabase), the other one is a blogsphere in a lifelong learning platform (European eTwinning Network). We conclude with our findings in Section 4.

## 2   Learning Analytics Approach

We specify two perspectives in the learning analytics approach for learning blogospheres: structural analysis and content analysis. We explore the social network

---

[1] http://www.google.com/analytics

properties drawn from different blog features in combination. For example, the users' comments can be represented as a social network. Thus, we conduct the structural analysis and content analysis to those blogger or content networks. We employ social network analysis (SNA) methods with computation on real data sets. Although recent research in networked learning and CSCL has employed SNA methods to describe and understand the patterns of learner interaction or for content analysis, it has focused more on empirical experiments than on large-scale network data computation [13].

## 2.1   Structural Analysis

Learning communities as the main actors in learning blogospheres are the target of structural analysis. How do learners acquire their knowledge and what changing roles do they play as individuals or sub-communities? And how can social capital be identified through the analysis of the underlying network structures of blogospheres?

SNA methods have been applied in many domains, e.g. knowledge discovery in digital libraries [14] and analysis of community of practice [6,8]. SNA is widely used in sociology to study social behavior of actors, emerging phenomena like the small-world effect [18,19], and diffusion of innovation – the spread of new ideas and technology through cultures [16]. The emergence of Web 2.0 applications such as blogs, wikis and social networking opens new challenges for studying the social behavior. Among the others, blogs can be greatly studied by means of SNA methods, especially with a focus on social capital [2,3].

**SNA measures.** Several SNA measures have been proposed to study the static and dynamic properties of social networks in order to help us gain an insight into the network structure such as community structure, and how it evolves over time. Formally, given the network $G = (V, E)$, where $V$ is the set of vertices or nodes, and $E$ is the set of edges, measures are defined as follows:

- Local clustering coefficient measures the probability that two nodes having a common neighbor are connected. The local clustering coefficient $C(u)$ of a node $u \in V$ is defined as the fraction of connected pairs in its neighborhood, and it measures the extent by which a node is clustered into a community, where $d(u)$ is the possible maximal degree of Node $u$.

$$C(u) = \frac{|\{(i,j) \in E : (u,i) \in E \wedge (u,j) \in E\}|}{\frac{d(u)(d(u)-1)}{2}}$$

- Global clustering coefficient is the average local clustering coefficient of all nodes in the network and shows whether the network exposes a community structure or not.
- Betweenness measures the extent to which a particular node lies between the other nodes in $G$: a node of low degree may play an important role and be very central to the network. Betweenness of a node $u \in V$, denoted by $B(u)$, is defined as the number of shortest paths from all vertices to all other vertices that pass through $u$.

$$B(u) \equiv \sum_{u \neq i \neq j} \frac{\sigma^u(i,j)}{\sigma(i,j)}$$

- Largest connected component measures the fraction of nodes that are connected with each other in the largest sub-network and shows the emergence of a giant component in a network.
- Diameter is defined as the greatest geodesic distance between any two nodes.
- Average path length is the average geodesic distance between any two nodes in $G$, and is one of characteristics to detect the small-world effect in real networks [19].

**Social capital in blogospheres.** Social capital stands for the ability of actors to derive benefits from the membership in social networks or other social structures. In social network research, studies are concerned with the identification of network structures that are the most effective factor for creating social capital. Coleman [3] emphasizes the benefits of being embedded into densely connected groups, regarding to the confidence, trust and secured relationship in the community. This form of social capital is defined as *closure*. In addition, Burt [2] discusses social capital as a tension between being embedded into communities and brokerage – the benefits arising from the ability to "broker" interactions at the interface between different groups, which is defined as *structural hole*. Both forms of social capital can be identified via SNA measures: structural holes are nodes which have high betweenness, while closures are nodes with high local clustering coefficient. In blogospheres, social capital stands for the informational benefit that a blogger obtains from the interaction with others. Here, the informational benefit is twofold: a blogger can update and be informed of the new content from diverse sources quickly; she can exert influence by spreading her own content and thoughts that she has posted on her blog.

## 2.2 Content Analysis

Content analysis is conducted on the blog content including blog entries and comments. It is used to analyze rising and falling topics, utterances and sentiments [5], e.g. for opinion mining in politics. Blog hosting services typically offer tagging features, and many bloggers make intensive use of it to organize and categorize blog entries, less to capture the actual meaning of the blog entry [1]. Tags attached to blog entries can be used to navigate in the blogosphere, and also to mine blogger community structures based on overlapping tag use. In analyses of learning blogospheres, content and topic bursts can support learners and educators in tracing the history of rising and falling topics and in identification of content-based clusters. Moreover, exposing trendy topics and topic shifts may facilitate self-reflection by showing the learners their position within in the overall "topic flows" in their blogosphere.

Generally speaking, bursts refer to topics which appear, gain popularity, and then fade [11]. They are therefore a particularly interesting study object for content analysis. The word sets found in the blog entries are processed by a burst detector process, which identifies bursty words (i.e. frequently occurring words) in the plain entry text; i.e., each blog entry is reduced to its main message(s). Analysis of bursty topics is conducted on word bursts in the context of particular time frames. Furthermore, visual burst analytics is applied to visualize the burst analysis results. Each word burst is associated with a burst power value that allows ranking and visualization of bursts, e.g. via a word cloud. Burst co-occurrences analytics is the study of co-occurrence of different terms within the same bursts. This can be performed as a structural-semantic analysis, where the co-occurrences are modeled as graphs. Thereby, the terms represent nodes (which can be sized according to SNA centrality measures), and the frequency of co-occurrence of each pair of terms can be used to provide a weight for the edges.

## 3   Case Studies

Based on analyses introduced in the previous section, two kinds of learning blogospheres are analyzed: the European eTwinning Network (a blogsphere in a lifelong learning platform) in Section 3.1, and the Mediabase (a blogosphere for technology enhanced learning) in Section 3.2.

### 3.1   Structural Analysis on Lifelong Learning Project Blogs

In eTwinning, the lifelong learning platform for European school teachers, teachers communicate and collaborate with each other using messaging and blogging. We apply SNA to analyze the structure of teacher blog network in order to understand its evolution. In eTwinning, teachers use blogs to document, communicate and report about their projects (called project diaries). This mechanism features all standard blogging functionalities, including post, comment, reference and multimedia operations. The data set consists of 20,963 blogs, 49,604 blog entries and 7,184 comments made by 3,264 teachers. In this project diary network $G$, nodes are teachers and a directed edge is established between two teachers if one teacher comments on at least one blog entry created by the other, weighted by the number of comments.

Those SNA measures are computed: global and local clustering coefficient, degree distribution, betweenness, diameter, average path length, number of components and largest connected component. We got very low global clustering coefficient (0.0009), high diameter (22), and average path length (7). The network is disconnected with many components (552 components) and the giant component consists of 62% of all nodes. It shows that although the network exposes the community structure, communities are not cohesively connected. The topology of these communities is a star, where there is a super node that connects to many other nodes while there are not so many connections between its neighbors. The power law degree distribution (a fat-tail distribution) in Fig. 1a, with exponent $\alpha = 1.625$, indicates the existence of hubs (or super connectors), which ensures connectivity, information spreading, knowledge sharing, and behavior cascading in networks.

Given the hubs in the networks, what is their local structure? Are they structural holes or closures? Fig. 1b depicts the betweenness and local clustering coefficient as a function of node degree. It is clear that betweenness increases and clustering coefficient decreases as degree increases for teachers with low degree (less than 20 and 50 respectively). For greater degree, betweenness and clustering coefficient do not follow this trend: although the clustering still decreases, the betweenness does not increase as degree increases. Together with other measures in the project diary network, high-degree teachers are placed in the center of a local group like a star, where many other teachers connect to the stars; but few of them connect to each other. The stars also do not connect to other stars in the network. Few connections between members surrounding a star create shortcuts and therefore decrease the betweenness, while they are not enough to increase the clustering coefficient. This observation provides evidence for the limitation in using project diaries as a communication means within the eTwinning community. Of course, these findings were drawn by exclusively considering the social network perspective, and a complementary content analysis of project diary might produce valuable additional insights.

## 3.2   Content Analysis on Mediabase Blogs

Content analysis is able to observe and evaluate the dynamics of blogosphere content as learning material in learning blogospheres. In this regard, the Mediabase aims to provide communities with cross-media digital information obtained from mailing lists, newsletters, blogs, RSS/Atom feeds, websites, and other web sources [11]. In the research on learning blogospheres, the Mediabase concept is adopted for facilitating roadmapping, forecasting and weak-signal analysis endeavors in communities of practice. Among other ingredients, this requires a content-based perspective on blogospheres. The data set consists of over 800 blogs related to technology enhanced learning (TEL) added by community members and over 340,000 blog entries as of end of 2011.

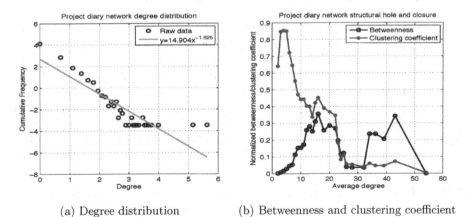

(a) Degree distribution          (b) Betweenness and clustering coefficient

**Fig. 1.** Properties of project diary network

**Bursty Topics.** The word bursts for all sources are grouped by year and analyzed for tendencies of rising and falling frequency. Standard word stemming procedures and stop-word lists are applied. 2,640 word stems started to appear in 2011 and never had bursts before 2011. In Fig. 2, a word cloud of the top 100 word stems shows highly diverse topics from various areas such as politics (e.g. gaddafi, mubarak), tools (e.g. bitcoin, itwin), hardware (e.g. chromebook) conferences (e.g. acmmm11, itsc11), websites (e.g. bestcollegesonline.com) etc. Some bursts of particular relevance to TEL include:

- Screencastcamp: a screencastcamp gathers screencasters for networking, learning, and collaborating [http://screencastcamp.com].
- MobiMOOC: A MOOC is a massive open online course, i.e. it involves many participants and is open to anyone who wants to join. [http://www.mooc.ca]; MobiMOOC adopts this concept in a mobile learning context.
- Edcamp: follows an open ad-hoc gathering approach for sharing and learning including demos, discussions, and interaction.[http://www.edutopia.org/blog/ ].
- Studyboost: an interactive social media platform for studying by answering self- or teacher-prepared questions using SMS text messaging and instant messaging [https://studyboost.com/about_us].

**Fig. 2.** Bursty terms appearing in the TEL blogosphere only in 2011

These four bursts in 2011 all point to a model of leveraging web technology (in particular: mobile technology) for an open and inclusive approach to education and learning. In addition, we identified bursty words that have been rising in power over the last three years. 3,641 word stems match this criterion. Again, these word bursts expose many terms with no particular TEL provenance. However, there are mentions of technologies and trends that are highly relevant to TEL (and appearing to point into a similar direction as the bursts exclusively appearing in 2011 as presented above). For instance: *Screencastcamp*; *ds106* (an open online course on digital storytelling; *transmedia* (often used together with storytelling); *mobilelearn*, *mlearncon*, and *tablet*.

**Visual Burst Analytics.** To provide interactivity with the bursty topics in the blogosphere content, we used the Google Motion Chart to visualize the rise and fall of bursty topics over time. This charts allows users to select particular terms and use a slider to animate the change of frequency and intensity of burst

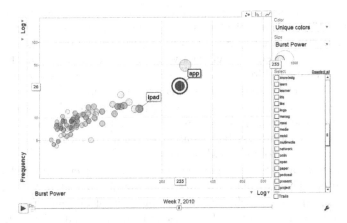

**Fig. 3.** Interactive chart of rising and falling bursts in the blogosphere

occurrence (Fig. 3), supporting them in exploratory data analysis, which is one main pillar of visual analytics [4]. For learning blogospheres such a visual tool could be very helpful in identifying current trends and for tracing particular topics, since the motion chart also allows to focus on a subset of the terms (e.g. 'ipad' and 'app' in the figure).

**Burst Co-Occurrences.** In an example of this content analysis method shown in Fig. 4, the co-occurrences of the word stem 'game' (which represents words like games, gaming, gamer, etc.) are displayed. It shows that 'game' frequently co-occurs with the words stems 'design', 'episdem', 'play' and 'learn'. In learning blogospheres such burst networks can be used to support topic-oriented exploration of the blogosphere, i.e. to explore relevant issues in the blogosphere based on links between (co-)related topics. We also found during this analysis that bursty terms in blogs often co-occur with event-related terms (e.g. conference, workshop, project), which underlines the relevance of blogospheres in learning contexts as an immediate source of information.

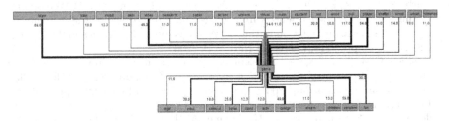

**Fig. 4.** Co-occurrence of words in bursts including the word "game"

## 4   Conclusions

In this paper, we proposed and demonstrated learning analytics methods to analyze and monitor the learning processes taking place in learning blogospheres.

The results of structural analysis on eTwinning and content analysis on the Mediabase show that outputs of blogging activities (e.g. comments, postings) can be modeled and measured by SNA methods. Structural analysis is able to identify learners' blogging activities via analysis of network structures of the learning blogs. Two social capital forms were observed: structural hole and closure, which are measured by betweenness and local clustering coefficient. They relate to influential bloggers and tight community structures, respectively. Content analysis is conducted on the learning content to observe term development trends based on learning blog content. As blog content develops over time the dynamics is captured through the content analysis as well.

The learning processes on blogosphere consist of bloggers' knowledge sharing and blog content development. Our current research results show that knowledge sharing in blogospheres is reflected in identification of bloggers' role in the network and analysis of blog topics. Bloggers with strong social capital play a more important role in knowledge sharing. Bursty topics show the popular learning content on learning blogospheres over time. Only an integrated learning analytics approach featuring an interplay of structural and semantic analysis methods will be able to provide a comprehensive image of the learning processes, social structures, and content in learning blogospheres.

**Acknowledgment.** This work was supported by the EU EACEA LLP project TeLLNet and by the EU FP7 ICT Support Action TEL-Map.

# References

1. Brooks, C.H., Montanez, N.: An analysis of the effectiveness of tagging in blogs. In: AAAI Spring Symp. on Comput. Approaches to Analyzing Weblogs. AAAI (2005)
2. Burt, R.: Structural Holes: The Social Structure of Competition. Harvard (1995)
3. Coleman, J.S.: Social capital in the creation of human capital. The American Journal of Sociology 94, S95–S120 (1988)
4. Fekete, J.-D., van Wijk, J.J., Stasko, J.T., North, C.: The Value of Information Visualization. In: Kerren, A., Stasko, J.T., Fekete, J.-D., North, C. (eds.) Information Visualization. LNCS, vol. 4950, pp. 1–18. Springer, Heidelberg (2008)
5. Harb, A., Plantié, M., Dray, G., Roche, M., Trousset, F., Poncelet, P.: Web opinion mining: how to extract opinions from blogs? In: Proceedings of the 5th International Conference on Soft Computing as Transdisciplinary Science and Technology, CSTST 2008, pp. 211–217. ACM, New York (2008)
6. Hoadley, C.M.: The shape of the elephant: scope and membership of the cscl community. In: Proceedings of th 2005 Conference on Computer Support for Collaborative Learning: Learning 2005: the Next 10 Years!, CSCL 2005, pp. 205–210. International Society of the Learning Sciences (2005)
7. Johnson, L., Smith, R., Willis, H., Levine, A., Haywood, K.: The 2011 Horizon Report. In: The New Media Consortium, Austin, Texas (2011)
8. Kienle, A., Wessner, M.: Analysing and cultivating scientific communities of practice. Int. J. Web Based Communities 2, 377–393 (2006)
9. Klamma, R.: Emerging research topics in social learning. In: Dirckinck-Holmfeld, L., Hodgson, V., Jones, C., de Laat, M., McConnell, D., Ryberg, T. (eds.) Proceedings of the 7th International Conference on Networked Learning 2010, Aalborg, Denmark, pp. 224–231 (2010)

10. Klamma, R., Cao, Y., Spaniol, M.: Watching the Blogosphere: Knowledge Sharing in the Web 2.0. In: Nicolov, N., Glance, N., Adar, E., Hurst, M., Liberman, M., Martin, J.H., Salvetti, F. (eds.) Proceedings of the 1st International Conference on Weblogs and Social Media, Boulder, Colorado, USA, March 26-28 (2007)

11. Klamma, R., Spaniol, M., Denev, D.: PALADIN: A pattern based approach to knowledge discovery in digital social networks. In: Tochtermann, K., Maurer, H. (eds.) Proceedings of I-KNOW 2006, 6th International Conference on Knowledge Management, Graz, Austria, September 6-8, pp. 457–464. Springer (2006)

12. Kovachev, D., Cao, Y., Klamma, R., Jarke, M.: Learn-as-you-go: New Ways of Cloud-Based Micro-learning for the Mobile Web. In: Leung, H., Popescu, E., Cao, Y., Lau, R.W.H., Nejdl, W. (eds.) ICWL 2011. LNCS, vol. 7048, pp. 51–61. Springer, Heidelberg (2011)

13. Laat, M.D., Lally, V., Lipponen, L., Simons, R.-J.: Investigating patterns of interaction in networked learning and computer-supported collaborative learning: A role for social network analysis. I. J. Computer-Supported Collaborative Learning 2(1), 87–103 (2007)

14. Pham, M., Klamma, R., Jarke, M.: Development of computer science disciplines: a social network analysis approach. Social Network Analysis and Mining, 1–20 (2011), doi:10.1007/s13278-011-0024-x

15. Robes, J.: What's in it for me? Über den Nutzen von Weblogs für Wissensarbeiter. IM - Information Management & Consulting (3) (2005)

16. Rogers, E.M.: Diffusion of Innovations, 5th edn. Free Press (2003)

17. Thomas, J.J., Cook, K.A. (eds.): Illuminating the Path: The Research and Development Agenda for Visual Analytics. IEEE Press (2005)

18. Travers, J., Milgram, S.: An experimental study of the small world problem. Sociometry 32(4), 425–443 (1969)

19. Watts, D.J., Strogatz, S.H.: Collective dynamics of 'small-world' networks. Nature 393(6684), 440–442 (1998)

20. Wenger, E.: Communities of Practice: Learning, Meaning, and Identity. Cambridge University Press, Cambridge (1998)

# Towards an Integrated Approach for Evaluating Textual Complexity for Learning Purposes

Mihai Dascălu[1,2], Stefan Trausan-Matu[1], and Philippe Dessus[2]

[1] Politehnica University of Bucharest, Computer Science Department, Romania
{mihai.dascalu,stefan.trausan}@cs.pub.ro
[2] LSE, UPMF Grenoble-2 & IUFM–UJF Grenoble-1, France
philippe.dessus@upmf-grenoble.fr

**Abstract.** Understanding a text in order to learn is subject to modeling and is partly dependent to the complexity of the read text. We transpose the evaluation process of textual complexity into measurable factors, identify linearly independent variables and combine multiple perspectives to obtain a holistic approach, addressing lexical, syntactic and semantic levels of textual analysis. Also, the proposed evaluation model combines statistical factors and traditional readability metrics with information theory, specific information retrieval techniques, probabilistic parsers, Latent Semantic Analysis and Support Vector Machines for best-matching all components of the analysis. First results show a promising overall precision (>50%) and near precision (>85%).

**Keywords:** textual complexity, Latent Semantic Analysis, readability, Support Vector Machines.

## 1 Introduction

Measuring textual complexity is in general a difficult task because the measure itself is relative to the reader and high differences in the perception for a given lecture can arise due to prior knowledge in the specific domain, familiarity with the language or to personal motivation and interest. Readability ease and comprehension are related to the readers' education, cognitive capabilities and background experiences. Therefore a cognitive model of the reader must be taken into consideration and the measured complexity should be adapted to this model. Additionally, software implementing such functionalities should be adaptive in the sense that, for a given target audience, the estimated levels of textual complexity measured for specific texts should be adequate and relevant. Fortunately, the target texts processed in this paper were accessible from a syntactical and vocabulary viewpoint by primary school pupils, and the required level of knowledge to grasp the read story was also on the same range.

Assessing the textual complexity of the material given to pupils is a common task that teachers encounter very often. However, this assessment cannot be performed without taking into account the actual pupils' reading proficiency and this point makes it time-consuming. Moreover, the impact of textual complexity on instruction and learning is important: pupils read faster and learn better if textual materials are

E. Popescu et al. (Eds.): ICWL 2012, LNCS 7558, pp. 268–278, 2012.

not too complex nor too easy. A web-based system can help teachers select and calibrate the appropriate texts presented to students and also help the latter attain their own learning objectives in selecting not too simple nor too difficult reading materials.

Our aim is to design and implement a system that automatically gives a measure of the complexity of texts read by children by studying the relations between human vs. computer measures of this textual complexity, similar to some extent to [9]. Although there are numerous applications that give estimates regarding textual complexity, they often do not rely on cognitive models of human reading or use only simple lexical or syntactic factors. An example of a complex system covering multiple perspectives of discourse analysis is *Coh-Metrix 2* [1] that automatically calculates the coherence of texts and determines how text elements and constituents are connected for specific types of cohesion. Besides lexical and syntactic factors, POS tagging and Latent Semantic Analysis (LSA), used also within *Coh-Metrix 2*, we provide an integrated approach through Support Vector Machines (SVMs) that covers in a novel manner all previous dimensions, tightly connected to the implemented discourse model. Therefore, our model is capable of automatically adapting its categories based on the training corpus, enabling us to personalize even further the classification process and the assigned weights to each evaluation factor.

Due to the fact that textual complexity cannot be determined by enforcing a single factor of evaluation, we propose a multitude of factors, categorized in a multilayered pyramid [3], from the simplest to the more complex ones, that combined provide relevant information to the tutor regarding the actual "hardness" of a text. The first and simplest factors are at a surface (*word*) level and include readability metrics, utterance entropy at stem level and proxies extracted or derived from Page's [4] automatic essay grading technique. At the *syntactic* level, structural complexity is estimated from the parsing tree in terms of max depth and size of the parsing structure [6]. Moreover, normalized values of occurrences of specific parts of speech (mostly prepositions) provide additional information at this level. *Semantics* is addressed through topics that are determined by combining *Tf-Idf* with cosine similarity between the utterance vector and that of the entire documents. The textual complexity at this level is expressed as a weighted mean of the difficulty of each topic, estimated in computations as the number of syllables of each word. Moreover, textual complexity is evaluated in terms of semantic cohesion determined upon social networks analysis metrics applied at macroscopic level upon the utterance graph [5]. Discourse markers, co-references, rhetorical schemas and argumentation structures are also considered, but are not included in current experiments.

By considering the disparate facets of textual complexity and by proposing possible automatic methods of evaluation, the resulted measurement vectors provide tutors valuable information regarding the hardness of presented texts. The remainder of this paper details the various metrics. All the measures used to evaluate textual complexity are then unified into a single result by using SVMs in the effort to best align automatic results to the classes manually assigned by teachers. The paper ends with conclusions and future improvements

## 2    Surface Analysis

Surface analysis addresses lexical and syntactic levels and consists of measures computed to determine factors like fluency, complexity, readability taking into account lexical and syntactic elements (e.g., words, commas, phrase length, periods).

### 2.1    Readability

Traditional readability formulas [7] are simple methods for evaluating a text's reading ease based on simple statistical factors as sentence length or word length. Although criticized by discourse analysts [8] as being weak indicators of comprehensibility and for not closely aligning with the cognitive processes involved in text comprehension, their simple mechanical evaluation makes them appealing for integration in our model. Moreover, by considering the fact that reading speed, retention and reading persistence are greatly influenced by the complexity of terms and overall reading volume, readability formulas can provide a viable approximation of the complexity of a given text, considering that prior knowledge, personal skills and traits (e.g. intelligence), interest and motivation are at an adequate level or of a similar level for all individuals of the target audience. In addition, the domain of texts, itself, must be similar because subjectivity increases dramatically when addressing cross-domain evaluation of textual complexity. Starting from simple lexical indicators, numerous mathematical formulas were developed to tackle the issue of readability. The following three measures can be considered the most famous:

1. The **Flesch Reading Ease** Readability Formula scores texts on a 100 point scale, providing a simple approach to assess the grade-level of pupils: the higher the score, the easier the text is to read (not necessarily to be understood).
2. The **Gunning's Fog Index** (or **FOG**) Readability Formula estimates the number of years of formal education a reader of average intelligence needs to understand the given text on the first reading. Although considering that words with more than two syllables are complex can be seen as a drawback, we chose this estimation due to its high precision and simplicity.
3. The **Flesch Grade Level** Readability Formula uses the same factors as the first readability metric and rates texts based on U.S. grade school levels.

### 2.2    Trins and Proxes

Page's initial study was centered on the idea that computers can be used to automatically evaluate and grade student essays using only statistically and easily detectable attributes, as effective as human teachers [4, 5]. In order to perform a statistical analysis, Page correlated two concepts: *proxes* (computer approximations of interest) with human *trins* (intrinsic variables - human measures used for evaluation) for better quantifying an essay's complexity. A correlation of 0.71 proved that computer programs could predict grades quite reliably, similar to the inter-human correlation. Starting for Page's metrics of automatically grading essays and taking into consideration Slotnick's method of grouping proxes based on their intrinsic values, the following categories were used for estimating complexity (see Table 1).

**Table 1.** Surface analysis proxes

| Quality | Proxes |
| --- | --- |
| Fluency | Normalized number of commas |
| | Normalized number of words |
| | Average number of words per sentence |
| Diction | Average word length |
| | Average number of syllables per word |
| | Percent of hard words (extracted from FOG Formula) |
| Structure | Normalized number of blocks (paragraphs) |
| | Average block (paragraph) size |
| | Normalized number of utterances (sentences) |
| | Average utterance (sentence) length |

Normalization is inspired from Data-Mining and our results improved by applying the logarithmic function on some of the previous factors in order to smooth results, while comparing documents of different size. All the above proxes determine the average consistency of sentences and model adequately their complexity at surface level in terms of the analyzed lexical items.

## 2.3    Complexity, Accuracy and Fluency

Complexity, accuracy, and fluency (CAF) measures of texts have been used in linguistic development and in second language acquisition (SLA) research. *Complexity* captures the characteristic of a learner's language, reflected in a wider range of vocabulary and grammatical constructions, as well as communicative functions and genres [2]. *Accuracy* highlights a text's conformation to our experience with other texts, while *fluency*, in oral communication, captures the actual volume of text produced in a certain amount of time. Similar to the previous factors, these measures play an important role in automated essay scoring and textual complexity analysis. Schulze [2] considered that selected complexity measures should be divided into two main facets of textual complexity: sophistication (richness) and diversity (variability of forms). The defined measures depend on six units of analysis: letter ($l$), word form ($w$), bigram ($b$ – groups of two words) and period unit ($p$), word form types ($t$) and unique bigrams ($u$). Additionally, textual complexity is devised into *lexical* and *syntactic* complexity:

**Lexical Complexity**

- *Diversity* is measured using Carroll's Adjusted Token Type Ratio (Eq. 1) [2]:

$$v_1 = \frac{t}{\sqrt{2w}}, with \ \frac{1}{\sqrt{2w}} \leq v_1 \leq \sqrt{\frac{w}{2}} \tag{1}$$

- *Sophistication* estimates the complexity of a word's form in terms of average number of characters (Eq. 2) [2]:

$$v_2 = \frac{l}{w}, with\ 1 \le v_2 \le l \qquad (2)$$

**Syntactic Complexity**

- *Diversity* captures syntactic variety at the smallest possible unit of two consecutive word forms. Therefore Token Type Ratio is also used, but at a bigram level (Eq. 3) [2]:

$$v_3 = \frac{u}{\sqrt{2b}}, with\ \frac{1}{\sqrt{2b}} \le v_3 \le \sqrt{\frac{b}{2}} \qquad (3)$$

- *Sophistication* is expressed in terms of mean number of words per period unit length and it's intuitive justification is that longer clauses are, in general, more complex than short ones (Eq. 4) [2]:

$$v_4 = \frac{w}{p}, with\ 1 \le v_4 \le p \qquad (4)$$

All the previous measures can be integrated into a unique measure of textual complexity at lexical and syntactic levels. Following this idea, these factors were balanced by computing a rectilinear distance (Raw Complexity - RC) as if the learner had to cover the distance along each of these dimensions [2]. Therefore, in order to reach a higher level of textual complexity, the learner needs to improve on all four dimensions (Eq. 5) [2]:

$$RC = \left| v_1 - \frac{1}{\sqrt{2w}} \right| + |v_2 - 1| + \left| v_3 - \frac{1}{\sqrt{2b}} \right| + |v_4 - 1| \qquad (5)$$

Afterwards, CAF is computed as a balanced complexity by subtracting the range of the four complexity measures (max - min) from the raw complexity measure (Eq. 6):

$$CAF = RC - (\max(v_1, v_2, v_3, v_4) - \min(v_1, v_2, v_3, v_4)) \qquad (6)$$

The ground argument for this adjustment is that if one measure increases too much, it will always be to the detriment of another. Therefore, the measure of raw complexity is decreased by a large amount if the four vector measures vary widely and by a small amount if they are very similar. Moreover, the defined measure captures lexical and syntactic complexity evenly, provides two measures for sophistication and two measures for diversity and, in the end, compensates for large variations of the four vector measures.

## 2.4    Entropy

Entropy, derived from Information Theory, models the text in an ergodic manner and provides relevant insight regarding textual complexity at character and word level by ensuring diversity among the elements of the analysis. The presumption of induced complexity pursues the following hypothesis: a more complex text contains more information and requires more memory and more time for the reader to process. Therefore, disorder modeled through entropy is reflected in the diversity of characters and of word stems used, within our implemented model, as analysis elements. The use of stems instead of the actual concepts is argued by their better expression of the root form of related concepts, more relevant when addressing diversity at syntactic level.

## 3     Part of Speech Tagging and Parsing Tree Structure

Starting from different linguistic categories of lexical items, our aim is to convert morphological information regarding the words and the sentence structure into relevant metrics to be assessed in order to better comprehend textual complexity. In this context, parsing and part of speech (POS) tagging play an important role in the morphological analysis of texts, in terms of textual complexity, by providing two possible vectors of evaluation: the normalized frequency of each part of speech and the structural factors derived from the parsing tree. Although the most common parts of speech used in discourse analysis are nouns and verbs, our focus was aimed at prepositions, adjectives and adverbs that dictate a more elaborate and complex structure of the text. Moreover, pronouns, that through their use indicate the presence of co-references, also indicate a more inter-twined and complex structure of the discourse. On the other hand, multiple factors can be derived from analyzing the structure of the parsing tree: an increased number of leafs, a greater overall size of the tree and a higher maximum depth indicate a more complex structure, therefore an increased textual complexity. Our implemented system uses the log-linear Part of Speech Tagger publicly available from Stanford University [11] with the "bidirectional-wsj-0-18.tagger" package as English tagger, therefore ensuring an accuracy of 97.18% on WSJ 19-21 concepts and of 89.30% on unknown words.

## 4     Semantic Analysis – Coherence through LSA

Coherence is a central issue to text comprehension and comprehension is strongly related to textual complexity. In order to understand a text, the reader must first create a well-connected representation of the information withheld. This connected representation is based on linking related pieces of textual information that occur throughout the text. Coherence is determined and maintained through the links identified within the utterance graph [5]. Our implemented discourse model characterizes the degree of semantic relatedness between different segments through means of Information Retrieval (Term Frequency – Inverse Document Frequency) reflected in word repetitions [3] and of LSA, capable of measuring similarity between discourse segments through concepts of the vector space [1].

The power of computing semantic similarity with LSA comes from analyzing a large corpus from which LSA builds relationships between a set of documents and terms contained within. The main assumption is that semantically related words will co-appear throughout documents of the corpus and will be indirectly linked by concepts after the Single Value Decomposition specific to LSA.

Coherence is determined using the utterance graph modeled as a Directed Acyclic Graph (DAG) of sentences, ordered sequentially through the ongoing discourse. The first thing that needs to be addressed is semantic cohesion between two sentences which is seen as the degree of inter-connection among them [3]. This similarity is computed by combining *repetitions* of stems and *Jaccard similarity* as measures of lexical cohesion, with semantic similarity computed by means of LSA (Eq. 7 and 8):

$$coh(u, v) = |repetions| \times \frac{|stems\ in\ common\ u,v|}{|stems\ in\ u\ or\ v|} \times cos(vector(u), vector(v)) \quad (7)$$

$$vector_k(u) = \sum_i (1 + |word_i \in u|) \times \left( \frac{|D|}{|word_i \in D|} \right) \times U_k[word_i] \quad (8)$$

where $U_k[word_i]$ is the vector of $word_i$ in the $U_k$ matrix from LSA.

After determining all possible connections between the sentences of a text through the previous equations, the utterance graph is built by selecting the links that have their corresponding values above a threshold (in our experiments, the best empirical value was the mean value of all viable cohesion values determined for any possible link within our initial text). Overall, coherence is evaluated at a macroscopic level as the average value for all links in the constructed utterance graph. Co-references and other specific discourse analysis methods (e.g., argumentation acts) will be used to further refine the previous DAG.

# 5     Support Vector Machines

All the measures previously defined capture in some degree different properties of the analyzed text (readability, fluency, accuracy, language diversity, coherence, etc.) and therefore can be viewed as attributes that describe the text. In order to use these attributes to estimate the complexity of the text, we have used a classifier that accepts as inputs text attributes and outputs the minimum grade level required by a reader to comprehend the specified text. Therefore multiple Support Vector Machine (SVM) classifiers are used to achieve the desired result. A SVM is typically a binary linear classifier that maps the input texts seen as $d$-dimensional vectors to a higher dimensional space (hyperspace) in which, hopefully, these vectors are linearly separable by a hyperplane.

Due to the fact that binary classifiers can map objects only into two classes, our multiclass problem can be solved using multiple SVM, each classifying a category of texts with different predefined classes of complexity. A one-versus-all approach implementing the winner-takes-all strategy is used to deal with the problem of multiple SVM kernel returning 1 for a specific text (the classifier with the highest output function assigns the class).

LIBSVM [10] was used to ease the implementation of the classifier. An RBF with degree 3 was selected and a *Grid Search method* was enforced to increase the effectiveness of the SVM through the parameter selection process. Exponentially growing sequences for $C$ and $\gamma$ were used ($C \in \{2^{-5}, 2^{-3}, ..., 2^{13}, 2^{15}\}$, $\gamma \in \{2^{-15}, 2^{-13}, ..., 2^1, 2^3\}$) and each combination of parameter choices was checked using a predefined testing corpus. In the end, the parameters with the best obtained precision were picked.

# 6     Preliminary Validation Results

The preliminary validation experiments were run on 249 reading assignments given by teachers to pupils ranging from 1st grade to the 5th grade (29 – C1, 41 – C1, 66 – C3, 71 – C4, 42 – C5). All the previous measurements have been automatically extracted for each these texts and were later used as inputs for the SVM. The split between the training corpus and the testing one was manually performed by assigning 166 texts as training set and the remaining for evaluation. Additional to data normalization that was previously performed, all factors were linearly scaled to the [-1; 1] range. Two types of measures were used to evaluate the performance of our model: *Precision* (P), as the percent to which the SVM predicted the correct classification for the test input, and *Near Precision* (NP), as the percent to which the SVM was close in predicting the correct classification (i.e. answered $n^{th}$ grade instead of $(n+1)^{th}$ grade). NP was introduced due to the subjectivity of the evaluation of the corresponding grade level and also due to the fact that the complexity of the finishing $n^{th}$ year text may be very close to one from the beginning of the $(n+1)^{th}$ year.

Table 2 presents in detail the optimum $C$ and $\gamma$ parameters determined for the SVMs via Grid Search method, precision and near precision for all classes, average and weighted average of both precision and near precision.

**Table 2.** Precision (P%) and Near Precision (NP%) for all evaluation factors

| Factor | C | $\gamma$ | C1 P/NP | C2 P/NP | C3 P/NP | C4 P/NP | C5 P/NP | Avg. P/NP | Weig. Avg. P/NP |
|---|---|---|---|---|---|---|---|---|---|
| Readability Flesch | 128 | 0.125 | 90/90 | 14/64 | 27/91 | 78/100 | 14/86 | 44.6/86.2 | 44.5/88.2 |
| Readability FOG | 32 | 0.5 | 80/90 | 29/64 | 32/100 | 83/91 | 7/79 | 46.2/84.8 | 47.4/86.8 |
| Readability Kincaid | 32768 | 2 | 90/90 | 7/57 | 45/95 | 57/100 | 14/57 | 42.6/79.8 | 42.2/83.2 |
| Normalized no. of commas | 0.5 | 2 | 0/80 | 29/57 | 14/100 | 83/91 | 0/71 | 25.2/79.8 | 32.2/83.1 |
| Avg. sentence length | 32 | 2 | 80/80 | 7/93 | 55/82 | 61/100 | 36/50 | 47.8/81 | 48.5/83.3 |
| Normalized no. of words | 2048 | 0.008 | 50/100 | 79/86 | 0/91 | 83/83 | 0/71 | 42.4/86.2 | 42.5/85.6 |
| Avg. word length | 2048 | 0.008 | 80/80 | 43/93 | 50/86 | 61/96 | 29/50 | 52.6/81 | 51.9/83.2 |
| Avg. no. of words/ sentence | 128 | 0.031 | 100/100 | 0/21 | 5/95 | 100/100 | 0/93 | 41/81.8 | 41.5/84.5 |
| Avg. no. of syllables/word | 2 | 0.125 | 60/60 | 0/71 | 41/100 | 87/100 | 0/79 | 37.6/82 | 42.7/87 |
| Percent of complex words | 0.5 | 0.5 | 70/70 | 0/86 | 41/91 | 83/100 | 0/79 | 38.8/85.2 | 42.7/88.3 |

**Table 2.** (*Continued*)

| | | | | | | | | | |
|---|---|---|---|---|---|---|---|---|---|
| Word Entropy | 0.125 | 8 | 80 / 100 | 57 / 100 | 23 / 95 | 65 / 83 | 0 / 64 | 45 / 88.4 | 43.3 / 87.8 |
| Character Entropy | 8 | 0.5 | 70 / 70 | 7 / 14 | 18 / 100 | 87 / 96 | 0 / 86 | 36.4 / 73.2 | 38.9 / 78.8 |
| Lexical diversity | 2 | 0.125 | 50 / 100 | 79 / 100 | 27 / 100 | 74 / 87 | 0 / 79 | 46 / 93.2 | 47.1 / 92.8 |
| Lexical sophistication | 8 | 8 | 40 / 60 | 14 / 64 | 45 / 86 | 65 / 100 | 14 / 50 | 35.6 / 72 | 39.8 / 77.3 |
| Syntactic diversity | 0.5 | 2 | 40 / 40 | 0 / 64 | 45 / 100 | 91 / 100 | 0 / 93 | 35.2 / 79.4 | 42.5 / 85.9 |
| Syntactic sophistication | 32768 | 8 | 80 / 90 | 0 / 93 | 50 / 82 | 61 / 96 | 21 / 50 | 42.4 / 82.2 | 43.5 / 83.3 |
| Balanced CAF | 512 | 0.5 | 70 / 100 | 79 / 100 | 50 / 100 | 57 / 91 | 0 / 71 | 51.2 / 92.4 | 50.7 / 92.5 |
| Average number of nouns | 2 | 0.125 | 0 / 0 | 0 / 79 | 68 / 100 | 74 / 100 | 0 / 71 | 28.4 / 70 | 39.1 / 80 |
| Average no. of pronouns | 128 | 2 | 40 / 60 | 14 / 71 | 50 / 91 | 39 / 96 | 7 / 64 | 30 / 76.4 | 32.5 / 81 |
| Average no. of verbs | 128 | 0.5 | 80 / 80 | 0 / 36 | 5 / 77 | 96 / 96 | 0 / 93 | 36.2 / 76.4 | 38 / 78.7 |
| Average no. of adverbs | 2 | 8 | 40 / 60 | 14 / 64 | 27 / 95 | 61 / 91 | 29 / 79 | 34.2 / 77.8 | 36.4 / 82 |
| Average no. of adjectives | 32 | 0.125 | 30 / 30 | 0 / 93 | 55 / 100 | 70 / 100 | 0 / 71 | 31 / 78.8 | 38 / 85.8 |
| Average no. of prepositions | 128 | 8 | 30 / 70 | 50 / 79 | 36 / 91 | 65 / 96 | 14 / 64 | 39 / 80 | 42.2 / 83.4 |
| Average POS tree depth | 2048 | 8 | 80 / 90 | 14 / 93 | 55 / 82 | 65 / 96 | 14 / 50 | 45.6 / 82.2 | 47.1 / 83.3 |
| Average POS tree size | 512 | 2 | 80 / 80 | 0 / 93 | 45 / 77 | 57 / 100 | 36 / 64 | 43.6 / 82.8 | 43.6 / 84.3 |
| Avg. doc. cohesion | 2 | 2 | 40 / 50 | 0 / 64 | 32 / 95 | 74 / 100 | 0 / 71 | 29.2 / 76 | 34.2 / 82 |
| **Comb. lexical-syntactic** | **512** | **0.002** | **100 / 100** | **43 / 93** | **41 / 82** | **48 / 100** | **36 / 86** | **53.6 / 92.2** | **49.4 / 91.7** |
| **Combined POS** | **2** | **0.125** | **80 / 80** | **14 / 93** | **55 / 82** | **52 / 100** | **29 / 71** | **46 / 85.2** | **45.9 / 86.9** |
| **Combined semantic** | **2048** | **0.008** | **70 / 70** | **7 / 86** | **45 / 91** | **70 / 96** | **0 / 79** | **38.4 / 84.4** | **41.2 / 87.1** |
| **Combined all** | **32768** | **0.008** | **100 / 100** | **57 / 100** | **55 / 86** | **35 / 91** | **50 / 64** | **59.4 / 88.2** | **54 / 87.7** |

Taking into consideration the previous experiment, we have obtained a promising overall precision (>50%) and an excellent near precision (>85%), taking into consideration the difficulty and the subjectivity of the task at hand. Moreover, as expected, the effectives of our method increased by combining multiple factors and, although simple in nature, readability formulas, average sentence length, average word length and balanced CAF provided the best alternatives at lexical and syntactic level. Also, character entropy proved to be a lesser relevant factor than word entropy that reflects vocabulary diversity. In term of parts of speech tagging, prepositions had the highest correlation of all types of parts of speech, whereas depth and size of the parsing tree provided a good insight of textual complexity. In contrast, semantic factors had lower scores because the evaluation process at this level is based on the links between sentences; but texts used in educational environments are characterized by a low variance between different classes in terms of the computed semantic cohesion function (a text belonging to C3 does not necessarily have to be more cohesive than a text from C1). Also, the most difficult class to identify was the last one because, in general, there are relatively small changes in comparison to the previous class and it's difficult to highlight the differences.

## 7     Conclusions and Future Development

By combining different factors as readability, lexical and syntactic complexity, accuracy and fluency metrics, part of speech evaluation and characteristics of the parsing tree with LSA embedded within the discourse model, we obtained an elaborate and multi-perspective model capable of providing an overall balanced measure for textual complexity. In order to fine-tune even further the results, additional investigations and experiments are to be conducted to find the best parameters for the SVM, making predictions more reliable, whereas additional coherence measurement techniques will be included for enriching the semantic perspective of our analysis. Our research can be easily extended to any online materials and can be considered a cornerstone in developing an adaptive system for proposing personalized reading materials. This adaptive system would also assess the relation between textual complexity and pupils' understanding, as measured by online questionnaires.

## References

1. McNamara, D.S., Louwerse, M.M., McCarthy, P.M., Graesser, A.C.: Coh-Metrix: Capturing linguistic features of cohesion. Discourse Processes 47(4), 292–330 (2010)
2. Schulze, M.: Measuring textual complexity in student writing. In: Proc. AAAL, Atlanta (2010)
3. Trausan-Matu, S., Dascalu, M., Dessus, P.: Textual Complexity and Discourse Structure in Computer-Supported Collaborative Learning. In: Cerri, S.A., Clancey, W.J., Papadourakis, G., Panourgia, K. (eds.) ITS 2012. LNCS, vol. 7315, pp. 352–357. Springer, Heidelberg (2012)
4. Page, E.: The imminence of grading essays by computer. Phi Delta Kappan 47, 238–243 (1966)
5. Trausan-Matu, S., Rebedea, T.: A Polyphonic Model and System for Inter-animation Analysis in Chat Conversations with Multiple Participants. In: Gelbukh, A. (ed.) CICLing 2010. LNCS, vol. 6008, pp. 354–363. Springer, Heidelberg (2010)
6. Gervasi, V., Ambriola, V.: Quantitative assessment of textual complexity. In: Merlini Barbaresi, L. (ed.) Complexity in Language and Text, pp. 197–228. Plus, Pisa (2002)
7. Brown, J.D.: An EFL readability index. JALT Journal 20, 7–36 (1998)

8. Davison, A., Kantor, R.: On the failure of readability formulas to define readable texts: A case study from adaptations. Reading Research Quarterly 17, 187–209 (1982)
9. Petersen, S.E., Ostendorf, M.: A machine learning approach to reading level assessment. Computer Speech and Language 23, 89–106 (2009)
10. Chang, C.-C., Lin, C.-J.: LIBSVM: a library for support vector machines. ACM Transactions on Intelligent Systems and Technology 2(3), 1–27 (2011)
11. Klein, D., Manning, C.D.: Accurate Unlexicalized Parsing. In: Proceedings of the 41st Meeting of the Association for Computational Linguistics, pp. 423–430 (2003)

# How about Using the PCA
# to Analyze Changes in Learning Styles?

Federico Scaccia[1] and Carlo Giovannella[1,2]

[1] ISIM Garage - Dept. of Science and Technology of Education
[2] Scuola IaD
Tor Vergata University of Rome
giovannella@scuolaiad.it, info@mifav.uniroma2.it

**Abstract.** Nowadays collaborative educational processes require the use of increasingly sophisticated analytical tools to help teachers, tutors and students to identify, at best, emergent behaviors. In this paper we describe the use of a module that has been designed and developed to perform Principal Component Analysis as internal facility of the on-line learning place LIFE to identify groups of students characterized by similar learning styles and, as well, to study the evolution (one or two years away) of such styles.

**Keywords:** PCA, docimology, learning styles.

## 1    Introduction to Research Problems on Learning Styles

Since few years we are assisting to a progressive diffusion of more collaborative and open learning processes and, at the same time, to a growing attention toward all meaningful dimensions of learning "experiences". Due to all this today we are facing two main problems: (a) a quite old one related to the definition of satisfactory models of personal styles and, more in general, of the experience [1-3]; (b) a newer one concerning the need for new and more powerful techniques of monitoring, analysis and visualization [4]. As far as problem (a), after more than fifty years of research, the present situation is well summarized in a comprehensive overview [5] where authors criticize the concept of learning styles (LS) whose utility they do not believe has been demonstrated convincingly. A conclusion, that in our opinion, may depend on the lack of a reasonable attempt to unify the theoretical backgrounds of various models in a more general framework capable to take into account the whole complexity of the educational experience and, at same time, clearly distinguish among dimensions describing the process, those describing the context and, finally, those describing the individual styles. Accordingly to all this we need: (i) to rethink the theoretical foundations of the learning styles; (ii) to explore new analytical approaches that can overcome problems such as the possible non-orthogonality of the spaces of representation [8, 9]. In trying to give an answer to need (i) we have introduced a new framework - the "experience style" one – based on a 3D representational space of the experience that decouples process', context's and individual's dimensions [6,10]. The "experience style" framework, however, requires a relevant effort (currently in

E. Popescu et al. (Eds.): ICWL 2012, LNCS 7558, pp. 279–284, 2012.
© Springer-Verlag Berlin Heidelberg 2012

progress) to identify methodologies and strategies to track relevant traces and work out meaningful indicators useful to describe all dimensions of the personal and contextualized learning experience. In the meantime, also to prepare the use of the new framework, it is useful to develop a deeper understanding of limitations and potentialities of previous models: recently we have shown how changes in the mean values of the Felder-Silverman LS (FSLS) characterizing groups of homogeneous or identical individuals could be probably used to measure changes induced by specific training environments or curricula. Intensity of the detected variations, however, was quite low due to limited sensitivity of the measurement tool (FSLS questionnaire) [11]. To investigate further the level of meaningfulness of such variations and, at the same time, to explore the possibility to overcome the problem of the non-orthogonality of the FSLS' space of representation we have implemented a procedure and a tool to perform a Principal Component Analysis (PCA). In the following we first remind the operational principles of the PCA and then we will present its application to a set of data collected, over three years, to trace variations in the individual LS values during the attendance of the bachelor's degree in Media Science and Technology of the University of Rome Tor Vergata.

## 2     The Methodological Approach and PCA Implementation

The PCA is a method of the factorial analysis widely used whenever one has to do with quantitative variables and a multidimensional space of representation (multivariate distribution) characterized by an incertitude on the orthogonality of the axes forming its basis: in our case the 4 dimensions of the FSLS model. The PCA, in fact, allows to carry out a linear transformation of the initial space into a new Cartesian space of representation whose dimensions, linear combinations of the original ones, are othogonal. The ultimate goals, in fact, are the orthogonalization of the initial space of representation and the concentration of the largest part of all significant information (at least 70% of the whole information) into a limited number of dimensions (called Principal Components, PCs) so as to obtain an optimal two-dimensional representation of the original information. Given an initial dataset $X_i$, the less time consuming method to achieve such goals foresees the diagonalization of the correlation matrix whose elements are defined as:

$$R_{i,j} = Cov(X_i,X_j)/SQRT(Var(X_i)Var(X_j))$$

followed by the derivation of a set of eigenvalues, the definition of the corresponding eigenvectors forming the new orthogonal space of representation, where data set consisting of a linear combination of observables will be positioned.

Once that the datasets have been represented according to the PCs, one needs also to develop an appropriate interpretation strategy that in our case implied: a) the display of the contributions provided by each dimension of the old space of representation to the new one; b) k-means clustering algorithm [12] to perform an unsupervised search for potential clusters. Accordingly, we have implemented and integrated in LIFE [13] a module that allows to apply PCA to any dimensional subset of the initial observational space and to compare two different sets of data on a unique

Principal Component Space of Representation (PCSR) to investigate for cluster formation and/or evolution. It allows also to visualize eigenvalues and eigenvectors matrices, the scree-plot, and to choose the axis of representation (by default those corresponding to the two highest eigenvalues).

# 3    Datasets, Analysis and Discussion

The groups of students that have been involved in the study are listed in Table 1. All subjects were asked to fill the ILS questionnaire [11] at the beginning of the course in Physics held in the second half of the first year of the Bachelor degree and again/or at the beginning of the course of "Multimodal Interfaces and Systems" (ISM) which is held in the second half of the third and final year of the same Bachelor degree.

**Table 1.** Groups of students involved in the overall study

| Course & Academic Year | N. of regular students | N. of students repeating the course |
|---|---|---|
| Physics - a.y. 08-09 | 22 (6 female) | 7 (1 female) |
| Physics - a.y. 09-10 | 47 (6 female) | 9 (2 female) |
| Physics - a.y. 10-11 | 27 (11 female) | 22 (1 female) |
| Physics – a.y. 11-12 | 24 (8 female) | 7 (2 female) |
| ISM - a.y. 08-09 | 17 (6 female) | 4 (no female) |
| ISM - a.y. 09-10 | 31 (6 female) | - |
| ISM - a.y. 10-11 | 16 (4 female) | - |
| ISM - a.y. 11-12 | 16 (5 female) | - |

The age of participants ranged between 19 and 23 years old for students attending the first year and between 21 and 26 years old for those attending the third year of the Bachelor. For the present study we decided to investigate changes in LS induced by one or two years attendance of the Bachelor's course on the same group of individuals and thus we considered only the subset of students listed in Table 2: (a) all students that attended the course in Physics on the second year and the ISM course on the third year of the Bachelor  (1 year away check); (b) all students that attended on regular time both courses in Physics and ISM (2 years away check).

A description of the study conducted an all student involved can be found in ref. [14].

*Descriptive statistics:* the observed changes in LS mean value describing propensities of group of same individuals one or two years away, max 17% of the full scale, indicate a tendency toward a reinforcement of sensitive and global styles while more controversial is the tendency toward the development of stronger visual and active styles (more evident in the 2 year away check). It is worthwhile to stress that variations in the LS mean values are much smaller than the variability range of individual LS (in brackets). This last observation legitimates doubts about the appropriateness of using FSLSM to design strategies aimed at supporting customized educational experience on individual level. The overall trend, however is not unreasonable and in our case can be justified by the nature of the Bachelor, offering many workshops and courses on visual media.

**Table 2.** Differences between LS mean values of groups of same individuals one or two years away, along with the range of individual LS variability (in brackets)

| Differences between LS mean values of student subgroups composed by the same subjects | Act(-)<br>Ref(+) | Sen(-)<br>Int(+) | Vis(-)<br>Ver(+) | Seq(-)<br>Glo(+) |
|---|---|---|---|---|
| 2 years - Number of subjects: 16 (4 female)<br>ISM 10-11 – Phys. 08-09<br>& ISM 11-12 – Phys. 09-10 | -1.50<br>(-8,8) | -0.25<br>(-6,12) | -1.00<br>(-10,6) | 0,94<br>(-6,6) |
| 1 years - Number of subjects: 12 (2 female)<br>ISM 09-10 – Phys. 08-09<br>& ISM 11-10 – Phys. 09-10 | 0,00<br>(-4,4) | -1.83<br>(-8,2) | 0.17<br>(-4,4) | 0,67<br>(-10,8) |

The correlation matrices worked out for all subset of data confirm the existence of a relevant correlation between sensing/intuitive and sequential/global dimensions and an anti-correlation between sequential/global and visual-verbal dimensions [8, 9] and offer a good reason to carry on a more detailed investigation of data by means of PCA. Another good reason to use the PCA is to make emerge the dynamics that are hidden behind the variations of the LS mean values.

*Inferential statistics:* a particularity of this study with respect to usual PCA studies is that we want to compare subset of data taken one or two year away that, after the application of the space transformation would lead each one to a different space of representation not easily comparable. Because of this we decided to use the PCA to operate a space transformation on the "initial" subset of data (i.e. the data collected during the Physics course of the Bachelor) and to use the same Principal Components to visualize also data collected one year or two years away. To verify the meaningfulness of the transformation obtained by diagonalizing the correlation matrices of the two subsets of data (see table 2) collected during the Physics course we checked the respective scree-plots: in both cases the sum of the weight of the first two eingevalues was higher than 70% and in the first case was even more than 85%.

Figure 1 shows the comparisons between the subsets of data recorded at the beginning of the course in Physics (blue dots) and those collected one year (top - Group 1) and two years (bottom - group 2) away, at the beginning the course of the ISM (red dots). We would like to recall that the points represented in the plot are no longer the data collected through the questionnaire LS, but the result of a linear combination of observables. To make the reader better understand which is the contribution that each learning style provides to the two Principal Components, Y1 and Y2 of the orthogonal space of representation, we have positioned on fig. 1 the initials of each learning style, accordingly to the weight they have in the linear combinations that defines the news axis.

In the first case, students attending the second year of the Bachelor, (top figures) we observe the formation of a cluster characterized by active and sequential styles. This cluster in one year moves almost rigidly toward positive Y1 as a consequence of an increase in global and visual styles, counterbalanced by a decrease of the sequential characteristic of the cluster. In the same period we observe also the formation of a smaller cluster acting as attractor for few elements characterized by a dominant sequential style.

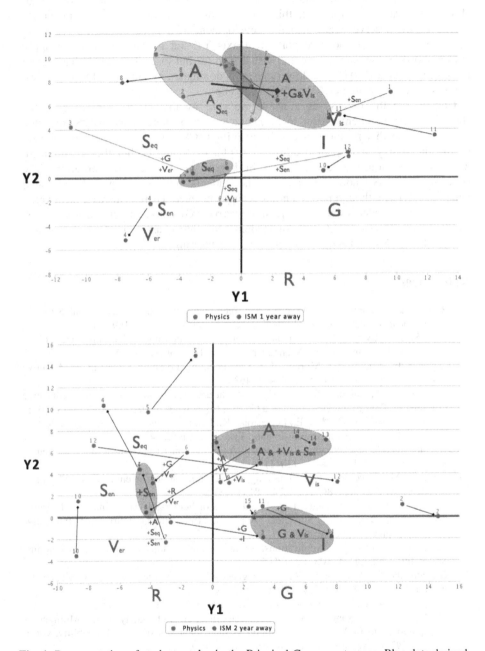

**Fig. 1.** Representation of students styles in the Principal Component space. Blue dots derived from data collected at the beginning of the course in Physics, red dots derived from data collected before the ISM course. Comparison are among data collected one year away (top), and two years away (bottom). Arrows indicate the displacements of the points.

In the second case (bottom figures) we observe once again the formation of a small cluster of attraction dominated, this time, by the sensitive style of its members. Moreover we observe again also the development of a large clustering region in correspondence of the positive portion of axis Y1, but it splits in two: the upper cluster shows a dominant active and visual features but loses the global character in favor of the sensitive style; the lower cluster is dominated by global and visual styles, but it is no longer characterized by the active one.

Considering the process as a whole we can say that at the beginning of the Bachelor course students seem to be characterized by heterogeneously distributed propensities so that no clusters can be identified. Clusters start to develop already during the first year (see blue ellipse, top plot of figure 1), but they continue to develop throughout the second and third year of the bachelor program. The educational process induces in most of the students more active, global and visual behaviors/styles, although not in a homogeneous manner. There is always, however, a small group of students that develops more verbal, sequential and/or sensitive styles. Finally, there is also a minority of students who are characterized by completely independent styles, and are not attracted by the clustering areas.

# References

1. Brusilovsky, P., Peylo, C.: Adaptive and Intelligent Web-based Educational Systems. International Journal of Artificial Intelligence in Education 13, 156–169 (2003)
2. Graf, S.: Adaptivity in learning management systems focusing on learning styles, Ph.D. Thesis, Faculty of Informatics, Vienna Univerity of Technology (2007)
3. Popescu, E., Badina, C., Moraret, L.: Accomodating Learning Styles in an Adaptive Educational System. Informatica 34, 451–462 (2010)
4. Giovannella, C., Carcone, S., Camusi, A.: What and how to monitor complex educative experiences. Toward the Definition of a General Framework, IxD&A, 11&12, 7–23 (2011)
5. Coffield, C., Mosely, D., Hall, E., Ecclestone, K.: Learning styles and Pedagogy in Post-16 Learning. LSRC. Univ. of Newcastle upon Tyne, London (2004)
6. Giovannella, C., Spadavecchia, C., Camusi, A.: Educational Experiences and Experiences Styles, IxD&A, 9&10, 104–116 (2011)
7. Felder, R.M., Silverman, L.K.: Learning and teaching styles in engineering education. Engineering Education 78(7), pp. 674–681 (1988)
8. Viola, S.R., Graf, S., Kinshuk, Leo, T.: Analysis of Felder-Silverman Index of Learning Styles by a Data-driven Statistical Approach. International Journal of Interactive Technology and Smart Education 4, 7–18 (2007)
9. Felder, R.M., Spurlin, J.: Applications, Reliability and Validity of the Index of Learning Styles. Int. J. Engng. 21, 103–112 (2005)
10. Giovannella, C., Moggio, F.: Toward a general model of the learning experience. In: ICALT 2011, pp. 644–645. IEEE Publisher (2011)
11. http://www.engr.ncsu.edu/learningstyles/ilsweb.html
12. MacQueen, J.B.: Some Methods for classification and Analysis of Multivariate Observations. In: Berkeley Symposium on Mathematical Statistics and Probability, vol. 1, pp. 281–297. University of California Press, Berkeley (1967)
13. Learning in an Interactive Framework to Experience, http://life.mifav.uniroma2.it
14. Giovannella, C.: What can we learn from long-time lasting measurments of Felder-Silverman's learning styles? In: ICALT 2012. IEEE Publisher (2012)

# An Automated Analysis and Indexing Framework for Lecture Video Portal

Haojin Yang, Christoph Oehlke, and Christoph Meinel

Hasso Plattner Institute (HPI), University of Potsdam, Germany
{Haojin.Yang,Meinel}@hpi.uni-potsdam.de,
Christoph.Oehlke@student.hpi.uni-potsdam.de

**Abstract.** This paper presents an automated framework for lecture video indexing in the *tele-teaching* context. The major issues involved in our approach are content-based lecture video analysis and integration of proposed analysis engine into a lecture video portal. In video visual analysis, we apply automated video segmentation, video OCR (*Optical Character Recognition*) technologies for extracting lecture structural and textual metadata. Concerning ASR (*Automated Speech Recognition*) analysis, we have optimized the workflow for the creation of a German speech corpus from raw lecture audio data. This enables us to minimize the time and effort required for extending the speech corpus and thus improving the recognition rate. Both, OCR and ASR results have been applied for the further video indexing. In order to integrate the analysis engine into the lecture video portal, we have developed an architecture for the corresponding tasks such as, e.g., data transmission, analysis management, and result visualization etc. The accuracy of each individual analysis method has been evaluated by using publicly available test data sets.

**Keywords:** Lecture videos, video indexing, ASR, video OCR, video segmentation, lecture video portal.

## 1 Introduction

Multimedia based education has become more and more popular in the past several years. Therefore, structuring, retrieval and indexing of multimedia lecture data has become an especially useful and challenging task.

Nowadays, the state-of-the-art lecture recording systems normally record two video streams synchronously: the main scene of lecturers which is recorded by using a video camera, and the second that captures the presentation slide frames projected onto the computer screen through a frame grabber card (as e.g., cf. Fig. 1(a)). Since two video streams can be synchronized automatically during the recording, the indexing task can be performed by using slide video only.

Text in lecture video is directly related to the lecture content. In our previous work [7], we have developed a novel video segmenter for key frames extraction from the slide video stream. Having adopted text detection and recognition algorithms on each slide shot in order to recognize the indexable texts. Furthermore,

E. Popescu et al. (Eds.): ICWL 2012, LNCS 7558, pp. 285–294, 2012.
© Springer-Verlag Berlin Heidelberg 2012

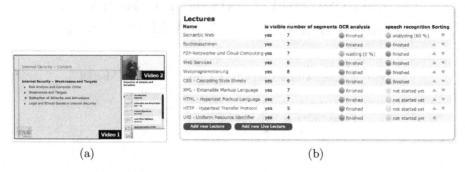

<table>
<thead>
<tr><th colspan="7">Lectures</th></tr>
<tr><th>Name</th><th>is visible</th><th>number of segments</th><th>OCR analysis</th><th>speech recognition</th><th>Sorting</th></tr>
</thead>
<tbody>
<tr><td>Semantic Web</td><td>yes</td><td>7</td><td></td><td>finished</td><td>analyzing (60 %)</td><td>▼</td></tr>
<tr><td>Suchmaschinen</td><td>yes</td><td>7</td><td></td><td>finished</td><td>finished</td><td>▲ ▼</td></tr>
<tr><td>P2P-Netzwerke und Cloud-Computing</td><td>yes</td><td>7</td><td></td><td>waiting (0 %)</td><td>finished</td><td>▲ ▼</td></tr>
<tr><td>Web Services</td><td>yes</td><td>6</td><td></td><td>finished</td><td>finished</td><td>▲ ▼</td></tr>
<tr><td>Webprogrammierung</td><td>yes</td><td>8</td><td></td><td>finished</td><td>finished</td><td>▲ ▼</td></tr>
<tr><td>CSS - Cascading Style Sheets</td><td>yes</td><td>6</td><td></td><td>finished</td><td>finished</td><td>▲ ▼</td></tr>
<tr><td>XML - Extensible Markup Language</td><td>yes</td><td>7</td><td></td><td>finished</td><td>not started yet</td><td>▲ ▼</td></tr>
<tr><td>HTML - Hypertext Markup Language</td><td>yes</td><td>7</td><td></td><td>finished</td><td>not started yet</td><td>▲ ▼</td></tr>
<tr><td>HTTP - Hypertext Transfer Protocol</td><td>yes</td><td>5</td><td></td><td>finished</td><td>not started yet</td><td>▲ ▼</td></tr>
<tr><td>URI - Uniform Resource Identifier</td><td>yes</td><td>4</td><td></td><td>finished</td><td>not started yet</td><td>▲</td></tr>
</tbody>
</table>

Add new Lecture     Add new Live Lecture

(a)                                        (b)

**Fig. 1.** (a) An example lecture video. Video 2 shows the speaker giving his lecture, whereas his presentation is played in video 1. (b) Management page of the lecture video portal for the video analysis

unlike most of the existing OCR-based lecture video indexing approaches [2,1] we utilize the geometrical information and the stroke width value of detected text bounding boxes for extracting lecture structure from the slide video frames. In this paper, we have integrated and adapted our visual analysis engines in an automated framework of the lecture video portal.

Speech is the most natural way of communication and also the main carrier of information in nearly all lectures. Therefore, it is of distinct advantage that the speech information can be used for automated indexing of lecture videos. However, most of existing lecture speech recognition systems have only low recognition accuracy, the WERs (*Word Error Rates*) having been reported from [6,5,3,4] are approximately 40%–85%. The poor recognition results limit the quality of the later indexing process. In this paper, we propose a solution that enables a continued improvement of recognition rate by creating and refining new speech training data. It is important that the involved tasks can be performed efficiently and even fully automated, if possible. For this reason, we have implemented an automated procedure for generating a phonetic dictionary and a method for splitting raw audio lecture data into small pieces.

In order to make the analysis engine applicable for our lecture video portal, we have designed and implemented an architecture so that the analysis process could be easily handled and the efficient indexing functionalities could be provided to the users.

The rest of the paper is organized as follows: section 2 describes our automated analysis architecture. Section 3 and section 4 details the proposed analysis methods. Section 5 concludes the paper with an outlook on future work.

## 2   An Automated Analysis Framework

The major components of the framework are the analysis management engine, video analysis engine and result storage/visualization engine. The analysis management and result storage/visualization engines are associated with the video

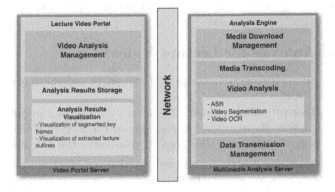

**Fig. 2.** Architecture of our multimedia analysis framework

portal server, while the video analysis engine is associated with the multimedia analysis server. Fig. 2 shows the framework architecture.

## 2.1   System Workflow

The analysis management engine handles the start of the analysis and reports the processing status. As shown in Fig. 1(b), we can start both, the OCR and ASR analysis for each video in the *staff* page of the lecture video portal. In order to manage each analysis request efficiently, we have defined a class "analysis job object" with the following properties: media id, date time, media URL, analysis type and language. Once the analysis for a lecture video is started, a job object will be created and encoded in the XML format. The XML request will then be sent to the analysis engine on the multimedia analysis server.

The analysis engine manages four major processes: media download, video transcoding, video analysis for each request, and analysis result transmission to the video portal server. Since the analysis engine is designed fully configurable, it is therefore suitable to be extended and work with a multi-process workflow or a distributed computing system. Once a video is downloaded, a transcoder will convert it to a predefined format with an uniform resolution which is most appropriate for the video segmentation and OCR analysis. For ASR, we extract the audio track with a format of 16KHz and 16 Bit which meets the requirements of the speech recognition software.

After the analysis, the results will be automatically sent to the destination place on the portal server. Subsequently, we send HTTP-POST requests for saving the corresponding results to the portal database. Thanks to the plugin architecture of our video portal, once the analysis result data is saved, the corresponding GUI elements will be created automatically by refreshing the web page.

For our purpose, we apply this framework to analyze the lecture videos from our institute. However, using it for the videos from other sources (as e.g., Youtube[1],

---

[1] http://www.youtube.com

Berkeley[2] etc.), we would only need to adapt the configuration file of the analysis engine.

## 3   Visual Analysis for Lecture Videos

Our video visual analysis system consists of two parts: unique slide shots detection and video OCR.

In [7], we have proposed a novel CC-based (*Connected Component*) video segmenter to capture the real slide transitions in the lecture video. The video OCR system is applied on each slide shot. It consists of the following steps:

- Text detection: this process determines whether a single frame of a video file contains text lines, for which a tight bounding box is returned (cf. Fig. 3(a)). We have developed a two-stages approach that consists of a fast edge based detector for coarse detection and a *Stroke Width Transform* (SWT) based verification procedure to remove the false alarms.
- Text segmentation: in this step, the text pixels are separated from their background. This work is normally done by using a binarization algorithm. Fig. 3(b) shows the text binarization results of our dynamic contrast and brightness adaption method. The adapted text line images are converted to an acceptable format for a standard OCR engine.
- Text recognition: we applied a multi-hypotheses framework to recognize texts from extracted text line images. The subsequent spell-checking process will further filter out incorrect words from the recognition results.

(a)                                    (b)

**Fig. 3.** (a) Text detection results. All detected text regions are identified by bounding boxes. (b) Text binarization results of our dynamic contrast-brightness adaption method.

After the text recognition process, the detected text line objects and their texts are further utilized in the lecture outline extraction method. Unlike other approaches, we observe the geometrical characteristics of detected text line objects, and apply size, position and average stroke width information of them to classify the recognized OCR text resources. In this way, the lecture outline can be extracted based on the classified OCR texts. Which can provide an overview about the lecture content, and help the user with a navigation within the lecture video as well (cf. Fig. 4).

More technical details as well as the evaluation results of proposed visual analysis methods can be found in [7].

---

[2] http://webcast.berkeley.edu

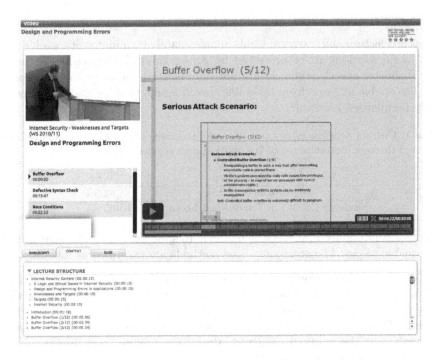

**Fig. 4.** Visualization of the segmenter slide shots and extracted outline (lecture structure) of the lecture video underneath the video player

## 4   Speech Recognition for Lecture Videos

In addition to OCR, ASR is an effective method for gathering semantic information about lecture videos. Combining both OCR and ASR offers the chance to improve the quality of automatically generated metadata dramatically. For that reason, we decided to build a speech model with the help of the CMU Sphinx Toolkit [3] and the German Speech Corpus by Voxforge[4] as a baseline. We collected hours of speech data from our lecturers and the corresponding transcripts in order to improve speech recognition rates for our special use case. Using a random assortment of speech segments from our lecturers as a test corpus, Table. 1 shows how the WER decreases when adding 7.2 hours of speech data from our lecturers to the training set.

However, manually collecting appropriate speech segments and transcripts is rather time consuming and costly. There is a number of steps to be performed to acquire high quality input data for *SphinxTrain*, as shown in Fig. 5(a). This entire process is described more detailed in the following subsections.

---

[3] http://cmusphinx.sourceforge.net/
[4] http://www.voxforge.org/

## 4.1    Creating the Speech Training Data

A recorded lecture audio stream yields approximately 90 minutes of speech data, which is far too long to be processed by *SphinxTrain* or the decoder at once. Several shorter speech segments are not only easier to manage by ASR tools, they also enable us to perform tasks like speech model training and decoding on highly parallelized hardware.

**Table 1.** Current progress of our speech model training. The WER results have been measured through a random set of 708 short speech segments from 7 lecturers.

| Training Corpus | WER |
|---|---|
| Voxforge (23.3h) | 82.5% |
| Voxforge (23.3h) + Transcribed Lectures (7.2h) | 62.6% |

Therefore, we looked for efficient methods to split the long audio stream into manageable pieces. The commonly used methods are described as follows:

- Combine segmentation and selection processes by using an audio file editor like Audacity[5]. Both steps are performed manually by selecting parts with a length of 2–5 seconds from the audio stream and save them as separate audio files. This approach results in high quality segments without any cropped words, but the required time and effort (50+ minutes real time/1 minute transcription) is not acceptable.
- Split the input audio stream uniformly every $n$ seconds, where $n$ is a constant between 5–30. This method is fast, but it yields a significant disadvantage: a regular subdivision of speech often results in spoken words being partly cropped, which makes a lot of segments useless in the ASR context. Selection of bad segments has to be performed manually in order to achieve adequate database quality. For 1 minute of transcribed speech data, we need approximately 35 minutes in real time.

Compared to these rather inefficient methods, our current approach is to fully automate segmentation and partly automate selection without suffering from quality drawbacks like dropped word endings. Fig. 5(b) describes the fundamental steps of the segmentation algorithm. The audio curve is first down-sampled, then blurred and split according to a loudness threshold. Too short or too long sentences are sorted out automatically. The effort to transcribe 1 minute of speech decreases to 15–20 minutes in real time.

In order to obtain the best recognition rates in the long run, we have to ensure that all speech segments used for speech model training meet certain quality requirements. Experience has shown that approximately 50% of the generated audio segments have to be sorted out due to one of the following reasons:

- The segment contains acoustical noise created by objects and humans in the environment around the speaker, as e.g., doors closing, chairs moving, students talking.

---

[5] http://audacity.sourceforge.net

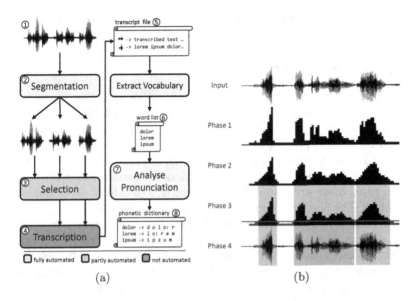

(a)    (b)

**Fig. 5.** (a) Workflow for extending our speech corpus. First, the recorded audio file (1) is segmented into smaller pieces (2) and improper segments are sorted out (3). For each remaining segment, the spoken text is transcribed manually (4), and in doing so, a line of text is added to the transcript file (5). As an intermediate step, a list of all used words in the transcript file is created (6). In order to obtain the phonetic dictionary (7), the pronunciation of each word has to be represented as phonetics (8).

(b) General idea of the algorithm used in our automatic audio stream segmenter. Phase 1: compute the absolute values of the input samples to get a loudness curve, which is then down-sampled (e.g. by factor 100). Phase 2: a blur filter (e.g. radius=3) is applied to eliminate outliers. Phase 3: a threshold (red horizontal line) determines which areas are considered *quiet*. Every connected area which is not quiet is a potential utterance (highlighted with green). Phase 4: all those green areas that are longer than a specified maximum length (e.g. 5 seconds) are dropped. Finally, the computed borders for each remaining block are remapped to the original WAVE samples and form a segment.

- The lecturer misspeaks some words, so that they are completely invalid from an objective point of view.
- The speaker's language is clear, but the segmentation algorithm cut off parts of a spoken word so that it turns invalid.

The classification of audio segments in good/bad quality is not yet solvable automatically, as the term 'good quality' is very subjective and strongly bound to the human perception.

Subsequently, the manual transcription process is performed. By definition, this step has to be done by a human, which is the reason why it is not perfectly optimizable. However, we speed up this process with the help of our transcription software. It provides a simple GUI where the user can play the audio segments and type the transcription with very few key presses and without doing anything unnecessary. File playing, naming, and saving is completely managed by the software. Furthermore, it provides a Sphinx compatible output format.

## 4.2   Creating the Phonetic Dictionary

The phonetic dictionary is an essential part of every ASR software. For every word occurring in the transcripts, it defines one or more phonetic representations. To build them, we use a customized phonetic alphabet which contains 45 phonemes used in German pronunciation.

As our speech corpus is still growing continuously, the extension and mainte-nance of the dictionary is a common task. Experience has shown that for each transcribed lecture, there are about 100 new words which have to be added to the vocabulary. The Voxforge community proposes to use eSpeak[6] to create the phonetic representation for each word. This method works fine, but yields some striking disadvantages: first, the output generated by eSpeak is only partly usable. For almost every word, corrections have to be made manually. eSpeak uses its own format for phonetic spelling. The conversion into a representation accepted by Sphinx is complex and error-prone. In addition, dictionary man-agement is inflexible. Discarding the dictionary and regenerating it with new parameters or changed transcripts is expensive, because all manual corrections will be discarded. For these reasons we have built an own phonetics generator. In order to maximize the output quality, our approach operates on three different layers of abstraction while successively generating the phonetic representation string $P$.

On *word level*, our so-called *exemption dictionary* is checked whether it con-tains the input word as a whole. If so, the phonetic representation $P$ is com-pletely read from this dictionary and no further steps have to be performed. Otherwise, we have to scale down to *syllable level* by applying an extern hy-phenation algorithm[7]. The exemption dictionary particularly contains foreign words or names whose pronunciation cannot be generalized by German rules, as e.g., byte, phänomen, and ipv6 etc.

On *syllable level*, we examine the result of the hyphenation algorithm, as e.g., com-pu-ter for the input word computer. For a lot of single syllables (and also pairs of syllables), the *syllable mapping* describes the corresponding phonetic representation, e.g. au f for the German prefix auf and n i: d er for the di-syllabic German prefix nieder. If there is such a representation for our input syllable, it is added to the phonetic result $P$ immediately and we succeed with the next part. Otherwise, we have to split the syllable even further into its char-acters and proceed on *character level*.

On *character level*, a lot of German pronunciation rules are utilized to deter-mine how the current single character is pronounced. Typical metrics are:

- Character type (consonant/vowel).
- Neighboring characters.

[6] An open source speech synthesizer (cf. http://espeak.sourceforge.net)
[7] http://swolter.sdf1.org/software/libhyphenate.html

- Relative position inside the containing syllable.
- Absolute position inside the whole word.

First and foremost, a heuristic checks if the current and the next 1–2 characters can be pronounced natively. If not, or the word is only one character long, the character(s) is/are pronounced as if they were spelled letter by letter such as, e.g., the abbreviations abc (for alphabet) and zdf (a German TV channel).

Next, we determine the character type (consonant/vowel) in order to apply the correct pronunciation rules. The conditions of each of these rules are checked, until one is *true* or all conditions are checked and turned out to be *false*. If the latter is the case, the standard pronunciation is applied, which assumes *closed* vowels. This is an example for the rules we use in our heuristic:

- A vowel is always *open* if followed by a double consonant, e.g. a̲ffe, we̲tter, bi̲tte.
- A vowel is always *closed* if followed by the German consonant ß, e.g. stra̲ße, grö̲ße, fu̲ßball.
- If the consonant b is the last character of a syllable and the next syllable does not begin with another b, then it is pronounced like the consonant p. Examples: hub̲schrauber, leb̲kuchen, grab̲.

An evaluation with 20000 words from transcripts shows that 98.1% of all input words where processed correctly, without the need of any manual amendments. The 1.9% of words where application of the pronunciation rules failed mostly have an English pronunciation. They are corrected manually and added to a special 'exemption dictionary'. Besides the striking advantage of saving a lot of time for dictionary maintenance, Table. 2 shows that our automatic dictionary generation algorithm does not result in worse WER. The recognized ASR texts are further used by search and key-word extraction functions.

**Table 2.** Comparison of the Voxforge dictionary and our automatically generated dictionary with an optimized phone-set for the German language. The used speech corpus is a smaller version of the German Voxforge Corpus which contains 4.5 hours of audio from 13 different speakers. It is directly available from the Voxforge website including a ready-to-use dictionary. Replacing this with our automatically generated dictionary results in a slightly better recognition rate.

| Phonetic Dictionary | WER |
| --- | --- |
| Voxforge German dictionary | 22.2% |
| Our dictionary with optimized phoneset | 21.4% |

## 5    Conclusion and Future Work

In this paper, we have presented an automated framework for the analysis and indexing of lecture videos. The proposed video analysis methods consist of video segmentation, video OCR, and automated speech recognition. In order to integrate the analysis engine into our lecture video portal, we have designed and implemented an architecture which enables an efficient processing of analysis management, multimedia analysis, data transmission, and result visualization.

As the upcoming improvement, we plan to implement an automated method for the extraction of indexable key words from ASR transcripts. In [4], the course-related text books have been used as the context reference for refining ASR results. In our case, the high accurate OCR texts from each video segment can be considered as a hint for the correct speech context. In this way, a more accurate refinement and key word extraction from ASR transcript could take place. It may solve the issue of building search indices for imperfect ASR transcripts. Furthermore, our research will also address the following issues: search-index ranking for hybrid information resources (as e.g., OCR, ASR, user-tagging etc.); usability and utility evaluation for our indexing and video navigation functionalities in the lecture video portal.

# References

1. Adcock, J., Cooper, M., Denoue, L., Pirsiavash, H.: Talkminer: A lecture webcast search engine. In: Proc. of the ACM International Conference on Multimedia, MM 2010, Firenze, Italy, pp. 241–250. ACM (2010)
2. Wang, T.-C.P.F., Ngo, C.-W.: Structuring low-quality videotaped lectures for cross-reference browsing by video text analysis. Journal of Pattern Recognition 41(10), 3257–3269 (2008)
3. Glass, J., Hazen, T.J., Hetherington, L., Wang, C.: Analysis and processing of lecture audio data: Preliminary investigations. In: Proc. of the HLT-NAACL Workshop on Interdisciplinary Approaches to Speech Indexing and Retrieval (2004)
4. Haubold, A., Kender, J.R.: Augmented segmentation and visualization for presentation videos. In: Proc. of the 13th Annual ACM International Conference on Multimedia, pp. 51–60. ACM (2005)
5. Lee, D., Lee, G.G.: A korean spoken document retrieval system for lecture search. In: Proc. of the SSCS Speech Search Workshop at SIGIR (2008)
6. Leeuwis, E., Federico, M., Cettolo, M.: Language modeling and transcription of the ted corpus lectures. In: Proc. of the IEEE ICASSP, pp. 232–235. IEEE (2003)
7. Yang, H., Siebert, M., Lühne, P., Sack, H., Meinel, C.: Lecture video indexing and analysis using video ocr technology. In: Proc. of 7th International Conference on Signal Image Technology and Internet Based Systems (SITIS 2011), Dijon, France (2011)

# Towards a Design Theory for Educational On-line Information Security Laboratories

Sarfraz Iqbal and Tero Päivärinta

Department of Computer Science, Electrical and Space Engineering,
Luleå Tekniska Universitet, Luleå, Sweden.
{sarfraz.iqbal,tero.päivärinta}@ltu.se

**Abstract.** Online learning for educating information security professionals has increased in popularity. The security curriculum and technology, as well as hands-on laboratory experiences implemented in information security labs, are important elements in an online education system for information security. We drew our motivation from an on-going information security lab development initiative in our own institution, and this paper aims to provide an integrated overview on reported instances of online hands-on education in information security. Our review contributes to the existing knowledge by using the anatomy of design theory framework as a basis for literature analysis, as this provides a common basis to examine theories about human-created information technology artifacts such as information security labs and how such knowledge has been communicated to academia. Our results show that none of the articles studied here puts forward a well-grounded and tested design theory for on-line information security laboratories. This hinders accumulation of knowledge in this area and makes it difficult for others to observe, test and adapt clear design principles for security laboratories and exercises.

**Keywords:** Information security, Information security education, online information security laboratory.

## 1    Introduction

Education of information security professionals is not a trivial issue [1]. An educational curriculum must prepare security professionals for mastering and develop ever-changing security solutions [2]. Hence, the information security curriculum needs dynamic and timely pedagogical tools that support an interdisciplinary and holistic approach to learning [1, 2, 3]. Graduates also need to master the 'hands-on' approach in addition to straightforward theoretical education [1, 2]. However, curricula development for information security education is a relatively recent phenomenon [4]. For example, less than a decade ago, the ACM (Association for Computing Machinery) guidelines for computer science –related educations specified no topics, courses, or course sequence for information security topics [8].

Since the mid-1990s, hands-on education in information security has been largely conducted through isolated laboratories, where the students have been able to practice

E. Popescu et al. (Eds.): ICWL 2012, LNCS 7558, pp. 295–306, 2012.
© Springer-Verlag Berlin Heidelberg 2012

attacks and defenses in well-secured server environments on campus [e.g., 1, 2]. Beyond campus-located education, however, blended or e-learning approaches have been regarded as even more effective e.g. for end-user security education [5]. Web-based instruction allows students and instructors to communicate on-line with providers of resources from all over the world [6]. Students find it more convenient to take classes online without the expense and time constraints involved in commuting to a campus facility and university administrators are seeing the online trend as a major revenue and recruitment tool involving the use of less staff and more students [7]. As our literature review below will show, the on-line learning approach targeted at educating information security professionals (in addition to end-users) has also been regarded as being desirable in a number of educational institutions.

Several key elements need to be considered with regard to an online education system for information security, including the security curriculum and technology needed to deliver the education. Distance learning classes have unique requirements if compared to campus-focused education, and accordingly, the information security curriculum needs to keep up with new teaching methods [8]. Hands-on laboratory experiences, implemented in information security labs, thus form a core feature of many information security curricula. An internet-based information security lab is an artifact which involves a collection of systems and software used for teaching information security, and which is accessible through the Internet. A lab is used for exercises, which provide the students with practical experience with security vulnerabilities, security testing, and defenses. For example, students studying topics in cyber security benefit from working with realistic training labs that test their knowledge of network security [10]. An educational lab for information security comprises at least four kinds of entities: servers, sources and targets of attacks, and exercises [9].

As we are motivated by the existence of an on-going security lab development initiative in our own institution, the aim of this paper is to provide an overview on reported instances of online hands-on education in information security. We aim to integrate the existing knowledge by using the "anatomy of design theory" framework [11] as a basis for our literature analysis. The framework provides a common basis for looking at what has been "theorized" with regard to human-created information technology artifacts such as security labs. The rest of the paper is organized as follows. The next section summarizes the design theory framework used as the analysis framework for our literature review. Section 3 summarizes the review results, Section 4 presents the analysis in light of the design theory framework while we discuss about the contribution of our review in section 5. The last section concludes with suggestions for future research.

## 2    Anatomy of Design Theory

In the discipline of information systems (IS), a research stream implies the establishment and evaluation of design theories with regard to promoting systematic research that involves development of information technology artifacts [26, 27] (such as information security laboratories). By articulating and developing design theories, research can guide design, development, maintenance, and improvement of IT artifacts and help individuals accumulate knowledge, as well as learn about the effectiveness and feasibility of IT artifacts in general, in a disciplined way. In connection to a design theory, one or more "kernel" theories (i.e. theories from the reference disciplines through which knowledge of IT utilization and benefits can be justified and evaluated) may help to provide a further foundation for the design theory [26]. Our focus here will be on design knowledge with regard to the development of online information security laboratories, and on how related knowledge is transcribed and communicated to the community researchers and educators of information security. We will assume that it is beneficial to examine the existing knowledge of on-line information security labs in light of the "anatomy of design theory" [11], in order to summarize what we currently know about design(s) and experiences from previous on-line labs. This may potentially reveal gaps in the existing knowledge in terms of a common framework. In general, we share Hrastinski's justification for such research in the field of e-learning, according to which "the rationale of developing design theory for e-learning is that such theory can support practitioners to understand which mechanisms that may lead to desired outcomes" [12]. Design Exemplars are developed through an iterative process (comprising theory and empirical grounding) which involves testing in contextual settings, by which outcomes can be used as an input for further development and knowledge sharing. Design exemplars provide contextual information to practitioners about when and how to manage and use a specific design. Ideally, in our case, design exemplars thus should guide information security educators to choose well-functioning laboratory exercises to be conducted through on-line laboratories, in order to serve the students better. Table 1 summarizes the design-theory-based framework which we used to define the questions that which guided our literature analysis.

**Table 1.** A design theory analysis framework for literature review

| Design theory issues [11] | Issues to analyze from the literature concerning on-line information security labs. |
|---|---|
| Purpose and scope of interesting designs | Any academic article, which discusses about the implementation of an on-line information security lab was considered relevant for our review. |
| Constructs | - Technological challenges to implement the laboratory (servers, sources, targets [9])?<br>- Designs of exercises [9]? |
| Principles of Form and Function | - Technological requirements and solutions available for labs?<br>- Elements of curriculum and their rationale?<br>- "Best practices" suggested for collaboration through the lab and on-line communication tools?<br>- How do all these relate together, if that has been studied at all? |
| Artifact mutability | - Description and suggestions for improving the current methods of utilizing lab facilities for distance education?<br>- Lab utility claims? |
| Testable propositions | - Measures for improvements and utility used for evaluating the existing labs in the literature, if any?<br>- Claims for lab design adaptability for other organizations?<br>- Are any design exemplars [12] proposed? |

**Table 1.** (*Continued*)

| Justificatory knowledge | - Do the improvement statements relate to any given theory / theories? (Kernel theories from social sciences governing the design process to provide the foundation knowledge on which other aspects of the ISDT are built [26-27]) (Or is knowledge still in the form of technical/practical "lessons learned", or even in the form of contextual suggestions only) |
| --- | --- |
| Principles of implementation | - Implementation guidelines observed for the servers, sources and targets, exercises? |
| Expository instantiation | - Where and how has the lab in question been implemented? (Conceptual idea, prototype, system in production – how long it has been in use?) |

We used Google Scholar for our literature search by using key words such as "information security laboratory", "information security lab", "virtual information security lab", "information security curriculum", "information security education", "information security course" and "information security pedagogy" in the article title. This provided us with 181 articles. We went through all the articles one by one and found 13 relevant articles which specifically discuss information about the security lab concept in an on-line context. We omitted articles discussing the campus-located, isolated laboratory concepts, as well as purely curriculum-related discussions.

## 3    Results

In the review process we have analyzed the articles against four important entities of an information security lab: Servers, Sources, Targets and Exercises [9]. The chosen articles discuss at least one of the entities of an information security lab.

**Servers:** Security equipment (hardware, software etc.) is costly, which makes it challenging for universities to build and maintain an information security laboratory. This increases the value of server virtualization platforms which provide the opportunity to implement cost effective solutions in order to provide students hands-on experimentation. Virtualization plays an important role in reducing cost providing the opportunity of utilizing same computer resources by many operating systems. A wide variety of servers, operating systems, and virtualization techniques have been demonstrated in the literature [14, 15, 17, 18, 19, 20, 21, 22, 24, 25] (table 2).

**Virtualization Benefits for Distance Education:** Our review reveals that most of the labs make use of virtualization technologies in one way or another. Virtualization Technologies are an important element of Information Security labs, and provide such benefits as lower hardware cost, increased deployment flexibility, simplified configuration management, customization of software & hardware resources, increased accessibility of computing resources, remote access to multiple single-user & multi-user computer systems and multiple virtual machines, classrooms system administration and ease of isolating the virtual networks [17,19,20-22]. Virtual computing labs are especially helpful for distance students as they can access the software packages hosted on virtual machines remotely instead of going to the university lab physically [15,16]. Virtual and physical labs configuration and cost has been compared [19] which reveals that virtual labs are far less expensive than physical labs which makes it an ideal tool for experimentation. Several virtual technologies have been discussed which have their own pros and cons, depending on how you intend to use them. Some of the popular products that received attention from authors include VNC Server, VNC client, VMware workstation, VMware server, Vlab Manager, VPN Concentrator, Virtual center, Apache Virtual Computing lab, Microsoft HyperV, Xen, and VMLogix Lab Manager [15, 17, 18, 24].

**Sources & Targets:** Sources and targets are two important entities of an information security lab for experimentation which has been discussed briefly in e.g. [13, 14, 15, 22, 23, 25] (table 2). The sources and/or targets need to be implemented to provide a basis for any information security exercise. For example, one team or individual will use a virtual machine to run some services and use the host operating system to attack. Once the user enters the lab through the server then the sources and targets are put into action to do further activities including attack / defend etc. options.

**Exercises:** Exercises for the information security lab have also been discussed briefly [13, 14, 15, 16, 18, 22, 23, 25] (table 2). The exercises include usage of tools such as SNORT (traffic monitoring tool), Vulnerability analysis, Firewall configuration, modification & testing, Passwords policies, traffic analysis, security auditing [14, 15, 18], ceaser cipher, Symmetric key encryption/decryption, public and private keys, Ethereal [16], Network Discovery and surveillance, Network Intrusion Detection [22], Attack – Defense exercises[1], SQL and Php injections, host discovery and port scanning, traffic filtering, web security, and intrusion detection [13, 25].

**Table 2.** Entities of InfoSec Lab

| Ref No | 13 | 14 | 15 | 16 | 17 | 18 | 19 | 20 | 21 | 22 | 23 | 24 | 25 |
|---|---|---|---|---|---|---|---|---|---|---|---|---|---|
| **Servers** |  | X | X |  | X | X | X | X | X | X |  | X | X |
| **Sources** | X | X | X |  |  |  |  |  |  | X | X |  | X |
| **Targets** | X | X | X |  |  |  |  |  |  | X | X |  | X |
| **Exercise** | X | X | X | X |  | X |  |  |  | X | X |  | X |

Only four articles include discussions about all the four information security lab entities (table 2). However, even these have mainly general-level discussions, involving scarce descriptions of the actual design and implementation. The next section will analyse the reported on-line security laboratories further in light of the design theory framework.

---

[1] Attack-defense exercises are usually performed by teams to test the skills and develop knowledge about how to detect vulnerabilities in a system and strengthening its security against any intended attack and from learning to counter-attack as in a real-world scenario.

# 4    Analysis in Light of the Design Theory Framework

The analysis below is based on the anatomy of design theory including purpose and scope of laboratory designs, key constructs used for conceptualizing the laboratory implementations, principles of form and construction, artifact mutability claims, testable design propositions, justificatory knowledge, principles of implementation, and examples of laboratory instantiations [26].

**Table 3.** Purpose and Scope of Design

| Component examples |
| --- |
| An application for "educational hacking" [13]. |
| Evaluating IDS/IPS technology and deriving outlines for remote lab [14]. |
| Aim to describe matters of practical importance to instructors, etc to implement Vlab [17]. |
| To improve students access to university resources [16, 19]. |
| To develop a platform to set up logically isolated virtual networks easily [22]. |
| Providing hands on practice to students for defensive/offensive mechanisms [23, 25]. |

The analysis shows that some articles present aims and goals very clearly e.g. the aim of most of the labs has been to provide hands on practice to network security class students [23, 25] by improving students access to university resources [16, 19] whereas laboratories have also been purposely designed to allow for exploitation that yields desirable results for hackers [13]. Some labs aim at describing matters of practical importance to instructors, administrators etc. [17], while others focus at particular technological exercises (IDS/IPS) [14]. The purpose and scope of design remained slightly unclear in five articles [15, 18, 20, 21, 22] while they discuss more generally about teaching information security classes to distance students and about how to improve their access to university resources for online education.

**Table 4.** Constructs

| Design of Exercises | Technological challenges |
| --- | --- |
| Design of exercise [13], sample assignments [22] and lab module assignments [25] discussed briefly. Inner team and inter-team tasks described shortly [23]. | Technical issues of online lab [14], differences of Plab vs Vlab [19] and challenges regarding configuration, administration etc., discussed briefly [22]. Vlab challenges discussed [17, 24]. |

The analysis shows that the two major categories have been investigated under the subject of Constructs i.e. technological challenges and design of exercises. Challenges include technical issues like low internet bandwidth for accessing the online lab resources, monitoring network traffic, host communication, durable network configuration [14], browser support for virtual labs (limited active-x browser plug-ins), browser security settings, storage management tasks, practical concerns of accessibility, training, security, configuration flexibility, reliability, resource management, lab network access, sufficient CPU capacity & memory [17, 19], configuration errors and misuse of administrative privilege [22]. Furthermore, management of virtual machines (including software applications and virtualized hardware components), users, isolating the lab network & virtual machines on the operational network [24] to eliminate the danger of contaminating other university resources and also provide the remote access to the students is a challenging issue as are student background and technical skills in using and operating a virtual computing lab. Cost is an economic challenge in terms of buying the necessary equipment and implementing the lab solution [19]. With regard to the design of exercises, some articles discussed design of assignments only briefly [13,22,23,25]. Nine articles provided no clear designs for assignments [14,15,16,17,18,19,20,21, 24].

Table 5. Principles of Form and Function

| Technological requirements & solutions for labs | Elements of Curriculum & rationale |
|---|---|
| Brief technological requirements and solution discussed[14,15,22] | Three courses as elements of curriculum discussed with some explanations [15]. |
| VLab technological challenges and solutions described [17, 21, 19, 24]. | Exercise modules discussed as elements of curriculum with brief supported reasoning [25]. |

The analysis revealed that Technological requirements & solutions for labs have been discussed in general level [14, 15, 22] including discussions about virtual technologies [17, 19, 21, 24]. The best practices for collaboration through lab and online communication tools have been largely ignored. Only two articles discussed the courses as elements of a curriculum designed to provide some support for reasoning in favor of a selected approach [15, 25]. Six articles describe no such characteristics or remained relatively unclear about the matter [13, 16, 18, 20, 21, 23].

Table 6. Artifact mutability

| Description and suggestions for improvement | Lab utility |
|---|---|
| Remote lab solutions for IDS/IPS technology for distance education [14]. Virtual lab with remote access eases software availability [15]. Virtual computing environment components suggested for improvement [17]. | 24/7 remote access for operating systems and applications [15, 24]. Lab utility in terms of saving cost & student access [19, 21]. |

With regard to artifact mutability, two categories were investigated in the articles; Descriptions and suggestions for improvement and Lab utility. Descriptions and suggestions for improvement has been discussed in terms of lab solutions for a particular technology (IDS/IPS) [14] as well as providing remote software access for distance education [15] and highlighting the virtual computing environment components role for improving the situation [17]. The issue of Lab utility claims shows that some authors claim that their labs provide 24/7 remote access for distance education [15, 24] whereas others consider lab utility in terms of providing students easy access to lab resources with cost saving solutions [19, 21]. Seven articles remained unclear on these issues [13, 18, 20, 22, 23, 24, 25].

**Table 7.** Testable Propositions

| Improvement & utility measures for existing Labs | Lab design adaptability | Design exemplars |
|---|---|---|
| Discussion drawbacks of HackQuest, WebGoat etc., [13]. Shift from Physical labs to Virtual labs discussed [19]. | None | None |

In the testable propositions category [13] has discussed and compared existing applications such as HackQuest and WebGoat, pointing out their drawbacks. Another paper provided measures for a shift from physical lab towards virtual lab infrastructure including cost and configuration [19]. The issues of lab design adaptability for other organizations and concrete design exemplars have been completely ignored.

**Table 8.** Justificatory Knowledge, Principles of implementation & Expository instantiation

| Relevant Theory |
|---|
| Cooperative learning strategy has been discussed [23]. |
| **Implementation guidelines** |
| Guidelines discussed briefly regarding exercises [13]. VLab implementation discussed [17, 18, 19, and 24]. Physical +remote networking lab topology implementation discussed [21]. Isolated virtual network lab software implementation with brief discussion about exercises [22]. |
| **Place of implementation** |
| Northern Kentucky University [13], North Carolina State University [15], University of New Mexico [17], Columbus State University [18], Anderson School of Management, University of Mexico [19], East Carolina University [21], Michigan Technological University [24], James Madison University USA [25]. |

In the category of justificatory knowledge, we tried to explore whether any relevant kernel theories had been used, in the light of which the designs could have been assessed in a larger context of knowledge claims. However, only one article referred to cooperative learning strategy [23] whereas the rest of the articles failed to provide any such kernel theory or related concepts, in light of which one could hold further discussions about the designed labs [13, 14, 15, 16, 17, 18, 19, 20, 21, 22, 23, 24, 25].

We could identify that the implementation guidelines for exercises were, at best, rather briefly discussed by [13, 22]. Virtual lab implementations have been discussed [17, 18, 19, 24] whereas network lab topology [21] and isolated virtual network lab software implementation [22] were mentioned as the technological bases for implementation. Seven articles communicated no such information [14, 15, 16, 20, 23, 25]. Eight articles specifically defined the university context, in which the reported security laboratory is located (table 8).

## 5    Discussion

All in all, our review shows that disciplinary literature on on-line education of information security is in its infancy. The reviewed academic reports seldomly referred to each other. Rather, the articles mostly simply presented each laboratory idea as such. Such an approach to reporting IT artifacts is in contrast to the design theory approach of research. In order to make knowledge of online security labs more cumulative and comparable, the literature should focus more systematically on the design theory viewpoint, with regard to which the framework we used for the literature review may give a disciplinary basis.

Our review reveals that several articles lacked a clear design purpose and scope. They simply aimed to improve students' access to University resources and to provide them hands on practice for information security classes. Technological challenges pertaining to physical and virtual online labs were discussed briefly [14,17,19,22,24]. However, our analysis revealed that no article discussed a full-fledged design theory [26], and that technological and pedagogical challenges for online information security labs still need to be discussed in a more precise and detailed manner in order to facilitate real sharing and accumulation of such knowledge. Another knowledge gap yet to be filled is the design of actual on-line assignments, which has not been discussed in detail. Elements of the Curriculum and the rationale behind them are fundamental for any information security laboratory. This element was discussed briefly in only two articles [15, 25], revealing a clear knowledge gap that needs to be filled by providing/suggesting suitable elements of the curriculum for on-line lab usage. Any "best practices" of collaboration through the lab and on-line communication tools was largely ignored. Thus, the literature focuses mainly on the technological implementations of the labs, instead of discussing about how the stakeholders could make use of them. None of the articles discussed the relationship between technological requirements and actual solutions for particular exercises, elements of curriculum and their rationale and best practices for collaboration through lab and online communication tools. Artifact mutability is a very important issue for establishing the criteria for the progress of any IT artifact. The utility of a laboratory and its ability to respond to the requirements better than the competing approaches should be measured and reported in order to bring positive changes and to improve the efficiency and effectiveness accordingly. Among the reviewed papers, only two [15, 24] made utility claims about providing 24/7 remote access. However, the articles provided few, if any, specific measurement criteria for validating such mutability claims.

Also, an absence of testable design exemplars for online information security labs was evident. Hence, it remains unclear which approaches would really be superior for which particular purposes, and whether knowledge and any guidelines for implementing the on-line laboratories yet would involve any verifiable components, let alone "best practice" solutions. Only one article [23] referred to kernel theory (i.e., "cooperative learning strategy"), in the light of which any deeper theoretical approach to discuss the usefulness or theoretical implications of the selected lab design could have been used. However, diverging theoretical assumptions, such as varying pedagogical approaches, would surely have had a profound impact on the actual design and evaluation parameters of any exercises and perhaps even the technological laboratory implementations. For example, if we contrast the above-mentioned cooperative learning strategy [in 23] to the pedagogical approach of "mass-customization" [cf. 28], the latter approach might highlight individually flexible interactions with the lab equipment instead of co-operative group efforts. This would, furthermore, have implications on the lab design as well as selection of evaluation criteria of the whole artifact in the first place. The introduction of pedagogical kernel theories would help the researchers and developers of this domain to crystallize the actual contributions of their laboratory concepts and to position them in relation to each other to form a more coherent body of knowledge. The current knowledge exists, at best, on the level of vaguely evaluated, even anecdotal, lessons learned from contextual suggestions.

In its current form, our review makes a contribution to the literature in that it represents the first attempt to locate the hitherto scattered reports of educational on-line information security laboratories in a common frame of reference. The review is thus a useful overview for other developers and researchers of information security pedagogy, providing an index for the previous literature. Our work primarily addresses the general-level absence of design theories for on-line laboratories and, in particular, research opportunities for pursuing such theories about particular on-line laboratory artifacts.

# 6    Conclusion

This paper provides an overview of reported instances of online educational information security laboratories by providing a literature review of the topic and analyzing 13 relevant articles. Our analysis was based on a framework for defining elements of design theory related to IT artifacts, such as on-line information security laboratories. The analysis showed that the contemporary literature on the topic is relatively scattered and that there is a need for more systematically formed design theories through which the academia and developers of security laboratories could enhance knowledge sharing and accumulation. In the future, our aim is to develop an online information security laboratory for our own educational institution, with a clear purpose and scope to provide on-line information security exercises for the master's students of our dinstance education program in information security. We will focus on systematic development of a design theory of on-line educational information security laboratories. A solid design theory is expected to form a further basis to introduce methods and techniques of conducting hands-on training based on  selected pedagogical approaches, and, furthermore, to develop systematic evaluations for enhancing continuous improvement of our educational products in this field.

# References

1. Yurcik, W., Doss, D.: Different Approaches in the Teaching of Information Systems Security. In: Information Systems Education Conference, Cincinnati OH, USA, ISECON (2001)

2. Woodward, B.S., Young, T.: Redesigning an Information System Security Curriculum through Application of Traditional Pedagogy and Modern Business Trends. Information Systems Education Journal 5, 1–11 (2007)
3. Yngstrom, L., Bjorck, F.: The Value and Assessment of Information Security Education and Training. In: Proceedings of the IFIP TC11 WG 11.8 First World Conference on Information Security Education, Stockholm, Sweden, pp. 271–292 (1998)
4. Crowley, E.: Information System Security Curricula Development. In: Proceeding of the 4th Conference on Information Technology Curriculum on Information Technology Education, pp. 249–255 (2003)
5. van Niekerk, J.F., Thomson, K.-L.: Evaluating the Cisco Networking Academy Program's Instructional Model against Bloom's Taxonomy for the Purpose of Information Security Education for Organizational End-Users. In: Reynolds, N., Turcsányi-Szabó, M. (eds.) KCKS 2010. IFIP AICT, vol. 324, pp. 412–423. Springer, Heidelberg (2010)
6. Khan, B.H.: Web‐Based Instruction (WBI): An Introduction. Educational Media International 35, 63–71 (1998)
7. Kosak, L., Manning, D., Dobson, E., et al.: Prepared to Teach Online? Perspectives of Faculty in the University of North Carolina System. Online Journal of Distance Learning Administration 7, 1–13 (2004)
8. Hentea, M., Dhillon, H.S., Dhillon, M.: Towards Changes in Information Security Education. Journal of Information Technology Education 5, 221–233 (2006)
9. McDermott, J., Fox, C.: Using Abuse Case Models for Security Requirements Analysis. In: Proceedings of the 15th Annual Computer Security Applications Conference (ACSAC 1999), Phoenix, Arizona, pp. 55–64 (1999)
10. Stewart, K.E., Humphries, J.W., Andel, T.R.: Developing a Virtualization Platform for Courses in Networking, Systems Administration and Cyber Security Education. In: Proceedings of the Spring Simulation Multi-Conference. Society for Computer Simulation International, San Diego (2009)
11. Gregor, S., Jones, D.: The Anatomy of a Design Theory. Journal of the Association for Information Systems 8, 312–335 (2007)
12. Hrastinski, S., Keller, C., Carlsson, S.A.: Design Exemplars for Synchronous e-Learning: A Design Theory Approach. Comput. Educ. 55, 652–662 (2010)
13. Crawford, E., Hu, Y.: A Multi-User Adaptive Security Application for Educational Hacking. In: Proceedings of the World Congress on Engineering and Computer Science, WCECS 2011, vol. I, San Francisco, USA, October 19-21 (2011)
14. Lahoud, H.A., Tang, X.: Information Security Labs in IDS/IPS for Distance Education. In: SIGITE 2006, Minneapolis, Minnesota, USA, October 19–21, pp. 47–52. ACM (2006)
15. Li, P., Toderick, L.W., Lunsford, P.J.: Experiencing Virtual Computing Lab in Information Technology Education. In: Proceedings of the 10th ACM Conference on SIG-Information Technology Education, SIGITE 2009, Fairfax, Virginia, USA, October 22–24, pp. 55–59. ACM (2009)
16. Choi, Y.B., Lim, S., Oh, T.H.: Feasibility of Virtual Security Laboratory for Three-Tiered Distance Education. In: Proceedings of the ACM Conference on Information Technology Education, pp. 53–58 (2010)
17. Burd, S.D., Gaillard, G., Rooney, E., et al.: Virtual Computing Laboratories using VMware Lab Manager. In: Proceedings of the 44th Hawaii International Conference on System Sciences, pp. 1–9. IEEE (2011)
18. Summers, W.C., Martin, C.: Using a Virtual Lab to Teach an Online Information Assurance Program. In: Proceedings of the 2nd Annual Conference on Information Security Curriculum Development, pp. 84–87. ACM, New York (2005)

19. Burd, S.D., Seazzu, A.F., Conway, C., et al.: Virtual Computing Laboratories: A Case Study with Comparisons to Physical Computing Laboratories. Journal of Information Technology Education 8, 24 (2009)
20. Gaspar, A., Langevin, S., Armitage, W., et al.: The Role of Virtualization in Computing Education. In: Proceedings of the 39th SIGCSE Technical Symposium on Computer Science Education, pp. 131–132. ACM, New York (2008)
21. Li, C.: Blur the Boundary between the Virtual and the Real. Journal of Computing Sciences in Colleges 24, 39–45 (2009)
22. Krishna, K., Sun, W., Rana, P., et al.: V-NetLab: A Cost-Effective Platform to Support Course Projects in Computer Security. In: Proceedings of the 9th Annual Colloquium for Information Systems Security Education (CISSE 2005), Atlanta, GA, June 6-9 (2005)
23. Chen, F.-G., Chen, R.-M., Chen, J. -S.: A Portable Virtual Laboratory for Information Security Courses. In: Lin, S., Huang, X. (eds.) CSEE 2011, Part V. CCIS, vol. 218, pp. 245–250. Springer, Heidelberg (2011)
24. Wang, X., Hembroff, G.C., Yedica, R.: Using VMware VCenter Lab Manager in Undergraduate Education for System Administration and Network Security. In: Proceedings of the 2010 ACM Conference on Information Technology Education, pp. 43–52 (2010)
25. Aboutabl, M.S.: The Cyberdefense Laboratory: A Framework for Information Security Education. In: Proceedings of the 2006 IEEE Workshop on Information Assurance United States Military Academy, West Point, NY, pp. 55–60 (2006)
26. Jones, D., Gregor, S.: An Information Systems Design Theory for e-Learning. In: Proceedings, Australasian Conference on Information Systems: 15th Annual ACIS Conference, pp. 51–61. University of Tasmania, Hobart, Tasmania (2004)
27. Walls, J.G., Widmeyer, G.R., El Sawy, O.A.: Building an Information System Design Theory for Vigilant EIS. Information Systems Research 3, 36–59 (1992)
28. Friedman, R.S., Deek, F.P.: Innovation and Education in the Digital Age: Reconciling the Roles of Pedagogy, Technology, and the Business of Learning. IEEE Transactions on Engineering Management 50(4), 403–412 (2003)

# Pedagogy-Driven Design of Digital Learning Ecosystems: The Case Study of Dippler

Mart Laanpere, Kai Pata, Peeter Normak, and Hans Põldoja

Tallinn University, Institute of Informatics, Narva mnt 25, 10120 Tallinn, Estonia
{Mart.Laanpere,Kai.Pata,Peeter.Normak,Hans.Poldoja}@tlu.ee

**Abstract.** In most cases, the traditional Web-based learning management systems (e.g. Moodle, Blackboard) have been designed without any built-in support for a preferred pedagogical model or approach. The authors and proponents of such systems have claimed that this kind of inherent "pedagogical neutrality" is a desirable characteristic for a LMS, as it allows teachers to implement various pedagogical approaches. This study is based on an opposite approach, arguing for designing next-generation online learning platforms – so called digital learning ecosystems – with built-in affordances, which promote and enforce desirable pedagogical beliefs, strategies and learning activity patterns while suppressing others. We describe the pedagogy-driven design, development and implementation process of a digital learning ecosystem based on Dippler platform, which was guided by a combination of four contemporary pedagogical approaches: self-directed learning, competence-based learning, collaborative knowledge building and task-centered instructional design models.

**Keywords:** digital learning ecosystems, pedagogy-driven design.

## 1    Introduction

This study was initially motivated by emerging opposition to the imperative of pedagogical neutrality of tools and platforms built for Technology-Enhanced Learning [1]. Among others, Koper [2] has argued that e-learning systems should not be biased towards any specific pedagogical approach, in order to allow every teacher to implement the teaching methods of his/her own choice. Some authors have argued that it is almost impossible to build technological tools that are completely pedagogically neutral or theory-agnostic. This is why we follow alternative path, proposed by Norm Friesen [3] who advocated the development of *'pedagogically "engaged" or "committed" conceptions of content and systems that serve specifiable educational purposes, situations and methods'*.

The main research problem for our study is: how to design next-generation Technology-Enhanced Learning (TEL) systems with built-in pedagogical affordances, which enhance innovative teaching and learning practices and reflect modern learning theories?

This paper is seeking the answers to the following research questions:

- What constitutes the model for pedagogy-driven design?
- Which pedagogical approaches could/should be promoted by the pedagogy-driven design of the next-generation online learning platforms?

E. Popescu et al. (Eds.): ICWL 2012, LNCS 7558, pp. 307–317, 2012.
© Springer-Verlag Berlin Heidelberg 2012

- How to implement the pedagogy-driven model in the process of developing a new type of online learning platform: a digital learning ecosystem?

Methodologically, the study follows the tradition of design-based research, where theorizing is combined with participatory design sessions involving potential users and followed by design experiments where prototypes are validated in real-life situations.

## 2     Digital Learning Ecosystems

Laanpere, Põldoja & Normak [4] have described undergoing generation shift in Technology-Enhanced Learning (TEL) systems, arguing that closed and static Learning Management Systems belonging to the second-generation are going to be replaced by third generation, open and evolving Digital Learning Ecosystems.

**Table 1.** Generations of TEL systems

| Dimension | 1st generation | 2nd generation | 3rd generation |
|---|---|---|---|
| *Software architecture* | Desktop software | Single-server monolithic system | Cloud architecture, mobile clients |
| *Pedagogical foundation* | Stimulus-response-reinforcement | Pedagogical neutrality | Social constructivism, connectivism |
| *Content management* | Content was integrated | Separated from software, re-usable | Open, web-based, embeddable, placed outside, rich metadata |
| *Dominant affordances* | Presentation, drill, test | Presentation, assignments | Reflection, sharing, remixing, tagging, mashups, recommenders |

Several proposals considering ecological principles in e-learning have appeared in last decade [5][6], but their uptake into the system design has been quite passive until the recent massive usage of social software for e-learning. Adopting ecology in digital e-learning systems suggests using the "digital learning ecosystem" concept that has been proposed by several researchers [7][8][9], but this concept has various modifications, particularly in how the biotic/abiotic component is modeled in ecosystem.

Biological ecosystems are usually divided in two parts: biotic component contains living organisms (species) and abiotic part is environment (air, temperature, humidity, soil, lighting). We define DLE as an adaptive socio-technical system consisting of mutually interacting digital species (tools, services, content used in learning process) and communities of users (learners, facilitators, experts) together with their social, economical and cultural environment. While the second generation of TEL systems presented software systems as an environment where learners and teachers interacted with each other as well as with learning resources, we propose to turn the roles upside down for DLE. In DLE, the "species" or "organisms" are various interacting software tools and services together with their users, while larger technological landscape, social and cultural contexts play the role of the "environment". This is a change of paradigm, which will help us better understand, analyse and design the future tools and services to enhance learning. We are not using ecological concepts as metaphors, we propose to extent the ecosystems theory towards the digital world. Let us examine, how the three main principles of ecology translate into digital ecosystems.

The first principle in ecology is that the flow of energy and the exchange of matter through open ecosystem is regulated by the interactions of species and the abiotic component (by the web of energy and matter). Reyna [9] conceptualized "teaching and learning" as this energy that empowers digital learning ecosystems to changing "information to knowledge". The permeability of a digital learning ecosystem to the export and/or import of information and knowledge depend on the nature of the 'architecture' of the components of the system (e. g. connectivity, clustering), the characteristics of species, and their diversity and distribution, and interactions between them (such as commensalism).

The second important ecological principle is existence of the feedback loop to and from the environment that enables species to be adaptive to the environment and the environment to change as a result of species. A recent literature in evolutionary theory elaborates the notion of niche construction [10] as an ecological factor that enables organisms to contribute for and benefit from environmental information. If organisms evolve in response to selection pressures modified by themselves and their ancestors, there is feedback in the system. In our approach to digital learning ecosystems, the "service-species" are activated by users with different roles (learner, facilitator) and their learning intentions. Ecological psychology [11] suggests that learner's/teachers' direct perception of the learning environment's action potentialities (or so-called affordances) varies and this would give the variability to the actual use of services in the e-learning system. The niches for each service-species in the digital ecosystem may be collected from this user-behaviour, for example by learning analytics.

The third important principle that we extend from ecology to technology-enhanced learning domain is associated with the communicative. interactions between species. The digital community is a naturally occurring group of "service-species" populations in e-learning ecosystem who inhabit the same habitat (but use different niches) and form temporary coalitions (communities). For example the mutualisms such as parasitism, symbiosis or commensalism may appear between service species are associated with sharing the resources and associate with our first principle (energy and matter exchanges in the network). Other type of interactions, based on communication, which assumes mutual awareness, signaling between agents (or using the accumulated signals left into the environment) may be distinguished as well.

As a result of applying these three ecological principles on designing the next-generation online learning platforms, an open, loosely coupled, self-organised and emergent digital learning ecosystem can evolve.

## 3      Conceptualizing the Pedagogy-Driven Design

Braha and Maimon [12] have identified five different design paradigms:

- **Analysis-Synthesis-Evaluation** (**ASE**): iterative process, going back and forth between 3-7 phases, starting from analysis and ending with validation of proposed solution (e.g. ADDIE model);

- **Case-Based:** making use of previous experiences within a community of practice in order to solve design problems;
- **Cognitive:** representation of how designers perform mental task or activity in real life, along with techniques to enhance creativity (brainstorming, checklists, trigger questions, Gordon technique);
- **Algorithmic:** semi-automated execution of an effective domain-specific procedure that yields a satisfying design solution, matching well-defined initial requirements in a finite number of steps (e.g. "waterfall" model);
- **Artificial Intelligence:** attempts to make computers perform tasks that usually require human intelligence.

We argue that the first learning management systems (WebCT, Moodle) were designed by software engineers (and not by educationists) in line with the case-based paradigm, taking over existing solutions from other, non-pedagogical domains. For instance, to solve the problem of sharing the learning resources, designers provided file upload functionality in LMS. For synchronous communication, a chat module was provided, for asynchronous communication: forum. In contrast, designers of FLE3 [13] demonstrated, how asynchronous communication can be designed in the cognitive paradigm, in the pedagogy-driven manner. After outlining the characteristic phases of collaborative knowledge building (setting up the context, defining initial research problem, creating working theories etc.) they designed quite different discussion tool with strong pedagogical affordances.

We have combined ASE and cognitive paradigm to define the pedagogy-driven design framework that would suit for next-generation TEL systems – Digital Learning Ecosystems.

Design is increasingly social activity, the traditions of user-centered and participatory design are drawing inputs to design process from potential users. Our pedagogy-driven design approach is combining the visions gathered from participatory design sessions involving users (learners, facilitators) with design concepts and decisions derived from the pedagogical foundation of Digital Learning Ecosystem.

Three main structural components for explicating our pedagogy-driven design framework are:

- **Software architecture:** software elements, relations among them and properties of both;
- **Affordances:** functionalities and process models designed into user interface, invoking certain activities of users;
- **Vocabulary:** metaphors and concepts implemented in user interface.

The initial pedagogy-driven design model was applied by us on designing the architecture and user interface of our first learning management system IVA back in 2003. The pedagogical foundation of IVA was Jonassen's 3C model [14]. IVA was a second-generation TEL system, which has been used by more than 25 educational institutions and 28000 users within the last decade. On 2010, we initiated pedagogy-driven design and development of a third-generation TEL system called Dippler: Digital Portfolio-Based Personal Learning Ecosystem.

# 4    Pedagogical Foundation of Dippler

We identified four contemporary pedagogical frameworks or approaches to inform and direct the pedagogy-driven design of Dippler platform, taking into account four selection criteria. First, the approach should be compatible with contemporary mainstream pedagogy, which we define as the art and science of facilitating the students' learning. Secondly, it should be operationalisable to the level of affordances of user interface, as there are several attractive and well-known frameworks (e.g. Wenger's Communities of Practice or SECI model by Nonaka and Takeuchi), which are suitable only for hermeneutic analysis of learning or for heuristic guidelines for teachers. Thirdly, it should be compliant with other components of the framework and with the concept of digital learning ecosystems (internal consistency). Fourthly, the selected set of frameworks should cover both learning process and its outcomes from learners and facilitator's perspective.

These four selection criteria helped us to identify four contemporary pedagogical frameworks (both theoretical and practice-based), which formed the core of the pedagogical foundation for Dippler:

- **self-directed learning (SDL)**: introduced by Knowles (1975) [15], based on assumptions that learner's capacity and need to be self-directing grows and should be nurtured, that learner's experience is a valuable input to learning process, that learner's natural orientation is task/problem-centered, and internal incentives for learning are more important than external. Väljataga and Laanpere [16] extended the model of SDL to include learners' control over building and adapting their personal digital learning environment.
- **competence-based learning (CBL)**: a new approach to disputed model of outcome-based education. Supports SDL, as it gives learners more control over their learning paths by fixing only generic performance-based learning outcomes in the form of competences [17], which are defined as personal characteristics (e.g. knowledge, skills, attitudes, social capital) of an individual, which are needed for performing an authentic task in a real-life context. Tammets et al [18] have demonstrated how e-portfolios can be used effectively for competence-based learning.
- **collaborative knowledge building (CKB)**: a framework which distinguishes tacit and hardly observable process of learning from knowledge building that results with shareable (digital) artifacts - knowledge objects [18].
- **task-centered instructional design** models. Although traditional instructional design models were criticized for their incompatibility with dominant pedagogical paradigm (social constructivism), the new generation of instructional design models, e.g. 4C/ID [20] support SDL by reducing prescriptive components, situating learning in authentic context and suggesting problem-based approaches.

Figure 1 below illustrates how these four frameworks can be mapped to facilitator-learner and process-outcome dimensions to cover the most important aspects of pedagogical domain.

**Fig. 1.** Mapping of selected frameworks to pedagogical dimensions

The selected pedagogical frameworks were then analysed from the perspective of their potential contribution to the design decisions guiding the specification of software requirements for Dippler. Table 2 below provides a brief summary of these design decisions in relation to three structural components of our pedagogy-driven design model.

**Table 2.** An initial set of design decisions inferred from pedagogical foundation

| | Architecture | Affordances | Vocabulary |
|---|---|---|---|
| Self-directed learning | Learner controls, adapts and expands her blog-based PLE | Self-directed goal setting, planning and document-ing learning paths, scaf-folds | Learning outcomes, learning path, scaffold-ing, goals, context |
| Competency management | Institutional repository of competency definitions, learning analytics module | Performance-based as-sessment, Binding artifacts with domain concepts, present-ing evidences | Portfolio, competence, competence profile, evidence, competence record, level, badge |
| Collaborative knowledge building | Semantic layer, domain ontology evolution me-chanism | Co-construction Remixing Social tagging Recommendation Peer-scaffolding | Knowledge object, arti-fact, share, annotate, thinking types, remix, project, product |
| Task-centered instruc-tional design models | | Binding tasks, resources with learning outcomes Embedded scaffolds | Course design, strategy, task types, learning activity stream, pattern |

## 5     Design Process and Product

Our research group has dedicated more than ten years to iterative research-based design process, which eventually led us to development of Dippler platform – a distributed set of core services for a next-generation digital learning ecosystem. Figure 2 illustrates the three iterations of this process, each iteration contains both pedagogy-driven and user-centered design phases, as well as the analysis phase. The first iteration started with pedagogy-driven design of IVA learning management system, where the main design decisions were derived from social constructivist learning theory and Jonassen's 3C model [14]. The system was developed in a user-centered manner (phase 1.2) and 5 years after its wide-scale adoption, the design was evaluated (phase 1.3) through analysis of pedagogical activity patterns [21].

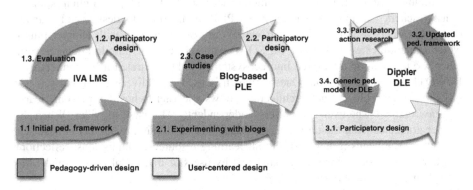

**Fig. 2.** Three iterations of research-based design of Dippler platform

Pedagogy driven design decisions can be informed both by pedagogical theories and experiences from educational practice. In 2008, when IVA LMS reached its stability and social media started to have influence on e-learning, we initiated a number of pedagogical experiments using blogs, wikis and others social media tools in formal higher education courses (phase 2.1). In these courses learners were encouraged to build their personal learning environments. We have studied how students perceive these distributed learning environments and their affordances [22]. These experiments have also indicated several issues that make it time-consuming to follow and to coordinate learning activities in blog-based courses. To address these limitations we developed two alternative software prototypes (phase 2.2): LePress and EduFeedr. LePress is a WordPress plugin that connects teacher's blog with those of students and creates a course coordination space for efficient management of course enrolments, assignments and assessments [23]. EduFeedr is an educational feed aggregator for blog-based courses and it doesn't require any plugins to be installed for teacher's and learners' blogs [24]. User-centered and participatory design approaches were used in both of these projects. We have also studied the pedagogical design challenges of various open, blog-based course formats (phase 2.3) [25].

Experiences gained from development of IVA LMS and also from experiments with blog-based courses led us to the third iteration: design of Dippler. The design process of Dippler started with a participatory design phase (3.1) where we developed five personas and four narrative scenarios that described typical use cases of Dippler: (1) facilitator designs a course, (2) learner sets up a weblog and enrolls to the course, (3) submitting assignments and giving feedback, and (4) learner graduates and re-affiliates her Dippler blog with another university. The scenarios were validated in a series of a participatory design sessions involving lecturers and students representing different persona's. This paper focuses mostly on the phase 3.2: pedagogy-driven design of Dippler. Above we have described the pedagogical framework and related design decisions that guided the development of Dippler. Currently we are in the end of phase 3.3, which involved conducting two pilot courses in Dippler ecosystem and related participatory action research experiment.

Figure 3 below illustrates the architecture of Dippler, consisting of a single centralised middleware application BOS, which is accessed by three types of client applications: teachers use institutional client (a PHP application) to design and manage courses, learners use either their personal Wordpress (enhanced with Dippler plugin which communicates with BOS via SOAP web services) or mobile client. Several other services can be integrated into ecosystem, we demonstrated it by connecting a IMS QTI compliant quiz tool Questr[1], which is used for delivering test and self-test tasks to learners' blogs. Such architecture allows a learner to host her personal learning environment wherever she prefers, independently of course provider. When the learner graduates from the university or changes her affiliation to another educational institution, she keeps in her portfolio all learning resources, submissions, reflections and communications which are usually lost by users of traditional institutional LMS after their user accounts expire.

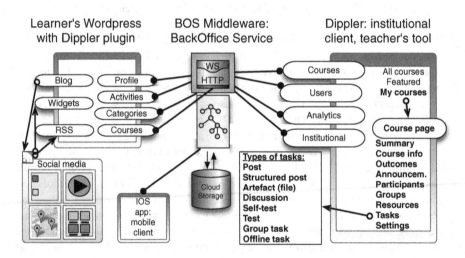

**Fig. 3.** The main components of Dippler platform

A self-directed learner is able to enhance her Personal Learning Environment by adding plugins or sidebar widgets to her Wordpress blog and change the "look and feel" of her PLE by modifying the Wordpress theme. Learner does not have to visit the institutional Dippler environment after initial registration, as all course related content - course announcements, assignments, teacher's feedback, grades - is displayed in learner's blog. Learner's responses to assignments are submitted as blog posts, which are automatically annotated with a specific category (domain concept

---

[1] http://trac.htk.tlu.ee/iva2

from teacher-created taxonomy), linking the submission with a given learning outcome. Figure 4 below shows the list of learning outcomes and their mapping to domain ontology concepts in the Dippler's institutional client. Teachers can use these
categories also for annotating the learning resources and announcements, which are
related to a specific learning outcome or assignment. Learners can annotate any blog
post with the relevant domain ontology concept, which allows them to advance their
competence in self-directed manner, in addition to assignments given by the teacher.
All submissions from learners' blogs, which are annotated with concepts from domain
taxonomy, are copied to the BOS database. Even if the learner removes or updates her
blog posts later, the original versions of submissions are kept within institutions.

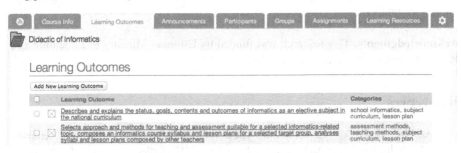

**Fig. 4.** Dippler's institutional client: mapping learning outcomes with domain concepts

By restricting uploading of learning resources (these can only be linked or embedded into Dippler course) and by establishing explicit connection between learning
outcomes, learning resources and various types of learning tasks, Dippler enforces
teachers to implement good practices of task-centered instructional design. Dippler
also promotes self-directed and competence-based learning, as the learners have more
control over their learning environment, yet they are guided by learning outcomes and
tasks. Learners can easily create a competence-driven presentation portfolio by selecting a set of their blog posts and other self-created knowledge objects related to a given
set of learning outcomes. Detailed activity stream (based on Activity Base Schema[2]
enhanced with educational action and object verbs) displays all recent activities on the
course in both, the teacher's client and in the learner's blog, helping all participants to
have a quick overview of the course in Facebook style. And, finally, the category annotations and activity streams of Dippler allow conducting a different kind of learning
analytics, which is not supported by traditional LMS: analyzing distribution of activities and resources in relation to domain topics, addressed by the course. The biggest
challenge for a blog-based PLE is supporting collaborative knowledge building, but
Dippler addresses this through providing collaborative tasks, where the learners either
share one copy of a blog post or embed to their joint blog post some external collaboration tool, e.g. typewith.me for collaborative writing or wiki for project work. Eventually, all four pedagogical frameworks selected to guide our pedagogy-driven design
model have been implemented on three levels in developing the Dippler: in its software
architecture, affordances and the vocabulary of the user interface.

---

[2] http://activitystrea.ms/specs/json/schema/activity-schema.html

# 6     Conclusions

This paper proposed a three-component model for pedagogy-driven design of next-generation technology-enhanced learning systems: digital learning ecosystems (DLE). We extended the concept of ecosystem from biological world to the digital one and more specifically, to the domain of technology-enhanced learning, going beyond using DLE as a metaphor. Further on, we explained how our pedagogy-driven design model was implemented in the development of a DLE called Dippler: a distributed and adaptable portfolio-based learning platform, which combines the strengths of institutional Learning Management Systems with those of blog-based Personal Learning Environments.

**Acknowledgments.** This research was funded by Estonian Ministry of Education and Research targeted research grant No. 0130159s08.

# References

1. Laanpere, M., Põldoja, H., Kikkas, K.: The Second Thoughts about Pedagogical Neutrality of LMS. In: Kinshuk, L.C.K., Sutinen, E., Sampson, D., Aedo, I., Uden, L., Kähkonen, E. (eds.) The 4th IEEE International Conference on Advanced Learning Technologies, pp. 807–809. IEEE Computer Society, Los Alamitos (2004)
2. Koper, R.: Modelling Units of Study from a Pedagogical Perspective: the Pedagogical Meta-model behind EML. OUNL, Heerlen (2001)
3. Friesen, N.: Learning Objects and Standards: Pedagogical Neutrality and Engagement. In: Kinshuk, L.C.K., Sutinen, E., Sampson, D., Aedo, I., Uden, L., Kähkonen, E. (eds.) The 4th IEEE International Conference on Advanced Learning Technologies, pp. 1070–1071. IEEE Computer Society, Los Alamitos (2004)
4. Laanpere, M., Põldoja, H., Normak, P.: Designing Dippler – a Next Generation TEL System. In: Tatnall, A., Ruohonen, M., Ley, T., Laanpere, M. (eds.) Open and Social Technologies for Networked Learning. Springer, New York (2012)
5. Pata, K.: Revising the framework of knowledge ecologies: How activity patterns define learning spaces? In: Lambropoulos, N., Romero, M. (eds.) Educational Social Software for Context-Aware Learning: Collaborative Methods & Human Interaction, pp. 1–23. IGI Global, Hershley (2009)
6. Normak, P., Pata, K., Kaipainen, M.: An Ecological Approach to Learning Dynamics. Educational Technology and Society (2012)
7. Uden, L., Wangsa, I.T., Damiani, E.: The future of E-learning: E-learning ecosystem. In: Inaugural IEEE International Conference on Digital Ecosystems and Technologies, pp. 113–117. IEEE, Cairns (2007)
8. Ficheman, I.K., de Deus Lopez, R.: Digital Learning Ecosystems: Authoring, Collaboration, Immersion and Mobility. In: Díaz, P., Kinshuk, P., Aedo, I., Mora, E. (eds.) Eighth IEEE International Conference on Advanced Learning Technologies, pp. 371–372. IEEE Computer Society, Los Alamitos (2008)
9. Reyna, J.: Digital Teaching and Learning Ecosystem (DTLE): A Theoretical Approach for Online Learning Environments. In: Williams, G., Statham, P., Brown, N., Cleland, B. (eds.) Changing Demands, Changing Directions. Proceedings Ascilite Hobart 2011, pp. 1083–1088. University of Tasmania, Hobart (2011)

10. Odling-Smee, F.J., Laland, K.N., Feldman, M.W.: Niche Construction: The Neglected Process in Evolution. Princeton University Press, Princeton (2003)

11. Young, M.F.: An ecological psychology of instructional design: Learning and thinking by perceiving-acting systems. In: Jonassen, D.H. (ed.) Handbook of Research for Educational Communications and Technology, 2nd edn. Lawrence Erlbaum Associates, Mahwah (2004)

12. Braha, D., Maimon, O.: A Mathematical Theory of Design: Foundations, Algorithms, and Applications. Kluwer Academic Publishers, Dordrecht (1998)

13. Rubens, W., Emans, B., Leinonen, T., Skarmeta, A.G., Simons, R.-J.: Design of web-based collaborative learning environments. Translating the pedagogical learning principles to human computer interface. Computers & Education 45(3), 276–294 (2005)

14. Laanpere, M., Kikkas, K., Põldoja, H.: Pedagogical foundations of IVA Learning Management System. In: Hudson, B.G., Kiefer, S., Laanpere, M., Rugelj, J. (eds.) eLearning in Higher Education, pp. 143–155. Universitätsverlag Rudolf Trauner, Linz (2005)

15. Knowles, M.S.: Self-directed learning: A guide for learners and teachers. Prentice Hall/Cambridge, Englewood Cliffs (1975)

16. Väljataga, T., Laanpere, M.: Learner control and personal learning environment: a challenge for instructional design. Interactive Learning Environments 18(3), 277–291 (2010)

17. Sampson, D., Fytros, D.: Competence Models in technology-enhanced Competence-based Learning. In: Handbook on Information Technologies for Education and Training, pp. 155–177. Springer, Heidelberg (2008)

18. Tammets, K., Pata, K., Laanpere, M., Tomberg, V., Gašević, D., Siadaty, M.: Designing the Competence-Driven Teacher Accreditation. In: Leung, H., Popescu, E., Cao, Y., Lau, R.W.H., Nejdl, W. (eds.) ICWL 2011. LNCS, vol. 7048, pp. 132–141. Springer, Heidelberg (2011)

19. Bereiter, C.: Education and Mind in the Knowledge Age. L. Erlbaum, Mahwah (2002)

20. van Merriënboer, J.G., Clark, R.E., de Croock, M.: Blueprints for complex learning: The 4C/ID-model. Educational Technology Research and Development 50(2), 39–64 (2002)

21. Laanpere, M., Pata, K., Tomberg, V.: Evaluating Pedagogy-Driven Design of IVA LMS with Activity Pattern Analysis. In: Spaniol, M., Li, Q., Klamma, R., Lau, R.W.H. (eds.) ICWL 2009. LNCS, vol. 5686, pp. 210–214. Springer, Heidelberg (2009)

22. Väljataga, T., Pata, K., Tammets, K.: Considering Students' Perspectives on Personal and Distributed Learning Environments in Course Design. In: Lee, M.J.W., McLoughlin, C. (eds.) Web 2.0-Based E-Learning, pp. 85–107. IGI Global, Hershey (2011)

23. Tomberg, V., Laanpere, M., Lamas, D.: Learning Flow Management and Semantic Data Exchange between Blog-Based Personal Learning Environments. In: Leitner, G., Hitz, M., Holzinger, A. (eds.) USAB 2010. LNCS, vol. 6389, pp. 340–352. Springer, Heidelberg (2010)

24. Põldoja, H.: EduFeedr: following and supporting learners in open blog-based courses. In: Open ED 2010 Proceedings, UOC, OU, BYU, Barcelona, pp. 399–408 (2010)

25. Väljataga, T., Põldoja, H., Laanpere, M.: Open Online Courses: Responding to Design Challenges. In: Ruokamo, H., Eriksson, M., Pekkala, L., Vuojärvi, H. (eds.) Proceedings of the 4th International Network-Based Education 2011 Conference The Social Media in the Middle of Nowhere, pp. 68–75. University of Lapland, Rovaniemi (2011)

# The Use of Expert Systems in Building the Quality Model of a Web-Based Learning Platform

Traian-Lucian Militaru, George Suciu, and Gyorgy Todoran

University POLITEHNICA of Bucharest, Romania
gelmosro@yahoo.com, george@beia.ro, todoran.gyorgy@gmail.com

**Abstract.** This paper proposes an expert system that can be used to build the quality model of a web-based learning platform. The main advantages of using such a tool instead of a human expert are the increased availability, low-cost and fast service. The quality framework used is called SEEQUEL and the proposed expert system was built using CLIPS, a productive development and delivery expert system tool which provides a complete environment for the construction of rule based expert systems.

In the first part of this paper, the SEEQUEL Core Quality Framework and CLIPS expert system generator are presented, showing the advantage of using an expert system for this task. In the second part, a case study of using the SEEQUEL framework and CLIPS tool to build an expert system for building the quality model of a web-based learning platform is presented. The final conclusion of the experiment was that an expert system can successfully replace a human expert for the proposed task.

**Keywords:** expert system, web-based learning, quality model, evaluation, SEEQUEL Core Quality Framework, computer assisted.

## 1    Introduction

E-learning covers all forms of electronically supported learning and teaching. This article only refers to computer-based e-learning which is essentially the computer and network-enabled transfer of skills and knowledge. The content is considered to be delivered via the Internet to browser-equipped learners. It is also called web-based learning and it can be or not instructor-led and includes media in the form of text, image, video and audio streaming.

Due to the rise of the informational volume available on the Internet, more and more users choose to use web-based environments for the learning process. Like for any other product, the necessity to select those virtual environments which satisfy the demands of the users appears. The extent to which user expectations are met is called quality. In order to evaluate the quality, relevant characteristics must be selected, weighted and then measured. This paper is presenting an automated method for building of the quality model for web-based learning platforms using an expert system. The building of the quality model is the process of selecting and weighing the

E. Popescu et al. (Eds.): ICWL 2012, LNCS 7558, pp. 318–327, 2012.
© Springer-Verlag Berlin Heidelberg 2012

quality characteristics and also of establishing the relations between them. The main advantages using an automated solution are the increased availability, low-cost and fast service.

## 2   Building the Quality Model

Usually, a quality evaluation method includes the following steps:

1.  the definition and specification of the demands referring to quality;
2.  the building of the quality model;
3.  the measurement;
4.  the aggregation of the scores;
5.  the analysis of the scores, the formulation and gathering documentary evidence for conclusions.

A similar method is Web Quality Evaluation Method (WebQEM) developed between 1998-2000 by a group of researchers from the National University of La Pampa (Argentina) led by Luis Olsina which was used as an inspiration resource for formulating this generalized evaluation method.

When a quality evaluation is started, the first thing which must be done is to establish the expectations the users have. The next step is to identify the quality characteristics which determine those expectations and then to link them in a tree-like model where the top is the total quality and the bottom is the set of basic, measurable characteristics. This model is also called the quality model. Then the measurements and the calculations of the composed quality characteristics indicators (including the total quality) can be started. Once the evaluators calculate those scores, the analysis can be started to observe which week points are detected in order to formulate some advices that help developers to improve the quality (only if it is necessary).

In this study the SEEQUEL Core Quality Framework (http://www.menon.org/) will be used, this proposing a tree organized set of characteristics. Those sets that are considered relevant will be selected to build the quality tree. This framework is a part of the SEEQUEL project, supported in frames of the EU e-learning initiative, originated from the collaboration between the e-learning Industry Group (eLIG) with a number of European expert organisations and associations, co-ordinated by the MENON Network. The project activities addressed the need for a common strategy to define and implement international e-learning quality standards. The SEEQUEL Core Quality Framework is based on a matrix where a list of common quality criteria applicable to the whole e-learning experience can be weighted by the various user (people or organisation), enabling any category of stakeholders to position their perception of quality with respect to the perceptions of another stakeholders' category [1]. So the only remaining challenge is choosing quality characteristics, determining their weights and building the mathematical model used for aggregation. All these will be handled by the proposed expert system.

The SEEQUEL Core Quality Framework proposes three main quality characteristics:

- The Learning sources which contain all the involved sources: the technical infrastructure, the learning materials and the human resources in their functions of teaching and supporting learning.
- The Learning processes: Any learning experience consists of a series of processes. There are two main types of processes. Firstly there are those that occur during the actual learning experience – learning processes. Secondly, there are a series of processes set up around a given learning experience. These support processes underpin any learning experience, but are separate from the learning experience itself – for example recruitment of teachers, which does not take place as part of the learning experience, but still has a definite impact on the learning experience itself. The processes identified are typical of any training action such as: training needs analysis, guidance, recruitment, design (macro and micro), delivery and assessment/evaluation.
- The Learning context is the environment in which learning takes place. It is viewed in its double perspectives: intrinsic and relative. The quality of a learning experience depends both on the quality of the context itself and on the relationship of the designed and implemented experience to the context in which it occurs.

The SEEQUEL Quality conceptual framework proposes the following scale for weights.

- 2 = key/ core criteria for defining quality of the object
- 1 = important criteria for defining quality of the object
- 0 = non relevant for defining quality of the object

For getting more accurate results, this article propose a modified scale for weights, the [0..1] scale, where 0 means the characteristic is not important for the research and 1 means a maximum importance. The sum of weights of all subcharacteristics of a characteristic must be 1.

The next step is to identify the quality characteristics which are determining those expectations and decompose them to basic ones. A tree-like quality model will be obtained where the top is the total quality and the bottom is the set of basic quality characteristics. Then, the aggregation model must be built. This study is using Logic Scoring of Preferences (LSP) proposed by Dujmovic [2] as aggregation method. In LSP, the E aggregated preference of some $E_i$ preferences from a subsequent inferior level is the following function [2]:

$$E(r) = (w_1 * E_1^r + w_2 * E_2^r + ... + w_k * E_k^r)^{\frac{1}{r}} \tag{1}$$

$$where - \infty \le r \le \infty, 0 \le E_i \le 1, 0 \le w_i \le 1$$

$$w_1 + w_2 + \cdots + w_k = 1$$

$$E(-\infty) = min(E_1, E_2, ..., E_k), E(\infty) = max(E_1, E_2, ..., E_k)$$

The r parameter is given by the simultaneity level of preferences which are to be aggregated. Small values of r lead to small values of the E(r) function, which inside CPL (Continuous Preference Logic) means conjunction while high values of r lead to high values of the E(r), the equivalent of disjunction. So, low values of r are chosen when they wish to punish the lack of simultaneity of the preferences which are aggregated while high values appear in opposite cases. This aggregation method also offers the opportunity to achieve more accurate results.

The proposed expert system will determine the value of r parameter, considering the preferences which will be aggregated. The aggregation is done 'from down to up', in several steps, in the tree-like structure of quality characteristics. The final result is a global plan which allows the calculation of the quality indicators for all the characteristics and also the total quality indicator. This last global preference represents the general satisfaction level referring to fulfilling the requirements concerning quality valued.

## 3    CLIPS Expert System Generator

An expert system is a computer system that emulates the decision-making ability of a human expert [3]. They are designed to solve complex problems by reasoning about knowledge, like an expert, not by following the procedure of a developer as is the case in conventional programming [5]. It can be concluded that if a human expert can specify the steps and reasoning by which a problem may be solved, then an expert system can be created to solve the same problem [4].

The architecture of an expert system is illustrated in the following figure:

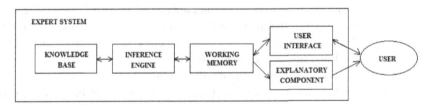

**Fig. 1.** The structure of an expert system

The knowledge base of expert systems is a collection of rules encoded as metadata in a file system, or more often in a relational database and contains both factual and heuristic knowledge. Factual knowledge is that knowledge of the task domain that is widely shared and commonly agreed. Heuristic knowledge is the less rigorous, more experiential, more judgmental knowledge of performance. In contrast to factual knowledge, heuristic knowledge is rarely discussed and is largely individualistic. It is the knowledge of good practice, good judgment and plausible reasoning in the field. It is the knowledge that underlies the "art of good guessing".

Knowledge representation formalizes and organizes the knowledge. The one used in CLIPS is the production rule, or simply rule. A rule consists of two parts: an IF part (also called a condition) and a THEN part (also called action). The IF part is a logical combination of some conditions. The piece of knowledge represented by a particular production rule is relevant to the line of reasoning being developed if the IF part of the rule is satisfied; consequently, the THEN part can be conclude or its problem-solving action taken. Expert systems whose knowledge is represented in a rule form are called rule-based systems.

The working memory initially contains the data that is received from the user as task input which is used to evaluate antecedents (the IF parts of the rules) in the knowledge base. Fired consequents from rules (actions whose conditions are true) in the knowledge base may create new values in working memory, update old values or remove existing values.

The inference engine is that part of an expert system which is designed to produce reasoning on rules. CLIPS uses forward chaining and rule prioritization for reasoning. The inference engine inspects the condition part of every rule from the knowledge base until it matches one for which the logical of condition is truly based on the data available in the working memory. When the rule condition part is true, the inference engine executes the action part of that rule which is determining the change of the working memory. This process continues until the solution to the problem is found or no new rules can be fired (in this case, the user can be prompted for offering new information) or the necessary resources (time, memory, etc.) are over.

In an expert system (especially a large one with a large amount of rules), at any moment in time there may be a series of rules that are ready to fire which are known as the conflict set. A conflict resolution strategy is required to make the decision as to which rule should be fired first. CLIPS provides seven conflict resolution strategies: depth, breadth, simplicity, complexity, LEX, MEA, and random. The default strategy is depth, which means the newly activated rules are placed above all rules of the same salience. For example, given that fact- a activates rule- 1 and rule- 2 and fact- b acti-vates rule- 3 and rule- 4, then if fact- a is asserted before fact- b, rule- 3 and rule- 4 will be above rule- 1 and rule- 2 on the agenda. However, the position of rule- 1 rela-tive to rule- 2 and rule- 3 relative to rule- 4 will be arbitrary [5].

The engine has two ways to run: batch or conversational. In batch, the expert system has all the necessary data to process from the beginning. For the user, the program works as a classical program: he provides data and receives results imme-diately. Reasoning is invisible. The conversational method becomes necessary when the developer knows he cannot ask the user for all the necessary data in the begin-ning, the problem being too complex. The software must "invent" the way to solve the problem, request the missing data from the user, gradually approaching the goal as quickly as possible. The result gives the impression of a dialogue led by an expert [5].

CLIPS is a productive development and delivery expert system tool which pro-vides a complete environment for the construction of rule based expert systems. An expert system generator consists of an empty knowledge database which can be filled through an interface by a knowledge engineer, a customizable inference engine, user

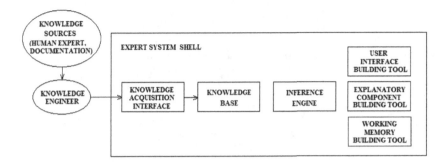

**Fig. 2.** The structure of an expert system generator

interface and explanatory component building tools and a working memory building tool as it is illustrated in Fig. 2. The inference engine, the filled database, the user interface and the explanatory component (both created by the system engineer) and the working memory will form the future generated expert system.

## 4    Case Study

The proposed expert system was used to build the quality model of the web-based learning platform belonging to the Open University from UK (http://www. open.ac.uk).

The SEEQUEL Core Quality Framework is permitting a quality evaluation from the perspective of any of the stakeholders, be it student, teacher or technical staff. In this study, the evaluation has been carried out from the student's perspective, the person who wants to accumulate knowledge. This type of visitor is considered an experimented internet user, with a high cultural level and intelligence.

There is no simple definition of quality in e-learning and any definition we might wish to consider runs the risk of constraining people vision of what quality means and it significance in their particular context [3]. In other words, quality is different for different people and even for the same person in a different context. In order to have the right user perception about quality, we must communicate with the user to feel what is really important for him. Knowing the user expectation from the web-based learning platform, we can select and weigh the quality characteristics in the proper way to obtain his right perception about quality.

The expert system is constructing the problem which must be solved by filling the working memory with information provided by the user. In order to find the users perception about quality the expert system is trying to find which of the quality characteristics (proposed by the SEEQUEL Core Quality Framework) are considered important and also how important they are considered by questioning the user.

```
CLIPS> (reset)
CLIPS> (run)
```

```
Select the stakeholders category where you are:
                1)students
                2)teachers
             3)supporting team
```

```
Enter your choise:
1
```

1. Do you have communications problems? (yes/no)
   Your Answer: yes

2. On a scale from 1 to 10 which is your communication
   skils level?
   Your Answer: 7

3. Do you have communications problems? (yes/no)
   Your Answer: yes

4. Can you motivate enough yourself during the
   learning process or do you necessarily need
   teacher help in order to have the desired results?
   (yes, I can motivate myself / no, I can't)
   Your Answer: no

5. On a scale from 1 to 10 which is your ability level to
   motivate yourself strong enogh to have the desired
   results?
   Your Answer: 4

**Fig. 3.** The proposed expert system

Of all proposed features of SEEQUEL Core Quality Framework the expert system selected and weighed those that were considered important for the present study:

1.  Learning sources (w=0.4)

  1.1.  Teaching staff (w=0.4)

     1.1.1  Ability to support learning (based on past experience) (w=0.5)

     1.1.2  Ability to support the motivation to learn (w=0.2)

     1.1.3  Adaptability to change/ flexibility (w=0.05)

     1.1.4  Communication skills (w=0.15)

     1.1.5  Ability to monitor learning progress (w=0.05)

     1.1.6  Ability to assess learning progress (w=0.05)

  1.2.  Learning materials (w=0.4)

     1.2.1  Content reliability and updated (w=0.35)

     1.2.2  Technical quality (w=0.2)

     1.2.3  Aesthetic quality (w=0.05)

     1.2.4  Conformance to standards (w=0.2)

     1.2.5  Ease of use (w=0.05)

1.2.6  Interactivity (w=0.05)

1.2.7  Materials are learner driven (w=0.05)

1.2.8  Low cost (w=0.05)

1.3.  Learning infrastructure (w=0.2)

1.3.1  Accessibility (e.g. people with disabilities, organizational difficulties) (w=0.05)

1.3.2  Adaptability to users' need (w=0.3)

1.3.3  Interoperability with other systems (w=0.05)

1.3.4  Ease of use (w=0.2)

1.3.5  Reliability of the Technical infrastructure (w=0.2)

1.3.6  Availability of different communication tools (w=0.1)

1.3.7  Uniform interface (w=0.05)

1.3.8  Personalized interface (w=0.05)

2.    Core learning processes (w=0.4)Learning design (w=0.4)

2.1.1  The learning course is aimed at developing knowledge (w=0.1)

2.1.2  The learning course is aimed at developing competences (w=0.1)

2.1.3  Clear definition of the target groups (w=0.1)

2.1.4  Coherence of the didactic strategy with course objectives (w=0.2)

2.1.5  Granularity of the content (w=0.2)

2.1.6  Flexibility of the learning path is assured in the module or course (w=0.1)

2.1.7  Learning accreditation system is available and linked to the national/ European accreditation system context (e.g. ECTS) (w=0.1)

2.1.8  Technical assistance in course development is assured (w=0.1)

2.2.  Learning Delivery (w=0.6)

2.2.1  Accessibility (w=0.4)

2.2.2  Reliability and robustness of the online services (w=0.4)

2.2.3  Throughout the course students are provided with technical and pedagogical support for using the services available (individual and group level) (w=0.15)

2.2.4  Measures to monitor and rectify common technical problems (w=0.05)

3.    Learning context (w=0.2)Learning Environment (w=0.7)

3.1.1  Supporting personalization (w=0.2)

3.1.2  Supporting competence representation (mapping) and recognition (w=0.05)

3.1.3  Supporting interaction/ communication (w=0.4)

3.1.4  Supporting team work (w=0.2)

3.1.5  Supporting individual behavior patterns rather than common behavior patterns (w=0.1)

3.1.6  Supporting divergent thinking (w=0.05)

3.2.  Legislation (w=0.1)

3.2.1  IPR and Copyrights related to the materials' content are respected (w=0.5)

3.2.2  The accreditation system is recognized by professional associations (w=0.5)

3.3.  Financial setting (w=0.2)

3.3.1  Specific financial aid measures are devoted to disadvantaged categories (e.g. grants, participation fees) (w=1)

Next, the proposed expert system will build the aggregation model by selecting the appropriate values of r, according to the desired conjunction/ disjunction degree (andness/orness) [6]. The information regarding the simultaneity level of preferences which are to be aggregated is provided by the human expert.

To realize a continuous transition from disjunction to conjunction with 16 equidistant steps of andness/orness the expert system can use the following special particular cases:

D ( r = +∞ ), D++ ( r = 20.63 ), D+ ( r = 9.52 ),

D+- ( r = 5.8 ), DA ( r = 3.93), D-+ ( r = 2.79 ),

D- ( r = 2.018 ), D-- ( r =1.449 ), A ( r =1),

C-- ( r = 0.619 ), C- ( r = 0.261),

C-+ ( r = −0.148 ), CA ( r = −0.72 ),

C+- ( r = −1.655 ), C+ ( r = −3.51),

C++ ( r = −9.06 ), C ( r = −∞ ) .

For example, the aggregation model for "Learning materials" is shown in the following figure:

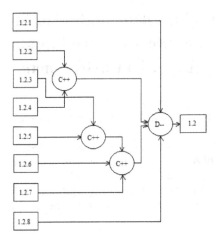

**Fig. 4.** The aggregation model for "Learning materials"

The result of the proposed expert system analysis is a tree-like quality model. Using this model, a questionnaire having questions which covers the user interest can be generated and the evaluation can be started.

## 5    Conclusions

Using an expert system to build a custom quality model adapted to the evaluator's profile, the guarantee of an evaluation which will offer a complete image of the user's perception on the quality of the evaluated e-learning environment is ensured. The expert system software can successfully replace a human expert for this task, the main advantages being the increased availability, low-cost and fast service.

## References

1. Ehlers, U.-D., Pawlowski, J.M. (eds.): Handbook on Quality and Standardisation in E-Learning. Springer, New York City (2006)
2. Dujmovic, J.J.: LSP: A Method for Evaluation and Selection of Complex Hardware and Software Systems. In: The 22nd International Conference for the Resource Management and Performance Evaluation of Enterprise Computing Systems, CMG 1996 Proceedings, vol. 1, pp. 368–378 (1996)
3. Giarranto, J.C., Riley, G.D.: Expert Systems: Principles and Programming. Thompson Course Technology, Boston (2005)
4. CORPORATE JTEC Panel. Knowledge-based systems in Japan, Communications of the ACM 37(1) (January 1994)
5. CLIPS Basic Programming Guide vol. I (June 2, 1993)
6. Dujmović, J.J.: Characteristic Forms of Generalized Conjunction/Disjunction. In: Proceedings of the IEEE World Congress on Computational Intelligence, Hong Kong (June 2008)

# A Prototypical Implementation of the Intelligent Integrated Computer-Assisted Language Learning (iiCALL) Environment

Harald Wahl[1] and Werner Winiwarter[2]

[1] Dept. of Information Engineering and Security,
University of Applied Sciences Technikum Wien, Vienna, Austria
wahl@technikum-wien.at
[2] Research Group Data Analytics and Computing, University of Vienna, Vienna, Austria
werner.winiwarter@univie.ac.at

**Abstract.** Since the late nineties, several Computer-Assisted Language Learning (CALL) platforms have been developed. By using Natural Language Processing (NLP) and Artificial Intelligence (AI) technologies, CALL has become Intelligent CALL (ICALL). Our research additionally deals with language learning integrated in different environments, be it Web browsers or Email clients. Therefore, we develop a Web-based e-learning solution, called Intelligent Integrated Computer-Assisted Language Learning (iiCALL) platform. Requirements engineering for iiCALL has primarily been done on the basis of identifying suitable use cases with respect to different learning types. Moreover, we face varying levels of learners.

The paper illustrates relevant use cases and describes the yielding Web-based and distributed system architecture of iiCALL. Furthermore, it draws specific attention to a first prototype integrated into Mozilla Firefox that implements a simple learning scenario for language learners on a beginner's level. Finally, it points out open issues and future work.

**Keywords:** iiCALL, Computer-Assisted Language Learning, Web-Based Learning, Integrated Learning, Intelligent Learning.

## 1 Introduction

Since the first introduction of *Computer-Assisted Language Learning* (CALL) in 1997 [12], several improvements in functionality and quality of CALL platforms have been made. By applying *Natural Language Processing* (NLP) and *Artificial Intelligence* (AI) technologies, CALL has become *Intelligent CALL* (ICALL) [8, 12, and 18]. Our specific interest additionally concentrates on integrated environments, which brings language learning to common working environments like Web browsers or Email clients. Therefore, we call it *Intelligent Integrated Computer-Assisted Language Learning* (iiCALL) [17].

E. Popescu et al. (Eds.): ICWL 2012, LNCS 7558, pp. 328–333, 2012.

## 2    Requirements Engineering and System Architecture

The flexibility of iiCALL is given by the requirement to ensure context-related learning; it should allow language learning in arbitrary scenarios. For instance, in the context of health and medicine, nursing stuff can use it to learn specific medical words and phrases, whilst tourists can use it in a context of travel and communication. Engineers focus on technical terms, or business persons are in need of financial and economical language use [20].

Progress and success of learning highly depend on a balanced support of individual learning types and methods designed for different levels of learners [20]. Therefore, we started with learning theories (behaviorism, cognitivism, and constructivism) and identified corresponding learning methods with respect to levels of learners.

Relevant use cases have been selected in [20], i.e. the use case "Vocabulary trainer" which follows behaviorism theory and is best suited for beginners, the use case "Cloze text" for intermediate learners, or the use case "Social translation" for advanced learners which uses constructivism elements. Based on those conditions, the core functional requirements yield to the following system architecture.

From a technological point of view, the iiCALL environment is a Web-based e-learning platform that allows arbitrary clients to connect using the SOAP Web service interface. Ideally, clients should be able to access a local database to ensure storage of one's preferences and allows offline learning. A counterpart database at the server side, to which local data can be synchronized, allows individual users to learn locally independent using any kind of client. At the server side, iiCALL runs inside an Apache Tomcat using Hibernate and MySQL for persistence purposes. The NLP tasks at the server side are fulfilled by the *General Architecture for Text Engineering* (GATE) framework. NLP toolkits and frameworks were evaluated in [18], and because of its open architecture, its extension possibilities, and its interface to semantic data using the Web Ontology Language (OWL, at the level of OWL-Lite), GATE has been chosen as the best candidate to fulfill the NLP functionalities in the iiCALL environment. Currently, the version 6.1 of GATE Embedded is installed at the iiCALL server. The core software framework is implemented in Java, and it is chiefly responsible for controlling data transfer, managing users, and communication to the iiCALL clients. Furthermore, it handles processes designed by a workflow engine, and it implements the interface to GATE. More details are available in [19].

## 3    A First Prototype Environment

A first iiCALL client prototype (currently in an early alpha-release stage) has been implemented as a Firefox extension by using the *XML User Interface Language* (XUL) and *JavaScript*. It implements the use case "Vocabulary trainer", a method for a language learner on a beginner's level. Integrated learning must be understood in a way that the plugin uses the current browser content as underlying data for learning purposes.

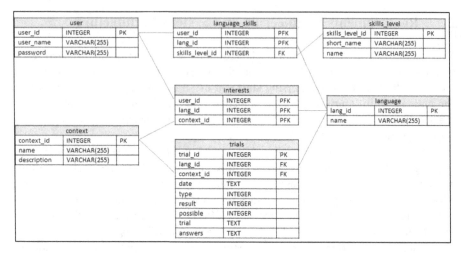

**Fig. 1.** Local data model (the part of user preferences) of the iiCALL prototype plug-in

During the first installation process, the program looks for a local iiCALL database. If the database is not available it will initially be created. The local database mainly stores user information like language skills, levels of learners, or areas of interest. It is implemented using the SQLite database, which meshes with Mozilla Firefox as Mozilla itself uses SQLite for database purposes. Additionally, it is easy to be managed by the Mozilla Firefox add-on "SQLite Manager", which is currently installed in version 0.7.7. The first draft of the data model, i.e. the part that handles user preferences and has relevance for the prototype implementation, can be viewed in Fig. 1.

The GUI of the iiCALL plug-in appears as a sidebar in parallel to the browser content. The plug-in adapts the language to the operation system's locale, so the following GUI screens show the German language occurrence.

The vocabulary trainer works on basis of the displayed content of the browser tab to which the iiCALL sidebar is adhered. In Fig. 2 the browser content shows the abstract of a white paper in the area of pharmacy standards in hospitals. The iiCALL client sends the whole content to the iiCALL server where a specific GATE plug-in tries to find out the core language and the context the text is about. Currently, texts can be assigned to combinations of languages (English, German, or Italian) and context types (medicine, information technology (IT), or sports). The plugin uses *thesauri* and some *machine learning* algorithms to identify language and context. In future versions, users will be able to train the context plug-in by making suggestions and corrections. So far, the context plug-in returns language-context combinations with a calculated probability. In the example of Fig. 2, the combination "English in medicine" is calculated with a probability of 68 percent, the combination "English in information technologies" comes with a probability of 26 percent, and the combination "Italian in sports" comes with a probability of 6 percent. The algorithm will be improved for future versions; so far, the user has to manually choose the combination that seems the most proper one. In the example of Fig. 2 the recommendation of the plug-in is consistent with the real world.

**Fig. 2.** Recommendation of language and context

After selecting language-context combination (this is sent back to the server), a multiple choice (and single answer) vocabulary test is created and sent to the client. The test contains 10 questions with 3 options each. The vocabularies come from the text (e.g. word indicated by the yellow marker signs on the right side in Fig. 3). The feedback to the user's test trial is given by an evaluation report. The report gives the amount of correct answers in relation to the total amount of questions. Correct answers are displayed in green and wrong answers are displayed in red (cf. Fig. 3). In future versions, the storage of information about user behavior enables replays of single tests. Additionally, the learner's skill level can be re-calculated.

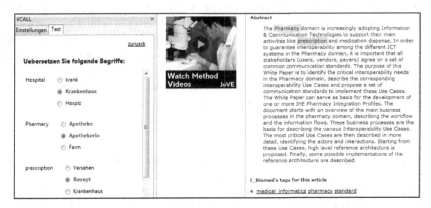

**Fig. 3.** Analysis and feedback of multiple choice vocabulary test

## 4     Outlook

The demonstrated prototype of the iiCALL environment offers places for improvement. User management, storage of user behavior, flexible learning methods, data synchronization to a generic data model, etc. are upcoming issues.

### 4.1     Improvements on the Server Side

The database at the iiCALL server mainly organizes the Hibernate issues, upcoming data models allow user management and user evaluations and can interact with workflow engines to offer flexibility in learning methods. The current iiCALL proto-type does not include lots of NLP tasks, grammar concerns will have to be added. GATE integration is solely used by a first version of the plug-in that tries to find out language and context of a given text. Not least, the evaluation of proper workflow engines and the integration itself become future tasks.

### 4.2    Improvements on the Client Side

The iiCALL client currently just implements the use case "Vocabulary training"; it is not able to understand any other workflow. The local database is more or less limited to user preferences. In future versions, the data model has to become more generic to store historical user actions and user behavior as well. Clients will be able to syn-chronize data to the centralized server database and they will support offline learning.

### 4.3    Cloud Learning and Multiple Users

The idea of the iiCALL environment is that language learning can be done every-where and every time, by oneself or within a team, self-conducted or even coached by a tutor. The iiCALL server will be the "heart" where most calculations will be done, the features are provided to lots of simultaneous users. Thus, thinking of scalability will be an important issue. Communication purposes and NLP functionalities (GATE) will run on individual virtual machines that can be mirrored whilst authentication, load balancing, and caching can be fulfilled by a prior proxy server. The database that is currently at the same server as GATE will be transferred to a centralized database that can be accessed from each virtual machine. The workflow engine is also trans-ferred outside to interact with the database server and the virtual machines.

## References

1. Amaral, L., Meurers, D.: On Using Intelligent Computer-Assisted Language Learning in Real-Life Foreign Language Teaching and Learning. ReCALL 23(1), 4–24 (2011)
2. Antoniadis, G., Echinard, S., Kraif, O., Lebarbé, T., Loiseau, M., Ponton, C.: NLP-based scripting for CALL activities. Proceedings of eLearning for Computational Linguistics and Computational Linguistics for eLearning. In: International Workshop in Association with COLING 2004, COLING, Geneva, Switzerland, pp. 18–25 (2004)
3. Antoniadis, G., Granger, S., Kraif, O., Ponton, C., Zampa, V.: NLP and CALL: integration is working. In: Kubler, N. (ed.) Proceedings of TaLC7, 7th Conference of Teaching and Language Corpora. Coll. Etudes Contrastives, Bruxelles, Belgium (2009)
4. Boulton, A.: Data-driven Learning: Reasonable Fears and Rational Reassurance. Indian Journal of Applied Linguistics 35(1), 81–106 (2009)
5. Buzzetto-More, N.A. (ed.): Advanced Principles of Effective e-Learning. Informing Science Press, CA (2007)
6. Callmeier, U., Eisele, A., Schäfer, U., Siegel, M.: The DeepThought Core Architecture Framework. In: Proceedings of LREC 2004, Lisbon, Portugal, pp. 1205–1208 (2004)

7. Domjan, M. (ed.): The Principles of Learning and Behavior, 6th edn., Wadsworth, CA, USA (2009)
8. Gamper, J., Knapp, J.: A Review of Intelligent CALL Systems. Computer Assisted Language Learning 15(4), 329–342 (2002)
9. Greene, C.E., Keogh, K., Koller, T., Wagner, J., Ward, M., van Genabith, J.: Using NLP technology in CALL. In: InSTIL/ICALL 2004 Symposium on Computer Assisted Learning, Venice, Italy, June 17-19 (2004) ISBN 88-8098-202-8
10. Huang, C., Calzolari, N., Gangemi, A., Lenci, A., Oltramari, A., Prevot, L.: Ontology and the Lexicon: A Natural Language Processing Perspective. Cambridge University Press, Cambridge (2010)
11. Indurkhya, I., Damerau, F.J. (eds.): Handbook of Natural Language Processing. Chapman & Hall/CRC Machine Learning & Pattern Recognition (2010)
12. Levy, M.: CALL: context and conceptualisation. Oxford University Press, Oxford (1997)
13. Meurers, D., Ziai, R., Amaral, L., Boyd, A., Dimitrov, A., Metcalf, V., Ott, N.: Enhancing Authentic Web Pages for Language Learners. In: Proceedings of the 5th Workshop on Innovative Use of NLP for Building Educational Applications, NAACL-HLT 2010, Los Angeles (2010)
14. Meurers, D.: Natural Language Processing and Language Learning. In: Chapelle, C.A. (ed.) Encyclopedia of Applied Linguistics, Blackwell (in press), available as PDF version from the authors homepage http://www.sfs.uni-tuebingen.de/~dm/publications.html (accessed on May 10, 2012)
15. Ott, N., Meurers, D.: Information Retrieval for Education: Making Search Engines Language Aware. Themes in Science and Technology Education. Special Issue on "Computer-Aided Language Analysis, Teaching and Learning: Approaches, Perspectives and Applications" 3(1-2), 9–30 (2010)
16. Semple, A.: Learning Theories and Their Influence on the Development and Use of Educational Technologies. Australian Science Teachers' Journal 46(3), 21–22, 24–28 (2000)
17. Wahl, H., Winiwarter, W., Quirchmayr, G.: Natural Language Processing Technologies for Developing a Language Learning Environment. In: Proceedings of the 12th International Conference on Information Integration and Web-based Applications & Services (iiWAS 2010), pp. 379–386. ACM, Paris (2010)
18. Wahl, H., Winiwarter, W., Quirchmayr, G.: Towards an intelligent integrated language learning environment. International Journal of Pervasive Computing and Communications 7(3), 220–239 (2011)
19. Wahl, H., Winiwarter, W.: A Technological Overview of an Intelligent Integrated Computer-Assisted Language Learning (iiCALL) Environment. In: Proceedings of the World Conference on Educational Multimedia, Hypermedia and Telecommunications (ED-MEDIA) 2011, Chesapeake, Lisbon, Portugal, June 27–July 1, pp. 3832–3837 (2011)
20. Wahl, H., Winiwarter, W.: The Intelligent Integrated Computer-Assisted Language Learning (iiCALL) Environment – Work in Progress. In: Proceedings 13th International Conference on Information Integration and Web-based Applications & Services (iiWAS 2011), Ho Chi Minh City, Vietnam, pp. 426–429. ACM (2011) ISBN: 978-1-4503-0784-0
21. Watson, J.B.: Psychology as the Behaviorist Views it. Etext Conversion Project - Nalanda Digital Library (1913)

# E-Learning - The Bologna Process, the European Credit Transfer System (ECTS), Learning Outcomes and ReProTool

Philippos Pouyioutas, Harald Gjermundrod, and Ioanna Dionysiou

University of Nicosia Research Foundation (UNRF), Cyprus
{pouyioutas.p,gjermundrod.h,dionysiou.i}@unic.ac.cy

**Abstract.** This paper discusses e-learning in relation to the Bologna Process, the European Credit Transfer System (ECTS), Learning Outcomes (LOs) and ReProTool, a software tool that supports the automation of the process of adopting LOs into the educational curriculum of Universities. It provides suggestions as to how to extend e-learning platforms and environments so as to conform to the Bologna Process directives. It briefly addresses why the Bologna Process and the reforms in the European Higher Education Area have not really focused on e-learning. It then addresses those concepts of the Bologna Process that can be adopted by e-learning platforms and environments and then presents Repro-Tool and its features that can be implemented in such environments. ReProTool is a software tool which automates the process of adopting Learning Outcomes into educational curriculum thus re-engineering academic programmes and courses. The tool will be the result of the project "ReProTool, A Software Tool for the ECTS and Bologna Process Re-engineering of University Programmes", which is co-financed by the European Regional Development Fund and the Republic of Cyprus through the Research Promotion Foundation.

**Keywords:** E-learning, Learning Outcomes, ECTS, ReProTool, Bologna Process.

## 1    Introduction

The Bologna Process [1] aims at developing a European Educational Framework of standards, definitions and concepts so as to provide the basis for European countries to transform their educational system according to this framework. This will result in comparability/compatibility of the various European educational systems which will then result in collaborations amongst educational institutions, exchanges of students and teachers within Europe and transparency and transferability of qualifications, all being very important when looked from the point of view of students, faculty, Erasmus co-ordinators, prospective employers and ENIC/NARIC networks.

One of the first and most important concepts developed by the Bologna process is the European Credit Transfer System (ECTS) that provides the framework for measuring the student workload in courses/modules/programmes and thus calculating the

E. Popescu et al. (Eds.): ICWL 2012, LNCS 7558, pp. 334–342, 2012.
© Springer-Verlag Berlin Heidelberg 2012

credits of these courses/modules/programmes. Another important concept is Learning Outcomes (LOs) [2], which allows courses/programmes to be expressed in terms of what a learner/student is expected to know by the end of the course/programme. Student input is very important for defining and reviewing LOs. The student workload calculated by both students and teachers leading to the course/programme ECTS, and the development of the LOs of the courses/programme viewed from the student perspective, ensure that the student has an active role in the development and re-engineering of academic curriculum.

Furthermore, a student-center environment requires that students provide input on regular basis with regards to curriculum development, delivery and assessment methods and quality assurance of education. The Standards and Guidelines for Quality Assurance in the European Higher Education Area require student participation in Internal Quality Assurance Committees, External Quality Assurance Evaluation Committees and in the Boards of Quality Assurance Agencies.

This paper discusses how e-learning platforms can be extended to fully support the aforementioned concepts and thus make e-learning environments to conform to the Bologna Process directives. This is explained by discussing how e-learning platforms support some of these concepts and how they can be extended by adopting feature of ReProTool, a tool which has been created to automate the process of adopting LOs into University programmes and courses. To this end, ReProTool is explained and discussed.

The rest of the paper is organized as follows. Section 2 briefly discusses the Bologna Process in relation to e-learning. Section 3 explains ReProTool. Section 4 discusses how e-learning platforms can be extended to adopt ReProTool features and thus conform to the Bologna Process and European Higher Education Area reforms. Finally, conclusions summarize the ideas presented in the paper.

## 2    The Bologna Process and E-Learning

One could wonder why the Bologna Process Declaration, which was signed back in 1999 has not yet really addressed the concept of e-learning. One actually should probably not wonder but be certain why this is the case. One of the top priorities of the European Union (EU) and thus of the Bologna Process is the increase of people mobility (students, graduates, employees, etc.). The main aim is to achieve a better and quicker integration of Europe through the interaction and blend of the various cultures that comprise EU. To this extent, EU has been generously funding projects and activities that lead to increased people mobility. Towards this end, EU Higher Education officials have set a target of 20% student mobility by the year 2020 [3]. This will be achieved through various funded activities such as Erasmus (targets mobility of students and academics across European Universities) and Tempus and Erasmus Mundus (targets the creation of joint and double postgraduate degrees to be offered by consortiums of European and other Universities thus offering opportunities to students to study in different countries; also offers funds and scholarships for students and academics and for projects), etc. [4].

Bearing in mind the strategic aim of EU with regards to mobility and considering the fact that e-learning breaks the barriers of space and is thus more appropriate for those students who do not wish/are not able to travel, one can then understand why the Bologna Process has not focused on e-learning. One can argue that e-learning could help towards the mobility aim by offering virtual mobility (through probably social network facilities, chat rooms, wikis, etc.) but this cannot be really a substitute to physical mobility. An attempt to achieve virtual mobility can be found in the VIRQUAL project [5].

Finally, as pointed out before, one very important concept of the Bologna Process is the adoption of a learner-center environment, according to which the learning process should be built focusing on the student and not the teacher and the teaching process (teacher-learning model). Learner-centered learning moves away from traditional teaching environments through which students are spoon-fed with information provided by the teachers, and thus utilizes teaching/learning methods/techniques, through which students assume an active role and teachers become facilitators and co-coordinators of the student learning process, rather than information providers. Such methods/techniques include amongst others, problem-based learning, simulation exercises, group projects, research work, etc. Thus, it is of paramount importance that any E-Learning environment takes into consideration the aforementioned methods/techniques and builds its learning process in line with the learner-centered learning model and thus conforms to the Bologna Process aims and directives.

## 3     ReProTool

ReProTool is a software tool that is currently being developed at the University of Nicosia, Cyprus. The rationale for the tool, its design and a prototype implementation has been presented at international conferences and published in their proceedings [6-9]. The tool provides the means and ensures that academic curriculum design/re-engineering takes place considering various learner-centered pedagogical methods that are crucial for the success of e-learning environments. The use of ReProTool also provides the opportunity to rethink the delivery and assessment methods employed in academic programmes of studies and learning environments. The tool focuses on the Bologna Process and LOs, which provide the basis for setting up a learner-centered learning environment. It provides facilities for academics to define LOs and students to provide input with regards LOs and the educational curriculum.

ReProTool will eventually be a web-based application that will be freely available to any University that would like to use it. So each university can have access to its own copy of the tool. The underlying database of the tool will be loaded with data that can be exported from the University's Information System (UIS). These will be the data needed to perform the tasks provided by the tool. Data and information could also then be exported to the UIS if needed. An XML schema will be defined that specifies the format that is needed by the ReProTool import/export script. Each University will be responsible for providing the interface required between its UIS and ReProTool.

The tool will provide three access methods. The first is through a web service that will support open access to a limited set of the data. Example of such data is information on programs and courses along with their associated information such as learning methods, learning outcomes, etc. Such data can be useful to other Universities who may want to use such resources in order to build their own programmes or compare their programmes with ones of other Universities. The second access method will be also through the web-service interface and will be restricted to students that are currently taking courses from the specific University. This will be an authenticated access method, i.e. the students will need to provide their credentials in order to log into the system. Through this interface the students could view all the courses that they are currently taking. In addition, they will have write access to part of the data in order to record the weekly number of hours that they spend on the various courses per week. The last access to the ReProTool will be through the ReProTool client application that will be installed on the faculty computers. This will also be an authenticated access method; hence faculty must provide their login credentials first. The client application will communicate directly with the database, and will allow faculty to modify and add data to the database tables that they are authorized for. There will be multiple roles for the faculty such as program coordinator, course leader, and teacher. The architecture of the tool is shown in Figure 1.

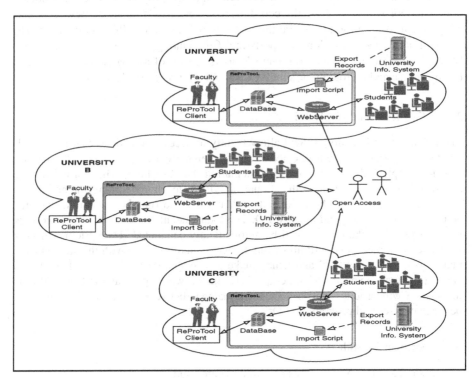

**Fig. 1.** The Architecture of ReProTool

RePeoTool will thus provide three password-controlled authorized areas and modules, namely programme coordinators, faculty members and students. The system will also support a system administrator module.

### 3.1    System Administrator Module

The System Administrator Module will provide the administrator the tools for managing (creating/editing) the end-users of the system and assigning them authorization privileges. Thus, the administrator will be responsible for the maintenance of the data pertaining to institutions, programmes of studies, faculty, coordinators and students. The administrator will also be able to declare the number of hours associated with one ECTS and set the semesters/trimesters start and end dates. The system should be flexible enough to cater for different requirements/rules across European countries and across institutions and departments within countries.

### 3.2    Programme Coordinator Module

The Programme Coordinator Module will assist academic faculty to set up programmes and create/edit courses and assign them to the programme under consideration. The tool will also allow the coordinator to select LOs or create new LOs and assign them to the programme. Furthermore its will provide a Reports menu choice that will allow the generation of reports including amongst others, LOs of a course, LOs of a programme vs. the programme's courses, LOs of a programme not covered by any course and a Programme's total ECTS and Semester's total ECTS.

### 3.3    Faculty Member Module

The Faculty Member Module will allow faculty to access the courses that they teach and thus authorized to modify. Once a faculty member chooses a course, s/he will be able to complete the Course ECTS Calculation Teacher form. This form lists the course's LOs, the associated educational activities (teaching/learning methods), the assessment methods and the estimated student workload (number of hours) that students are expected to spend on each LO. The total student workload in hours and thus the total ECTS of the courses will be automatically calculated. The system will provide a Reports menu that will allow one to access and compare with the student estimated workload and ECTS and hence make any amendments if needed. It will also allow a lecturer to specify which course LOs match which programme LOs and thus the system will produce matrices showing matches between these LOs and matches between courses and programme LOs.

### 3.4    Student Module

The Student Module has already been implemented and:

- allows lecturers to record student absences; thus calculating in-class attendance work load

- allows students record the number of hours they spend every week in a course (Figure 2)
- calculates the total number of hours (in class, out of class and total) spent by each student in each course
- calculates the average total number of hours spent by all students in the course and thus calculates the average student workload that is translated into the course ECTS as estimated by the students; provides this workload and ECTS number to the faculty module for the lecturer to compare with his/her own calculated work-load and number of ECTS
- allows student provide feedback to their lecturers on a weekly basis
- provides E-portfolio facilities allowing students to reflect on their work and future plans for studying
- produces statistics and charts such as
  - (weekly and cumulative weekly) student workload (in-class, out-of-class, total) for a course and comparison with the class average student workload and the expected workload set by the faculty – bar chart (Figure 3)
  - (weekly and cumulative weekly) student workload (in-class, out-of-class, total) for all courses taken by student and comparison with the class average workload and the expected workload set by the faculty – bar chart
  - Percentage of student workload (in-class, out-of-class, total) devoted for each course (weekly and cumulative weekly) and comparison with the expected workload percentages – pie chart (Figure 4).

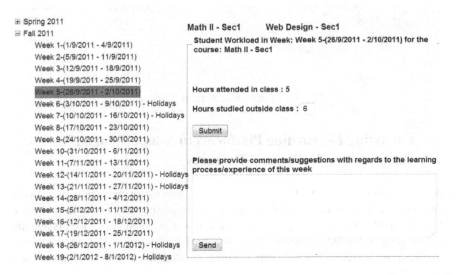

**Fig. 2.** Recording Student workload and Providing Feedback to Lecturer

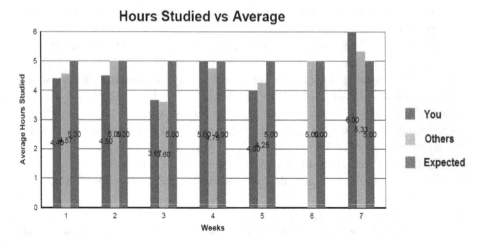

Fig. 3. Comparison of Student Workload

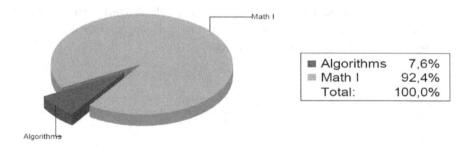

Fig. 4. Distribution of Student Workload

## 4      Extending E-Learning Platforms to Adopt Bologna Process Concepts and ReProTool Features

E-learning platforms and environments have been around for more than two decades now and have transformed/created many universities, especially in the United States. The Bologna Process is a European initiative that was initiated thirteen years ago after the flourish of e-learning systems. There is a need for European Universities providing e-learning services to adapt their learning environments to the Bologna Process requirements.

Firstly, and very importantly, the e-learning environments should fully support a learner-centre approach. E-learning platforms are indeed built around this concept with academics being more of facilitators of the learning process rather than teachers.

Students are expected to be more independent learners and take control of their learning process. However, e-learning environments may not (and many do not) support a learner-centre environment through the adoption of student-oriented learning methods such as Problem-Based Learning, simulation exercises, etc. Such methods have been very successful in traditional learning environments.

Secondly, e-learning environments should provide students with facilities to provide feedback to their lecturers with regards the courses they take, their delivery, assessment and quality assurance. Again, one can argue that e-learning environments are built around these concepts, however when it comes to the cross-checking of student workload as compared to the expected workload then clearly they do not provide such facilities as the ones supported by ReProTool and illustrated in Figures 2, 3 and 4.

Finally, e-learning environments should allow academics to create the LOs of the programmes and courses and associate them with the on-line delivery and assessment methods. Thus students will be able to check on-line the extent to which they achieved the expected LOs and how the way (delivery, assessment) they achieved them. Lecturers will also be able to monitor the progress of students with regards to the LOs and also receive feedback from students in relation to the workload they have devoted in each LO. This will enable them to review the programmes/courses and align them in a learner-center environment.

## 5     Conclusions

This paper has addressed the need for e-learning environments to conform to the Bologna Process and to the reforms taking place in the European Higher Education Area. More specifically it has addressed the need for e-learning environments to support facilities for allowing lecturers to create LOs and associate the e-learning material and assessment with the specific LOs. In doing so, e-learning lecturers would also record the associated time needed for achieving these LOs. E-learning platforms will monitor the time spent by students in learning and completing assessment and will also prompt students to record any additional time spent outside the e-learning platform. The platforms will then be able to monitor each student with regards to the assessment completed and thus LOs achieved and present to the student a record of his/her own LOs achieved and the ones remaining to be achieved. A student will also be able to compare his/her workload with the one estimated by the lecturer for each LO and assessment and provide appropriate feedback to his/her lecturer.

Enhancing e-learning platforms with the LOs approach will also encourage e-learning lecturers to rethink of the curriculum and its delivery and assessment methods, considering also student feedback. The LO approach will encourage lecturers to adopt problem based learning and other learner-centre methods, thus enhancing the learning process of students.

In order to illustrate how to extend such platforms, the paper has presented ReProTool, a software tool that automates the process for the adoption of LOs into the educational curriculum and thus the re-engineering of academic programmes. The tool is currently under development and is expected to be publicly released in July 2013.

Some screenshots of the already implemented Student Module of the tool have been presented to exemplify the functionality of the tool and the way e-learning platforms can be similarly extended to support such features.

**Acknowledgements.** The authors would like to thank the Cyprus Research Promotion Foundation. The project "ReProTool, A Software Tool for the ECTS and Bologna Process Re-engineering of University Programmes" is an eighteen months project (February 2012 - July 2013), co-financed by the European Regional Development Fund and the Republic of Cyprus through the Research Promotion Foundation.

# References

1. European Commission Education and Learning (2008), The bologna process, http://ec.europa.eu/education/policies/educ/bologna/bologna_en.html
2. Kennedy, D., Hyland, A., Ryan, N.: Writing and using learning outcomes, a practical guide. EUA Bologna Handbook (2006), http://www.bologna-handbook.com/docs/frames/content_c.html
3. http://www.ehea.info/Uploads/Irina/Working%20paper%20on%20Mobility%20strategy%202020%20for%20EHEA.PDF
4. http://ec.europa.eu/education/lifelong-learning-policy/mobility_en.htm
5. VIRQUAL Network for integrating Virtual Mobility and European Qualification Framework in HE and CE Institutions, http://virqual.up.pt/
6. Pouyioutas, P., Gjermundrod, H., Dionysiou, I.: ReProTool, A Software Tool for the ECTS and Bologna Process Re-engineering of University Programmes. In: IADIS International Conference on e-Society, Berlin, Germany, pp. 42–49 (March 2012)
7. Pouyioutas, P.: Hybrid Learning Curriculum Development Using the ReProTool – Lessons From Ancient Philosophy. In: Tsang, P., Cheung, S.K.S., Lee, V.S.K., Huang, R. (eds.) ICHL 2010. LNCS, vol. 6248, pp. 160–170. Springer, Heidelberg (2010), http://hkuspace.hku.hk/ichl2010
8. Pouyioutas, P., Gjermundrod, H., Dionysiou, I.: The Development of ReProTool, A Software Tool for Developing Programmes Using Learning Outcomes. In: IADIS International Conference e-Learning, Germany, vol. II, pp. 96–100 (2010), http://www.elearning-conf.org/2010
9. Pouyioutas, P., Gjermundrod, H., Dionysiou, I.: The Development of the TunTool, A Software Tool for the Tuning Methodology. In: 2nd International Conference on Computer Supported Education, Spain, vol. II, pp. 401–406 (2010), http://www.csedu.org/CSEDU2010/index.htm

# The Implementation of the E-Learning Systems in Higher Education – Sharing the Work Experience from Petroleum-Gas University of Ploieşti

Gabriela Moise, Mihaela Suditu, and Loredana Netedu

Petroleum-Gas University of Ploiesti, Romania
gmoise@upg-ploiesti.ro, {msuditu,lorenetedu}@yahoo.com

**Abstract.** In this paper there are presented the partial results obtained after the implementation of the European Social Fund Project entitled *Development of the Universities' Staff Skills in Order to Be Able to Use an E-learning System* at Petroleum-Gas University of Ploieşti. The general objective of the project is to develop and modernize the initial educational and continuing professional system in order to cope with the challenges of the nowadays ever-changing society through an e-Learning system implemented by the University of Petroşani and a repository of e-courses, built by the trainees within PGU of Ploieşti.
   Within the framework of the project, there have been realized two studies. The former analyzes the necessity of initiating and developing formation courses in the field of e-learning that are dedicated to the staff functioning within higher education and the latter deals with the impact of the project's unrolling on PGU employees. The conclusions drawn from the research studies and the outcomes of the project reveal the active role of the e-Learning systems in the higher education from Romania and the increasing number of teachers that are currently using e-Learning in their professional activities.

**Keywords:** e-Learning system, higher education, Lectora, digital competences.

## 1 Introduction – European Context of ICT-Based Learning's Development

The preoccupations of the European Commission regarding the usage of the information and communication technologies in the learning activities were outlined in 1999 through the *eEurope initiative* [1], focused on issuing a new Internet technologies-driven economy. The *Lisbon Strategy* (2000) contained a 10-year action plan having as a major goal "to make the EU the most competitive and dynamic knowledge-based economy in the world capable of sustaining more and better jobs and with greater social cohesion" [2]. In June 2010, the *Lisbon Strategy* was replaced by *Europe 2020 Strategy*. *Education and Training 2020* continues the *ET2010* programme and defines a framework for European cooperation in education with the following strategic objectives: "making lifelong learning and mobility a reality; improving the quality and efficiency of education and training; promoting equity, social cohesion and active

E. Popescu et al. (Eds.): ICWL 2012, LNCS 7558, pp. 343–348, 2012.

citizenship; enhancing creativity and innovation, including entrepreneurship, at all levels of education and training" [3].

E-learning involves both traditional and modern learning and teaching techniques based on information and communication technologies, conducting to knowledge and skills acquisition. As a result, teachers' digital competences should be satisfactory, if not advanced, in case of e-courses design. Therefore, a possible drawback in the implementation of e-learning systems is the low level of ICT competences of the Romanian academic staff. On the plus side, one mentions that e-learning systems implementation provides to the learning process the three "any"-s: anytime, anywhere, any place and facilitates the achieving of *ET2020* objectives. This strategy outlines eight key competences which are necessary to both young people and adults, among which there is digital competence. Considering it, e-learning programmes offer opportunities for the academic staff to be trained and to professionally develop.

## 2    Description of the project *Development of the Universities' Staff Skills in Order to Be Able to Use an E-learning System*

In the context of the new European educational strategies, in Romania there have been initiated several projects having as their main objectives the implementation of e-learning systems in higher education and the usage of informational technologies in the learning and teaching activities. Human resources are essential in the educational process, so they are to be prepared in order to adequately use e-learning systems.

Nowadays, in Romania, this component of the e-learning systems implementation is achieved through the projects co-financed by the European Union through the Sectorial Operational Programme for Human Resources Development 2007-2013 (SOP HRD). In the report (31$^{st}$ March 2012) comprising the contracted projects through the SOP HRD, there are listed 2468 projects financed by the European Union, the national budget and beneficiary's contributions [4].

The project entitled *Development of the Universities' Staff Skills in Order to Be Able to Use an E-learning System* started in 2010 and will finish in 2013. The project is co-financed from the European social Fund through Sectorial Operational Programme for Human Resources Development 2007-2013, Priority axis 1, Key Area of Intervention 1.3 "Human resources development in education and training", contract code: POSDRU/87/1.3/S/64273. Petroleum-Gas University of Ploiesti (PGU) is a partner in this European project, alongside the University of Petro□ani and two IT firms, namely Memory LTD and Euro Jobs LTD.

The objectives of the project are the development and modernization of the Romanian higher education system by implementing an e-learning system and building a repository of e-courses. The operational objective of the project is to train academic community so that they may introduce the e-Learning system in further education and training and use the system, by posting teaching materials. The final target group constituted at PGU consists of 60 academic persons from different educational areas. At the date of the 31$^{st}$ of March 2012, there have been trained two groups summing 28 persons, with the following gender and age structure: 20 female and 8 male teachers, 21 persons (24-45 years), 6 persons (45-54 years) and 1 person (55-64 years).

The academic staff having already been trained within the project followed customized courses in order to build an e-course, by using MS Word, PPT and Lectora, and to use CourseMill. Lectora Inspire represents a complex software application and an authoring tool that enables its users to quickly create dynamic e-contents. Lectora includes as e-learning tools Camtasia for Lectora to create professional tutorials, SnagIt for Lectora to capture anything on the screen and Flypaper for Lectora to develop professional, custom interactive exercises [5]. Lectora relies on two concepts: "book metaphor" and "inheritance" [6]. The book metaphor helps users to create a hierarchy of content. An e-course built with Lectora is organized in chapters, sections, subsections and pages, each subordinate structure keeping the general objects (that is titles, keywords, objectives etc.) established at the level of the chapter, feature which is defined as inheritance [6]. Lectora supports all standard formats of e-contents. The electronic content can be published as a single executable file: "the option compacts the entire title and all supporting files into a single file for easier distribution, for example, as a downloaded file from the Web", a file on a CD: "this option compresses the entire title and all supporting files into a single file and creates an auto-start file that will automatically launch the title when the CD is placed into a CD-ROM drive"; HTML file: create web pages; A compatible CourseMille file; an AICC/Web standard-based file; a SCORM/Web standard-based file; a compatible Learning Resource Interchange (LRN) descriptor [6]. CourseMill is a Learning Management System developed by the same firm as Lectora, Trivantis that enables to manage and take online courses. The trainees involved in the projects have assimilated the taught lessons and realised e-courses which are stocked on the CourseMill platform (http://webserver.upet.ro/wps/portal). There were recorded 11 e-courses by 31 March.

## 3    The Impact of the Project on the Target Group

The major objectives of the project are to train and develop the skills of academic teachers in order to improve their ability to use interactive teaching-learning methods through the e-Learning system.

Teachers are trained to use modern methods of teaching and learning (eLearning), combining traditional education with modern and flexible learning methods, thus becoming more competent and more competitive on the labour market. The academic staff is aware of the fact that, in the future, any academic teacher will have to access an e-Learning system and to participate in professional discussion forums with students, exchange experience etc. Teacher training in this direction is an urgent need to which the present project responds directly. A further plus is the implementation of innovative activities, namely the implementation of an e-learning system in PGU, as well as the training of teachers to populate the system with course materials.

The necessity of this programme was determined after the application of an initial assessment questionnaire for teachers in PGU. Initial evaluation aimed to reveal the knowledge and computer skills to be used both for the development of courses and in teaching. The data of the participants' initial assessment questionnaire are necessary for trainers in order for them to better adapt and harmonize the content with the knowledge the participants need, while still complying with the fundamental objectives of the project. The initial assessment has been conducted through a questionnaire with the following areas of interest:

— Internet usage in professional documentation / information;
— Usage of email, Facebook, Skype, messenger as ways of communication;
— Usage of IT technologies (PPT presentations, electronic courses, educational platforms, etc.) in teaching (lectures/seminars);
— Address the different ways of presenting courses for distance learning and part-time learning: PPT presentations, e- course, educational platform and course book;
— Developing working skills in specialized IT programmes, as a result of participation in other courses;
— Expressing the need to participate in the training course that is part of the project to improve teaching and learning strategies.

After applying the initial quiz, the results are as follows:

— 92% of the participants use the Internet in their professional documentation work; 92% of participants use various electronic tools (mail, messenger, etc.) as a means of communication; 75% of participants use IT technologies in teaching;
— the most used electronic ways of presenting scientific contents are the following: PPT (75% of the trainees), course in electronic format (75% of the trainees), educational platforms (33% of the attendants);
— for distance learning or part-time education, the most often used ways to present the lecture by the participants in the target group are: PPT (35%), lectures in electronic format (67%), the educational platform (35%) and course books (67%);
— 83% of the participants have not attended a training course before to develop the skills needed for the programs used in creating a course in electronic format;
— 100% of the participants consider the project as useful and welcome.

The results presented above lead to the conclusion that the training activities proposed to academic teachers within the project meet their training needs for IT skills. It is necessary to improve learning and teaching strategies and to efficiently use modern teaching-learning methods for full time and distance learning or part-time education, fact of which all the participants in the project are aware of. As a proof, 100% of the trainees expressed their opinion in favour of such courses.

The experimental phase of the project consists in effectively covering (in consecutive series of four groups of academic teachers) the programme involving the acquisition of knowledge needed to use e-Learning as a modern method of teaching and learning. At the end of each series, trainees go through a specific assessment and obtain the certification of the acquired skills. Certified teachers will also populate the system database with the courses they teach, with assistance from trainers. In support of the applications that participants must realize, it was designed a *Study Guide for Developing e-Materials*, as an additional working support that aims towards the acquisition of the following skills: *Pedagogical skills*, expressed in the design, management, evaluation of content, learning units for both lecture and the laboratory activities specific to each field of expertise; *Online communication skills*, expressed in the ability of the participants to design the contents while complying with the format of an electronic course. The authors of the guide consider useful to begin by presenting a short glossary of terms to achieve a good and necessary separation and specification of the working concepts, followed by several psycho-pedagogical aspects that refer to the design and evaluation elements of a unit. Last but not least, the guide offers elements related to the rigors of designing a course in electronic format.

The assessment of satisfaction degree is achieved by applying to each series of trainees a final impact survey to obtain feedback for further improvement of the project. The questionnaire on the quality of the training course offered within the project is structured in eight areas of interest, as follows:

1. Analysis of the adequacy / novelty / applicability of the presented content.
2. Evaluating the presentation of the course.
3. Organization of teaching - learning activities.
4. Analysis of the teaching style introduces by the trainer.
5. The organization of the activities of the training course
6. Ergonomic conditions.
7. Mentioning items that could improve training activity in this course.
8. Specify weaknesses noticed throughout the training activities.

The analysis of responses to questions in the applied questionnaire led to the following conclusions: course content is 100% available; it shows a high degree of novelty at a rate of 60%; the applicability rate is as high as 50%. With regards to the manner of presenting the content covered in course, participants appreciate it as: highly attractive: 100%; manner of presentation, generating reflections: to a very large extent (60%); applied character: to a large extent (90%).

As far as the type of activity organization is concerned, participants work frontally, in groups or in pairs, on the theoretical parts and individually for the application part when trainees build their e-courses by using Lectora programme. Regarding the trainers' teaching activity, there are considered in the final quiz the following aspects to be assessed by the attendants: the trainers motivate the participation in the course - 60%, provides immediate feedback - 75% and complies with the time schedule of meetings - 100%, approaches the democratic teaching style - 100%, foster the curiosity of participants - 67%.

Regarding the organization of activities in the course, this was appreciated as follows: consistency to a large extent (85%), activities organized according to course objectives to a very large extent (92%) and ergonomic conditions offered were deemed appropriate to a large extent (70%). The suggestions the first 28 participants made on items that would improve future training activity in this course are: more applications in Lectora software; more examples; more time allocated for the applications. There have not been remarked flaws in conducting the course. As shown in the analysis above, this type of human resources training finds its maximum utility and the participants' assessments are revealing in this respect. The course achieves its full role by developing digital competence and computing skills of the academic teachers so that they may work with software systems specific to e-Learning. The project also fulfills its mission to prepare and to support teachers in transition from being a "traditional" teacher to the status of a moderator and/or a facilitator of learning.

## 4     Conclusions

The project *Development of the Universities' Staff Skills in Order to Be Able to Use an E-learning System* meets the demands of nowadays general educational policies that aim at improving the quality and efficiency of the educational systems and professional training in the EU, and at improving the education and training of teachers and trainers. As teachers should play an active role in any strategy of stimulating the development of a society, the initiators of this project considered the following as key elements of the project [7]: supporting teachers and trainers so that they may further cope with the challenges of a knowledge-based society, defining competences, including ICT competences, that teachers should have, given their major role in a society of knowledge, facilitating the access for all to the systems of education and professional training. The project *Development of the Universities' Staff Skills in Order to Be Able to Use an E-learning System* values, through its objectives and scheduled activities, the priorities of the Romanian educational system as a member of the EU: embracing the idea of teacher education, their continuous pedagogical training, focusing on higher education, complex academic certification.

**Acknowledgment.** The SOP HRD project entitled *Development of the Universities' Staff Skills in Order to Be Able to Use an E-learning System,* Code Contract: POSDRU/87/1.3/S/64273, provides the data analyzed in this paper and financially supports the dissemination of the current results.

## References

1. Before i2010: eEurope initiative, http://ec.europa.eu/information_society/eeurope/2002/index_en.htm
2. Europe in 12 lessons, http://bookshop.europa.eu/en/europe-in-12-lessons-pbNA3110652/
3. Education and Training 2020 (ET 2020), http://europa.eu/legislation_summaries/education_training_youth/general_framework/ef0016_en
4. List of SOP HR Projects contracted, http://www.fonduri-strurturale.ro/
5. The official site of Trivantis, http://www.trivantis.com/e-learning-software
6. Lectora User Guide, http://www.trivantis.com/downloads/Lectora_User_Guide.pdf
7. Velea, S., Neacşu, I. Zgaga, P. (coord.): Formarea cadrelor didactice. Experienţe europene. Editura Universitară, Bucureşti (2007)

# Enhancing Online Class Student Engagement through Discussion

## A Case Study on Modern Educational Technology[*]

Fengfang Shu, Chengling Zhao, and Liyong Wan

Information Technology Department, Central China Normal University,
Wuhan, China
sff265@163.com, {zhcling,wanliyong}@mails.ccnu.edu.cn

**Abstract.** Online student engagement is the premise of online learning. This paper firstly stated the characteristic of online engagement and discussion's key role in enhancing student engagement, and then took modern educational technology's online theory class as example, designed and implemented the online discussion teaching method, and analyzed the learning effect. The result shows that through online discussion, student engagement, especially behavior and emotional engagement were greatly improved.

**Keywords:** Student Engagement, Online Discussion, Modern Educational Technology.

# 1    Theoretical Framework

## 1.1    Introduction

Researchers have proposed many different ways to describe quality learning, and student engagement has been identified as an important precursor to student effective learning [1]. Student engagement refers to a set of cognitive, affective, and behavioral states, usually involves commitment, involvement, participation, and motivated and strategic interaction with materials. It is hypothesized to mediate between teaching and learning and to be affected by instructional practice [2]. Levin reviewed that lots of studies specifically point to the engagement value of case discussion for enhancing student interest in, enjoyment of (affective engagement), reflection upon, and learning from (cognitive engagement) teaching cases. In the teacher-centered class, learner's learning engagement, especially learning affective engagement, is low and negative. Discussion can make learners be more engaged than no discussion because discussion might enhance student cognitive engagement by requiring them to express their ideas

---

[*] This paper was supported by the projects 985 ZB05 and BCA100024.

E. Popescu et al. (Eds.): ICWL 2012, LNCS 7558, pp. 349–354, 2012.

to peers, and to articulate views to peers may stimulate behavioral engagement by motivating learners to spend more time on cases and engaging with course materials to support their views.

## 1.2    Student Engagement Definition and Assessment

A widely used definition of student engagement was comprised of three subtypes: behavioral, cognitive, and affective [3]. Behavioral–refers to participation in academic, social and extracurricular activities; Cognitive – concerns involvement in learning, motivation to learn, willingness to exert effort to learn difficult concepts and skills, the use of strategies; and affective–encompasses emotional aspects, feelings, attitudes, and perceptions towards the educational environment, relationships with teachers and classmates. Behavior engagement is a kind of basic engagement. Some researchers think that behavior engagement mainly refers to the student's behavior in the classroom that can be observed. According to the definition and relationship between different subtypes of engagement, we work out concrete standards to evaluate students engagement (table 1).

**Table 1.** Assessment of student's engagement

| Kinds of engagement | Measurement method |
|---|---|
| Behavioral engagement | The participation frequency in discussion and class. |
| Cognitive Engagement | The depth of understanding on problems or discussion cases and reflections about learning process and method. |
| Affective engagement | Interest, belonging, and attitude toward learning. |
| | |

The teacher can use the software ROSTCM (a content mining software created by Wuhan University) to analyze learners' chat log in the QQ chatting room (OpenICQ, ICQ stands for I SEEK YOU, a Chinese popular instant messaging software created by Pony Ma) and YY channel (Multiplayer online voice chat software, http://www.yy.com/s/download.html). The software can calculate the number of questions learners asked to receive information and expand knowledge, the number of explanations learners gave to express individual knowledge, the amount of on-task discourse, and learners' learning emotional tendency in discussion. The teacher can estimate the depth of learner's cognitive engagement's by observing and analyzing the learner's discourse by hand.

## 1.3    Discussion Based on Case or Problem

Online Discussion, whether synchronous or asynchronous, has several qualities likely to facilitate learners' motivation to analyze cases and improve their ability to analyze cases critically. Discussion may expose students to more viewpoints and require them to clarify and analyze their own ideas. Wisdom spark may appear after discussion and debate collisions, and we naturally understand the connotation of knowledge and truth. Levin's (1995) studies have found that pre-service and beginning teachers engaging in discussion were more likely to elaborate on their original ideas, while those who did not discuss tended simply to consolidate their original ideas [4]. So may be learning from listening to peers in online classroom can prompting students' meta-cognitive ability. However, explanations have to follow certain criteria to foster deeper understanding. Some findings [5] show that certain discourse practices elicit substantive student engagement, with teachers taking students seriously, and acknowledging and building on what they say. So for discussion, teachers should make it clear that, before class they should design the discussion seriously, search for learning resource, teaching cases, design the discussion process, and make guidance for students to participate better in online class discussion. During the discussion, they need to be open minded, encourage students' good ideas timely, give objective comments on learners' point of view. As to students, they need some discussion requirements.

Asynchronous online discussion is more flexible, discussion of the topic commonly occurs during the same time period that students are engaged in case, task, or problem analysis and reflection. Also, during discussion, asking questions can be seen as a constructive activity that promotes understanding [6]. Compared with face to face class, online discussion presumably gives students more time and opportunities to reflect [7].

## 2     Case Design and Implementation

### 2.1     Course Design

**Course introduction and design.** Modern educational technology is a common compulsory course for Pre-service teachers in normal university. The course contains face to face experiment class and online theory class. The organization of online theory class' learning contents is topic-centered. Designed discussion problems should: firstly focused on the mastery of core course subject matter; then linked to practical teaching problems; last but not the least, related to students' mind controversial issues. The sub discussion topic can be designed as questions, study cases or authentic tasks. The designed topics should be open-ended, and can stimulate learners' learning interest and motivation and train the learners' advanced thinking. According to the characteristics of the topic and the time limited, the discussion form can be divided into various forms, like individual freedom discussion, group discussion and intergroup discussion.

### 2.2     Course Implementation Process and Effect

**Participants.** There are 51 learners in the modern educational technology network classroom. They come from nine majors-biological science, English, histories, music, mathematics, psychology, physical education, chemistry, and Chinese literature.

**Implementation process.** Firstly, we tell learners the importance of discussion and provide some practical discussion tips. Then, according to the point view of online discussion teaching, teachers organized the classroom discussion as follows: Before the start of the discussion, prepared for the material carefully, designed discussions procession, and posted it online. During the discussion, paid attention to the direction of the students' discussion, encouraged and guided the student to speech and arguing, so that all the students have a chance to speak in the discussion, and made sure to complete the discussions as far as possible within the prescribed period of time. In the end of the discussion, gave an overall evaluation to student's viewpoint.

We used QQ group and YY channel as the course learning platform. The teacher posted topic's task list in QQ group BBS a week before the online synchronous class. The online synchronous class was divided into two parts: learners' individual learning, and teachers' teaching and learners' online discussion. In the first time period, learners learned and reflected the teaching case or problem autonomously according to the learning task list. In the second time period, the teacher guided the learners to discuss the study cases or problems.

**Affective engagement.** We collected data from QQ BBS, QQ chatting, YY text chatting and YY voice chatting from September 1, 2011 to December 18, 2011. Text sentiment analysis, also referred to as emotional polarity computation. It is the process of analyzing, processing, summarizing and reasoning the subjectivity text with emotional color. [8] ROSTCM can analyze the emotional features of statements. The results are as table 2.

**Table 2.** Students emotional state

| Positive motions | Neutral emotions | Negative emotions |
|---|---|---|
| 31.05% | 61.14% | 7.81% |

From this table, we can know that most students' emotions are neutral and positive, only few students' emotions are negative. The online discussion theory class can lead to students' better affective engagement.

**Behavioral engagement.** Through ROSTCM, we calculate students' behavioral engagement, including the number students of chatting log in QQ chatting room (Table 3) and the number of discussion posted by students in QQ BBS (Table4).

**Table 3.** Students' chatting frequency in QQ chatting room

| students' chat frequency | 1~19 | 20~39 | 40~59 | 60~79 | 80~99 | >=100 |
|---|---|---|---|---|---|---|
| number of students | 20 | 10 | 9 | 6 | 3 | 3 |

The largest chatting log number is 193, the smallest number is 1, the mean and standard deviation number is 35.6 and 35.55, there is a big difference among the learners chatting frequency in QQ group chatting room. The largest post number is 18, the smallest number is 0, the mean and standard deviation number is 7.16 and 5.795, also there is a big difference among the learners post frequency.

**Table 4.** The number of students' postings in QQ BBS discussion

| posting frequency | 1~5 | 6~10 | 11~15 | 16~20 | >=20 |
|---|---|---|---|---|---|
| number of students | 21 | 14 | 12 | 4 | 1 |

The correlation coefficient between speech and post is 0.578, they are related. From the two chats we can know that, as the students' post frequency and students' chat frequency ascend, the student number descends.

To analysis the online class's teacher and students interaction in YY platform, we take the topic Learning resources development and media cognitive psychology as example, it has three synchronous class discussion; every discussion topic has about ten students' opinion posting. We recorded and calculated the teachers' and learners' speaking time duration in online YY voice interaction (figure 1). In the 80 minutes (4800 seconds) discussion, the ratio of the teacher's speaking time and all the students' total speaking time is 1.7:1. But when the teacher is speaking, the students can key in text. The students' text interaction is much more. The total number of the students text posts is 332, 131 posts is about the students' opinion, and 201 posts expresses agree or disagree and other things. From the YY voice and text, we can know that in contrast to conditional class-where the students do not have the opportunity to interrupt the teacher in the form of text, the online class contact intensity is high.

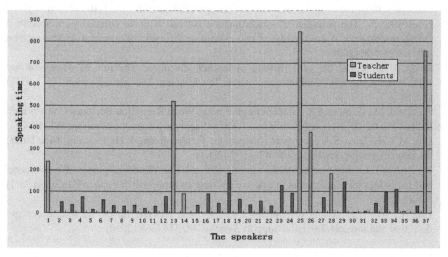

**Fig. 1.** The voice interaction in online class discussion

**Student cognitive engagement.** Students' cognitive engagement in learning activities is linked to thinking level. Cognitive engagement contains active engagement and superficial engagement. During the online discussions, students positively gave their opinions, analyzed peers' comments, and reflected on their learning to increased individual's cognitive growth and development. Through the students' works, test grades, and learner's self-evaluation, we can found that their cognitive strategies and meta-cognitive strategies were improved.

# 3    Conclusion

In contrast to the face to face learning, online class interaction is based on free social software learning platform. It can break through time and space limitation and can in the form of text or voice. It can provide learners with better learning support and improve the students' learning enthusiasm. In the information era, learning cognitive and meta-cognitive strategies is very important. The empirical research of the design and application of online discussion class, which is centered on topic or teaching case, first self-study and then discussion, proved that discussion can enhance online class students' behavioral engagement, improve learners' learning interest, cognitive and meta-cognitive engagement. But how to change the learner's habit in online learning and discussion still remains to be done.

# References

1. Reeve, J., Tseng, C.-M.: Agency as a fourth aspect of students' engagement during learning activities. Contemporary Educational Psychology 36(4), 257–267 (2011)
2. Fredericks, J.A., Blumenfeld, P.C., Paris, A.H.: School engagement: Potential of the concept, state of the evidence. Review of Educational Research 74, 59–109 (2004)
3. Hrastinski, S.: The potential of synchronous communication to enhance participation in online discussions: A case study of two e-learning courses. Information & Management 45(7), 499–506 (2008)
4. Levin, B.B.: Using the case method in teacher education: The role of discussion and experience in teachers' thinking about cases. Teaching and Teacher Education 11(1), 63–79 (1995)
5. Nystrand, M., Gamoran, A.: Student Engagement: When Recitation Becomes Conversation, Date: 1990-02-00, National Center on Effective Secondary Schools, Madison, WI (1990)
6. Chi, M.T.H., Siler, S.A., Jeong, H., Yamauchi, T., Hausmann, R.G.: Learning from human tutoring. Cognitive Science 25(4), 471–533 (2001)
7. De Bruyn, L.L.: Monitoring online communication: Can the development of convergence and social presence indicate an interactive learning environment? Distance Education 25(1), 67–81 (2004)
8. Lia, N., Wu, D.D.: Using text mining and sentiment analysis for online forums hot spot detection and forecast. Decision Support Systems 48, 354–368 (2010)

# Author Index